# TOWARD A THEOLOGY OF SCIENTIFIC ENDEAVOUR

Foundations of science are specific conditions of the cosmos, of human intelligence, of cultural beliefs, and of technological structures that make the pursuit of modern science possible. Each of the four foundations of scientific endeavour can be studied as a topic on its own. The concurrent study of all four together reveals several tensions and interconnections among them that point the way to a greater unification of faith and science.

This book explores four foundations of scientific endeavour and investigates some of the paradoxes each of them raises. Kaiser shows that the resolution of these paradoxes inevitably leads us into theological discourse and raises new challenges for theological endeavour. In order to address these challenges, Kaiser draws on the wider resources of the Judeo-Christian tradition and argues for a refocusing of contemporary theology from the perspective of natural science.

# Ashgate Science and Religion Series

*Series Editors*:

Roger Trigg, *University of Warwick, UK*
J. Wentzel van Huyssteen, *Princeton Theological Seminary, USA*

Science and religion have often been thought to be at loggerheads but much contemporary work in this flourishing interdisciplinary field suggests this is far from the case. The Ashgate Science and Religion series presents exciting new work to advance interdisciplinary study, research and debate across key themes in science and religion, exploring the philosophical relations between the physical and social sciences on the one hand and religious belief on the other. Contemporary issues in philosophy and theology are debated, as are prevailing cultural assumptions arising from the 'post-modernist' distaste for many forms of reasoning. The series enables leading international authors from a range of different disciplinary perspectives to apply the insights of the various sciences, theology and philosophy and look at the relations between the different disciplines and the rational connections that can be made between them. These accessible, stimulating new contributions to key topics across science and religion will appeal particularly to individual academics and researchers, graduates, postgraduates and upper-undergraduate students.

*Other titles published in this series:*

*Explorations in Neuroscience, Psychology and Religion*
Kevin S. Seybold
978-0-7546-5563-3 (HBK)

*God's Action in Nature's World*
*Essays in Honour of Robert John Russell*
Edited by Ted Peters and Nathan Hallanger
978-0-7546-5556-5 (HBK)

*From Human to Posthuman*
*Christian Theology and Technology in a Postmodern World*
Brent Waters
978-0-7546-3914-5 (HBK)
978-0-7546-3915-2 (PBK)

# Toward a Theology of Scientific Endeavour

## The Descent of Science

CHRISTOPHER B. KAISER
*Western Theological Seminary, USA*

**ASHGATE**

Published by
Ashgate Publishing Limited
Gower House
Croft Road
Aldershot
Hampshire GU11 3HR
England

Ashgate Publishing Company
Suite 420
101 Cherry Street
Burlington, VT 05401-4405
USA

Ashgate website: http://www.ashgate.com

**British Library Cataloguing in Publication Data**
Kaiser, Christopher B.
   Toward a theology of scientific endeavour: the descent of science – (Ashgate science and religion series) 1. Research – Philosophy 2. Religion and science 3. Philosophical anthropology
   I. Title
   261.5'5

**Library of Congress Cataloging-in-Publication Data**
Kaiser, Christopher B.
   Toward a theology of scientific endeavour: the descent of science / Christopher B. Kaiser.
      p. cm. – (Ashgate science and religion series)
   Includes bibliographical references and index. 1. Religion and science. 2. Science – Philosophy. I. Title.

   BL240.3.K35 2007
   261.5'5–dc22

                                                                     2006035624

ISBN 978-0-7546-4159-9 (Hbk)
ISBN 978-0-7546-4160-5 (Pbk)

Printed and bound in Great Britain by MPG Books Ltd, Bodmin, Cornwall.

*For the Very Reverend Professor Thomas Forsyth Torrance,
mentor and friend.*

*And for professionals who may be inspired
to apply the method of this essay to their own disciplines.*

# Contents

# List of Figures

# Acknowledgements

Many people have supported me in this project. My Edinburgh professor, Thomas Torrance, strongly encouraged me to organize my career-long thinking on science and faith in a fresh, accessible form. My wife, Martha, read early drafts and listened to endless explanations over breakfast and dinner. The library staff of Western Theological Seminary has supplied me with numerous interlibrary loans. I have been encouraged and challenged by colleagues who have read or discussed parts of the manuscript with me, particularly Western Seminary Professors Thomas Boogaart and Jim Brownson; Hope College Professors Don Cronkite, Tim Evans, and Tim Pennings; Del Ratzsch at Calvin College; and Max Tegmark at the University of Pennsylvania. The original illustrations were produced by Reformed Church in America (RCA) staff artists Maria Orr and Carl Meinke in consultation with Phil Tanis. I am indebted to the series editors, Wentzel van Huyssteen and Roger Trigg, for their encouragement and support, to my friend, Laurie Z. Baron, for help in editing the manuscript.

# Four Foundations of
# Scientific Endeavour

A thick description of natural science inevitably leads to theological questions and cultivates a thick description of nature, humanity, history and God. This is the overall thesis for the four studies that make up the main body of this book. Each of these studies begins with some aspect of natural science and raises questions about what makes such an endeavour possible. Each study uses appropriate scientific disciplines to address those questions and in the process raises further questions and paradoxes that are of theological interest. We then review the resources of the historic Judeo-Christian tradition in search of concepts that will help address those questions. The studies conclude with suggestions for thickening our description of nature, history, and God.

This book is not a study in 'natural theology' in the traditional sense of the term. Natural theology begins with assumed features of the natural world, for example, motion or design, or with the scientific theories that describe them, and develops a rational argument for the existence and attributes of God.[1] Our starting point, in contrast, will be the foundations of natural science as a human endeavour. Instead of using discursive reason, we shall use the tools of various natural and social scientific disciplines to investigate the conditions that make that endeavour possible and then explore the theological dimensions embedded in those conditions. Instead of examining the structure and the origin of the natural world, we shall examine the deep structure and origin of scientific endeavour. Instead of trying to demonstrate the existence of God, we shall demonstrate the need for sustained theological discourse as part of any attempt to carry out the investigation and complete the objectives of scientific endeavour.

We shall map out some of the relationships between scientific and theological discourse in order to show the coherence among various scientific and theological concepts when viewed in relation to the foundations of scientific endeavour.[2] As in the

---

1 See Alister E. McGrath, *A Scientific Theology, Volume 1: Nature* (Edinburgh: T&T Clark, 2001), 305, for a good review of 'The Purpose and Place of Natural Theology'. In addition to the observable world of nature, McGrath includes human rationality (in general) and human culture among the possible grounds for natural theology. Our starting point does not fit any of these categories.

2 Technically one may distinguish between several levels of argumentation. In Chapter 2 (Anthropological Foundation) I shall offer a level-2 argument for the existence of a spirit world and a level-3 argument for the existence of God. An argument for the existence of something (say the planet Neptune or God) from features of the natural world may be termed a level-1 argument. An argument that posits the existence of something (like Dirac's positively charged electrons) in order to achieve completeness and consistency may be termed a level-2 argument. An argument

study of any map, a reader can follow a particular route without deciding to go there personally. Each step in our argument involves choices that can be assessed rationally if not dispassionately. The style is open ended and invitational, sometimes even playful, rather than foundational or demonstrative. Since my goal is to develop an approach to theology based on the study of science as a human endeavour, I call this a 'theology of science', or, more exactly, a 'theology of scientific endeavour'. It is based on insights and questions that arise from a thorough examination of the conditions that must be fulfilled in order for scientific research to be a viable enterprise.

In the remainder of this introduction, I shall explain the need for a thick description of science – one that takes the life and work of scientists into account – and then proceed to thicken the description by describing four preconditions that illustrate the contingency of scientific endeavour. Each of these preconditions will become the starting point for a chapter to follow.

## Toward a thick description of science

Scientists are human beings.[3] They need relaxation and sleep like all other humans. Each day they also need to resume their work and exert themselves, often under considerable pressure, in order to make progress in their work. Scientists struggle with motivation and direction in their lives like the rest of us.

What makes natural scientists different from most other people, and what often makes their work so difficult, is the fact that they work on topics so far removed from everyday life and try to solve problems that have never been solved, or in many cases even articulated before.

A good analogy would be helpful here. The closest example I can think of is that of an Olympic athlete training for years to break a world record. The athlete also struggles with pressure and motivation and is often pressing the limits of what the human frame can accomplish. In this respect, scientists are like athletes. However, the scientist is not simply trying to gain a fraction of a second or centimeter (although the technologies that sustain modern science often work with even smaller margins). Scientists have to face directly the qualitative difference between the known and the unknown.[4] Certainly this is true of what Thomas Kuhn has termed 'revolutionary science' in contrast to the ordinary process of experiment-construction and data-verification. However, the design of experiments and confirmation of known data can themselves lead to confrontations

---

that draws tentative implications from the results of a level-2 argument is a level-3 argument. Such arguments are heuristic and must be corroborated by other lines of investigation.

3    These paragraphs are adapted from my article, 'Scientific Work and Its Theological Dimensions: Toward a Theology of Natural Science', in Jitse Van der Meer (ed.), *Facets of Faith and Science*, Vol. 1 (Lanham, Md.: University Press of America, 1996), 229.

4    Thomas Kuhn, *The Structure of Scientific Revolutions*, 2nd edn (Chicago: University of Chicago Press, 1970). A similar distinction has been drawn for observational astronomy between analysis of known phenomena and the search for new cosmic phenomena; Martin Harwit, *Cosmic Discovery: The Search, Scope, and Heritage of Astronomy* (Cambridge, Mass: MIT Press, 1984), 19, 24. The way the latter search depends on new technologies will be discussed in Chapter 4.

with the unexpected or unknown. The work of scientists is always just a step away from the unknown. So perhaps the term 'revolutionary science' is overly dramatic. A more ethnographic category like 'independent, risky work'[5] may be more helpful in conveying the uncertainty involved in all scientific research. In any case, if we are to do justice to the actual practice of science, and not just its documented results, we must include in our description a consideration of the conditions that enable our scientists to do what they do.

For convenience, I shall refer to such a consideration of practical conditions as a 'thick description' of science. The phrase is borrowed from the work of Clifford Geertz, who argued against strictly cognitive views of cultural anthropology in the early 1970s. Taking exception to the notion that a culture consists in rules of human behavior and interpretation, Geertz argued for a 'thick view' of culture that includes the actual contexts that make both behavior and interpretation possible.[6]

In the case of science-fostering societies, culture is just one of many aspects of such a thick description,[7] and anthropology is just one of many tools of analysis. So there is some semantic stretching involved in extrapolating the idea of 'thick description' from anthropology to our entire project. However, the concept will prove useful as a way of summarising the main points of the following chapters in an easily recognizable form. Those summaries will have the following form: a thicker description of natural science leads to a thicker description of some area of theology, for example: (1) the relation of God to creation; or (2) the cosmos; or (3) the history of theology; or (4) the attributes of God. This formulation helps to make the overall case that theological questions and options flow naturally out of a consideration of scientific endeavour.

In arguing for a thick description of science – one that takes the life and work of scientists into account – I am tilting against the conception of science fostered by most media and by the teaching of science in most of our schools and universities. In most people's minds and in most science-theology discussions, science consists primarily of scientific 'facts', scientific theories, and sometimes scientific applications.[8] More sophisticated discussions may include simplified scientific methods. But only rarely do students get to know anything about the actual history of science or even about the lives and the projects of the scientists whose ideas they study.

The problem with understanding human enterprises is not unique to science. The usual approach is a little like studying visual art simply by going to lectures and

---

5    The phrase 'independent, risky work' comes from Sharon Traweek, *Beamtimes and Lifetimes: The World of High Energy Physicists* (Cambridge, Mass: Harvard University Press, 1988), 87.

6    Clifford Geertz, *The Interpretation of Cultures: Selected Essays* (New York: Basic Books, 1973), 9-13, 17.

7    Some other ways of thickening the description of natural science would be to look at the way in which it is taught and studied in our schools and to consider its technological applications or social and environmental impacts.

8    A good critique of the presentation of science in American middle-school textbooks can be found in John Hubisz, 'Middle-School Texts Don't Make the Grade', *Physics Today* 56 (May 2003), 50-54. Such truncations of the thickness of scientific endeavour are comparable to the reduction of human cultures to ideas and rules in the cognitive anthropology against which Geertz argued so passionately.

visiting museums rather than visiting artists' studios. Both science and art are important human endeavours, but most of us have very thin views of either. Our culture almost always enforces a separation of the private aptitudes and motivations of producers from the public marketing of goods for consumers. So the problem I am addressing here should not come as a complete surprise.

Some light can be shed on the problem by considering the few endeavours that are exceptions to this cultural norm. Two areas of Western culture that do not generally separate personal aptitude and motivation from public performance are politics (where other kinds of obfuscation are often at work) and sports. To focus on the latter for a moment: it would be unthinkable to publicize a sports event today without conveying information about the health and morale of the athletes. The rigours of the sport and the conditions imposed by the aging process are commonly discussed in relation to the limits of what is physically possible. The contrast to disciplines like science and the visual arts could not be greater. We are used to very thick descriptions of sports events – everything from detailed statistics to Mother's Day greetings. Our understanding of science is rather thin by comparison.

The reasons for these differences among disciplines have yet to be investigated. Clearly the fact that athletes have to perform in real time in the presence of the public has a lot to do with it. But the same is not true for professional musicians. We do not learn very much about the lives of symphony musicians or ballet dancers. On the other hand, we do get to know a good deal about very special kinds of scientists, like astronauts, who happen to fascinate the public. So media exposure is an important factor. The separation of the products of science from our knowledge about the life and work of scientists is a cultural artifact based on the fact that our relationships transcend the traditional limits of small communities: only the mass media are in a position to reconnect producer and consumer and thereby thicken the description of marketable human endeavours. The issue of public knowledge bears further consideration.

For now it is sufficient to conclude this part of the discussion with the following result: limiting 'science' to its cognitive dimensions (a set of ideas or theories or methods) is a relatively thin abstraction. If science is viewed abstractly, all kinds of problems naturally arise for the dialogue with theology (also viewed abstractly) – different views of creation, different approaches to human nature, different epistemologies. These are certainly important problems, and they deserve all the attention that they get in current discussions.[9] But a thicker view of science will engage theological endeavour more directly. Apparent tensions between the two disciplines can be viewed in a more positive light when they are seen to result from questions and paradoxes in the description of science's foundations. Then theological endeavour is part of a thicker description, leading to a broader rationality that makes more sense out of scientific endeavour itself.[10]

---

9    For a wide-ranging review of the various models for dialog, see Ian G. Barbour, *When Science Meets Religion* (San Francisco: Harper, 2000). For an analysis of Barbour's typology, see C. Kaiser, 'Scientific Work and Its Theological Dimensions: Toward a Theology of Natural Science', in Jitse Van der Meer (ed.), *Facets of Faith and Science* (Lanham, Md.: University Press of America, 1996), 1:223-46 (224-8, 240 n.63).

10    Lesslie Newbigin posited a 'wider and more inclusive rationality' that makes room for key Christian doctrines in contrast to reductionist views of science in his 1984 Warfield

## The contingency of scientific endeavour

Let us start with the purpose of natural science: its general purpose is to explore all accessible features of the space-time world and to explain them by positing principles and laws. In order to carry out this endeavour it is necessary to collect ever-wider fields of information by developing new technologies and to interpret them by constructing mathematical models and histories.[11] Progress results from a cycle that alternates between experimentally derived information and theoretically constructed models: models are built in order to explain the available information, and information is gathered in order to test available models. As a rule there are always 'anomalies' – features that are not accounted for by any available model. So, new models need to be constructed. But new models are usually underdetermined – their validity is generally not decidable on the basis of available information. So, new experiments must be designed to gather further information. And the cycle goes on.

All of this adds up to the crucial observation that science is a highly contingent enterprise. There is nothing either automatic or guaranteed by its progress. This outlook could be termed 'scientific fallibilism'. It can be compared with the traditional philosophical fallibilism, for which all predictions are viewed as being uncertain. Strictly speaking, no one knows for sure that a warmer spring season will follow winter or even that the sun will rise again after it sets. In the case of these regular cycles, however, we can discover natural mechanisms that at least make the recurrence of phenomena like the seasons highly probable. We can be sure that spring will come again unless there is a catastrophe of some sort. At least, that is true for the short to moderately long term.[12] In the case of scientific endeavour, however, there are no natural mechanisms to ensure such a probability. Scientists are continually facing the unknown. They do succeed in solving problems, but there is always the nagging possibility that they may be wasting their time.[13] The wonder is that they succeed as much as they do.

---

Lectures, published as *Foolishness to the Greeks: The Gospel and Western Culture* (Grand Rapids: Eerdmans, 1986), 90. A similar point was made by John Polkinghorne, 'The Reason Within and the Reason Without', in Ronald E. Mickens (ed.), *Mathematics and Science* (Singapore: World Scientific, 1990), 181.

11   In terms of information theory, such laws and histories can be described as algorithmic compressions of the information we have about the universe; cf. John D. Barrow, *Theories of Everything: The Quest for Ultimate Explanation* (Oxford: Clarendon Press, 1991), 10-11; Paul Davies, *The Mind of God: The Scientific Basis for a Rational World* (New York: Simon & Schuster, 1992), 135-6. However, most laws and histories are originally derived as speculative hypotheses rather than actual compressions of data.

12   On the longer scales of tens of thousands, millions, and billions of years we can look forward to a new glacial era and the eventual destruction of earth; Peter Ward and Don Brownlee, *The Life and Death of Planet Earth: How the New Science of Astrobiology Charts the Ultimate Fate of Our World* (New York: Times Books, 2002).

13   See Traweek, *Beamtimes and Lifetimes*, 75-6, 100-101 for a realistic description of the anxieties that high energy physicists live with. This entire study is a good example of a thick description in Geertz's sense.

Following our previous statement of the purpose of natural science, we can suggest two kinds of contingency: those on the side of information gathering and those on the side of model building.[14] Information gathering is of course limited by the technologies that are available. For example, in the early nineteenth century, Auguste Comte stated that scientists would never know what the stars are made out of.[15] Although his pessimism sounds incredibly short-sighted today, when he made this statement the tools need for optical spectroscopy were only beginning to be developed, and their possible impact on science was unforeseen. One might argue that Comte should have been more circumspect about his strictures. We have come to take progress in technology for granted. A new space probe or more powerful computer is always just around the corner. However, a degree of agnosticism about developing technologies is always in order. The fact that we have to work with material substances places limits on what we can do – we simply cannot build a particle accelerator the size of the solar system or run a computer program for $10^{127}$ years as would be required to solve some important scientific problems.[16]

There are also economic and even political limits: even relatively feasible technologies cannot be built and deployed unless they can be paid for. One of the most famous examples of a scientist's encounter with the contingency of government funding was Steven Weinberg's advocacy of the Superconducting Super Collider (SSC) in the early 1990s. According to Weinberg, 'The urgency of our desire to see the SSC completed comes from a sense that without it we may not be able to continue with the great intellectual adventure of discovering the final laws of nature.'[17] The SSC was designed to provide enough energy (up to 20 trillion electron volts) to reveal the existence of hypothetical particles needed for the unification of three fundamental forces and to account for the origin of the masses of elementary particles. But funding for the SSC was cut off by the US Congress in October 1993. It was felt that the cost of the project was greater than the American public would willingly support. As a result, physicists in America were forced to contemplate the possibility that the frontier of high energy particle physics might soon be closing – not the actuality, but at least the possibility.[18]

Here is another example of such a contingency – one that is still undecided at the time of my writing. On 30 April 2003 an ultimatum was delivered to the team of physicists and technicians who were developing a space mission designed to test important aspects of Einstein's General Theory of Relativity (Gravity Probe-B).

14    The following discussion is inspired by the work of John D. Barrow, *Impossibility: The Limits of Science and the Science of Limits* (Oxford: Clarendon Press, 1998), but it is organized differently.

15    Comte, *Cours de philosophie positive* (1830-42), cited in Gillispie, ed., *Dictionary of Scientific Biography*, 16 vols (New York: Scribner's, 1970-80), 3:377; cf Barrow, *Impossibility*, 47.

16    Aviezri S. Fraenkel has shown that computing the structure (folding) of even simple proteins (with 104 amino acids) would take a supercomputer $10^{127}$ years; John L. Casti, 'Confronting Science's Logical Limits', *Scientific American* 275 (Oct. 1996), 103; cf. Barrow, *Impossibility*, 104-107.

17    Steven Weinberg, *Dreams of a Final Theory* (New York: Pantheon Books, 1992), 274.

18    Charles Seife, 'Physics Tries to Leave the Tunnel', *Science* 302 (3 Oct. 2003), 36-8.

The outstanding technical issues were relatively simple ones involving a heater and some fuses. But the completion of the mission had already been delayed for years and the projected cost had escalated by hundreds of millions of dollars. The ultimatum delivered by the National Aeronautics and Space Agency (NASA) stated that funding would be terminated unless several tests and other conditions were fulfilled.[19] As it happens, much of the information to be derived from this mission could probably be obtained in other ways, but an awareness of the economics of the project thickens the description of science and illustrates one kind of contingency that underlies all modern scientific endeavour. We shall look at some of the conditions that underlie modern technology and the theological issues they raise in more detail in Chapter 4.

Information gathering may also have limits in principle. In astrophysics, most information is teased out of faint light signals (electromagnetic waves) from outer space. Other information is collected from high-energy particles and the measurement of magnetic fields in space. Eventually gravity waves may also be tapped. However, there may be regions of the universe, entirely different from our own, that are so distant that no electromagnetic signals from those regions would ever reach us. The theory of cosmic inflation, which is supported by a preponderance of recent observational data, pretty much guarantees this result.[20] Information may also be irretrievably lost in black holes and in the wormholes of space-time.[21] Information about our universe may also be affected by the very process of gathering and storing information.[22] We ought not be dogmatic about positing limits, but neither ought we to assume that we can get around them all. So much for information gathering.

Even when information is available, it must be interpreted, and this step results in further contingencies in scientific endeavour. Scientists usually account for observed patterns and anomalies in the experimental data by constructing mathematical models. The ingredients of these models may already be available, but they may have to be developed or even invented from scratch. Like technologies, new forms of mathematics must repeatedly be developed. There is no guarantee that the needed tools will be available at any given time. In fact, mathematics has its own limits:

---

19  'News of the Week – Space Physics – NASA Orders Make-or-Break Tests for Gravity Probe', *Science* 300 (9 May 2003), 880.

20  Barrow, *Theories of Everything*, 52-3; and idem, *Impossibility*, 166-9, 189. The 'ekpyrotic model' of cosmology, first proposed in 2001, can account for the origin of our universe without cosmological inflation. This fascinating theory has yet to be developed in detail but it would imply that even the most distant regions of the universe would probably look very much like our own and avoid the problem raised by Barrow. The observation of very long wavelength gravity waves (or their effect on the microwave background) could decide which of the two theories is to be preferred. The inflationary model predicts the existence of such waves whereas the ekpyrotic model does not; Alison Boyle, 'The Edge of Infinity', *New Scientist* 171 (29 Sept. 2001), 26-9.

21  Barrow, *Theories of Everything*, 109. Information can also be lost in bound entanglement states, which are the equivalent of black holes in quantum information theory; Barbara M. Terhal, Michael M. Wolf, and Andrew C. Doherty, 'Quantum Entanglement: A Modern Perspective', *Physics* Today 56 (April 2003), 49a.

22  Stephen Hawking has made this point in a conversation with Michael Brooks, 'The Impossible Puzzle', *New Scientist* (5 April 2003), 34-5.

some may be due to the limits of the human brain – even with the assistance of computers (back to the contingency of technology) – but others are due to the existence of noncomputable numbers and the impossibility of constructing self-contained deductive logical formalisms (Gödel's theorem).[23]

As a result, there are often patterns in data files that go unrecognized for lack of the needed mathematical models. Scientists hope they will be able go back to look for those patterns once the models become available – a process that involves a complex sequence of steps in insight, perseverance, and successful retrieval. When, for example, a team of high-energy physicists is fortunate enough to discover a new subatomic particle, other physicists can go back over previously collected data to confirm the new result. In such cases, the data were there long before their significance was recognized. There are even cases where looking at old data for confirmation of one new particle leads to the discovery of still further particles.[24] So scientists may sometimes have access to important information without even realizing its significance.

Often we assume that any pattern or anomaly can easily be seen once you look at it in the right way – computer programs can be developed to assist the human eye and textbooks try to make the patterns look obvious to the reader. But there is nothing automatic about the ability of the human brain to recognize subtle patterns, particularly when they have never been recognized before. Anyone who has tried to become proficient at chess or a complex card-game knows the difficulty from experience. Obviously all of the patterns we already know about are humanly recognizable. But in most cases they would not be recognizable to a frog or even to a chimpanzee. Even among humans, the ability to recognize complex patterns varies widely. Consequently, there may well be important features of the space-time world that are far too subtle for any human brain, even a human brain aided by a humanly designed computer.[25] We shall consider the conditions underlying the needed human intelligence in more detail in Chapter 2.

In view of the technological, economic, physiological and mathematical limits just described, we cannot be sure how far scientific endeavour will continue into the future. We should not take its progress for granted. But it is not my purpose to make readers pessimistic about the prospects. The amazing thing is that scientific endeavour works at all in arenas that are so far removed from everyday experience. Our next step is to turn the problem around and consider what general conditions have to be fulfilled in order for science to work as well as it has.

---

23   Barrow, *Impossibility*, 210, 215-16; cf. Davies, *The Mind of God*, 104-9, 126-34.

24   On 28 April 2003, researchers at the Stanford Linear Accelerator Collider (SLAC) announced the discovery of a new meson, $D_s$ (2317), which weighed in at 10 per cent lower than the mass that had been theoretically predicted and so challenged the 'Standard Model' known as quantum chromodynamics. Thereupon a team of physicists at Cornell University particle collider (CESR) looked back through their past experimental data and found evidence not only for the $D_s$ (2317), but also another underweight meson, the $D_s$ (2463); 'New Particles Pose Puzzle', *Science News* 163 (24 May 2003), 333. On the current status of the Standard Model itself, see Gordon Kane, 'The Dawn of Physics Beyond the Standard Model', *Scientific American* 288 (June 2003), 68-75.

25   Barrow, *Impossibility*, 89-90.

**Four foundations supporting scientific endeavour**

Examining the preconditions that make scientific endeavour possible is one way of thickening the description of scientific endeavour.[26] Scientific work has a set of necessary, cumulative preconditions or foundations that open avenues for thickening our way of doing theology (theological endeavour).

Some of these foundations were suggested already in our discussion of the contingency of the scientific endeavour. Among those contingencies were the development of information-gathering technologies and the capacity of the human brain for building effective theoretical models. Underlying the development of the needed technologies is the existence of industries, transportation systems, and means of communication that can exist only in a highly industrialized society. I shall refer to this as the *societal condition* of scientific endeavour. It will lead us to consider the possible role of industrialization and secularization in a biblical view of history and its implications for the attributes of God (a thicker doctrine of God).[27]

The development of industrial technologies is based on earlier (pre-industrial) developments in the sciences like Newtonian mechanics and thermodynamics. Therefore, advanced technology also requires the pre-existence of a cultural tradition that fosters the investigation of hidden recesses of the space-time world. I shall refer to this as the *cultural condition* of scientific endeavour.[28] The scientific revolution of the 16th and 17th centuries would not have been possible without such a science-fostering culture to sustain them. The cultural values and beliefs needed for an investigation are not unique to Western civilization, but neither are they universal. This condition will lead us to a review of the role of the 'creationist tradition' in Western civilization and to reevaluate the way the history of Western theology is presented in most courses and texts (a thicker historical theology).[29]

Unlike cultural traditions, the underlying ability of humans to create scientific models and theories is a cultural universal. I shall refer to this as the *anthropological condition* of scientific endeavour because it relates to intrinsic capabilities of the human

---

26   Some other ways of thickening the description of scientific endeavour would be to study the aesthetics of scientific endeavour or the psychological stresses and ethical issues that scientists face; cf. Traweek, *Beamtimes and Lifetime*, on the latter pair.

27   My analysis of the secularization issue was developed in 'From Biblical Secularity to Modern Secularism: Historical Aspects and Stages', in S. Marianne Postiglione and Robert Brungs (eds), *Secularism versus Biblical Secularity* (St Louis: ITEST Faith/Science Press, 1994), 1-43.

28   In 1924, Edwin Arthur Burtt's idea of 'metaphysical foundations of modern science' corresponds roughly to what I am calling the Cultural Foundation of scientific endeavour; Burtt, *The Metaphysical Foundations of Modern Physical Science*, 2nd edn (London: Kegan Paul; New York: Humanities Press, 1932).

29   The historic 'creationist tradition' is a composite of beliefs that supports scientific endeavour and is not to be confused with 'creation science'. I reviewed the history of the 'creationist tradition' in *Creation and the History of Science* (London: Marshall Pickering, 1991), and more extensively in *Creational Theology and the History of Physical Science: The Creationist Tradition from Basil to Bohr* (Leiden: Brill, 1997). Subsequent references will be made to the latter work.

species.[30] An evolutionary approach to the emergence of science-fostering intelligence will lead us to examine the evidence for the practice of soul journey in Paleolithic societies and to consideration of the spirit-matter complex (a thicker cosmology).[31]

Underlying all of these conditions, the most basic condition of all is the particular kind of universe we live in. Science would not be possible without the existence of a lawful cosmos. Of all the possible universes that might exist, only those that are governed by laws or symmetries of some sort can produce species capable of doing science.[32] I shall refer to this as the *cosmic condition* of scientific endeavour. Analysis of this condition will not lead to a cogent argument for the existence of God (the natural theology option), but it will raise the question of a Lawgiver and, given the biblical tradition, it will require a rethinking of God's role in creation and of the nature of the laws of nature (a thicker view of God in relation to creation).[33]

If we rearrange these preconditions and start with the most basic, we have the following necessary, cumulative conditions or foundations of scientific endeavour:

1. a cosmos with laws or symmetries (cosmic condition)
2. a species with brains capable of investigating those laws (anthropological condition)
3. a culture that fosters scientific investigation (cultural condition) and
4. an industrial society capable of producing the technologies needed to collect the needed information (societal condition).

Each of these conditions will be taken up and analysed in one of the following chapters. Detailed consideration of each one will lead to interdisciplinary questions that call for serious theological endeavour.[34]

---

30   There are various branches of anthropology. The capacity of the human brain to create scientific models is a subject for physical anthropology as distinct from cultural anthropology.

31   I first developed these ideas in reviewing the writings of my mentor, Thomas F. Torrance; Kaiser, 'Humanity in an Intelligible Cosmos: Non-Duality in Albert Einstein and Thomas Torrance', in Elmer M. Colyer (ed.), *The Promise of Trinitarian Theology: Theologians in Dialogue with T. F. Torrance* (Lanham, Md.: Rowman & Littlefield, 2001), 239-67.

32   The deepest laws of physics we know have the form of mathematical symmetries. Symmetries may be ultimate in one sense, but there is also the need for principles of symmetry-breaking and emergent phenomena; George Ellis, 'Physics and the Real World', *Physics Today* 58 (July 2005), 49-54.

33   The basis of these ideas were presented in two of my earlier articles: Kaiser, 'The Laws of Nature and the Nature of God', in Jitse Van der Meer (ed.), *Facets of Faith and Science* (Lanham, Md.: University Press of America, 1996), 4:185-97; and idem, 'The Integrity of Creation and the Social Nature of God', *Scottish Journal of Theology* 49 (1996), 261-90.

34   Theological endeavour is just one way of addressing the issues embedded in the foundations of scientific endeavour. Trajectories could also be traced into philosophy (esp. epistemology), economics, ethics, and politics. Theology and philosophy are perhaps the only disciplines of sufficient generality to address all of the foundations we have listed. Here we view the sciences as human endeavours rather than as bodies of knowledge, and we approach theological endeavour through the foundations of scientific endeavour, in contrast to Nancey Murphy and George F. R. Ellis, who locate theology (and ethics) at the summit of a hierarchy

These four conditions are all necessary for the origin and development of natural science, but they are not sufficient by themselves. A variety of other conditions could be added. For example, special properties of our universe like the force of cosmic expansion and the value of the fine structure constant are required to allow the formation of stars and planets and the evolution of life. This is the basis of the so-called 'Anthropic Principle' – the properties of our universe must be almost exactly the ones that we observe or else it would not have been possible for life to evolve.[35] Much has been written on the theological significance of this topic and its significance for purpose in the universe.[36] However, the Anthropic Principle is not relevant to the viability of scientific endeavour as such. As a condition for the evolution of life, it requires that the laws of nature have a particular form, but it is too specific to affect the most basic condition of the existence of laws of nature, and it is too general to guarantee the existence of species with the intelligent needed to do science. I shall only touch on the Anthropic Principle in Chapter 1.

Another necessary condition for the viability of scientific endeavour is the existence of a stable, habitable planetary environment. Such an environment may be very rare in our universe.[37] In fact, the very special (and fleeting) environmental conditions of planet Earth raise issues of for the study of eschatology – how humans will confront the inevitable deterioration of conditions in our 'habitable zone' around the sun and how that relates to biblical eschatology. Like the Anthropic Principle, however, the condition of habitable environments is not related to the viability of science as such. So, while other conditions could be considered, the four that we discuss here will suffice to demonstrate the method and to stimulate further discussion.

Besides being necessary, these four conditions of scientific endeavour are also cumulative and forward-contingent. The existence of a lawful cosmos does not necessarily lead to the emergence of science-fostering intelligence. The existence of science-fostering intelligence does not necessarily lead to the emergence of a science-fostering culture. The existence of a science-fostering culture would not necessarily produce an industrial base sophisticated enough to produce the technologies needed for modern science. The overall picture is one of necessary conditions and contingent developments.

I shall use the term 'foundations' in this study because it captures the complex idea of conditions that underlie scientific endeavour and that build on one another

---

of sciences; Murphy and Ellis, *On the Moral Nature of the Universe: Theology, Cosmology, and Ethics* (Minneapolis: Fortress Press, 1996), 16, passim.

35  Technically this is the 'Strong Anthropic Principle'; John D. Barrow and Frank J. Tipler, *The Anthropic Cosmological Principle* (Oxford: Oxford University Press, 1986, 1988), 21-2.

36  For good review of the debate concerning the Anthropic Principle and an able defense of its validity as evidence of purpose in the universe, see Karl Giberson, 'The Anthropic Principle: A Postmodern Creation Myth?' *Journal of Interdisciplinary Studies* 9 (1997), 63-90. For a discussion in the renewed interest in the principle since 2003, see Dan Falk, 'The Anthropic Principle's Surprising Resurgence', *Sky and Telescope* 107 (March 2004), 43-7.

37  On the special conditions required for habitable environments, see Kaiser, 'Extraterrestrial Life and Extraterrestrial Intelligence', *Reformed Review* 51 (1998), 77-91; Peter Ward and Don Brownlee, *Rare Earth: Why Complex Life is Uncommon in the Universe* (New York: Copernicus Books, 2003).

in a cumulative, forward-contingent manner. It is easy to visualize foundations of scientific endeavour by imagining a pyramid of blocks laid one on top of the other, with the most basic one, representing a lawful cosmos, on the bottom and the most dependent, scientific endeavour, on the top (see Figure I).

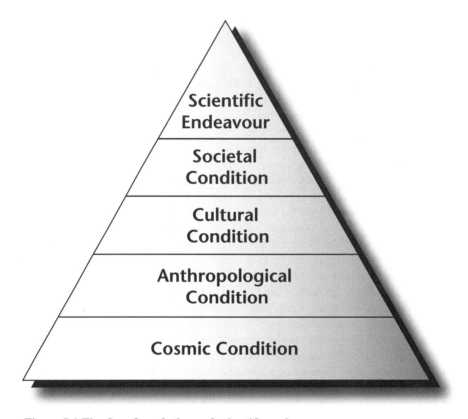

**Figure I.1 The four foundations of scientific endeavour**

The blocks in Figure I.1 represent the preconditions or foundations of scientific endeavour and illustrate the idea of thick description. The decreasing size of the blocks illustrates increasing contingency as one goes up. One could develop a drawing that includes endeavours besides science simply by adding summits supported by different blocks, all resting on the same Cosmic Foundation. A complete picture would look something like a tree with many branches and even more twigs and leaves to represent the variety of endeavours. The life of each leaf would draw from all the structures that support it.

The idea of foundations here has nothing to do with the idea of philosophic 'foundationalism' – the belief that certain basic presuppositions must be posited in order to sustain any rational discourse.[38] Our preconditions or foundations are actual

---

38   On the subject of classical foundationalism, see, for example, Alister E. McGrath, *A Scientific Theology, Volume 2: Reality* (Edinburgh: T&T Clark, 2002), 20-39.

features of the world in which scientists work rather than presuppositions.[39] Nor are all of these foundations appropriate for other forms of human endeavour. A different set of foundations would have to be explored in the investigation of social justice or music.

An alternative way to visualize the idea of conditions that underlie scientific endeavour would be to use a set of concentric spherical shells with the cosmic condition at the centre and the other conditions as concentric shells surrounding it (see Figure I.2).

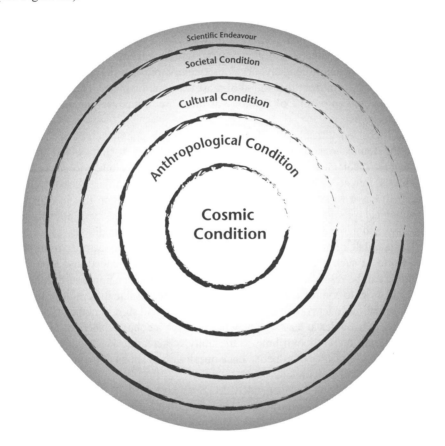

**Figure I.2 The interior shells supporting scientific endeavour**

The decreasing thickness of the spherical shells in Figure I.2 illustrates the increasing contingency or the preconditions of scientific endeavour. Once again, allowance must be made for a variety of other shells expanding out of the same center and supporting other endeavours besides science.

---

39  The Cultural Foundation involves the presupposition or belief that the world is comprehensible to humans (Chapter 3). However, we treat it here as a contingent cultural tradition rather than a logically necessary presupposition.

## Toward theological endeavour

Scientific endeavour occurs within specific cultures and traditions. The same is true of theological endeavour. The discussion of theology in this book will relate primarily to the biblical (Judeo-Christian) tradition – the tradition to which the author adheres. But our discussion will be rigorously science-based, contingent, open-ended, and ecumenically inclusive within that tradition.

Our approach to theology will be science-based in that theological doctrines will be brought in only as they address issues raised in our discussion of the foundations of scientific endeavour and as allowed by rigorously scientific analysis of those foundations. The theological resources drawn on will be derived from the biblical tradition, but the arrangement of the material will be governed by the outline of the foundations of scientific endeavour. Consequently, our theological discussion will take a different form from that found in most textbook theology. There are as many ways to develop an outline of theology as there are to analyse human endeavours like the sciences.

The discussion of theology will also be progressively contingent. Each observation about the foundations of scientific endeavour will lead to unresolved questions and suggest theological possibilities, but no attempt will be made to convert those possibilities into necessary inferences. This will show that scientific endeavour (thickly described) has a variety of seams or trajectories of investigation that lead naturally to theological questions. The theological payoff is in the necessity of addressing the questions, and in the discovery of resources in the theological traditions.

The mandate of modern science is to explore all accessible features of the space-time world in such a way that everything can be comprehended and all relevant questions can be resolved. It will be argued that some wider frame of rationality is needed in order to complete this project and make sense of scientific endeavour itself, i.e., for scientific endeavour to be self-referential. We will show that the invocation of theistic ideas provides at least one way to give such a coherent account of scientific endeavour and thereby contribute to the unity of scientific knowledge. Once you look beneath the surface of either science or religion as social phenomenon you find that they are deeply entangled.

Our discussion will be openended. In some cases, it will be possible to make predictions and test some steps in our argument. In other cases, suggestions will be made for the reordering of theological disciplines as suggested by the study of the preconditions of natural science. The basic point is that thickening the description of scientific endeavour will thicken our view of both Creator and cosmos. But, as already mentioned, a different analysis of the foundations of scientific endeavour could be developed, and a different theological tradition might provide resources for a very different interpretation of those foundations.

Let us return for a moment to our visual model of a series of blocks with the most basic one on the bottom and the smallest on the top. The small block on the top represents scientific endeavour, and the underlying blocks represent its foundations. There may be a large number of these foundations, but we are working with just four of them. The theological issues we will discuss can be visualized as lying in the same plane as the foundational blocks, but extending to one side. The theological resources from the biblical tradition can be visualized as a complementary set of blocks selected in such a way that they dovetail with first set. Each set of blocks can stand on its own, but a stronger arrangement (representing a broader rationality) can be achieved by viewing them together.[40]

Our discussion will also be ecumenical. No one theological tradition has the resources to address all of the issues that will be raised. Therefore, patristic and early Jewish sources will be employed in addition to commonly known Christian teachings. There is no attempt to be strictly confessional.

Each of the following four studies stands on its own and can be read independently of the others. Readers may wish to check the brief abstracts at the beginning of each chapter and pick out the chapters that most interest them. However, there are several interesting overlaps among the studies that contribute to a cumulative effect and there will be some cross-referencing along the way. The concluding chapter will address these overlaps more directly and synthesise the four studies into a unified vision of science as indicated in the title.

On an autobiographical note, I should explain that beginning this investigation with a description of scientific endeavour reflects my own growing experience. My university training in physics and astrophysics and my discovery of spirituality through anthropology and depth psychology are reflected in the observations I will make and the illustrations I will use. For me, this will not be interconnecting abstract ideas so much as reviewing real learnings and personal choices. A theology that is imposed on science from the outside is not likely to carry conviction for those who are not already believers. I hope to show that theological questions and confessional options emerge from analysing the foundations of scientific endeavour in much the same way that scientific questions come from analysing the features of the a space-time world. In short, a thick description of natural science leads to a thick description of nature, humanity, history and God.

---

40   In terms of Ian Barbour's typology of ways to interrelate science and theology, the method we are developing might be classed as either a 'Dialogue Model' with an emphasis on presuppositions and limit-questions or an 'Integration Model' along the lines of natural theology and continuing creation; see Barbour, *Religion in an Age of Science* (San Francisco: Harper & Row, 1990), 17-20, 24-6; *When Science Meets Religion*, 23-4, 28-30, 52-4, 59-61, 114-15. However, all of these models presuppose that theology is defined as a body of discourse separate from science, whereas I intend to discern theological issues and theological discourse within the foundations of scientific endeavour and follow those through in search of a thicker view of relevant theological doctrines. It is true that as formal bodies of knowledge theology and science are distinct and need to be interrelated, but as human endeavours they are inseparable. The integration in question is more like that of Maxwell's integration of electric and magnetic force fields than it is like the integration of two separate cultures. Paul Tillich's 'method of correlation' did something very similar for existential philosophy and Christian theology; Tillich, *Systematic Theology*, Vol. 1 (Chicago: University of Chicago Press, 1951), 61. However, Tillich did not work specifically with the natural sciences in this context or with the traditional theology of the fathers and rabbis. His main concerns were more soteriological than creational.

# CHAPTER ONE

# Cosmic Foundation: The Challenge of a Lawful Universe

**Abstract**

The viability of scientific endeavour places special conditions on the kind of universe in which we live and do natural science. Such a universe must be governed by laws or symmetries of some kind. Inquiry into the reasons for the existence of a lawful universe, based on the ideas of inflationary cosmology and the possible existence of a multiverse (multiple universes), leads to several theological questions and challenges. Addressing those challenges establishes some conditions for a viable doctrine of God. A thick description of scientific endeavour, therefore, leads to a thicker view of God's relationship to the natural world.

**Keywords**: cosmology, deism, divine council, God-of-the-gaps, laws of nature, Midrash, multiverse, personal God, transcendence and immanence, triune God.

In this first chapter, we discuss the *cosmic foundation* of scientific endeavour and the mystery of origins embedded within it. We proceed to use the tools of modern cosmology to investigate (but never quite resolve) the mystery and explore the possible implications for theological endeavour, particularly for the doctrines of God and creation.[1]

Readers hoping for an attempted proof of a Creator may be disappointed. The existence of God cannot be demonstrated from the study of the cosmic foundation of scientific endeavour any more than it can from the study of the cosmos itself. What can be demonstrated is the necessity of theological endeavour – discourse concerning the God question. We will demonstrate a smooth transition to theological discourse; we will develop an argument for *a posteriori* consistency between the existence of a lawful cosmos and belief in divine creation; and we will draw several mandates for revising traditional ways of thinking about the Creator. The primary theological purchase will be the viability of belief in the immanence and personality of a cosmic Lawgiver. Religious faith and theological doctrine can be interrelated with modern science and freshly articulated as a result of the encounter, but they cannot be demonstrated from science alone.

---

1    The use of the term 'mystery' is a way of focusing attention on an unsolved problem. As Henry Margenau has stated, 'a mystery is but a challenge' to inquiry and understanding; Margenau, *Open Vistas: Philosophical Perspectives of Modern Science* (New Haven: Yale University Press, 1961), 76.

We have defined natural science as the endeavour to explore all accessible features of the space-time world in such a way that everything can eventually be comprehended by positing laws and constructing histories using the tools of mathematics and logical inference (from the Introduction). The focus of this chapter is one of the ideas embedded in this definition: our universe is governed by mathematical laws and evolves in a way that can be described as a fairly coherent history.[2] This observation will lead us to the question of the origin of such laws and the possibility of divine creation. But first, we need some preliminary clarifications.

**Contingent lawfulness and complex realism: four clarifications**

Before we investigate the origin of cosmic laws, four general points need to be made for clarification – points that are general in the sense that they do not relate to a specific cosmic theory.

First, there is no need to suppose that our universe is entirely lawful or that its laws can be written in any simple form. Some laws are purely statistical. Some may change with time or with location in the universe, in accordance, perhaps, with some higher-order law. There might even be laws or symmetries that cannot be exactly formulated or that, even if they could be formulated, would defy human understanding (a topic for Chapter 2). For the purposes of our argument, we need only observe that no science would be possible in a universe that was not governed to some extent by definable laws. It is this contingent lawfulness that we need to inquire about.

The point made here is more general than the so-called Anthropic Principle. The Anthropic Principle states that the universe in which we live must be consistent with preconditions necessary for the existence of life.[3] If, for example, the strong nuclear force were slightly weaker than it is, there would be nothing in the universe but hydrogen. If, on the other hand, it were slightly stronger than it is, all of the hydrogen in the universe would have been combined into helium and there could be no water ($H_2O$). Conditions like the precise value of the nuclear force are of course necessary for the existence of intelligent life. On the other hand, an extremely hostile environment for life as we know it could still be lawful enough to allow scientific endeavour in principle, even if it did not allow the existence of beings capable of pursuing it. All that we require for our purposes in this chapter is the existence of cosmic laws or symmetries that can serve as the object of science. If required to use a label, I could call this a 'nomic principle' rather than an 'anthropic' one.

The second preliminary point to be made is that there is no a priori necessity for the existence of cosmic laws. Modern education has trained us to think in terms of scientific laws from primary school onwards. So we normally take a high degree of lawfulness for granted. In order for us to recapture an appropriate sense of wonder about such lawfulness, we need seriously to consider the alternatives. In principle a universe could exist that is entirely random in every respect. A universe could even

---

2    I shall refer here to 'our universe' in view of the possibility that there may exist many other universes – a topic we shall consider presently.

3    Barrow and Tipler, *Anthropic Cosmic Principle*, 21.

lack any well-defined space-time dimensionality or temporal order.[4] Our cultural history and our educational systems have equipped us well for life, but they may also have created an epistemological blind spot in our larger worldview. Why should the universe be lawful in any sense at all? Addressing this question will lead us to explore some of the latest theories of cosmology to see if they can explain the origin of the cosmic foundation of scientific endeavour.

The third point is that the wonder of cosmic lawfulness does not depend on a strongly realist epistemology. We recognize that the process of scientific endeavour and the forms of scientific theories and supporting technologies are socially conditioned. A scientific problem can only be solved by drawing on and perhaps modifying a culturally conditioned fund of concepts and tools. Even a physicist like Einstein, who worked very much on his own, could not have developed the General Theory of Relativity without matrix algebra and the formalism of non-Euclidean geometry, which were available through institutionally supported networks and publications. Isaac Newton, who invented a new mathematical calculus to solve problems, had to rely on a tradition of prior work in mathematics mediated by university training and available textbooks. In fact, the idea of laws of nature and belief in the possibility of doing meaningful science are themselves cultural artifacts – we shall discuss them in Chapter 3 (the cultural foundation). All scientific endeavour is historically and culturally conditioned.

The point, however, is that socially conditioned theories and technologies would not be sustainable in a world without any regularity or lawfulness at all. Most scientific theories make predictions that can, and sometimes do, turn out to be wrong. Technologies are also known to fail. As I argued in the Introduction, scientific endeavour is highly contingent – a fact that could not be explained by a subjective idealist epistemology in which science was nothing more than a projection of individual or social interests. On the other hand, products of modern physics like radio waves and nuclear chain-reactions are real enough in spite of their social and cultural conditioning.[5] So a complex realist epistemology can be sustained and will suffice for our purposes.[6] The lawfulness we are concerned with is whatever it is about our universe that allows us to develop formalisms and compress information in such a way that we can make new predictions and develop new technologies to test them.

---

4    Max Tegmark has shown that three space dimensions and one time dimension are needed for a world that is reasonably predictable; Tegmark, 'Parallel Universes', *Scientific American* 288 (May 2003), 45.

5    For an able defense of critical realism, see Alister E. McGrath, *A Scientific Theology, Volume 2: Reality* (Edinburgh: T&T Clark; Grand Rapids: Eerdmans, 2001–2003), 121-226. McGrath states the point I am making in slightly different terms on pp. 129-30.

6    I prefer a label like 'complex realism' or 'symmetrical realism' to the more common one of 'weak realism.' The point is not that socially conditioned views are weak or even false. Rather the existence of social and psychological factors must be taken into account in addition to the natural universe in which they occur. The world is complex, consisting of perceptions as well as things perceived, and it is all real. We encounter this problem again in Chapter 2, where we advocate attributing reality to the spirit world. The important point is that there is symmetry between the degree of reality we assign to the empirical world of supposed facts and the degree of reality we assign to the spiritual world, associated with human imagination.

The fourth point is that by focusing on the lawfulness of the universe as a source of theological insight, I hope to reverse a common perception of the relation between science and theology. Often this relationship is taken to be a zero-sum game: the more scientists come up with new laws and explanations for phenomena, the less room there is supposed to be for faith in God. Some popular science writers even contend that scientific explanation should replace conventional religious faith.[7] Many religious people feel threatened by the advancement of science for this very reason and insist that there will be gaps in the laws of nature that allow room for divine activity as described in the Bible. In the approach advocated here, however, it is the lawfulness of the cosmos, rather than the limits of such lawfulness, that will lead to possibilities for theological discourse.[8] As we shall find in our discussion of theological endeavour later in this chapter, the lawfulness of the universe can be viewed as expressing divine creation rather than detracting from it. We shall see that the very lawfulness of the universe we live in may help us revitalize some theological beliefs and clarify others.

## The origin of cosmic laws

With these four clarifications in mind, we can now focus on the main question of this chapter: why is our universe lawful? Why is this basic precondition of scientific endeavour – a lawful cosmos – fulfilled? In order to pursue this question we must, of course, make use of the tools of current cosmological thinking. Our working assumption is that using the resources of modern science can help us examine the preconditions of scientific endeavour.[9] Due to the preliminary nature of many

---

7     For example, biologist John Tyler Bonner states that 'for some [people] a religious or mystical explanation is the most satisfying. This is not so for me: the more rational and materialistic the explanation the better I like it'; Bonner, *The Evolution of Complexity by Means of Natural Selection* (Princeton: Princeton University Press, 1988), x. Even Paul Davies, who is among the popularizers of science most favorable to religious interests, states rather defensively that 'gaps left by the inadequacies of reductionist thinking should be filled by additional scientific theories ... and not by appeal to mystical or transcendent principles'; Davies, *The Cosmic Blueprint: New Discoveries in Nature's Creative Ability to Order the Universe* (New York: Simon and Schuster, 1988), 203. Such remarks undoubtedly reflect years of experience in which advocates of religion have rejected or attacked scientific endeavour.

8     According to Ernan McMullin, 'The appeal is not to a "gap" in scientific explanation but to a different order of explanation that leaves scientific explanation intact, that explores the conditions of possibility for there being any kind of scientific explanation'; McMullin, 'Natural Science and Belief in a Creator: Historical Notes', in Robert John Russell, William R. Stoeger, and George V. Coyne (eds), *Physics, Philosophy, and Theology: A Common Quest for Understanding* (Vatican City State: Vatican Observatory, 1988), 74; cf. Hugo Meynell, 'More Gaps for God?', in John M. Robson (ed.), *Origin and Evolution of the Universe: Evidence for Design?* (Kingston, Ont.: McGill-Queen's University Press, 1987), 253-4.

9     This use of current scientific ideas is an 'emic' description of science – one that takes its categories from the proponents of the discipline itself, in this case, the discipline of cosmology. There have been many reviews of current cosmological thinking in emic terms. What is different about the present study is the fact that emic descriptions are secondary to

current cosmic ideas, this inquiry will lead to more questions than answers, yet some general conclusions can be reached. It is to be hoped that future progress in cosmology will bring further clarification.

*Why is our universe lawful?*

The laws of our universe are bound up with its origin. At the origin of our universe, or prior to that origin (if priority can be suitably defined), one set of laws was somehow singled out from among all of the various possibilities, both regular and random. So it appears that there is an element of contingency at the foundation of cosmology, a contingency that could lead to theological questions.

In order to be more specific, we must refer to current theories of cosmology. Our objective, however, is not to integrate current cosmology with theology. It is rather to use current cosmic thinking as a way of exploring one of the foundations of science (the lawfulness of the universe) and to discern theological possibilities and challenges that reside in that foundation. Current cosmological theories can help us in that discernment by what they tell us about the origin and nature of the cosmos and what they tell us about its degree of lawfulness. Moreover, some personal experience of the mind-stretching character of current cosmological theories will provide important background for our discussion in Chapter 2 of the puzzling ability of the human brain for such cosmos-probing research.

At present there is considerable evidence that our universe originated in a spurt of cosmic inflation. According to this inflationary scenario, the details of which are still being worked out, some inflationary force caused a small region of space-time to expand by a factor of $10^{50}$ in a fraction of a second. As a result it was smoothed out to form a relatively homogeneous universe that was suitable for the formation of galaxies and planets and the eventual evolution of life.[10] If this basic idea is correct, a remarkable conclusion follows: many universes other than our own may exist as the result of the inflation of other regions of primordial space-time. These universes might have entirely different structures and conditions and hence be far

---

our earlier 'etic' description of science – the analysis of the preconditions or foundations of scientific endeavour.

10   On the origin and development of this theory, see Alan H. Guth, *The Inflationary Universe: The Quest for a New Theory of Cosmic Origins* (Reading, Mass: Addison-Wesley, 1997). The fact that our present universe has just the right balance of residual expansion and gravitation is one of the basic ideas behind the Anthropic Principle discussed earlier.

less hospitable to life than our own.[11] The ensemble of all these universes taken together is called the 'multiverse'.[12]

The idea of a multiverse is a controversial concept. The reason that such highly inflated regions are thought of as completely different universes, rather than distant parts of our own universe, is that their structures and properties cannot influence the other inflated regions. In fact, they are no longer able to communicate with each other with light signals because the initial inflation took place at speeds faster than that of light.[13] Such regions lie beyond our cosmic horizon, and they cannot provide us with any information. Some physicists and philosophers might argue that they are not a

---

11   Several alternatives to the standard inflationary cosmology must be kept in mind. The 'chaotic, eternally self-reproducing inflationary' model, developed by Andrei Linde and others, posits a repeated generation and inflation of new universes with various laws and different initial conditions. In this scenario, a viable theory of scalar fields and elementary particles must be assumed as well as some meta-law governing the mutation of the local laws of physics; see Linde, 'The Self-Reproducing Inflationary Universe', *Scientific American* 271 (Nov. 1994), 48-55.

The 'ekpyrotic model' of cosmology, proposed in 2001, can possibly account for the origin of our universe without resorting to the idea of cosmic inflation. In its present form the 'ekpyrotic model' posits a pair of parallel four-dimensional membrane-universes eternally moving back and forth in a five-dimensional space in accordance with the laws of a unified theory known as 'string theory'; see, for example, Marcus Chown, 'Cycles of Creation', *New Scientist* (16 March 2002), 26-30.

Both the eternal inflation and the ekpyrotic models create a succession of different expansions that constitute a multiverse comparable to that of the more common inflationary scenario. Max Tegmark includes them both as possible models for his Level 2 multiverse; Tegmark, 'Parallel Universes', 44-5.

The 'instanton' model, developed by Stephen Hawking and Neil Turok, avoids the idea of a multiverse by positing a primordial, apparently unique, seed or 'pea' out of which our universe inflated directly. One of the predictions of this model is a geometrically open (negatively curved) universe, whereas current evidence points toward a perfectly flat universe consistent with the inflationary and ekpyrotic models; see Tom Yulsman, 'Give Peas a Chance: Could an exotic object known as a pea instanton have given birth to our universe?', *Astronomy* 27 (Sept. 1999), 38, 44-6.

The 'emergent-universe model' uses loop quantum gravity to describe the initial state of a small closed universe; Martin Bojowald, 'Original Questions', *Nature* 436 (18 Aug. 2005), 920-21.

All of these theories assume a set of primordial laws and the existence of a multidimensional framework in which those laws function. Contingency is built in from the start.

12   Max Tegmark refers to this option as a 'Level 1' multiverse; Tegmark, 'Parallel Universes', 42-4. A simple introduction to the idea of the multiverse is given in Martin Rees, *Our Cosmic Habitat* (Princeton: Princeton University Press, 2001), chapter 1. The multiplicity of possible string theories leads Leonard Susskind to posit a 'cosmic landscape' of possible universes each with a different set of laws; Susskind, *The Cosmic Landscape: String Theory and the Illusion of Intelligent Design* (New York: Little, Brown, and Co., 2005).

13   Effective speeds faster than that of light are possible in some cosmologies because it is space itself that is expanding. All matter and energy move at speeds less than that of light with respect to their space-time continua.

proper subject for rigorous natural science.[14] Nonetheless, positing an ensemble of universes might be the best way to account for the origin and the peculiar properties of our own particularly if the same fundamental laws of physics apply to the origin and subsequent development of all of them.

## *Why is our multiverse lawful?*

The implication of cosmic inflation is that the ultimate laws and symmetries of physics must apply not only to our universe, but to the entire multiverse. If the laws vary from one universe to another, there must be a higher-order law, perhaps a statistical one, that governs the overall variation. For example, there might be a master equation governing the distribution of all the properties and laws of all the universes similarly to the way that the Maxwell-Boltzmann equation governs the distribution of velocities in a perfect gas. As Martin Rees has suggested rather wittily, the laws of our universe might turn out to be local bylaws of an overall theory governing the entire ensemble of 'pocket universes'.

This higher-order law existed before our particular universe came into being. In fact, it governed the origin and the peculiar properties of all universes in the multiverse. This move forces us to rephrase our original question and ask why our multiverse is lawful. Why was this particular law singled out from among all of the possibilities for our multiverse? Why is this even more basic foundation of scientific endeavour – a lawful multiverse – there in the first place? The move from universe to multiverse does not itself explain the lawfulness or eliminate the element of contingency in cosmology.

Earlier we cited the general point that the laws of our universe must be bound up with its origin. We see now that the laws governing the origin of our universe may be shared by all the universes in the ensemble we call our multiverse. So we may rephrase our original point to say that the laws of our multiverse are somehow bound up with its origin.

At present we have no way of describing scientifically the origin of our multiverse or even to know for sure whether its origin can be treated by science. It has been suggested is that our multiverse is one of an even larger ensemble of multiverses, each with its own set of laws and symmetries.[15] Again there would be no way for us to observe any of these other multiverses, but conceivably an even higher-order theory could be developed that would account for the origin of our multiverse within such an ensemble of multiverses. Such a theory would have to account for distribution of laws among the multiverses as well as their origins.[16]

---

14   For example, Neil Turok, a physicist at Cambridge University who has worked on several new cosmic models, has stated that the idea of a multiverse was too complex and untestable and that he preferred to work with a 'one-shot' universe; Yulsman, 'Give Peas a Chance', 45. Later, however, Turok helped develop the repeating 'ekpyrotic universe' model discussed in a footnote above.

15   Max Tegmark refers to this option as a Level 4 multiverse; Tegmark, 'Parallel Universes', *Scientific American* 288 (May 2003), 49-51. For simplicity I have conflated Tegmark's Level 2 and Level 4 multiverses and skipped over his Level 3 multiverse.

16   Rees, *Our Cosmic Habitat*, 173.

Such a higher-order theory would explain just about everything about the basic conditions of our multiverse as well as our universe. Of course, such ideas are purely speculative at this point. It is possible, as Stephen Hawking and Steven Weinberg have suggested, that a unique unified theory could be constructed – a theory that would be logically self-consistent and that would have no undetermined parameters.[17] Would such a breakthrough eliminate the contingency of lawfulness that has haunted modern cosmology?[18]

*Contingent lawfulness will not go away*

There are at least two ways in which the idea of contingency may come back to haunt us again (and happily so). One would be to accept, at least for the sake of discussion, the possibility of discovering a unique final theory and to query the appeal to logical self-consistency. James Trefil considered this possibility in his 1983 book, *The Moment of Creation*. After noting that physicists hope to press the laws that govern elementary particles back to the origin of the universe, Trefil concluded that this amazing accomplishment would confront us with a deeper contingency:

> This [accomplishment] does not, however, alter the fact that there is a frontier [of research]. All it does is transfer our attention from the material form of the universe to the laws that govern its behavior.... But who created those laws? And, even if, as some physicists have suggested, the laws of physics we discover are the only laws that are logically consistent with each other ... who made the laws of logic?[19]

Trefil's question exemplifies the 'nomistic turn' that has characterized recent discussions of cosmology: given the possibility that the origin of our universe can be explained in terms of simple laws, he asks where the laws come from.[20] The locus of contingency is shifted from the structure of the universe to the laws of physics and even to the laws of logic. The exact same reasoning can be applied to the origin of our multiverse.

In the Enlightenment era and its aftermath, it was believed that human logic was a given, self-evident, coherent system. But the advent of multi-valued quantum

---

17    Stephen Hawking, *A Brief History of Time: From the Big Bang to Black Holes* (Toronto: Bantam Books, 1988), 174; Steven Weinberg, *Dreams of a Final Theory* (New York: Pantheon Books, 1992), 239; cf. Barrow and Tipler, *Anthropic Cosmic Principle*, 257-8. Hawking actually hedged a bit by allowing for a small number of such theories, and, as stated above, he was thinking of equations that govern our particular universe rather than an ensemble of universes (a multiverse). On Hawking's later misgivings about finding a final theory, see the report of his views in Michael Brooks, 'The Impossible Puzzle', *New Scientist* 178 (5 April 2003), 34-5.

18    I am indebted to earlier discussions of this issue like Hugo A. Meynell, 'More Gaps for God?'; Michael Heller, 'Chaos, Probability, and the Comprehensibility of the World', in Robert John Russell, Nancey Murphy and Arthur R. Peacocke (eds), *Chaos and Complexity: Scientific Perspectives on Divine Action* (Vatican City State: Vatican Observatory, 1995), 110, 117-18.

19    Trefil, *The Moment of Creation*, 222-3.

20    The nomistic turn of focusing on the laws of physics rather than the cause of the origin of the cosmos is also made in Davies, *The Mind of God*, 203, 205, 222.

logic[21] and Kurt Gödel's 1931 proof of the incompleteness of deductive logical formalisms have made the idea of contingency more acceptable even in the field of logic. It seems likely that any recourse to pure logic would move cosmologists from the hot 'frying pan' of Big Bang physics back into the fire of human creativity (to be discussed in Chapter 2).

Another option for recovering contingency would be to question the finality of any meta-theory of the ensemble of multiverses. In order to do this one must try to anticipate the form that such a theory would likely take. For example, one could argue quite plausibly, as Max Tegmark does, that every possible set of laws gets a multiverse of its own to govern.[22] Such an arrangement would certainly be impressive in its simplicity, but it would not eliminate the idea of contingent lawfulness from cosmology. Most distribution functions have one or more maxima that determine which arrangements are more probable than others. A distribution that limited each arrangement to just one instance, just one multiverse in this case, would be very special indeed.

Other possible distribution functions would be special in ways of their own. A Gaussian ('normal') distribution of properties and laws is one likely possibility.[23] Such distributions are encountered frequently in natural phenomena that we observe in our own universe. A Gaussian distribution has a distinctive peak value, representing the arrangement that occurs most frequently in nature, and a distinctive width, representing the deviance from the peak value that is normally allowed. If this kind of meta-theory applies to the ensemble of multiverses, it would still be contingent – doubly contingent, in fact – and we would be invited to posit an even higher order law to account for it! In other words, we could be embarking on an infinite regress.

Even if physicists were to persevere in pushing the origin of our universe back into the multiverse and possibly beyond, contingent lawfulness would outlast their perseverance in the same way that the tortoise outran Achilles. In fact the double contingency of the infinite Gaussian distribution of multiverses would require a doubly infinite ensemble of ensembles of multiverses. From this point on, the tortoise might actually pull away from Achilles. Contingency just won't go away. The attribute of contingent lawfulness is apparently irreducible.

*Theological questions: Where do the laws come from?*

The assumption of contingent laws appears to be an irreducible feature of scientific endeavour. I do not propose to argue from the irreducible contingency of our universe to the necessity of a Creator. The only way to develop such an argument would be to require that all apparent contingency ultimately be referred back to a sufficient and necessary cause (a Being that exists necessarily). In effect, all contingency would

21  Patrick A. Heelen, 'Quantum Logic and Classical Logic', *Synthese* 21 (1970), 2-33.

22  Tegmark, 'Parallel Universes', 50a. A more technical version of Tegmark's work is available in 'Is "The Theory of Everything" Merely the Ultimate Ensemble Theory?', *Annals of Physics* 270 (1998), 1-51.

23  As discussed in Barrow and Tipler, *Anthropic Cosmic Principle*, 256-7.

then be eliminated by theological means. Such a move might lead us to the idea of God, but it might come back to haunt us when we appeal to the idea of divine freedom, which is contingency in another form, in order to attribute any thoughts or actions to this God. A worldview without any contingency is not likely to include a God that anyone would really want to know.

It might be more helpful to note some of the ways in which current cosmic thinking raises the question of God and to clarify its implications for faith in such a God. Are the cosmic ideas we have discussed consistent with faith in God as Creator or is there a conflict of some sort? What implications do they have for our understanding of God's immanence and current relationship to the world? Those whose minds are not completely closed to the God possibility are likely to be more interested in thinking the possibility through than in being dragged through the steps of an attempted proof.

Even though the contingency of the origin of the universe and the laws that govern it do not require us to assume a Creator, it does raise the question of where the laws come from. Recent cosmologists have asked the question in at least two ways: one way is based on the selection of a particular set of laws for our universe or multiverse (or the ensemble of multiverses); the other is based on the existence of a universe or multiverse with that (or any) particular set of laws. Let us look at one example of each type.

Reference has already been made to James Trefil's *The Moment of Creation*, published in 1983. The author is just one of a number of physicists who have provided literate laypeople with a scientific account of the origin of the universe and its history from the Planck time ($10^{-43}$ sec.) up to the present, some 14 billion years later, all in accordance with the laws of physics. At the very end of his book, Trefil asks, 'What about God?' There is interesting background for this question.

'What about God?' is the very question that Napoleon is reported to have asked Marquis Pierre Simon de Laplace after looking over his two-volume *Treatise on Celestial Mechanics* (1799). Laplace had tried to account for the formation and stability of the solar system in terms of natural laws and natural causes. When Napoleon asked why there was no mention of God in this account, as there had been in Newton's *Principia* a century earlier, Laplace is reported to have answered: *Sire, je n'ai pas eu besoin de cette hypothèse* – 'Sire, I had no need of that hypothesis.' The historicity of this conversation is in doubt, but it certainly captures the shift in thinking away from appeals to divine causation – a shift that continued in the eighteenth and nineteenth centuries.[24] The idea of God filling the gaps in the natural, scientific explanation, known as a 'God-of-the-gaps', has fallen into disfavour in scientific circles ever since.

Trefil's response to the God question is more guarded philosophically than Laplace's; it is also more positive theologically. Trefil argues that scientific progress

---

24   On the problem of documentation, see Herbert H. Odom, 'The Estrangement of Celestial Mechanics and Religion', *Journal for the History of Ideas* 27 (Oct. 1966), 535; Roger Hahn, 'Laplace and the Vanishing Role of God in the Physical Universe', in Harry Woolf (ed.), *The Analytic Spirit: Essays in the History of Science in Honor of Henry Guerlac* (Ithaca: Cornell University Press, 1981), 85-6.

will never answer all of the questions even if it makes continual progress indefinitely. Physics and cosmology make progress by postulating principles and laws and there will always be the question of where those principles and laws come from (even in an ensemble of multiverses, as we have seen). In effect, the amazing advances in cosmology since the time of Laplace have shifted our attention from the earlier issue of accounting for the material forms of the universe (like the solar system and the galaxies) to the issue of accounting for the principles and laws that govern the origin of universe and all its material forms.[25] 'No matter how far the boundaries are pushed back', Trefil concludes, 'there will always be room both for religious faith and a religious interpretation of the physical world.'[26] The appeal here is not to a 'God-of-the-gaps', which relies on exceptions to the laws of nature, but to a 'matrix-God', which relies on the validity and sufficiency of those laws all woven together like a fine fabric.

This shift between Laplace and Trefil is what I call the 'nomistic turn' in the cultural context of scientific endeavour. Whereas Laplace lived in a time when unfettered rational inquiry into questions of origins was still suspect, particularly in contexts of church politics, Trefil has the benefit of living in an era of unprecedented knowledge and freedom of speculation. The unexamined dogma that needed to be challenged in the eighteenth century was one that appealed to God or to the Book of Genesis in place of rigorous scientific endeavour. The unexamined dogma of the late twentieth century was just the opposite one – that a final theory would answer all questions about the universe and leave no room for God at all.

The shift between Laplace and Trefil can be pinned down more closely. A more recent example of the no-room-for-God dogma is Carl Sagan's *Cosmos*, which was released as a television series in 1980. Possibly because Sagan's series was aimed at a broad public audience, Sagan felt it necessary, much as Laplace had done two centuries earlier, to challenge any appeal to God in explaining the origin of the universe.

> In many cultures it is customary to answer that God created the universe out of nothing. But this is mere temporizing. If we wish courageously to pursue the question, we must, of course ask next where God comes from?... Or, if we say that God has always existed, why not save a step and conclude that the universe has always existed?[27]

The contrast between Trefil and Sagan is striking, but it must be interpreted in context. The difference is not that Sagan was less open to the God question than Trefil is. They were making different points because they were addressing different questions. Sagan was arguing against an appeal to God as an explanation for the origin of the universe out of nothing.[28] He rightly insisted on an explanation in terms

---

25  Trefil, *Moment of Creation*, 222.

26  Trefil, *Moment of Creation*, 223. Trefil still wants to move away from 'the old fashioned God who had to make it all, laboriously, piece by piece' (*Moment of Creation*, 223). The question concerning the kind of God involved in this religious faith will be taken up in the next section of this chapter.

27  Carl Sagan, *Cosmos* (New York: Random House, 1980), 257.

28  Sagan may have been responding to Robert Jastrow's appeal to divine creation in his *God and the Astronomers* (New York: Norton, 1978), 115-116.

of natural laws. Trefil does not appeal to God to account for the origin of the universe either. The difference between them is that Trefil takes the 'nomistic turn' and asks where the laws that govern creation come from – an entirely different question. This shift is theologically significant in that it protects the integrity of scientific enterprise and its necessary foundations, but at the same time it asks about the meaning of those foundations. This shift in questions makes the transition to theological discourse much smoother.[29]

*Theological questions: What actualizes lawfulness?*

Trefil is an example of a physicist who wonders why one particular set of laws is singled out from all possible sets. Another way to articulate the contingency of the origin of the universe is to express wonder at the actual existence of a universe or multiverse that obeys those (or any) laws.[30] Trefil's articulation starts with our existence in the lawful world that we know and asks about the possible ground for such a world. The second way starts with the possibility of a given set of laws or symmetries and asks about the actual existence of a world that embodies them. In this second alternative, it might look as if the question of the origin of the universe that was supposedly laid to rest by Laplace and Sagan has returned to haunt us again. But the question raised here is slightly different from theirs.

It will help us see the difference if we look closely at Stephen Hawking's *A Brief History of Time*, published in 1988. In a chapter about the origin of the universe, Hawking begins with the classic Napoleonic question of whether God need be invoked as an explanation for how things got started in the way that they did (the initial conditions of the universe). Hawking answers by stating that the universe might actually be self-contained, and he suggests that there is no need for a creator in this sense (as a first cause).[31]

In his concluding chapter, Hawking states that the universe did not necessarily have a temporal beginning (though it is still not infinitely old). Consequently, it does not have an initial condition that needs to be explained. It simply is.[32] However,

---

29   Ironically, Trefil's 'nomistic turn' reverses a mirror-image transition that took place in the Latin Middle Ages. The original biblical and patristic image of God's creativity was expressed in terms of God's word or will. The emphasis on God as efficient (first) cause began with the ascendancy of Aristotelian physics in the 13th century; see Kaiser, *Creational Theology and the History of Physical Science: The Creationist Tradition from Basil to Bohr* (Leiden: E. J. Brill, 1997), 102-9. The fact that modern physicists often fill the role of traditional theologians will be taken up in Chapter 3.

30   Michael Heller refers to this aspect of contingency as the 'ontological gap' between nonexistence and existence in contrast to the (previously discussed) 'epistemological gap' between incomprehensibility and intelligibility; Heller, 'Chaos, Probability, and the Comprehensibility of the World', 121. I find Heller's distinction helpful but prefer Ernan McMullin's plea for an order of explanation that avoids the idea of gaps and leaves scientific explanation intact; McMullin, 'Natural Science and Belief in a Creator', 74 (cited in note above).

31   Hawking, *Brief History of Time*, 140-41. Hawking was then working with an early version of the instanton theory (discussed in note above) rather than with an ensemble of universes.

32   Hawking, *Brief History of Time*, 174.

the being of the universe is described by a set of laws, and we may well ask where those laws come from. This is the 'nomistic turn' that we found previously in James Trefil's work. Hawking goes on to conclude that there may be only one set of laws that is logically self-consistent and that would allow for the existence of complex living creatures. One day, he hopes, physicists will discover that unified set of laws. But discovering and writing down such a set of laws would still not be the same as creating a universe with those laws. So Hawking asks rather poetically:

> What is it that breathes fire into the equations and makes a universe for them to describe? The usual approach of science of constructing a mathematical model cannot answer the questions of why there should be a universe for the model to describe. Why does the universe go to all the bother of existing?[33]

Hawking's question is not about the origin of the universe, but about the actualization of the laws of theoretical physics. The situation he depicts is something like that of politicians discussing a variety of possible budgets for the coming year. It is one thing to imagine a budget that will accomplish wonderful things. It is quite another matter to pass the budget and come up with the funding. Where does that come from?

Hawking is haunted by the why question: not just why the universe is the way it is – that question evokes the concept of laws – but why there is lawful existence in the first place.[34] This is another version of the question that underlies all of scientific endeavour: why there are laws that make scientific endeavour possible?

*Scientists as true believers*

Are cosmologists like Trefil and Hawking reflecting their own thoughts sincerely when they ask these questions? Some critics have suspected that they only want to enhance the sale of their books to a public that is still very interested in religious questions.[35] It has also been argued that Western cosmologists are simply conditioned by the root metaphor of lawgiving they inherited from medieval thought.[36] Like the earlier idea of cosmic design, which seemed to suggest the existence of a Designer, the idea of cosmic laws suggests the existence of a Lawgiver. Both ideas might be no

---

33   Hawking, *Brief History of Time*, 174.

34   Hawking's thought is echoed in Davies, *The Mind of God*, 171-2. Davies works it out in more detail, but the nomistic turn and the transition to theology are much the same as in Trefil and Hawking. A slightly different version is offered by Geoffrey Chew in his contribution to Henry Margenau and Roy Abraham Varghese, eds , *Cosmos, Bios, Theos: Scientists Reflect on Science, God, and the Origins of the Universe, Life, and Homo Sapiens* (LaSalle, Ill: Open Court, 1992). Chew concludes that an appeal to God may be needed in order to understand why the set of laws, those of quantum cosmology and their classical limits, are consistent with each other; *Cosmos, Bios, Theos*, 36.

35   For example, Robert Park of the American Physical Society criticized Leon Lederman for titling his own book about high-energy physics, *The God Particle*; Gregg Easterbrook, 'Science and God: A Warming Trend?', *Science* 277 (15 Aug. 1997), 891a.

36   Steven Weinberg calls the idea that laws of nature originate in the mind of Gods an 'irresistible metaphor' in his *Dreams of a Final Theory*, 242.

more than relics of an outmoded cultural worldview. The only difference would be that the metaphors of law and lawgiving appeal more to a more educated audience.

From a detached position, outside the practice of physics and cosmology, it may seem that lawfulness is simply a happy coincidence or perhaps a culturally constructed mirage. But for those who work in the scientific disciplines and find that the theories they construct sometimes actually work out in practice, there is an existential sense to the notion of lawfulness. It is as if someone had been there ahead of the physicist arranging the ideas and planting the clues. This experience does not prove that there is a Creator (a cosmic treasure-hunt master?),[37] but it does indicate that the willingness of many physicists to think about the God possibility flows directly out of their engagement with the scientific process. It is not just an afterthought that only comes out in popular books.

There is a good reason for this commitment to the idea of lawfulness that is at once sincere and culturally conditioned. All of the ideas of cosmology have been developed in the belief that some set of laws or symmetries undergirds all the processes of nature. Scientists are believers by training. Their belief is not religious in the conventional sense,[38] but it is belief all the same.[39] The vindication of this belief that scientists experience as their disciplines take small steps of progress only serves to strengthen the underlying faith. The possibility of believing in God is not as strange as it seems. God may be strange, of course – especially to those who actually believe in God – but the viability of belief is normal – even for scientists, in fact, especially for scientists.

Scientists are believers. A suitably 'thick description' of scientific endeavour must therefore include the dimension of faith[40] – in this case, a nomistic faith. A thick view of scientific endeavour has room for the question of God as Creator and leads quite smoothly into theological discourse. We shall examine the cultural foundation that underlies such belief in Chapter 3. Meanwhile, let us explore some of the theological possibilities and issues that emerge from the foundation of scientific endeavour in a lawful universe.

---

37   Paul Davies is an example of a physicist who raises the God question, but then affirms no more than that qualities like ingenuity, economy and beauty have a transcendent reality even if they cannot bring the universe into existence the way a traditionally conceived Creator God could; Davies, *The Mind of God*, 189, 214.

38   I take issue with Chet Raymo's characterization of good scientists as natural skeptics; Raymo, *Skeptics and True Believers: The Exhilarating Connection Between Science and Religion* (New York, MJF Books, 1998), 2-4. For Raymo, skeptics are people who 'trust the ability of the human mind to make sense of the world'. People who live by such trust are believers in the sense that I am using the term. Paul Davies points out that, while many scientists practice a conventional religion, most of them keep their scientific work separate from their religious practice; Davies, *The Mind of God*, 15.

39   Scientists frequently confess that they have a deep faith in the order of nature or intelligibility of the universe as discussed in Chapter 3. Some recent examples include the physicists, Paul Davies and Joel Primack, in interviews cited by Kim A. McDonald, 'Science Confronts the Ultimate Question: Does the Universe Hold Clues to God?', *The Chronicle of Higher Education* 39 (12 May 1993), A9.

40   The phrase 'thick description' is borrowed from the work of Clifford Geertz; see the Introduction under 'Toward a thick description of science'.

**Theological challenges and resources**

I have argued that an examination of the cosmic foundation of scientific endeavour is conducive to theological endeavour. Thus far we have focused on positive factors, ones that encourage us to think in terms of God as Creator. Probing the origin of cosmic law does not require the existence of God, but it certainly raises the possibility of God's role as the author of the laws that govern the universe or multiverse and as the Creator of the universe or multiverse that embodies those principles and laws.

But there are other ways in which examination of this foundation of science is theologically important. Our study can also provide a healthy challenge to theology, especially to any theology that works within the biblical tradition. There are at least two challenges to consider: one derives from the possible existence of a multiverse; the other is occasioned by the seemingly deistic image that can be derived from discussions of God as a Lawgiver. In the following sections, we shall sharpen those challenges and explore some theological resources in the theological tradition that might help address them. In the process I hope to highlight some neglected aspects of the Judeo-Christian tradition. In other words, the challenges arising from our analysis of the foundations of scientific endeavour can serve as a kind of lens to bring traditional theology into a fresh new focus.

*Multiple universes in the theological tradition*

The idea of a multiverse (or even an ensemble of multiverses) posits a plurality of universes as a way of accounting for the origin of our own universe with its particular laws and special initial conditions. The theological challenge here stems from the fact that students of the Bible have usually assumed that God created only one universe. The existence of a multiverse is far from proven scientifically – in fact, it may never be proven – so there is no point in forcing theology to adapt. Nonetheless, the assumption that the existence of a multiverse would necessarily contradict biblical thought would complicate open discussion of the issue. Therefore, consideration of the challenge and of the options that may be available is in order. We shall find that a number of early Jewish and Christian theologians viewed the idea of a plurality of universes as a fitting interpretation of Scripture and a corollary of belief in the power and goodness of God. In this discussion, our goal is to work through the possible implications of the first precondition of scientific endeavour, the existence of a lawful universe.

The common idea that our universe is the only one God created is suggested by various biblical texts. The most familiar of these, Genesis 1:1, is usually translated, *In the beginning God created the heavens and the earth.*[41] But the Hebrew text can also be translated rather differently: *In the beginning when God created the heavens*

---

41   So the Authorized King James Version, the Revised English Bible, and the New International Version. Some other biblical creation texts to look at are Ps. 104:2-5; Prov. 8:27-30; Isa. 40:12-13; 42:5; 51:13.

*and the earth....*[42] On the latter reading, Genesis 1 begins with a relative clause that describes the condition of the world before God began to work on it: *the earth was a formless void and darkness covered the face of the deep* (Gen. 1:2). On this alternative reading, nothing is stated or implied about an absolute beginning; the Hebrew text assumed the prior existence of the formless earth, water and darkness: *In the beginning when God created the heavens and the earth, the earth was a formless void and darkness covered the face of the deep...* (Gen. 1:1-2).

As far as English translations of the Bible are concerned, this alternate translation of Genesis 1:1-2 is a fairly recent development (the New English Bible introduced it in 1970). So it has not yet had much of an impact on modern Christian theology. But Jewish theologians had been working with the Hebrew text all along, and long ago some of them came to the conclusion that God had been active creating worlds before this one.

Early Jewish explorations of the biblical text and its possible meaning were called *midrāshîm*. The term, 'midrash', comes from the verb, *dārash*, meaning to seek, explore or inquire.[43] Various collections of these *midrāshîm* were compiled beginning around the third century of the Common Era (CE). One of the earliest of these collections, compiled in the fifth century, was Genesis Rabbah (*Běre'shît Rabbah*), the 'Great Genesis Collection'. In this compilation, we find a wide variety of interpretations of the Genesis text. This variety indicates a keen awareness of critical issues in the text and a wealth of ideas for resolving them. Here are a few examples that address the modern possibility of multiple universes.

In Genesis Rabbah 3:7,[44] the views of three rabbis are cited on the puzzling statement, *And there was evening and there was morning, one day*, which includes the very first creative act described in the Genesis account (Gen. 1:5). Their opinions are cited in such a way that each comment builds on those already made and an imaginary conversation is constructed. Rabbi Judah ben Rabbi Simon begins the discussion by pointing out that the wording assumes that the sequence of evening and morning, night and day, had already been established before the one 'day' described in Genesis 1. In other words, there must have been an earlier sequence of days that is not described directly. What was God doing during those very early days? Rabbi Abbahu draws the inference that God was creating other worlds:

> Said R. Abbahu, 'On the basis of that same formulation [*there was evening and there was morning* in Gen. 1:5] we learn that the Holy One, blessed be he, had been engaged in creating worlds and destroying them prior to the moment at which he created this one. Then he said, "This is the one that pleases me, but those did not please me."' (Genesis Rabbah 3:7)[45]

---

42   So the New English Bible, the New American Bible, and the New Revised Standard Version.

43   *Oxford Dictionary of the Jewish Religion*, ed. R. J. Zei Werblowsky and Geoffrey Wigoder (New York: Oxford University Press, 1997), 463a. On the use of imagination in *midrāshîm*, see, for example, Michael Fishbane, *The Exegetical Imagination: On Jewish Thought and Theology* (Cambridge, Mass: Harvard University Press, 1998).

44   The citation 3:7 refers to *parashah* three, subsection 7, which deals with Gen. 1:5 (not Gen. 3:7).

45   Jacob Neusner, trans., *Genesis Rabbah: The Judaic Commentary to the Book of Genesis*, 3 vols (Atlanta: Scholars Press, 1985), 1:33.

According to R. Abbahu, the 'beginning' of God's creativity depicted in Genesis 1:1 was just one of many similar beginnings. It was unique only in the sense that the world that resulted was pleasing to God, presumably because it was suited to the continuance of human life.

The third rabbi, Rabbi Phinehas, provides confirmation for this idea by referring to a small detail at the very end of Genesis 1: *God saw all that he had made, and behold, it was very good* (Gen. 1:31). The point here is that God ascribed goodness to just one thing, apparently one of 'all that he had made'. In other words, Genesis 1:31 also assumes that God created many worlds, consistent with the arguments of Rabbis Judah and Abbahu – quite a powerful argument.

The central point is the one made by Rabbi Abbahu. The historical Abbahu (d. 309) was a disciple of the outstanding Palestinian scholar, Rabbi Yohanan bar Nappaha. Rabbi Abbahu became a prominent biblical authority in his own right and served as the head of the rabbinical academy at Caesarea, which is credited with editing the juridical sections of the Jerusalem Talmud.[46] The words attributed to him must have made a deep impression on the editors of Genesis Rabbah because they also appear in a very different context in Genesis Rabbah 9:1-2. The text for discussion here is Genesis 1:31 itself: *God saw all that he had made, and behold, it was very good.* Whereas, in the earlier chapter of Genesis Rabbah, this text was brought in only at the end as corroboration for R. Abbahu's idea, here the punch line is stated at the beginning of the conversation and repeated at the conclusion.

There is also an important transitional text that supports the speculation. We hear (in Gen. Rab. 9:1) from Rabbi Levi in the name of Rabbi Hama bar Hanina (both of the third century), who cites a famous proverb, *It is the glory of God to conceal a thing, but the glory of kings is to search out a matter* (Prov. 25:2). The ensuing discussion establishes the point that a wise person (a 'king') can search out the mysteries of the world just as God did in the very beginning (before concealing them). This optimistic epistemology, which is part of the cultural foundation to be discussed in Chapter 3, prepares the ground for Rabbi Abbahu's speculation on a plurality of worlds, as described above.

It is clear that in the early centuries of the Common Era, there were a number of Rabbis who understood the creation story to imply a series of worlds – an ensemble of many universes in today's scientific terminology – the one most suitable for God's purposes being our own. It would be sophomoric to try to correlate this ancient speculation with present-day cosmology (the rabbinic accounts evidently assume a space-time continuity from one world to the next). The point here is that the biblical text can inspire a worldview that allows for a plurality of universes. Even though reflection on the contingency of cosmic law in a multiverse does not prove the biblical idea of creation, at least it does not lead to an overt contradiction with the biblical texts. In fact, the current idea of a multiverse may help us revitalize some older interpretations of Scripture that have not received the attention they deserve.

If we wish to find something similar to Rabbi Abbahu's view in early Christian literature, we must turn to the great Alexandrian theologians of the second and third centuries. We begin with a brief look at the late second-century writer, Clement of

---

46 *Oxford Dictionary of the Jewish Religion*, 1-2, 748.

Alexandria. At the end of the fifth book of his theological 'Miscellanies' (*Stromateîs*), Clement points out that God's goodness is eternal. Therefore, he argues, God's doing good things could have no absolute beginning.[47] Clement's primary concern here was to affirm God's beneficence and righteousness for all peoples, even for those who lived before the advent of Jesus Christ. However, the discussion could be interpreted as implying an eternal process of creation as well.

Clement's student Origen developed this idea in his text, *On First Principles*, which was written in the 220s, while he was still teaching in Alexandria. Origen's primary purpose was to establish the most basic teaching of the Church, the belief that God's Wisdom is coeternal with God. As the deuterocanonical ('apocryphal') book, the Wisdom of Solomon states, *She [Wisdom] is a reflection of eternal light* (Wis. 7:26a). If God's light is eternal, Origen reasoned, so must its reflection be.[48] Then the same reasoning should apply to all of the divine attributes listed in Wisdom 7, including God's power, might and goodness – all must be expressed eternally. If, to the contrary, we were to say that God began to express these attributes, we would be introducing substantive change into the Godhead. From this concession, Origen concludes that there must have been a world, or a sequence of worlds, prior to this one over which God was sovereign Lord and in which God demonstrated eternal goodness. The key passage reads as follows:

> But, if there was no time when God was not almighty, there must always have existed the things in virtue of which he is almighty, and there must always have existed things under his sway, which own him as their ruler.[49]

Origen here assumes an infinite past, based on the idea of God's eternity or everlastingness (Pss. 90:2; 93:2; passim).[50] Through this infinite duration God was always sovereign Lord, so there must always have existed a world of some sort over which God reigned.

Since our own world is apparently of finite age, it must have been preceded (and will be succeeded) by other worlds.[51] Origen describes one such scenario as follows:

> ...worlds may exist that are diverse, having variation by no means slight, so that for certain clear causes the condition of one may be better, while another for different causes may be worse, and another intermediate.[52]

---

47   Clement of Alexandria, *Stromateîs* V.4.262; *Ante-Nicene Fathers*, ed. Alexander Roberts and James Donaldson, 10 vols (Buffalo and New York, 1885-96), 2:476b.

48   Origen, *De princ.* I.2.9 (in Rufinus' Latin translation).

49   Fragment 5, a Greek fragment from *De princ.* I.2.10; ET in Origen, *On First Principles*, ed. G. W. Butterworth (London: SPCK, 1936; New York: Harper & Row, 1966), 24. The argument is restated in *De princ.* I.4.3-4 (Latin trans.).

50   Cf. *De princ.* I.2.2 (Latin trans.).

51   Origen argues that the material world in which we live is not eternal in *De princ.* I. pref. 4; 3.3: II.1.4; III.5.3.

52   So *De princ.* II.3.4 (Latin trans.); ET in Butterworth, trans., *Origen on First Principles*, 88. This is just one of three scenarios that Origen discusses in chapter II.3. In *De princ.* III.5.3 (Latin trans.), Origen gives scriptural support for the idea of a succession of worlds from Isa. 66:22 and Eccl. 1:9-10.

Origen's comparison of worlds sounds in many ways like that of Rabbi Abbahu described above. But, for Origen, the idea of an ensemble of universes demonstrated the infinite power and eternal sovereignty of God. In other words, the idea of a plurality of worlds came out of an investigation into the foundations of theology, much as the idea of a multiverse comes today out of an investigation into the foundations of scientific endeavour.

What were these other worlds like? Elsewhere in his theological treatise, Origen indicates that the world just prior to this one was a purely spiritual one in which all souls existed without bodies.[53] He concedes that this is a difficult concept and suggests that these disembodied souls probably existed in some ideal form within God's Wisdom.[54] So Origen's reasoning is rather different from that in Genesis Rabbah, and his assessment of prior worlds is somewhat more positive than that of Rabbi Abbahu (for whom prior worlds were not good enough to endure), but the speculative impulse is strikingly similar.[55] In the case of the Rabbis, the speculative impulse was inherent in the idea of midrash – exploration or inquiry. Origen explicitly states the speculative nature of his investigation and points out the fact that there are good arguments on both sides of the issue since it did not affect the Church's basic rule of faith.[56] Such speculative cosmic thinking was very much a part of both early Judaism and early Christianity and was not regarded as being in conflict with the study of Scripture.

Some of Origen's views on Christology became suspect after the fourth-century ecumenical councils began to define Christological orthodoxy, and his speculations about the fall of souls from their prior existence in the ideal spiritual world were condemned at the Second Council of Constantinople (Fifth Ecumenical Council, 553), but nothing was said against his ideas about the eternity of creation or a succession of worlds. Origen's views were never adopted by any school of Christian thought, but the orthodox fourth-century theologian, Basil of Caesarea, referred to Origen's ideas in his sermons, 'On the Six Days of Creation' (*In Hexaemeron*, c. 360 CE). Basil described the possible existence of a created order prior to our own. Like Origen, he thought that this prior order was one of pure spirits, by which he meant angels.[57]

In the early Middle Ages, speculation on a possible plurality of worlds, each with its own heaven and earth, recurred in Jewish *midrāshîm* like *Seder Rabbah de Běre'shît* and *Midrash Alef Bēth*.[58] But the idea was nearly lost in the Christian world. In the 13th century, Aristotelian cosmology began to dominate Christian

---

53  *De princ.* I.4.1 (apud Jerome, *Con. Joh. Hieros.* 16); in Butterworth, trans., *Origen on First Principles*, 40-41.

54  *De princ.* I.4.4-5 with Greek Fragment 10; in Butterworth, trans., *Origen on First Principles*, 42-3.

55  Coincidentally, Origen probably became aware of the exegetical ideas of R. Abbahu's teacher, R. Yohanan bar Nappaha in Caesarea in the 240s; Reuven Kimelman, 'Rabbi Yohanan and Origen on the Song of Songs: A Third-Century Jewish-Christian Disputation', *Harvard Theological Review* 73 (1980), 569-73.

56  *De princ.* I. pref. 2, 3, 7; 4.4 (Latin trans.).

57  Basil, *Hexaemeron* I.5; II.5, described below in Chapter 3.

58  Peter Schäfer (2004), 'In Heaven as in Hell: The Cosmology of Seder Rabbah di-Bereshit', in Ra'anan S. Boustan and Annette Yoshiko Reed (eds), *Heavenly Realms and*

natural philosophy in Western Europe. The issue of debate then was not that of other creations, but one of the existence of gravitational centers other than the earth within our universe, and even these speculations were often relegated to the fringes of orthodoxy.[59]

Neither the thinking of the Jewish rabbis nor that of the early Christian theologians corresponds very closely to present-day cosmological thinking about the multiverse. But the ideas of exegetes like Rabbi Abbahu and Origen do demonstrate possibilities in the biblical concept of God that might help make theological sense of current scientific discussions. Moreover, they demonstrate a profound similarity between the speculative imagination of early theologians like Origen and that of physicists like Max Tegmark.[60] If 'it is the glory of God to conceal a thing', it is still the glory of thinking people to search it out (Prov. 25:2).

*The problem of transcendence in theological endeavour*

Another way in which examination of the cosmic foundation of science relates to the theological tradition is the challenge of the seemingly deistic image of God that often emerges from the image of a Lawgiver. There are at least two distinct issues here. One is the seeming impersonality of a cosmic Lawgiver. The second is that a Creator who is outside all space and time may not have any immediate relationship to space-time creatures.[61] So positing a cosmic Lawgiver relates well to the contingent lawfulness of the universe, but it does not tell us whether such a God can be present and active in space and time. Before we turn again to the resources of the biblical tradition for possible insights, it will help to illustrate these challenges from a current physics writer.

One of the first physicists to discuss the challenges in any detail is Paul Davies. In his ground-breaking *God and the New Physics* (1983), Davies argued that the scientific study of cosmic origins provides ground for belief in the existence of

---

*Earthly Realities in Late Antique Religions*, Cambridge; Cambridge University Press, 233-74; Deborah F. Sawyer, *Midrash Aleph Beth* (Atlanta: Scholars Press, 1993), 108, 115.

59   Edward Grant, 'The Condemnation of 1277, God's Absolute Power, and Physical Thought in the Late Middle Ages', *Viator* 10 (1979), 217-19. The idea of many such centres was revived by Giordano Bruno in the late sixteenth century; see, for example, Alexandre Koryé, *From the Closed World to the Infinite Universe* (Baltimore: Johns Hopkins University Press, 1957), 39-57.

60   The consonance between speculation in cosmology and speculation in theology is not a mere coincidence. Historians have shown the beginnings of modern science in medieval speculations about cosmology in which theological issues were very much involved; for example, Edward Grant, *Much Ado About Nothing: Theories of Space and Vacuum from the Middle Ages to the Scientific Revolution* (Cambridge: Cambridge University Press, 1981); Amos Funkenstein, *Theology and the Scientific Imagination from the Middle Ages to the Seventeenth Century* (Princeton: Princeton University Press, 1986).

61   The issue here is whether God is a participant in space and time as required by traditional theology. In conversation about a multiverse, the issue would have to be generalized to a more comprehensive continuum like Hilbert space or a de Sitter space.

God as the cause of all things (in some broad conception of causation).[62] Davies concluded that science actually offers a surer path in the search for God than religion does.[63] The problem that he raises for Judeo-Christian theology is that a God whose existence is inferred as the origin or cause of the space-time universe (or ensemble of space-time universes) must transcend all space and time.

It should be noted that Davies bases his confidence in part on the remarkable coincidences that make our particular universe a suitable one for the evolution of life (the Anthropic Principle).[64] He prefers not to pursue the idea of an ensemble of many universes (a multiverse) as a way around this problem. Rather disarmingly, he states that it is simpler and easier to believe in a unique Designer than it is to believe in a potential infinity of unobservable universes.[65] In this respect, Davies' approach differs from the one we are taking here. We have allowed for the possibility of a multiverse and even an ensemble of multiverses and have argued that the way to belief in God as Creator is still open through the contingency of the underlying laws. Even though the route we have taken is somewhat different from Paul Davies', the entry point into theology is much the same. So Davies' observations about the concept of God that results from cosmic speculation are pertinent for the transition we are making to a reconsideration of theological tradition.

According to Davies, a God who is completely transcendent cannot do temporal things like plan the future or answer prayers.[66] As a result, the 'God' we have posited as an explanation for the existence and lawfulness of the universe (or multiverse) seems rather impersonal: 'He cannot be a personal God who thinks, converses, feels, plans and so on for these are all temporal activities.'[67] In fact, there is no need for this God once the basic structure and laws of the universe (or multiverse) are established.[68] The most we have for all our trouble is some form of deism.[69] If so, the God of physicists like Davies is not the same as the God of the biblical prophets.

It will not be our purpose to criticize Davies' amazingly honest and insightful discussion. The challenge of deism – an impersonal, transcendent God, who is not immediately involved in the lives of its creatures – has exercised philosophers and theologians at least since the impact of Aristotelianism on medieval Europe.[70] The issues are complex and not easily resolved. Our purpose here is simply to illustrate

---

62  Paul Davies, *God and the New Physics* (New York: Simon and Schuster, 1983), 39, 42-3. Davies is a professor at the Australian Centre for Astrobiology at Macquarie University in Sydney.

63  Davies, *God and the New Physics*, ix, 229.

64  Davies, *God and the New Physics*, 43, 186-9.

65  Davies, *God and the New Physics*, 189; cf. idem, *The Mind of God*, 190.

66  Davies, *God and the New Physics*, 38-9, 133.

67  Davies, *God and the New Physics*, 133-4; cf. idem, *The Mind of God*, 191.

68  Davies, *God and the New Physics*, 133; cf. idem, *The Mind of God*, 192.

69  As Ian Barbour points out, such arguments by themselves lead to a God of Deism. Resolving that issue requires an appeal to religious experience or theological tradition; Barbour, *When Science Meets Religion*, 30. Davies develops a tentative resolution of this problem using Whitehead's 'dipolar' concept of God; Davies, *The Mind of God*, 181-3, 189. We come back to theological resources, including Whitehead's ideas, later in this chapter.

70  Kaiser, *Creational Theology*, 98-112.

how our analysis of the foundations of science and the theological issues they raise may lead us to explore the resources of the biblical tradition and possibly to rethink our current understanding of theology.

Of the many theological resources we could draw on, I shall discuss three: the idea of God as ecstatic Creator; the idea of God as Lawgiver; and the idea of an interpersonal Lord. In each case, we need to ask whether such ideas have anything to offer in the current discussion and to see what implications the applicability of such ideas might have for our understanding of God.

*God as ecstatic Creator of all things*

In Hebrew Scripture (the Old Testament), the idea of creation is set in a narrative context in which God is a regular participant in historical events. This idea implies that the Creator is somehow projected and thereby imaged in the realm of finite form.[71] God moves outside of the properly divine frame of reference (eternity) into relationship with the space-time forms of the created order. We shall develop this idea in the next few paragraphs. Our purpose is to show that the issue of transcendence raised by an appeal to God as the ground of cosmic order can help resuscitate aspects of biblical theology that have often been overlooked.[72]

The idea of God as Creator is a primary tenet of the Jewish-Christian tradition. The Jewish morning prayer service opens with the Sanctification of the Creator, who *forms light and creates darkness*.[73] The baptismal creeds of Eastern and Western churches both start with the affirmation that God is 'Creator of heaven and earth.'[74] This foundational belief implies that God transcends the constitutional orders of creation: be they light and darkness; heaven and earth; or space and time. So God is not conditioned by space and time or any other created frame of reference. The challenges raised by theology-minded physicists like Paul Davies are helpful in reminding us of this essential fact.

In the biblical tradition, however, God's action in creation is ecstatic. The world is viewed as a cosmic temple – God creates it as a dwelling place. So God does not remain

---

71  In biblical terms, the realm of finite form includes both the space-time world and a spirit-world. The difference between the two levels does not concern us in this chapter but will be discussed in Chapter 2.

72  The idea of God's creating space (and time) and then entering it as a participant has recently been developed by Jürgen Moltmann, primarily in relation to the Incarnation and outpouring of the Spirit; Moltmann, *Science and Wisdom*, trans. Margaret Kohl (Minneapolis: Fortress Press, 2003), 121-4.

73  The words in italics are derived from Isa. 45:7, based on Gen. 1:3-5. See Lawrence A. Hoffman, ed. *My People's Prayer Book: Traditional Prayers, Modern Commentaries, Vol. 1 – The* Sh'ma *and Its Blessings* (Woodstock Ver.: Jewish Lights, 1997), 19, 41; cf. *Oxford Dictionary of the Jewish Religion*, 754b. In the twelfth century Moses Maimonides (Moshe ben Maimon) compiled Thirteen Articles of Faith (*Shloshah-Asar Ikkarun*) that form a credo for many Jews to this day (*Commentary on Mishnah Sanhhedrin* 10:1). The first article of this credo was the existence of the Creator, who is the Primary Cause of all things.

74  Especially the Apostles' Creed (based on the Old Roman Symbol) and the Nicene Creed; see John H. Leith, *Creeds of the Churches: A Reader in Christian Doctrine from the Bible to the Present*, 3rd edn (Atlanta: John Knox Press, 1963), 24, 33.

within the divine frame in isolated from creation, but rather enters into relationship with space-time creatures.[75] In order to enter into relationship, God takes on the forms of space and time and specific attributes like justice and mercy. In the properly divine frame, God can be said to be all of these things in an undifferentiated way, but God cannot be equated with any of them to the exclusion of others. In the world of finite form, however, God appears as one of the space-time creatures: a rider on the clouds or a king on a throne. It is as if white light had passed through a prism and been diffracted into a rainbow of colours, any one of which may be in focus at any given time.[76]

Difficult as this idea of divine self-projection might seem, it is amply illustrated in well-known biblical narratives like that of the divine encounter in the Garden of Eden:

> They heard the sound of the LORD God walking in the garden at the time of the evening breeze, and the man and his wife hid themselves from the presence of the LORD God among the trees of the Garden. But the LORD God called to the man and said to him, 'Where are you?' (Genesis 3:8-9)

This amazing game of hide and seek may seem to modern readers a mere fable, but to the proponents of the biblical tradition it was the archetype of God's relationship to humanity – the LORD God is seeking us, calling us, and finding us 'ready or not'.[77] God is portrayed as walking 'in the garden' – the very garden s/he had planted (Gen. 2:8). God is enclosed by the framework that God initially transcended.[78] God is there not immutably, but at a particular, identifiable time of day, 'at the time of the evening breeze' – part of the cycle of 'evening and morning' that God had previously created (Gen. 1:5). Such is the character that the Creator assumes in the biblical tradition. Surely this God is not locked out of the world s/he has created.[79]

---

75   The difference between male and female attributes is another way of expressing the diffraction that God undergoes in entering the realm of finite form. Unless the text being considered specifies a gendered attribute, I shall try to use gender-inclusive pronouns. The question of the personality of God will be taken up in due course.

76   The fullness of divine attributes was symbolized by a rainbow in Ezek. 1:28; cf. Sir. 50:7; Apoc. Abr. 11:3, 4QShirShabb[f] Frag. 23 2:7-10. The idea of the diffraction of divine attributes was common in Amoraic Rabbinic theology, most notably in Exodus Rabbah 6:1 and Mekhilta of R. Ishmael, *Shira* 4:22; *Ba-hodesh* 5:23; see Ephraim E. Urbach, *The Sages: Their Concepts and Beliefs* (Cambridge, Mass: Harvard University Press, 1987), 37-8, 448-61.

77   So said Rabi Samuel bar Ammi according to Gen. Rab. 3:9, 'From the beginning of the creation of the world, the Holy One, blessed be he, yearned to make for himself a partner among the creatures of the world down here'; Neusner, trans., *Genesis Rabbah*, 1:35; cf. Abraham J. Heschel, 'God, Torah, and Israel', in Edward LeRoy Long, Jr, and Robert T. Handy (ed.), *Theology and Church in Times of Change* (Philadelphia: Westminster Press, 1970), 86.

78   A rather different emphasis is found in texts like Jer. 23:24, *Who can hide in secret places so that I cannot see them? says the LORD. Do I not fill heaven and earth? says the Lord.* The notion of seeking and finding is assumed as in Genesis 3, but the LORD's attributes are scaled up to world dimensions.

79   The idea of God existing in two distinct frames of reference is not without parallels in physics. In the quantum theory of measurement, for example, the 'state vector' that represents

One of the difficulties that the narrative raises is that, as soon as the LORD God walks in one place at one time and speaks, s/he submits to limitations, and even the conflicts, of finite form. In order to search for the man and woman s/he has created, God chooses to be patient and wait until the evening. By walking in the garden, God may not see everything at once – so the man and woman can hide among the trees. God has to call for the man. It is up to the man to answer. Then patience gives way to judgment – God punishes humans with the famous curses (Gen. 3:14-19). The biblical account clearly lacks the timelessness and rigorous consistency that physicists prefer.[80] Biblical writers, on the other hand, show a high degree of tolerance for concreteness and conflict in the God they so lovingly portray.

In short, the God of the Genesis narrative is both transcendent Creator and immanent participant. The challenge of deism helps remind us of this. But, one might ask, is this not a sacrifice of consistency? Is anything to be gained by it? We shall look at several ways in which Jewish and Christian theologians have tried to address the apparent inconsistency. Their contributions will make the notion of an immanent Creator at least plausible. In subsequent chapters, we shall find that there is something to be gained: the complex picture of the deity developed here can help us address several other theological issues that are raised by investigating the foundations of scientific endeavour.

One of the very earliest ways developed to affirm the compatibility of immanence and transcendence was to think of God as the matrix for creation. A 'matrix God' is one who embraces and contains all things. Such a God can contain, but not be contained – an affirmation of transcendence. Such a God also pervades and fills all things s/he contains, both sustaining them and giving them coherence.

The idea of a matrix-God is indicated in several biblical narratives. At the dedication of the first Temple in Jerusalem, for example, the priests carried the Ark of the Covenant into the inner sanctuary of the Temple and, as soon as they left, the Shekhinah-Glory of the LORD filled the entire structure. Solomon addressed God in prayer, saying: 'Even heaven and the highest heaven cannot contain you, much less this house that I have built' (1 Kgs. 8:6, 10-11, 27). The very image of a temple implied to the Israelites that the transcendence of God did not preclude concrete immanence. The Shekhinah-glory of the LORD filled the temple and was present in a particular place, even though it could not be contained by that, or any other, spatial location.

One of the first theologians to give a rational form to the idea was the Jewish philosopher and exegete, Philo of Alexandria. Philo wrote extensive commentaries on the Hebrew Bible in the first half of the first century CE. He addressed the problem of immanence and transcendence as he tried to make philosophic sense of the texts. An example is his treatment of Genesis 11:5, which states that the LORD 'came down' to inspect the tower being built in Babel (Babylon) and to pass judgment – a good example of God's self-diffraction into the particularity of place, time and attributes.

---

a particle exists in a multi-dimensional Hilbert space. Upon measurement, however, it is 'projected' into ordinary space-time with a definable location.

80   Paul Davies points out the importance of the timelessness of concepts in mathematics and logic in the Cartesian tradition in the writing we reviewed earlier; Davies, *The Mind of God*, 178.

Philo finds this portrayal of God a bit too anthropomorphic, however, and restates it as follows:

> As we all know, when a person comes down [from anywhere] he must leave one place and occupy another. But God fills all things [Isa. 6:3; Jer. 23:24]; he contains but is not contained. To be everywhere and nowhere is his property and his alone. He is nowhere, because he himself created space and place…. He is everywhere, because he has made his powers [Greek, *dynámeis*] extend through earth and water, air and heaven, and left no part of the universe without his presence…. That aspect of him which transcends his potencies [*dynámeōn*] cannot be conceived of at all in terms of place, but only as pure being, but that Potency of his by which he made and ordered all things…holds the whole in its embrace and has interfused itself through the parts of the universe.[81]

Philo's statement is quite consistent: it is as carefully balanced as the equation for a chemical reaction. The fact that God created space, time[82] and matter means that God's potency or power (*dÿnamis*) holds all of these things in its embrace. God is 'nowhere' in the sense that God transcends all. But, by the same token, God fills all and is 'everywhere' in that his presence and powers penetrate to each part of the world he has created. By referring to the 'powers' or 'potencies' of God, Philo articulates the way in which God's undifferentiated being ('pure being') is diffracted into a variety of complementary attributes within space and time. We shall return to this aspect of God's immanence in Chapter 4 when we consider the paradoxes of the societal foundation of scientific endeavour and the possibility of an eschatological 'refocusing' of God's attributes.

The idea of God as the matrix of creation entered the Christian thought world along with many other of Philo's ideas, through the Alexandrian school of apologists and theologians, especially Origen and Athanasius. It was transmitted to Western Christendom in the writings of Saint Augustine (early fifth century) in terse formulas like this one:

> Without any distance or measure of space, by immutable and transcendent power [Latin, *potentia*], God is interior to all things because they are all in God and exterior to all things because God is above them all.[83]

The familiar Augustinian emphasis on transcendence and immutability are clearly stated here.[84] But the idea of God as matrix of creation ('all in God') ensured that for

---

81  Philo, *De Confusione Linguarum* 136-7; ET in Loeb Classical Library, *Philo*, 10 vols and 2 supplementary vols (Cambridge, Mass: Harvard University Press, 1929-62), 4:83-5, stylistically modified.

82  A very similar passage in *De Posteritate Caini* 14 speaks of God as the Cause of all place and time; Loeb Classical Library, *Philo*, 2:335.

83  Augustine, *On Genesis Literally* VIII.26.48; ET in *Ancient Christian Writers*, ed. Johannes Quasten et al. (New York: Paulist Press, 1949 to present), 42:67. In addition to earlier Christian writers, Augustine was influenced by passages in the philosophical writing of Plotinus like *Enneads* V.5.9, which he read in the Latin translation of Victorinus.

84  I document Augustine's emphasis on transcendence and immutability in my *The Doctrine of God: A Historical Survey*, revised edn (Eugene, Oregon: Wipf and Stock, 2001), 89-95.

one of the keenest minds of Western history, at least, there was no contradiction in simultaneously affirming God's proximity and interiority to all things. As for Philo, the paradoxical nature of the formulation actually provides a sense of consistency.

So far we have seen how the idea of divine self-projection can be found in biblical texts and in influential theological texts like Augustine. Strictly speaking, however, these texts only deal with the results of projection, not with the process itself. Here again we can find helpful ideas in the Hebrew Bible, in Philo, and in early Christian apologists and theologians. What we find in all of these texts is an interesting polarity within the Godhead.

We begin with the book of Proverbs 8, which is part of the Wisdom literature of the Hebrew Bible. Proverbs 8 is a self-description of Lady Wisdom, a hypostatic (concrete) form of divine creativity like the power or potency described by Philo and Augustine in the passages cited above:

> The LORD created me at [or 'as'] the beginning of his work,
> the first of his acts of long ago.
> Ages ago I was set up,
> at the first, before the beginning of the earth.
> When there were no depths I was brought forth,
> when there were no springs abounding with water....
> When he marked out the foundations of the earth,
> then I was beside him, like a master worker...
> rejoicing in his inhabited world,
> and delighting in the human race. (Prov. 8:22-31)

According to this passage, the process of creation begins, not with the creation of heaven and earth as in Genesis 1:1, but with the creation (or engagement)[85] of Lady Wisdom (Hokmah in Hebrew), who is the LORD him/herself in a finite form just like the Shekhinah-glory that filled the temple of Solomon.[86] This duplication or self-projection of the deity is stated as a precondition ('the beginning') for the formation of the cosmic structures as they were known in the ancient world: the earth, depths and springs described in the passage cited.[87] Just like Philo's 'Potency by which he made and ordered all things', Wisdom serves as God's craftsperson ('a master worker') in all the acts of creation and then dwells within the structures that result ('rejoicing in his inhabited world'). The 'wisdom theology' of Proverbs yields a polarity of transcendence and immanence similar to that we observed in Philo and Augustine, but it also attempts to describe the process that led to that polarity.

---

85    The Hebrew verb *qanah* has a variety of possible meanings, as footnotes to Prov. 8:22 in most English Bibles will indicate.

86    The parallel between Hokmah-Wisdom and Shekhinah-Glory is developed in texts like Sirach 24:3-12. Jewish exegetes appealed to the identification of Wisdom and 'beginning' in Prov. 8:22 to discern a reference to Wisdom in Gen. 1:1, 'In the beginning God created...'; for example, Fragment Targum to Gen. 1:1; Gen. Rab. 1:1.

87    Fragment Targum to Exod. 15:18 describes four special nights in which the LORD is revealed on earth. The first of these is as the Word (Aramaic, *memra*) in the midst of primordial darkness in Gen. 1:2-3, the Word being another of the a hypostatic forms of divine creativity.

From a Christian standpoint, the idea of God's self-projection and immanence in creation in the form of Lady Wisdom had obvious parallels to the incarnation of the divine Word (Greek, 'Logos') in Jesus of Nazareth. In the New Testament writings, Jesus was identified with the Wisdom of God as described in Proverbs 8.[88] In second-century apologists like Justin Martyr and Athenagoras, the idea of the divine projection was developed into a two-stage Christology using the Stoic concept of an 'expressed word' (*Lógos prophorikós*).[89] Prior to creation, the Word or Wisdom of God was within God like an idea in the mind (stage 1), but then it was expressed as an articulated, active Word in the realm of space and time (stage 2). Although later theologians bypassed this early Christological model (due to the implied subordination of the Word), it is still a useful way of conceptualizing the idea of God's self-projection in creation.

One of the clearest formulations of a two-stage Christology is found in Athenagoras' effort to explain the meaning of the phrase 'Son of God' in his *Plea on Behalf of the Christians*, written in the 170s:

> He [the Son] is the first offspring of the Father. I do not mean that he was created, for since God is eternal mind, he had his Word within himself from the beginning, being eternally wise. Rather did the Son come forth from God to give form and actuality to all material things…. The prophetic Spirit agrees with this opinion when he says, *The LORD created me as the first of his ways, for his works.* [Prov. 8:22a][90]

Athenagoras' description of the divine self-projection is based on the model of Wisdom in Proverbs 8, which he quotes. But his thinking differs from earlier presentations in that the divine polarity is located within the life of the divine Word (or Wisdom), rather than the LORD God and Wisdom as in Proverbs 8. As God's own Wisdom, the Son was eternally one with God (stage 1), but he proceeded into the realm of finite form in order to establish the structure of material world (stage 2). An important question raised by this two-stage Christology is whether, even though it is coeternal with God, the Word only assumed a hypostatic (concrete) form upon its projection into the realm of finite form. If the Word was eternally one with God the Father, it might not be hypostatically distinct. If it was distinct from God, it might not be truly divine.

In the fourth century Christian theologians debated these issues with considerable passion. The two alternatives just mentioned were both ruled out.[91] Orthodox theologians

---

88   See, for example, Matt. 11:27; John 1:1; 5:17; Col. 1:15; Rev. 3:14; see Kaiser, *The Doctrine of God: A Historical Survey*, revised edn (Eugene, OR: Wipf and Stock, 2001), 42-4. From a Rabbinic standpoint, the idea of God's self-projection and immanence in creation was paralleled in the giving of the Torah on Sinai. In various Jewish *midrāshîm*, the Torah was also identified with the Wisdom of God as described in Proverbs 8:22; for example, Gen. Rab. 1:1.

89   The etic category, 'twofold stage theory of the Logos', is from Henry Austryn Wolfson, *The Philosophy of the Church Fathers: Faith, Incarnation, Trinity*, third edn (Cambridge, Mass: Harvard University Press, 1970), 192-8.

90   Athenagoras, *Legatio* 10.3-4; ET in Cyril C. Richardson (ed.), *Early Christian Fathers*, Library of Christian Classics 1 (London: SCM Press; Philadelphia: Westminster Press, 1953), 309.

91   These two options are referred to as Modalism and Arianism, respectively. Both were ruled out by the Ecumenical councils of Nicea (325) and Constantinople (381).

became more consistent in affirming the hypostatic nature of the Word, even in its transcendent, eternal aspect. But the basic idea of a projection in the event of creation was retained by the chief advocate of Nicene orthodoxy, Athanasius of Alexandria.

The primary aim of Athanasius' treatise *On the Incarnation of the Word* (early fourth century) was to show that the only being capable of restoring humanity to its intended quality of life and knowledge was its Creator. In other words, there must be a correspondence between the ideas of incarnation and salvation, on the one hand, and creation, on the other. This correspondence led Athanasius to two important results. One was that the divine potency (Greek, *dýnamis*) that Philo had described as embracing all things and interfused through all could be identified with Christ, the Word:

> [It is a] thing most marvelous: Word as he was...he contained all things himself; and... while present in the whole of creation, he is at once distinct in being from the universe and present in all things by his own power [*dynámesi*] – giving order to all things, and over all and in all revealing his own providence, and giving life to each thing and to all things, including the whole without being included, but being in his own Father alone wholly and in every respect.... (*De Incarnatione* 17)[92]

The polarity of transcendence and immanence is affirmed in very much the same way as in Athanasius' Alexandrian predecessor, Philo. But rather than identifying the Word exclusively with the immanent side of the Godhead as Philo did, Athanasius portrayed both transcendence and immanence as modes of being in the life of the divine Word. The Word is present in all things, not just as the self-projection of God, but 'by its own power' (cf. Heb. 1:3).

On this basis, Athanasius was able to sum up his Christian faith by ascribing three distinct modes of being to the divine Word. The first two modes are transcendence ('in his own Father') and immanence ('present in the whole of creation'). The third mode is its bodily presence in Jesus of Nazareth. In other words, there are really three stages in the life of the Logos, corresponding to three distinct levels of being: (1) with God eternally; (2) in all of creation; and (3) in the person of Jesus. This summary of faith implies that the self-projection of the Word in the Incarnation is paralleled by a prior self-projection in creation. Athanasius stated it this way:

> ...we must speak also of the origin of humanity, that you may know that the reason for his coming down [in the person of Jesus] was because of us, and that our transgression called forth the loving-kindness of the Word [*tou Lógou tēn philanthrōpían*], that the Lord should both make haste to help us and appear among humans.... For...out of a former normal state of nonexistence they were called into being by the presence and loving kindness of the Word [*tē tou Lógou parousía kai philanthrōpía*].... (*De Incarnatione* 4)[93]

---

92   ET in Edward Rochie Hardy and Cyril C. Richardson, eds, *Christology of the Later Fathers*, Library of Christian Classics 3 (London: SCM Press, 1954), 70-71.

93   ET adapted from Hardy and Richardson, *Christology of the Later Fathers*, 58-9. The Greek text and a slightly different English translation are available in Athanasius, *Contra Gentes and De Incarnatione*, ed. Robert W. Thompson (Oxford: Clarendon Press, 1971), 142-5.

Note that Athanasius used the Greek term, *philanthropía*, meaning 'mercy' or 'loving-kindness', as a way of connecting the incarnation of the Word with its original presence (*parousía*) in creation.

Elsewhere Athanasius used the Greek term *parousía*, meaning presence or coming, to refer to the Incarnation.[94] The term expressed perfectly the idea of the immanence and self-projection of the Word in the world of finite form. The self-projection of the Word at creation was therefore a preview of Incarnation, the only difference being that this first self-projection diffracted the attributes in the vastness of space and time, whereas the Incarnation concentrated them in a single human being.[95]

Returning now to the challenge of deism raised with respect to the Cosmological foundation of scientific endeavour, our review of early Jewish and Christian thought demonstrates two things. First the idea of divine transcendence required by divine creation did not necessarily exclude God's presence within the space-time continuum. In fact, the early understanding of transcendence as containing or embracing all things implied the permeation of the universe with divine power (Philo, Athanasius, Augustine). Second, creation in the biblical tradition involved an ecstatic self-expression of God. The Word/Wisdom of God duplicated itself within the realm of finite form in space and time.

Medieval Latin Christian theologians stressed the simplicity and immutability of God and referred to creation as an 'external operation' (*opus Dei ad extra*) in order to differentiate it from the internal operations (begetting, proceeding) among the Trinity. That was a helpful way to make the earlier idea of the *Lógos prophorikós* conform with orthodox (Nicene) Christology. The idea of an external operation raised its own problems, however. It sometimes gave the impression that the tri-hypostatic Creator had a complete life of its own without regard to creation. God was only present in the world as a simple, undifferentiated, timeless whole without location or any other particularity.[96] The idea of transcendence took on a connotation of separation rather than embracing the whole of creation. Some theologians qualified the starkness of this

---

94  'Who, then, and how great is this Christ, who by his own name and presence [*parousía*] casts into the shade and brings to naught all [deceitful] things....' Athanasius, *De Incarnatione* 48. Earlier examples of this usage are found in the Apostolic Fathers (Ignatius, *Philadelphians* 9:2) and the Apologists (Justin, *1 Apology* 52.3; *Dialogue* 14.8; 40.4).

95  On Jesus as the fullness of the Godhead or the light of God, see John 8:12; 9:5; 2 Cor. 4:6; Col. 1:19; 2:3, 9; Rev. 1:16. The idea of the concentration in Jesus of the fullness of the Godhead, otherwise known throughout the world in only fragmentary ways, was developed by Justin Martyr, *2 Apology* 13. Instead of a diffraction of light, Justin used the image of the scattering of seed in the world. Justin recognized that there were other major projections or 'advents' of the Logos in the history of Israel, for example, in relation to Abraham and Moses; Justin *1 Apology* 63.11, 17; *Dialogue with Trypho* 56, passim.

96  For example, Thomas Aquinas, *Summa Theologiae* Ia. Q. 3, esp. art. 7; Q. 8, art. 3, passim, which assume that simplicity and spatio-temporal composition are mutually exclusive alternatives. But the idea is already found in Augustine's anti-Manichaean writings (cf. *On the Literal Interpretation of Genesis, Unfinished Version* 5.19; *Confessions* III.6.10; 7.12; V.10.19; VI.3.4; 4.5; 11.18; XII.5.18). For an influential critique of this scholastic idea, see Charles Hartshorne, *The Divine Relativity: A Social Conception of God* (New Haven: Yale University Press, 1948), 15, passim.

transcendence by referring it to the essence of God. For John Calvin, for example, the glory (or the powers) of God pervaded all of creation as they had for the early theologians.[97]

A similar polarity is ensconced in Eastern Orthodox theology, based on the contributions of theologians like St Gregory Palamas (d. 1359), for whom transcendent essence and immanent energies were two polar modes of the divine existence.[98] The energies are a procession of the Deity outside the divine essence as a multiple expression of the divine nature. The existence of a space-time order was made possible by this effusion of creative power.[99] In short, the act of creation involves an ecstatic self-expression of God in the realm of finite form.[100]

Since the early twentieth century, the idea of a polarity within the divine being has been widely discussed in relation to the process philosophy of Alfred North Whitehead. In Whitehead's understanding, God (like all actual entities) has two aspects, an antecedent nature and a consequent nature: the one being unconscious and unconditioned; and the other conscious in the conditions of temporal immanence. First worked out in his classic treatise, *Process and Reality* (1929),[101] Whitehead's ideas have had a major impact on Christian theologians like Charles Hartshorne and David Griffin.[102] They offer one more way in which the chasm between the notion of God as a transcendent Creator and an immanent participant in creation can be bridged.

*Other theological challenges*

In the previous section we showed that the ecstatic, self-projecting Creator portrayed in traditional theology is immanent within the space-time world of finite form. This idea enriches our understanding of creation and addresses the challenge of deism – that God is not immediately involved in the lives of its creatures – one of the issues raised by Paul Davies and others. But there are several other theological problems to address. So far, we have only enriched our understanding of creation to the point of

---

97  T. H. L. Parker, *Calvin's Doctrine of the Knowledge of God* (Edinburgh: Oliver and Boyd, 1952, 1969), 83-5.

98  Vladimir Lossky, *The Mystical Theology of the Eastern Church* (Cambridge: James Clarke, 1957), 86.

99  Gregory Palamas, *Hyper tôn hierôs hesychazontôn* III.2.7-8, passim; ET in Gregory Palamas, *The Triads*, ed. John Meyendorff (New York: Paulist Press, 1983), 95-6; cf. John Meyendorff, *A Study of Gregory Palamas* (London: Faith Press, 1964), 210-11, 220-21; Lossky, *Mystical Theology of the Eastern Church*, 74, 86, 89, 94.

100  John D. Zizioulas has interpreted the procession of the divine energies in writings of Pseudo-Dionysius, Maximus Confessor, and Gregory of Palamas in terms of the idea of divine *ekstásis*; Zizioulas, *Being as Communion: Studies in Personhood and the Church* (Crestwood, N.Y.: St Vladimir's Seminary Press, 1985), 91-2.

101  Alfred North Whitehead, *Process and Reality: An Essay in Cosmology* (New York: Macmillan, 1929). See, for example, pp. 33, 44-6, 135, 523, 527.

102  Hartshorne described the poles as 'abstract' and 'concrete' or 'maximally absolute' and 'maximally relative', respectively; Hartshorne, *The Divine Relativity*, ix, xi, 32, passim. Griffin adopted Hartshorne's terminology and used Trinitarian ideas to avoid the negative connotations of unconsciousness and restore personal attributes to the abstract essence of God; David Griffin, *A Process Christology* (Philadelphia: Westminster Press, 1973), 190-92.

allowing for God's immanence in finite relationships. Nothing has been said explicitly about divine activity, so the challenge of deism is still unresolved. I shall argue in the following section that divine activity is already implied by the idea of God as cosmic Lawgiver as portrayed in Scripture and as understood by early theologians. The God of the physicists is not incompatible with the God of the prophets.

A second problem for traditional theology is that a self-projecting, lawgiving God might be inherently impersonal. God enters into relationships with God's creatures, particularly humans, and is personal in his/her immanent mode of being. Does that mean that God only appears to be personal, something like a computerized robot? Is God truly personal within God's own frame of reference? As far as biblical narratives are concerned, God is clearly both transcendent and personal.[103] But in our exploration of the foundations of scientific endeavour we are confronted with the question of whether personality can in any sense be attributed to a cosmic Lawgiver. I shall argue that the traditional idea of God as Lawgiver addresses this challenge heuristically, and the idea of God as interpersonal (tri-hypostatic) Lord addresses it more directly.

A third problem has to do with the coherence of ideas. In our discussion of God as ecstatic Creator, the ideas of self-projection and immanence have simply been asserted (or read back into the Godhead from the creation story and other biblical narratives). Nothing has been said about a possible ground for self-projection within the eternal being of the Godhead itself. I shall argue that such a ground can also be found in the Christian idea of God as interpersonal Lord.

*God as cosmic Lawgiver*

The idea of God as Lawgiver can help us understand the contingent character of a law-governed creation and provide heuristic (analogical) grounds for belief in the personality of the Lawgiver. The writers of the Hebrew Bible viewed the lawfulness of our world as a direct expression of the will and word of God. There are two implications here. One is that God is believed to be active wherever God's laws are effective. Another implication is that the laws of creation are believed to be contingent on the will of God: they are either ratified or amended in each instance of their operation. We shall discuss each implication in turn.

Readers familiar with appeals to gaps in the laws of nature as evidence for divine activity may be surprised by the first of these implications: that the will and word of God are manifest and active wherever God's laws are effective. Laplace's contention that the activity of God is a hypothesis and that it is eliminated as the gaps in scientific explanation are filled in has greatly conditioned our thinking. We have come to view the laws of nature as autonomous and to associate them with the absence, or at least the hiddenness, of God even if it might be true that God decreed those laws in the beginning.

But the idea of cosmic natural laws goes back before the Enlightenment and even before the emergence of Western Europe as we know it. The idea that God organizes the cosmos by establishing laws has been documented in a variety of ancient Near

---

103 Kaiser, *Doctrine of God*, 2.

Eastern cultures.[104] It was mediated to the Western Europe through the Hebrew Bible and the historic 'creationist tradition' that provided the theological background for the origin of modern science.[105] I shall discuss this tradition in some detail in Chapter 3 as part of the cultural foundation of scientific endeavour. Here it will suffice to give a brief overview and a few examples in order to address the issue of divine activity and to describe how the modern idea of autonomous causation arose. The point to be established is that the original idea of cosmic natural laws intimately involved God in the operations of nature.

One of the first references to laws of nature in the Hebrew Bible occurs in the Book of Consolation, included among the prophecies of Jeremiah.[106] The context for this particular prophesy was one of the most discouraging phases of the history of Israel, their exile in Babylon following the destruction of the First Temple, which as we have seen was viewed as the residence of the Creator God on earth. Did the destruction of the Temple mean that God had abandoned the people if Israel? Would God ever abandon them? The consolation offered was couched in terms of the lawful motion of the celestial bodies:

> Thus says the LORD,
> who gives the sun for light by day
>  and the fixed order [Hebrew, *huqqot*] of the moon and the stars for light by night....
> If this fixed order [*huqqîm*] were ever to cease
>  from my presence, says the LORD,
> then also the offspring of Israel cease
>  to be a nation before me forever. (Jer. 31:35-36)

The term translated here as 'fixed order' (NRSV) is the Hebrew word, *hoq*, meaning a royal decree or law. It is translated as *nómos*, the Greek word for law, in the Septuagint, and as *lex* in Jerome's Latin translation, the Vulgate.[107] The biblical and theological use of these terms played a huge role in the development of the idea of cosmic natural law inherited by modern science. As shown by the passage cited, laws for motion of the sun, moon and stars were viewed as expressions of God's providence analogous to God's covenant faithfulness to Israel. Lawfulness implied the faithfulness and the activity of God through the regularities God had decreed. God is both immanent and personal, at least by analogy to the covenant with Israel.

---

104 For example, Henri Frankfort, et al., *The Intellectual Adventure of Ancient Man: An Essay on Speculative Thought in the Ancient Near East* (University of Chicago Press, 1946), chap. 5.

105 See also Kaiser, *Creational Theology*, esp. 18-21, 32-60.

106 The 'Book of Consolation' (Jer. 30-33) is generally thought to be a later addition to the prophecies of Jeremiah, but the part cited below was included in the Greek translation (Septuagint, Jer. 38:35-36). Issues of redaction and translation do not materially affect the points we are concerned with here.

107 Jer. 33:25 similarly refers to the 'ordinances [or laws, *huqqot*] of heaven and earth'. This passage is not present in extant versions of the Greek Septuagint, but it is included in the Latin Vulgate where *huqqot* is translated as *leges*.

The Book of Consolation cited laws only for the sun, moon and stars, for which it was fairly easy to see lawfulness and faithfulness at work. Elsewhere, the Hebrew Bible cited every possible aspect of creation as exemplifying God's law: even the tumultuous elements like the wind and the seas and meteorological phenomena like rain, lightning, thunder, snow and even hail (for example Job 28:25-6; Ps. 148:7-8). All of these elements are said to fulfill God's ordinances in a lawful way. Such texts were not unknown to later theologians. In fact they were celebrated as a way of magnifying God's wisdom. Augustine, for example, reveled in the idea that God's order could be seen in such potentially destructive phenomena as hailstorms. If humans cannot see that order, that does not mean that it is absent, only that it is hidden.[108]

Early Jewish and Christian theologians expressed this biblical idea using the Greek phrase for 'law of nature', *nómos physeōs*. The suspension of the earth, the orbits of the sun, moon and stars, and the alternation of the seasons were all established in the beginning by God's word and law.[109] One of the most influential of these texts was Basil of Caesarea's treatise 'On the Six Days of Creation' (*In Hexaemeron*), which we just discussed in connection with the idea of multiple universes and will take up again in Chapter 3. Neither Basil nor Augustine understood the 'six days' of Genesis 1 as a straightforward chronological account of events. They read them rather as a map of the structure and operation of the cosmos, all of which came into being instantaneously even though they could only be revealed to creatures in a sequence of steps.[110]

We conclude that, in its beginnings, the idea of laws of nature in no way detracted from the sense of the providence of God (or God's self-projection as Word) in the world. The analogy of the system of nature to a spinning top indicates that even the most regular of mechanical operations could be embraced in this vision of God's all-pervasive word. The operation of creatures in accordance with laws of nature actually demonstrated the immanence and action of that word.

The idea of lawfulness in creation as a manifestation of divine providence was not forgotten in the Jewish community either. The biblical belief that God's cosmic laws guaranteed God's immediate care for his people was celebrated in Jewish liturgies and in legal discussions. One example is the benediction attributed to Rab Judah in the Babylonian Talmud:

> Praised [is the Lord our God] who created the heavens with his word and all their hosts with the breath of his mouth. He appointed to them fixed laws and times, that they should not change their ordinance. They rejoice and are glad to do the will of their Creator. They work [alternate reading, 'he works'] truthfully for their action is truth. (b. Sanhedrin 42a)[111]

---

108 Augustine *De Gen. ad Lit.* V.26.42-27.43; ET in *Ancient Christian Writers*, 41:172-4, discussed in Chapter 3.

109 For example, Eusebius of Caesarea, *Prep.* VII.9, 10, which relies on Jewish authors like Aristobulus and Philo; see Chapter 3, for details.

110 Kathryn. E. Greene-McCreight, *Ad Litteram: How Augustine, Calvin, and Barth Read the 'Plain Sense' of Genesis 1-3* (New York: Peter Lang, 1999), 44, 58-9. The idea of simultaneous creation of all material things had precedent in Philo and is found in several Jewish *midrāshîm*.

111 I. Epstein (ed.), *Hebrew-English Edition of the Babylonian Talmud: Tractate Sanhedrin* (London: Soncino Press, 1969).

The idea of fixed laws and times in creation is quite compatible here with the belief in the personal care and covenant faithfulness of the LORD God. And so generations of Europeans who were instructed by the rabbis and theologians originally believed: the laws of nature were manifestations of the wisdom and care of the Creator.

The influence of Basil and Augustine was determinative in Western Europe where early modern science originated. The ideas we have discussed can be documented in medieval writers like Grosseteste and William of Ockham, in Renaissance writers like George Bauer Agricola and Richard Hooker. During the 'scientific revolution' of the 17th century, they were influential in the thinking of Francis Bacon, René Descartes, Benedict Spinoza, Robert Boyle, and Isaac Newton.

It is not possible in a brief review like this to go through all the links in the chain of tradition. But the continuity can readily be seen in a passage like the following from the early seventeenth-century 'Confession of Faith' by Francis Bacon. Among other things, Bacon believed:

> That God... created heaven and earth, and all their armies and generation [sun, moon and stars], and gave unto them constant and everlasting laws, which we call *Nature*, which is nothing but the Laws of the creation.... So as the laws of Nature, which now remain and govern inviolably till the end of the world, began to be in force when God first rested from his works and ceased to create [Gen. 2:2]....[112]

Bacon's credo is a typical recycling of motifs from biblical and patristic texts that were standard literature in the seventeenth century. The origin of the laws of nature in God, the continuing efficacy of those laws for all time as a reflection of the sovereignty of the Lawgiver, the idea of the rest of God from the first creative work,[113] and even the inviolability of the laws of nature are all themes derived from the biblical tradition. None of them were thought to diminish the immediacy of divine providence.

This is not to say that the Western concept of nature had not changed at all over twelve centuries of transmission. During the twelfth-century renaissance of natural philosophy in France and England, a clear distinction was made between the immediate activity of God and the operations of nature in accordance with God's laws.[114] In the 14th century, fascination with newly invented mechanical clocks and the philosophical idea of nature as a mechanical device like a clock promoted a further recession of the activity of God to the moments of initial creation and occasional miracles.[115] By the time of Descartes, Boyle and Newton, the most progressive thinking was that God had either stirred everything up or wound everything up in the beginning so that no further appeal to God's presence or activity was needed, at

---

112 Francis Bacon, *A Confession of Faith*, written c. 1602; in *The Works of Francis Bacon*, ed. James Spedding et al., 14 vols (London: Green, Longman and Roberts, 1857-74), 14:49-50.

113 God rested from the work of primary creation (Gen. 2:2) but continued to be active in the world; for example Odes of Solomon 16:12-14; Augustine, *De Gen. ad Litt.* V.4.11; idem, *De Civ. Dei* XXII.24.

114 Kaiser, *Creational Theology*, 54-9.

115 Kaiser, *Creational Theology*, 106-9, 125-9.

least, for 'mechanical' phenomena.[116] This mechanized image of the natural world inspired some very creative cosmological thinking among philosophers, but it also fundamentally altered our understanding of God as Creator and Lawgiver and provided the ideological basis for theological deism, on the one hand, and for the industrial revolution, on the other.[117]

We shall postpone further discussion of the challenge of mechanization and secularization for Chapter 4 (societal foundation). Our purpose here is simply to highlight resources of the biblical tradition that may help address the challenges raised by the theological implications of cosmic lawfulness. We have seen that originally the all-important idea of cosmic laws did not exclude the extension of God's presence and power to the created world. Nor did it remove God from personal (covenant) relationship to space-time creatures. There is, therefore, no necessity for a deistic recession of divine activity as far as the idea of laws is concerned. Deism is one option, but not by any means a necessary consequence of the cosmic foundation of scientific endeavour. Our familiar modern patterns of thought about God and the world are relatively recent constructs in the Western history of ideas.

In the modern world, we normally think of 'acts of God' as unpredictable exceptions to the laws of nature. We do not normally think of God acting through the laws s/he mandated in the beginning: the present unfolding of events is quite separate from the divine initiation.[118] One arena in which we still do observe continuity between initiation and consequence, however, is in affairs of state. When a governing officer issues an executive order, for example, the authority and intentions of the executive power are seen as operative in every case where that decree is applicable. Legal decrees are one of the few contexts in which the root metaphor that we found in the biblical texts about creation still survives and informs our lives. It may still be helpful to recall that image in thinking about God as Creator and Lawgiver in relation to the cosmic foundation of scientific endeavour.

The legal-decree metaphor leads us to a second implication of the idea of God as Lawgiver: the laws of creation are at all times contingent on the will of God.[119] In every instance of their applicability they must be ratified or amended or revoked.

---

116 For example, Descartes' imaginary world in which God created a pure chaos and subjected it to laws of nature so that the order of the present world emerged naturally; Descartes, *Discours de la méthode* V.45 (1637). The same idea occurs in Jonathan Edwards' 'Things to Be Considered'; in *The Works of Jonathan Edwards*, ed. Perry Miller and John E. Smith, 27 vols (New Haven: Yale University Press, 1957-2004), 6:265.

117 On the role of the mechanical philosophy in the secularization process, see Kaiser, 'From Biblical Secularity to Modern Secularism', 10-12, 18-19.

118 I say 'not normally', because there are significant theologians like Thomas F. Torrance who have responded to the challenge of the sciences and recovered the patristic insight that laws of nature are expressions of God's legislative word; Torrance, *Christian Theology and Scientific Culture* (New York: Oxford University Press, 1981), 123.

119 Earlier we argued (on cosmological grounds) for the contingency of the laws of physics that are singled out for our multiverse ('Why is our multiverse lawful?'). Here we are arguing (on biblical grounds) that the contingency of selection implies a contingency of continuation. The two contingencies are both related to the classical theological idea of God's 'absolute potency' (*potentia absoluta*).

The Christian writers discussed above viewed those laws as permanent (Basil) and inviolable (Bacon), but they did not view them as compulsory. Since the power of the Creator extends through the entire domain of the laws of nature, the contingency that lies at the root of those laws extends throughout time.

This sense of contingency is familiar to readers of the Hebrew Bible from stories like the Long Day of Joshua (Josh. 10:12-14). The element of contingency was still recognized by early modern scientists like Francis Bacon. In the same 'Confession of Faith' that we saw affirming the inviolability of God's laws for the creation, Bacon allowed quite explicitly for exceptions like miracles. In accordance with the theological tradition we have surveyed, such miracles were seen by Bacon as 'new creations.'[120] In other words, the initiative that God exercised in creating the world could without contradiction be exercised again in the cause of redemption. Bacon never doubted that nature was regular enough for scientific endeavour to succeed in discerning the underlying laws, but this did not make the Author of those laws seem either distant or inactive.

An ecstatic, self-projecting Creator is immanent in creation as well as transcendent. A lawgiving God is also active and creative in the operation of the laws and symmetries of creation. These two ideas help to addresses the challenge raised by Paul Davies concerning the role of a Creator in the history of the creation. They also show how an examination of the foundations of scientific endeavour can help retrieve neglected aspects of the biblical theological tradition. However, they do not provide any ground in the Godhead itself for such self-projection and expression. For this we turn to another motif in the theological tradition.

*God as interpersonal Lord*

In the traditional sources we have cited on God as ecstatic Creator and Lawgiver, the self-projection, personality and executive power of God were simply asserted as images embedded in biblical narrative and prophecy. We have shown that these images of God can be consistent with the assumption of cosmic laws and symmetries that constitute the deepest foundation of scientific endeavour. But these images also assume a particular kind of God: one who is dialogical: a God who is inherently social. In order to explore this possibility, we must posit a narrative behind the narrative: the narrative concerning God's own being. If you begin by positing absolute Being or an unmoved Mover, you are likely to encounter problems understanding the involvement of such a God in the operations of creation: this is precisely the problem that Paul Davies pointed out.[121] Here again we may look to the biblical tradition for resources that will give a better understanding of God's social nature.[122]

---

120 'Likewise that whensoever God doth break the law of Nature by miracles (which are ever new creations), he never cometh to that point or pass, but in regard of the work of redemption…'; Francis Bacon, *A Confession of Faith*, in *Works of Francis Bacon*, 14:50-51.

121 Davies, *God and the New Physics*, 38-9, 133, discussed above ('The problem of transcendence in theological endeavour').

122 The following ideas were worked out in detail in Kaiser, 'The Integrity of Creation and the Social Nature of God', *Scottish Journal of Theology* 49 (1996), 261-90.

In the ancient Near East, the social nature of God was portrayed by the image of a divine council. The LORD God presided at a council of divine beings (also known as angels) somewhere in the heavens. Issues of divine government were deliberated, decisions were made, and decrees were announced just like those in royal courts on earth. One particularly striking example is found in Psalm 82:1-2.

> God has taken his place in the divine council;
>  In the midst of the gods he holds judgment:
> 'How long will you judge unjustly
>  and show partiality to the wicked?'

The 'gods' who attend the council are powers that preside over the nations. On earth they are represented by the kings of the nations. The LORD God evaluates their performance and holds them accountable. This image of the divine council provides a simple model for understanding God's relational personality. As sovereign Judge, God exists in a relationship to all creatures.[123]

The divine council also provides the framework for God's descent from heaven to inspect the tower of Babel (Gen. 11:5-7). This is the very text on which Philo based his teaching about God's self-projection through powers or potencies, discussed above.

> The LORD came down to see the city and the tower which mortals had built. And the LORD said, 'Look, they are one people, and they have all one language…. Come let us go down, and confuse their language there….' (Genesis 11:5-7)

In this narrative, the self-projection of the LORD in history is referred back to the self-disclosure in the divine council. God's social nature in heaven provides the ground for God's interaction with humans on the terrestrial plane.

Similar deliberations of the divine council lay behind the original work of creation.[124] The ongoing deliberations ensured divine oversight and providence in all subsequent history. The fact that all creatures, even nonhuman ones, were God's subjects and adherents of God's law implied that all were potential members of the divine council. They were commissioned, and they could be summoned.[125] In all of these ways, precedent for the relational character of God in creation and history was given in the divine council.

The idea of the divine council provides a basis for understanding the relational character of God, but it also leads to further questions. Are the angels eternal like God? Do they have their origin in God's own proper frame of reference? If not, was there still a basis within God's frame for such social, dialogical behavior? Pressing the

---

123 See Kaiser, 'The Integrity of Creation', 286-90. The presiding role of God in the heavenly world is discussed further in Chapters 3 and 4.

124 For example, Gen. Rab. 8:5 (God and the angels); Gen. Rab. 8:7 (God and the preincarnate souls of the righteous).

125 For example, Ps. 147:4; Baruch 3:33-4; Gen. Rab. 5:5; see also E. Theodore Mullen, Jr, *The Divine Council in Canaanite and Early Hebrew Literature* (Chico, Cal.: Scholars Press, 1980), 194-7.

matter back into the Godhead itself leads us back to the figure of Lady Wisdom in the Hebrew Bible and to the Son and Spirit of God in the New Testament.

Of all the members of the divine council, one, Lady Wisdom, was truly divine like God. In fact she represented the self-projection of God into the realm of finite form. We have already looked at the primary text in Proverbs 8 in our discussion of God as ecstatic Creator. The primordial 'creating' (or 'engaging' or 'setting up') of Lady Wisdom (Prov. 8:22-3) and her collaboration in the work of creation (Prov. 8:30) take place in the context of a divine council with just two members (cf. Ps. 2:6).

In the Wisdom of Jesus, Son of Sirach, another of deutero-canonical books, Lady Wisdom (Hokhmah) is described as praising her divine origin in the larger divine assembly as follows:

> In the assembly of the Most High she opens her mouth,
>  and in the presence of his hosts she tells of her glory;
> 'I came forth from the mouth of the Most High....' (Sirach 24:2-3)[126]

In the background here is the same idea of the divine council we found in Genesis 11:5-7. Here, however, the Most High participates in the council through a self-duplication or projection in the person of Lady Wisdom ('from the mouth of the Most High'). The interpersonal character of God (and of Wisdom) is rooted in the divine council and in a self-duplication within the Godhead.[127]

The ideas of the divine council and of the God-Wisdom relationship show that God was not entirely alone prior to the creation of the space-time world. There was a narrative behind the biblical narrative – one involving a complex society of celestial beings, including the angels and one special figure, Hokhmah/Wisdom, who originated directly from the Most High.

In the New Testament and early Christian thought, the role of Lady Wisdom was assigned to Jesus Christ, who prior to his becoming incarnate was begotten 'before all worlds' as an only Son. Several aspects of early Christology are modeled on the Wisdom theology of earlier Jewish texts. The idea of the divine council is always there in the background, but the fellowship of Father and Son, like that of the Most High and Wisdom, takes the form of an antecedent, inner ('privy') council. This inner council can be seen quite clearly in some of the sayings attributed to Jesus:

> All things have been handed over to me by my Father; and no one knows the Son except the Father, and no one knows the Father except the Son. (Matt. 11:27)

---

126 The Wisdom of Jesus ben Sira, also know as Ecclesiasticus (The 'Church's Book'), is found in all collections of the Old Testament Apocrypha. It was originally written in Hebrew in the early second century BCE. Cf. Ps. 110 for the terrestrial counterpart of the 'assembly of the Most High.'

127 The duplication of the Holy and Blessed One is described as 'Jewish binitarianism' by Daniel Boyarin, *Border Lines: The Partition of Judaeo-Christianity* (Philadelphia: University of Pennsylvania Press, 2004), 113-14, 120-27.

I glorified you by finishing the work that you gave me to do. So now, Father, glorify me in your own presence with the glory that I had in your presence before the world existed. (John 17:3-4)

As Son of God, Jesus, like Lady Wisdom, enjoys the privileges of a special relationship to God and special knowledge of God's plans that antedate the creation of the world.[128]

In the New Testament this inner council does not involve the angels, but it does include one other figure, the Holy Spirit, generally known as the source of prophetic gifts. The sending of the Spirit, like that of the Son, is modeled on the sending of Hokhmah/Wisdom in the deutero-canonical scriptures (Gal. 4:2-6; cf. Wis. 9:10, 17). So we read that the Spirit, like the Son, has special knowledge of God's plans (1 Cor. 2:11), knowledge that is not shared by the angels (1 Pet. 1:12).

In these New Testament texts, we have an early form of what was later defined as the doctrine of the Trinity: Father, Son, and Spirit constitute one God in 'three persons', with the second and third persons being derived ('proceeding') from the first. Whatever one makes of the conceptual difficulties raised by the classical doctrine of the Trinity, it does have at least one positive value. The triune (three-in-one) character of the Godhead provides a foundation within the frame of eternal God for the self-projection and relationality of God in creation and history.[129]

With respect to the foundations of scientific endeavour, the idea of a self-projection of God (and God's Wisdom or Word) in creation is not just an arbitrary postulate of dogma. A God who eternally begets as Father and who is eternally begotten as Son and from whom a Spirit eternally proceeds is an inherently ecstatic, self-expressive God. External actions like self-projection and lawgiving are quite natural for such a internally self-duplicating, tri-hypostatic God. This is a fourth way in which our examination of the foundations of scientific endeavour and the challenges they raise for theological endeavour can highlight often-neglected resources in the theological tradition.

## Six mandates for theological endeavour

We have reviewed four distinct aspects of the Judeo-Christian tradition that are well worth considering in relation to the theological challenges raised by an examination of the cosmic foundation of scientific endeavour. We have seen that theological discourse is embedded in the question of origins, particularly in the idea of cosmic laws.

---

128 On the consultations between God and Wisdom, see Prov. 8:30; Wis. 8:4; 9:4. In Genesis Rabbah 1:1, Wisdom is identified with the Torah as the plan of creation. The logion in Mark 13:32 limits the knowledge of the Son, but still distinguishes it from that of the angels. The model assumed here is that of a human Messiah rather than divine Wisdom.

129 In technical theological language, the eternally 'hypostatic' character of the eternal Logos provides a ground for its hypostatization as *Lógos prophorikós* in creation and rehypostatization as *Lógos ensárkos* in incarnation. These ideas are not unique to Christianity. On various attempts to develop a narrative of God's inner life in early and medieval Judaism, see Peter Schäfer, *Mirror of His Beauty: Feminine Images of God from the Bible to the Early Kabbalah* (Princeton: Princeton University Press, 2002), chaps 4-6.

Some readers may be satisfied with the level of theological discourse that addresses the origin of cosmic laws without appealing to any particular theological tradition. James Trefil and Paul Davies are good examples of this. In order to address the challenges to traditional theology that Davies and others have raised, however, it is necessary to explore some of the theological ideas that have been developed by Jewish and Christian writers. The four ideas we have explored are, therefore, optional from the standpoint of the foundations of science. Nonetheless they may be helpful to those who wish to explore the theological traditions.

Before moving on to the second (anthropological) foundation of scientific endeavour, it will be helpful to suggest some mandates for current theological endeavour that arise out of our explorations. As I see it, six mandates can be drawn up that will be of interest to those who seek to do biblical theology in the context of a thick description of science.

First and foremost, theological endeavour needs to recover the importance of belief in God as Creator of all things, which is foundational for both Judaism and Christianity. The first article of the Christian baptismal creed begins with the words, 'I believe in God the Father Almighty, Creator of heaven and earth.'[130] Most popular Christianity, however, is based on the need for salvation and the quest for holiness in personal and family life – values that are more related to the second and third articles of the creed. A recovery of the meaning and importance of the first article will not only provide greater balance in faith and worship; it will be good news for those who struggle with issues of faith and ethics raised by modern science and technology. The God who creates all the parts of our world (heaven and earth, universe and multiverse) is one who can help us make sense of scientific and technological endeavour.[131]

Second, theological endeavour needs to recover a sense of the immensity and majesty of God. It is clear that a God who is responsible for creating a universe that is now billions of years old and billions of light years in size is far greater than our everyday concept of the deity. The same is true and more for a God who has created an infinite ensemble of such universes! Even speculative theologians like Rabbi Abbahu and Origen of Alexandria would have been staggered by the implications for our view of the Creator. The same may be true for the present-day believer who struggles to find any connection between a transcendent God and our earthly world. But it will be good news for believers who find the image of a 'man with a beard' unconvincing and unhelpful for purposes of worship. The God who creates an infinite multiverse is one who is far more majestic than anything we have yet imagined.

---

130 So the Apostles' Creed (based on the Old Roman Symbol) and the Nicene Creed; Leith, *Creeds of the Churches*, 24, 33.

131 Further reading for those interested in these issues might include Langdon Gilkey, *Maker of Heaven and Earth: A Study of the Christian Doctrine of Creation* (Garden City, N.Y.: Doubleday, 1959); Jürgen Moltmann, *God in Creation: A New Theology of Creation and the Spirit of God* (London: SCM Press, 1985); Robert Murray, *The Cosmic Covenant: Biblical Themes of Justice, Peace, and the Integrity of Creation* (London: Sheed & Ward, 1992); Colin Gunton, *The Triune Creator: A Historical and Systematic Study* (Grand Rapids: Eerdmans, 1998).

Third, theological endeavour needs to recover a sense of the ecstatic immanence of this majestic Creator. Most Jews and Christians believe that God transcends all of creation. Many are also familiar with the paradox of transcendence and immanence. In our review of the biblical and patristic literature, however, we have found that the idea of creation actually presupposes an ecstatic self-projection or diffraction of the Godhead into the realm of finite form. Theological endeavour must question any notion of transcendence that makes immanence seem paradoxical or contrived. This will be good news for those who struggle with the sense of distance and impersonality that modern awareness of the immensity of the cosmos can create. The God who creates all things also embraces the creation with divine potency and permeates it as divine Word or Wisdom.

Fourth, theologians may need to rethink the ideas of the omnipresence and omnipotence of God. God can certainly do all things, but not all at once. This mandate is a corollary of the idea of ecstatic self-expression. By ecstatically entering the realm of finite form, God takes on the limits of particularity just as a person who plays a role takes on and limits of the script or the rules of the game. Athanasius argued that there is a 'presence' or 'advent' (*parousía*) in creation as well as in the Incarnation of the divine Word. We might add that there is a 'self-emptying' (*kenōsis*) in creation and providence as there is in the Incarnation of the divine Word (Phil. 2:7a). This realization should come as good news to those who struggle with the questions of 'why' and 'why not' in divine providence. God can certainly be everywhere and do all things. But a God who truly enters the realm of finite form cannot be everywhere and do all things at once.

Fifth, theological endeavour needs to recover a sense of the law-governed processes of nature as the activity of God. Biblical and patristic writers saw God's word at work in the lawful processes of nature as well as in miraculous exceptions to the laws. Believers should see God in the fabric of creation's laws and symmetries as much as in any gaps that may be left. This will be good news for those who seek to live in the presence of God, but have to work in a world of science and technology. The God who grants laws by which creation can evolve and produce life is directly present and active both in the processes of nature and in their results.

One final mandate: theological endeavour needs to recover a sense of the intrinsic relationality of God as the ground for God's self-projection in creation. Real immanence and real relationship will always seem contrived if God is viewed as a simple Monad that transcends all relationships whatever. There are various alternatives here. The Christian doctrine of the Trinity views self-projection and relationship as an intrinsic feature of the Godhead even in its transcendent eternity. The ancient Near Eastern idea of a divine council and the Jewish idea of Lady Wisdom as the representative of the Most High in the council are some other ways of dealing with the same problem. In any case, the God who goes outside the divine frame into the realm of finite form is one who is intrinsically relational and interpersonal. This will be good news for those who seek a personal relationship to God in full awareness of God's immensity and majesty as Creator of all things.

We have found that belief in a Creator who is majestic, ecstatic, and interpersonal allows us to embrace the idea of God as cosmic Lawgiver in a way that can address the challenge of deism. Our investigation does not prove that God is personal or even that God exists. But it has demonstrated the viability of disciplined theological endeavour in the context of a thick description of science with a special focus on its cosmic foundation.

In the next chapter we shall examine a second (anthropological) foundation of scientific endeavour. Even though the starting point will be entirely different from the one in this chapter, the idea of a God who is both ecstatic and personal arises again as a result of a thick description of scientific endeavour.

# CHAPTER TWO

# Anthropological Foundation: The Paradox of Science-Fostering Intelligence

**Abstract** (with brief definitions of technical terms for reference)
The possibility of scientific endeavour places conditions on the evolution of intelligence, summed up in the phrase, Science-Fostering Intelligence. SFI enables people to make sense out of fragmentary perspectives on phenomena that are not directly observed and to intuit laws and principles that often differ from those exhibited in the everyday environment. Inquiry into the origin of SFI, based on the ideas of evolutionary anthropology, suggests that the cognitive demands of soul journey by paleoshamans played an important role in the survival and genetic formation of early *Homo sapiens*. This spirit-niche hypothesis could be corroborated with cross-cultural aptitude tests. One reasonable way to account for SFI, consistent with evolutionary biology, is to suppose that our space-time world coexists with a spirit world so that both together constitute a single psychophysical metaverse presided over by a unique Spirit. Further theological implications can be developed for a 'thick cosmology' and vestiges of the divine image in humanity.

**Keywords**: adaptive traits, creativity, divine council, evolution, image of God, multiple intelligences, Renaissance cosmology, Paleolithic era (African Stone Age), paleoshamanism, unity of scientific knowledge.

In the present chapter we discuss the *anthropological foundation* of scientific endeavour and its implications for theological endeavour. Our procedure will be the same as in Chapter 1: we begin with a description of the foundation in question and the outstanding mystery that scientists find embedded within it, and then proceed to use the appropriate scientific tools to resolve the mystery and explore the possible implications for theological endeavour, in this case, for theological cosmology and anthropology.

We have defined natural science as the endeavour to explore all accessible features of the space-time world in such a way that everything can be understood eventually by positing underlying laws of nature and constructing histories using the tools of mathematics and logical inference (from the Introduction). In Chapter 1 we examined the existence of a lawful universe as a precondition – the cosmic foundation – for scientific endeavour. The focus of this chapter is another of the features embedded in our definition: the fact that the species of *Homo sapiens* actually has the aptitude for pursuing natural science. Humans can be trained to construct principles, laws and histories that actually make sense of increasingly remote features of the world in ways that are testable. To state the point compactly, humans possess a Science-Fostering Intelligence (SFI) that can be developed through rigorous science education. SFI is a built-in, genetically based feature of human intelligence that enables the nurture of scientific intelligence in trained individuals and makes science possible.[1] It is the Anthropological (or, if you prefer, psychological) foundation of scientific endeavour.

Science-Fostering Intelligence is the aptitude for going beyond the limits of known scientific categories and methods to develop new categories and methods in order to discern and interpret novel, unforeseen patterns in natural phenomena. SFI is not a given 'scientific' method, or even a fixed skill, but the ability to generate new formalisms and methods in an effort to address unprecedented intellectual challenges.

To say that SFI is built in and genetic means that scientific endeavour, like all human behaviour, is both enabled and constrained by the coding of the human genome. Such a genetic base is permissive, not determinative: nutrition and education are also necessary. Cultural preconditions like these will be discussed in Chapter 3, but here we will focus on the genetic substratum of SFI.

There are several mysteries concerning SFI. One of them concerns its origin. As a trait with a genetic basis, it should be possible to account for it in evolutionary terms. Such an account will be necessary if natural science is ever to give an adequate explanation of its own origin. The most promising way to meet this challenge will be to posit a formative role for the spiritual dimension of Paleolithic era (African Stone Age) human life. Generalizing the human environment to include the spiritual will naturally engage us in further theological endeavour and further confirm our thesis that science and theology are loosely interwoven when viewed as human endeavours with real preconditions.

## The contingency of multiple intelligences: four clarifications

The quest for an evolutionary origin of built-in SFI is an ambitious task that is susceptible to a number of possible misunderstandings. In this section, four general points will be made for clarification.

---

1    The choice of new phrases is always difficult. I prefer the term 'science-fostering' because innate SFI enables the development of scientific endeavour even though innate SFI might originally have been adapted for other purposes. I prefer the term 'intelligence' because its meaning is widely recognized, even though it lacks precision. As David Lewis-Williams points out, the term places the emphasis on the human capacity for reasoning. He proposes using the use of the term 'consciousness' (in its medieval sense); Lewis-Williams, *The Mind in the Cave* (London: Thames & Hudson, 2002), 111-12. While agreeing with the tenor of Lewis-Williams' critique, I think the work of Howard Gardner has broadened the use of the term 'intelligence' to include artistic and social skills. But other terms like 'science-sustaining creativity' could also be useful. In an earlier study, I referred to this human capability as 'Copernican intelligence'; see Kaiser, 'How Can a Theological Understanding of Humanity Enrich Artificial Intelligence Work', *Asbury Theological Journal* 44 (Fall 1989), 65-7.

*Contingency of SFI for individuals*

I have defined SFI as an built-in, genetically driven aptitude for advancing scientific endeavour – the ability to construct, test and apply principles, laws and histories that capture basic features of phenomena in new realms of the space-time world. The first point to make is that such an aptitude is contingent at the individual level: it varies greatly from one person to the next. SFI should not be equated with the 'general intelligence' that many psychologists have claimed is common to most mature individuals.[2] Nor is it simply the intelligence profile of working scientists. Scientists rely on a vast array of cognitive skills, ranging from the power of sustained mental concentration (executive function) to a deep sense of aesthetic beauty, each of which contributes to many forms of human behaviour.[3] SFI is not just a high level of intelligence, but a distinct kind.

The fact that the degree of built-in SFI varies so much from one individual to another indicates that it depends on the collective effect of many different genes, any one of which may or may not be present in a particular genome.[4] Only in cases where most or all of these genes are present and activated (given adequate nurture) can built-in SFI be expressed in any particular individual as skill in scientific work.

Science-Fostering Intelligence occurs in some individuals more than in others. To some extent such differences in aptitude for science are the result of varying socialization, education and nurture. People cannot do rigorous scientific research unless built-in SFI has been cultivated and developed to a professional level. The relatively low participation of women and of some minority groups in such research indicates that only a small proportion of those with the aptitude for science have had the opportunity or motivation to develop it. This nurture barrier is particularly evident in cultures or subcultures where scientific research is viewed as an irrelevant

---

2    Several cognitive psychologists have developed experiments showing that so-called 'general intelligence' (G) actually depends on a number of relatively independent cognitive processes or operations. See, for example, the report on the 1999 symposium, 'The Nature of Intelligence' in N. J. Mackintosh, 'Evolutionary psychology meets G', *Nature* 403 (27 Jan. 2000), 378-9. Michael S. Gazzaniga argues for a 'selectionist' model of domain-specific predispositions and concludes that the human brain is a contingent collection of neural circuits devoted to specific capacities; Gazzaniga, *The Mind's Past* (Berkeley: University of California Press, 1998), 12-19, 173-4. Paul Davies appropriately distinguishes between general intelligence and 'intelligibility', the latter being that special form of intelligence that allows humans to understand the principles of the universe; Davies, 'The Intelligibility of Nature', in Robert John Russell, Nancey Murphy, and C. J. Isham (ed.), *Quantum Cosmology and the Laws of Nature: Scientific Perspectives on Divine Action* (Vatican City State: Vatican Observatory, 1993), 158.

3    Silvano Arieti has noted that scientific discovery often involves postulating a new class of objects some of which were previously thought to be quite dissimilar; Arieti, *Creativity: The Magic Synthesis* (New York: Basic Books, 1976), 270-74. This 'induction by creativity', as Areiti calls it, would be basic to the development of unified theories. Our concern, however, is the reformulation of scientific concepts and laws so that they will include such apparently dissimilar objects.

4    The technical term for the collective effect of many different genes is 'polygenic inheritance'; Ernst Mayr, *What Evolution Is* (New York: Basic Books, 2001), 107.

luxury. As a result, any tests designed to measure built-in SFI cross-culturally would have to be designed with cultural inclusivity in mind.

SFI is the ability to be trained in scientific disciplines.[5] In spite of the importance of individual nurture, some children benefit from science education and positive role-models far more than others. Readers of this book have had enough exposure to science education to realize their own aptitude for science in relation to their aptitudes for other disciplines like business or music.

Anyone who has worked with children or taught in elementary schools will know from experience that any human skill will progress more easily in some and only develop with difficulty in others. Each of these forms of intelligence has a genetic base of its own and is hard-wired (or pre-wired) into the brain in specific ways.[6] Hard-wiring is shown by the fact that patients suffering from injuries to one part of the brain may lose a single form of intelligence. In cases where the left parietal lobe has been damaged due to a stroke, a person's ability to use numbers can be seriously reduced without affecting language facility or other reasoning skills.[7]

Special limitations of intelligence can also be congenital. An example is the disability known as *dyscalculia*: a genetic defect in people who are unable to do elementary mental arithmetic even though they are capable of becoming PhDs in nonmathematical subjects.[8] Prenatal cerebral damage could possibly explain some of these cases, but others are clearly genetic in origin.[9]

The same is true of a disability known as congenital *amusia*. 'Amusics' are people who are unable to encode pitch and thereby differentiate simple tunes despite having normal memory and language skills. This limitation cannot be overcome by any amount of training.[10] So the intelligences that most people develop and rely on

---

5    Thirteenth-century philosopher Maimonides recognized that people differ widely in their innate ability to be trained in philosophical reasoning; Maimonides, *Guide for the Perplexed*, I.31.

6    Gary F. Marcus has argued that the brain is 'pre-wired', rather than 'hard-wired' because it still has a great deal of developmental flexibility within the limits of its 'built-in structure'; Marcus, *The Birth of the Mind: How a Tiny Number of Genes Creates the Complexities of Human Thought* (New York: Basic Books, 2004), 12, 40.

7    Cases described by Brian Butterworth, *What Counts? How Every Brain Is Hardwired for Math* (New York: Free Press, 1999), 149-54, also published in the UK as *The Mathematical Brain* (London: Macmillan, 1999). See the interview with Butterworth in *New Scientist* 3 July 1999, 46-7. All of this research applies to individuals living in cultures in which numeracy is cultivated. Numeracy can also be cultural as in the case of the Piraha of the Amazon rainforest, who do not have words for numbers larger than two; Constance Holden, 'Life Without Numbers in the Amazon', *Science* 305 (20 August 2004), 109. We take up cultural considerations in Chapter 3.

8    Cases described by Butterworth, *What Counts?* 240-45, 271-9.

9    Butterworth, *What Counts?* 8-9, 276, 280-81.

10   Amusics can easily detect normal pitch variations in the intonation of speech, which are much larger than those required for musical scales, thereby indicating the relative independence of different types of intelligence; see Krista L. Hyde and Isabelle Peretz, 'Brains that are Out of Tune but in Time', *Psychological Science* 15 (May 2004), 256-60.

in their vocations are multifaceted and hard-wired in the brain.[11] If this is true for mathematical and musical intelligence, we are safe in concluding that it is also true for a specialized form of intelligence like SFI.

The idea of multiple forms of intelligence has received widespread public attention since 1983, when Howard Gardner published a major study of the subject, entitled, *Frames of Mind: The Theory of Multiple Intelligences*. Gardner argued that there are at least seven types of intelligence in humans: linguistic (verbal), spatial (artistic), musical, logical-mathematical, kinesthetic, interpersonal (social), and intrapersonal. Gardner constructed these rather broad categories to ensure that all of the types would present in every individual to some degree based on the development of hereditary traits.[12] Gardner's work is a preliminary investigation of a complex subject.

In later research, Gardner added an eighth form, 'naturalist intelligence'.[13] He also recognized that there are many types of intelligence that humans have not yet developed – for example, those intelligences with which other species are specially gifted.[14] In short, intelligence is more a qualitative than a quantifiable trait. It is not so much a question of more or less intelligence, as it is a question of this or that kind of intelligence. Innate SFI, in the sense that we have defined it, is even more specialized than Gardner's categories, even naturalist intelligence, but Gardner's work supports our contention that all such forms are contingent at the individual level.

### Contingency of SFI for the species

Innate SFI is one of several traits of humanity that differentiates us from other species. Every metazoan species has its own special intelligence. Species of bird and squirrels, for example, are able to retrieve food that they have hidden in multiple locations. Humans are relatively stupid in this sense: we need to write it all down or draw a map. We appear to be unique, however, in the use of symbols (as distinct from simple signs).[15] Among the many symbol based activities for which we have an

---

11   On the complexity of the brain's response to music and the different brain regions involved, see Norman M. Weinberger, 'Music and the Brain', *Scientific American* 291 (Nov. 2004), 89-95.

12   Howard Gardner, *Frames of Mind: The Theory of Multiple Intelligences* (New York: Basic Books, 1983), 167-9.

13   'Naturalist intelligence' is the ability to recognize and classify species; Howard Gardner, *Intelligence Reframed: Multiple Intelligences for the 21ˢᵗ Century* (New York: Basic Books, 1999), 48-52. Gardner considered the possibility of adding a spiritual or existential intelligence but gave it up due partly to the difficulty of definition. Actually, humans are not as good at identifying plant species as chimpanzees; Tetsuro Matsuzawa, 'What Only a Chimp Knows', *New Scientist* 190 (10 June 2006), 48.

14   Gardner, *Frames of Mind*, 36.

15   This characterization of human uniqueness can be supported by observations of present-day hominoids. For example, chimpanzees can be taught to use a few hundred words (using signs), but not to use metaphors or to construct counter-factual sentences. For a hominoid, a sign can represent a particular thing, but that thing cannot then represent a more elusive thing or be combined in the imagination with other things to form a new creation; David Premack, 'Is Language the Key to Human Intelligence?' *Science* 303 (16 Jan. 2004), 318-20. The use

innate capacity, scientific endeavour is certainly unique to humans. The mystery is not that other species lack such a trait, but why humanity should exhibit it.

So innate SFI is not just a property of particular science-endowed individuals. Like other types of intelligence, it is a property of the entire human gene pool that manifests itself – due to both heredity and development – to varying degrees in various individuals. The question is why the genes that together code for built-in SFI occur with significant frequency in the human gene pool. This happy coincidence appears all the more remarkable when we realize, based on archaeological findings, that all modern humans are the descendants of a group of hominins, numbering no more that a few thousand individuals, who lived in Middle Stone Age Africa.[16] The original incidence of built-in SFI must have been very small indeed.[17] Therefore, built-in SFI is contingent to the human species as well as at the individual level. The mystery is why it was present in our ancestral population at all.

As physicist Paul Davies has argued, it is only with great difficulty that the code underlying the phenomena of nature can be discerned from the phenomena themselves.[18] Davies goes on to raise the question that will concern us here: why should we be so fortunate as to be able to discern these codes (principles and laws) at all? We shall explore this question in the body of this chapter as we discuss the mystery embedded in built-in SFI in detail. The scientific framework for this discussion will be the theory of evolution.

*Mystery in what science has already accomplished*

The fact that SFI is a human trait does not mean that humans are capable of understanding all the accessible features of our space-time world. In Chapter 1 we argued that science would not be possible if our universe (or multiverse) were not

---

of symbols is also likely to be unique to humans (*Homo sapiens*) in comparison to hominin ancestors that are now extinct.

16   Hominins include chimpanzees, bonobos, humans and extinct ancestors of human like the australopithecines. One must allow for interbreeding of African *Homo sapiens* with regional populations of *Homo erectus* in Asia and Neanderthals in Europe. However, both archeological evidence and the universality of SFI point to the group that migrated out of Africa between 85 000 and 65 000 years ago as the carrier of SFI.

17   The so-called 'founder effect' is sometimes attributed to a very small founder population or even to an individual female; for example, Mayr, *What Evolution Is*, 135-6, 179. However, computer models developed by population geneticists indicate that populations of at least a thousand individuals are needed for long-term genetic viability; cf. Jan Klein, Naoyuki Takahata and Francisco J. Ayala, 'MHC Polymorphism and Human Origins', *Scientific American* 269 (Dec. 1993), 82-3; Henry C. Harpending et al., 'Genetic Traces of Ancient Demography', *Proceedings of the National Academy of Sciences of the United States* 95 (17 Feb. 1998), 1961-7. In any case, the total number of individuals with SFI in the founding *Homo sapiens* population was much smaller than it is today.

18   Paul Davies, 'The Unreasonable Effectiveness of Science', in John Marks Templeton (ed.), *Evidence of Purpose: Scientists Discover the Creator* (New York: Continuum, 1994), 55. Davies is currently a professor at the Australian Centre for Astrobiology at Macquarie University in Sydney.

largely governed by definable laws and principles. However, the mere operation of such laws throughout the universe does not mean that they can all be discovered or understood by any of its inhabitants. So our focus on built-in SFI should not be taken to imply that scientists will someday understand everything about our universe. There is sufficient mystery to require explanation in the fact that scientists have accomplished anything at all beyond the observation of plants and animals and the production of simple tools.

To be sure, some simple laws are so much a part of everyday experience on earth that any species with simple skills of observation and reflection should be able to grasp them. Basic patterns like the connection between lightning and thunder can be noticed without much trouble. Aristotle's physics operated at a slightly greater degree of abstraction. His system of nature was based on simple observations like the fact that heavy things fall to earth, while light things like fire rise up and the stars move around the earth in regular circles. Such empirically based notions might be grasped without anything like built-in SFI as we have defined it.

The ability to probe more deeply into such phenomena is another matter. It requires the explanation or interpretation of the patterns of nature: figuring out how lightning produces thunder or finding out why the stars seem to travel in circles. Moreover, the phenomena treated in modern science are far more remote from everyday experience than lightning or falling frocks. Kepler's laws of planetary motion postulated elliptical orbits, which are quite unlike anything normally experienced on earth.[19] The apparent contraction of objects that move at high speeds (Einstein's special theory of relativity) and the passing of quantum objects through seemingly impenetrable barriers ('quantum tunneling') are just two more recent examples.

It is this contingent Science-Fostering Intelligence (built-in SFI) that we need to inquire about – intelligence that goes beyond known phenomena and systems of concepts and probes beneath the appearances to discern the underlying laws. The mystery is already there before our eyes.

## *A positive relation to theological endeavour*

Contrary to much popular thinking, the relationship between evolutionary science and theological endeavour is a positive one. By focusing on human scientific ability as a source of theological insight, I hope to reverse another common perception of the science-theology relationship.

It is often assumed that the larger scope there is for scientific research, the less room there is for spiritual realities. Many people believe that the validity of faith will be diminished if scientists succeed in explaining phenomena, particularly phenomena involving human origins. Many assume that the scope of scientific endeavour would have to be limited by any attempt to preserve space for theological endeavour. In the approach advocated here, however, it is the very proficiency of scientific endeavour that will suggest new possibilities for theological discourse – just the reverse of the common assumption.

---

19 Kepler's laws were based on the geometry of conic sections which dated back to Menaechmus and Euclid.

In the following sections, we shall argue that the existence of built-in SFI is the result of an evolutionary prehistory that involved human exploration of the spirit world as a new environment. In other words, we will argue that there is a spiritual basis for built-in SFI and offer a more robust argument for the role of a sovereign Creator, though still nothing like a proof. The result will be a demonstration of plausibility rather than one of existence. The point is to show that theology affirming results come from asking why scientific endeavour is successful rather than limiting it or challenging its validity at some point. A naturalist (evolutionary) methodology can lead to a thick ontology:[20] one that includes the spiritual as well as the natural.

## The origin of Science-Fostering Intelligence (SFI)

From an abstract standpoint outside the stream of practice, it might seem that built-in SFI is nothing more than a fortunate coincidence – that is the way things are, and we would not be here discussing the matter if they weren't. Logically speaking, an appeal to brute fact is always a possibility (compare the Anthropic Principle in cosmology). Every species has special attributes that differentiate it from others: gibbons happen to be that species limber enough to swing in the trees of Southeast Asia; *Homo sapiens* just happens to be that species creative enough to be able to analyse the processes of cosmic creativity. The consonance between the processes of the human mind and those of the cosmos might just be a fortunate coincidence.

Most thinking people would not be satisfied with this kind of appeal to good fortune. But there is an additional problem for those who spend their lives working in scientific disciplines. Practicing scientists with suitable training and years of hard work, who are courageous enough to tackle seemingly intractable research problems, often experience the discovery of amazing solutions. Since most researchers regard themselves as fairly ordinary people, they often experience a deep existential wonder at the success of their own creativity.

The fact that SFI is a highly contingent human attribute can not be appreciated on a purely cognitive level. It involves an existential sense of wonder about the success of scientific endeavour, and this sense of wonder is also a contingent attribute because it reflects a modest degree of personal confidence in one's own intellectual powers. Folks who have no self-confidence are not likely to think about such issues. On the other hand, those who are fortunate enough to have unquestioned confidence in the underlying rationality of the world and in their own ability to understand it are not likely to see that there is any problem. It is very difficult to engage either group in this sort of discussion.

In Chapter 1, we cited several physicists who were keenly aware of the wonder of the existence and the beauty of cosmic laws. Here we should look at natural scientists from various disciplines who have reflected on the wonder of Science-

---

20  I deliberately avoid using the word 'supernatural' in this context. The ontology suggested by our investigation could be described as super-natural because it includes the spiritual as an environmental niche within the broader framework of human life as understood by anthropologists. But it does not substitute the intervention of spirits in place of natural evolution.

Fostering Intelligence. This will illustrate the existential dimension of the questions we are considering as part of our thick description of scientific endeavour.

One of the best known writers to call attention to the mystery of built-in SFI was Eugene Wigner. Wigner was one of the pioneers of quantum mechanics in the twentieth century. In 1963 he was awarded the Nobel Prize in physics for his work on symmetry principles in quantum theory.

Just a few years earlier Wigner published a paper in a professional mathematical journal that has become the touchstone for subsequent discussions of the issue. The article had the rather playful title, 'The Unreasonable Effectiveness of Mathematics in the Natural Sciences'.[21] Here Wigner stepped back from his work to reflect on the amazing success of mathematical physics in recondite areas like quantum theory. Some of his contributions to physics were based on his own ability to discern mathematical symmetries in the equations of quantum physics and to draw important conclusions that could be tested experimentally from the form of those symmetries.

In this 1960 paper, Wigner described what he called the two 'miracles' or wonders that scientists experience.[22] Focusing on his own specialty of mathematical physics, Wigner asked why mathematical formulas that describe particular phenomena often turn out to have far wider applicability.[23] This was one of the 'two miracles' that Wigner thought about: the fact that patterns that are exhibited in special cases are often also of more general applicability; or, in the terms we used in Chapter 1, the fact that there exist universal laws of nature.[24]

---

21  Wigner, 'The Unreasonable Effectiveness of Mathematics in the Natural Sciences', *Communications on Pure and Applied Mathematics* 13 (Feb. 1960), 1-14. I shall use the more readily accessible reprint in Wigner, *Symmetries and Reflections* (Bloomington: Indiana University Press, 1967), 222-37.

22  Wigner, *Symmetries and Reflections*, 227, 229. Wigner used the term 'miracle' to indicate something that is surprising and unexplained, not a violation of the laws of nature. The usage came from Erwin Schrödinger's, *What Is Life?* (Cambridge: Cambridge University Press, 1944), 31, which used the English word, 'marvel'. Both words refer back to the German 'Wunder', which can be translated as either 'miracle' or 'wonder' or 'marvel', i.e., something that defies any simple explanation.

23  The examples Wigner cites of this effectiveness are Newton's law of universal gravitation, Max Born's matrix mechanics, and the theory of the quantum Lamb shift; Wigner, *Symmetries and Reflections*, 230-33. The issue of the extended applicability of mathematical formulas is rather different from Gottlob Frege's classic problem of the applicability of arithmetic to concepts, some of which will apply to the empirical world; Frege, *The Foundations of Arithmetic: A Logico-Mathematical Enquiry Into the Concept of Number* (Oxford: Blackwell, 1950, 1959), par. 87. Mark Steiner refines and defends Wigner's argument in his *The Applicability of Mathematics as a Philosophical Problem* (Cambridge, Mass.: Harvard University Press, 1998), 44-53, 72-3.s

24  Paul Davies has pointed out that the effectiveness of mathematics also depends on the approximate linearity and locality of the equations needed to describe most phenomena, conditions which in turn may depend on the initial conditions of our particular universe; Davies, 'Why Is the Universe Knowable?' in Ronald E. Mickens (ed.), *Mathematics and Science* (Singapore: World Scientific, 1990), 16-22, 26-8; idem, *The Mind of God*, 156-60. If, as seems likely, the conditions of approximate linearity and locality are prerequisite to the emergence of conscious organisms, or even all living organisms, Davies' observation is

Wigner's second 'miracle' is the one that concerns us here: the fact that the human mind has the capacity to intuit such patterns and construct appropriate mathematical formalisms on the basis of a few particular examples.[25] Wigner makes a strong case for the contingency and fallibility of such scientific endeavour that we discussed above and then concludes with these amazingly poetic thoughts:

> The miracle of the appropriateness of the language of mathematics for the formulation of the laws of physics is a wonderful gift which we neither understand nor deserve. We should be grateful for it and hope that it will remain valid in future research and that it will extend, for better or worse, to our pleasure, even though perhaps also to our bafflement, to wide branches of learning.[26]

As Wigner indicated, mathematical physics has been far more successful in probing the recesses of nature than an outside observer would ever have dreamed. We can not know for sure how far the continuing development of mathematics will take us in our quests for understanding, but we continue to rely on it in scientific endeavour as a matter of faith, hope and gratitude.[27]

Wigner's comments are limited to his specialization in mathematical science, but his observations about the effectiveness of scientific endeavour in this special case – like the patterns he described as being intuited in special cases within physics – turns out to have wider applicability in a range of sciences. In order to illustrate this wider applicability, I turn to a writer in the life sciences.

---

a special case of the Anthropic Principle, which can be resolved by an appeal to multiple universes (Chapter 1 above).

25   R. W. Hamming paraphrases Wigner's point this way: 'How can it be that simple mathematics, being after all a product of the human mind, can be so remarkably useful in so many widely different situations?' Hamming, 'The Unreasonable Effectiveness of Mathematics', *American Mathematical Monthly* 87 (Feb. 1980), 82. In yet another commentary on Wigner's paper, Paul Davies speaks of the fact that modern *Homo sapiens* is so 'unreasonably effective' at discovering appropriate algorithms; Davies, 'Why Is the Universe Knowable?', 28. In addition to SFI, there may be a 'pure mathematics-fostering intelligence' that functions in the realm of pure imagination. Marc D. Hauser has given an evolutionary account of the origin of human ability to represent and conceptualize numbers in relation to systems of exchange and trade; Hauser, 'What do Animals Think About Numbers?', *American Scientist* 88 (March-April 2000), 149-51. Keith Devlin gives an account of the origin of symbolic mathematical ability in relation to the mental representation of interpersonal relationships and gossip; Devlin, *The Math Gene: How Mathematical Thinking Evolved and Why Numbers are Like Gossip* (New York: Basic Books, 2001). Helpful as these accounts are, neither of them addresses the human ability to develop entirely new branches of abstract mathematics.

26   Wigner, *Symmetries and Reflections*, 237. Note that Wigner shifts from the idea of discovering laws of nature (*Symmetries and Reflections*, 227, 229) to 'formulating laws of physics'. Technically speaking, these are two distinct ideas; cf. Nicholas Saunders, *Divine Action and Modern Science* (Cambridge: Cambridge University Press, 2002), 60.

27   Willem B. Drees has tried to explain the 'effectiveness of mathematics' by arguing that it is a language of communication like any other that is applicable only to phenomena for which it happens to work; Drees, *Beyond the Big Bang* (LaSalle, Illinois: Open Court, 1990), 107-110. If so, the wonder is that mathematics works any better than other social constructs like astrology and faith-healing.

In 1999 Edward O. Wilson published his own manifesto for scientific endeavour, *Consilience: The Unity of Knowledge*. Wilson is renowned both as an entomologist and as a proponent of sociobiology, the endeavour to understand social behaviour and moral codes as the result of natural selection. The discipline of sociobiology is still a highly controversial subject, but as a human endeavour it perfectly illustrates the goal shared by all scientists, that of finding rational explanations for features of the space-time world.

Wilson's common ground with physicists like Wigner is shown in his definition of scientific endeavour:

> Science offers the boldest metaphysics of the age. It is a thoroughly human construct, driven by the faith that, if we dream, press to discover, explain, and dream again, thereby plunging repeatedly into new terrain, the world will somehow come clearer and we will grasp the true strangeness of the universe. And the strangeness will all prove to be connected and make sense.[28]

Wilson certainly does not view himself as a proponent of metaphysics in the narrow sense. However, his convictions about the unity of knowledge are profoundly metaphysical and potentially theological. As he points out so passionately, scientific endeavour rests on the belief that humans have the ability to 'plunge repeatedly into new terrain' of the space-time world in such a way that they can discern the basic features of that terrain and find a way to explain them. Even though the new terrain may seem inexplicable in relation to what has been experienced and understood previously, it is not beyond our grasp in the long run. Wilson's use of the language of dreaming is different from Wigner's image of 'miracle', but it similarly expresses his enthusiasm for scientific endeavour. Scientists are dreamers who find that their dreams often miraculously provide the clues needed to map out the extremities of the space-time world.

Other illustrations from scientific literature will be discussed in Chapter 3,[29] but those of Wigner and Wilson suffice to give us a sense of the wonder and dreaming experienced by those who engage in scientific endeavour. The ability of the human psyche to do research applies to a wide range of sciences and presents us with a mystery that calls for further investigation.

*Where does Science-Fostering Intelligence come from? The selection value dilemma*

In Chapter 1 we inquired into the origin of a lawful cosmos as the cosmic foundation of scientific endeavour. In order to do so we used the ideas of current cosmology, particularly current ideas about the origin of our universe (and multiverse). Our working assumption was that the current resources of sciences like cosmology can be

---

28 Edward O. Wilson, *Consilience: The Unity of Knowledge* (New York: Random House, 1998), 12. Wilson cites Wigner's article on pp. 48-9.

29 In Chapters 1 and 2, I cite the writings of these philosopher-scientists to illustrate the ideas of lawfulness and SFI. In chapter 3, I will cite these and similar writings again, but as evidence of a cultural tradition that has transmitted such ideas.

applied to the foundations of scientific endeavour. In other words, scientific endeavour can be self-referential in the sense of accounting for its own foundations.

Our present task is to inquire into the origin of built-in Science-Fostering Intelligence (SFI) as the anthropological foundation of scientific endeavour. In order to do so we must use the theory of evolution, particularly as it applies to the origin of *Homo sapiens*. Our working assumption is again that the resources of science can be applied to the foundations of scientific endeavour (a completeness or self-consistency argument). It should be understood that the resources of science are never finalized; they are continually being refined as new instrumentation is developed and new phenomena come within view. As the resources are refined, the quest for the origin of SFI must be adapted accordingly. The possibility of making scientific endeavour self-referential is itself a human endeavour, not a fixed dogma.

In comparison to the problem of the origin of the cosmos and its lawfulness, the problem of the origin of built-in SFI has not received as much attention from scientists. Many scientists simply pass the issue off as belonging to disciplines other than their own, like sociobiology or evolutionary psychology. Among scientists who take the problem seriously, there is considerable disagreement. One can define two different approaches here. Some anthropologists have tried to explain the emergence of a primitive scientific intelligence as the byproduct of adaptations to changing environmental and social conditions. The problem with most of these explanations is that they do not address the specialized type of intelligence that fosters scientific endeavour (built-in SFI). There are physicists and philosophers, on the other hand, who point out the special demands of scientific endeavour, but they frequently conclude that evolutionary biology can not possibly account for built-in SFI. Here are some examples.

An example of the first approach is archaeologist Steven Mithen. Mithen has developed a wide-ranging theory of the origin of human intelligence based on four general areas or 'modules' of intelligence. The four areas of intelligence Mithen proposes are technical, natural history, social and linguistic.[30] These particular modules are certainly prerequisite for most creative scientific work. However, none of them is specific enough to account for the creativity that scientists rely on in advanced research (built-in SFI).[31] They are necessary, but not sufficient conditions. Mithen's 'natural history intelligence', for example, is limited to typical hunter-gatherer skills like exploring a landscape, recognizing the change of seasons, and detecting the habits of potential game.[32] The physical intuition that he explains is exhibited by all children and consists of concepts like solidity, gravity (downward)

---

30   Steven Mithen, *The Prehistory of the Mind: A Search for the Origins of Art, Religion and Science* (London: Thames & Hudson, 1996), 69-70, 117-42. It is not clear whether the 'domain-specific modules' of evolutionary psychology are specific brain regions or functional networks. Compare Gardner's six/seven forms of intelligence, which include three of Mithen's four modules: naturalist, social (interpersonal) and linguistic, but are clearly functional in character.

31   See notes 2 and 3 on the variety of aspects of intelligence involved in scientific endeavour and the distinctiveness of SFI.

32   Mithen, *Prehistory of the Mind*, 124-5.

and inertia (at rest).[33] Everyday concepts like these would be sufficient for hunting and gathering, but they must actually be bracketed out in order for science to progress beyond the physics of Aristotle.

Sustained scientific endeavour requires the mental dexterity to bracket old forms of knowledge and generate radically new formalisms and methods in an attempt to deal with novel, unforeseen phenomena. As pointed out earlier, built-in SFI is not just a different degree of general intelligence found equally in all people. It is a particular type of intelligence that is highly contingent at the individual level as well as for the human species as a whole (see clarifications 1 and 2). In spite of its weaknesses, the great strength of Mithen's proposal is the fact that it is based on evolutionary biology and thereby avoids appeals to supernatural intervention. Mithen rightly tries to make scientific endeavour self-referential by applying evolutionary principles to the origin of the kind of intelligence that developed the theory of evolution in the first place.

The contrary viewpoint is maintained by scientists and philosophers who argue that evolutionary biology is not capable of accounting for built-in SFI. Paul Davies argues that natural selection is unable to account for SFI because the underlying laws of nature only emerge in scientific experiments using advanced technologies, and they have no direct relationship to the experiential world to which our ancestral hominins were forced to adapt.[34]

According to Davies, the demands of long-term survival in the Paleolithic era (or African Stone Age) period may account for the intelligence required to predict the trajectory of thrown objects or to recognize the migration patterns of animals.[35] However, the phenomena modern science investigates are entirely different from those of everyday experience. This difference holds true for the everyday experience of people living in modern technological societies, so it must be true for those who lived in preindustrial societies. This observation leads us to what Davies calls 'one of the great mysteries of the universe', the fact that intelligence adapted to Paleolithic conditions works in areas like nuclear physics and astrophysics.[36] Davies' mystery is basically the same as the 'miracle' to which Wigner pointed us, but it has the advantage that it is couched in evolutionary terms.

---

33  Mithen here relies on the child psychology of Elizabeth Spelke; Mithen, *Prehistory of the Mind*, 54-5.

34  Paul Davies, *The Mind of God*, 24; idem, 'Unreasonable Effectiveness', 54; idem, 'The Mind of God', in Jan Hilgevoord (ed.), *Physics and Our View of the World* (Cambridge: Cambridge University Press, 1994), pp. 233-4. In another work, Davies develops his own ideas about the origin of human intelligence in terms of the (not yet discovered) laws of complexity theory. In this effort, the meaning of 'intelligence' shifts back and forth between higher mental faculties in general and mere mental consciousness. It is not specific to SFI; Davies, *Are We Alone? Philosophical Implications of the Discovery of Extraterrestrial Life* (Harmondsworth: Penguin, 1995), 66, 80, 85, 89-90, 106-7.

35  The trajectories of projectiles are actually not intuited very accurately by humans. Modern standards for the computations of trajectories required the development of artillery and the experimental methods of Galileo, which broke with earlier Aristotelian notions concerning free-fall.

36  Paul Davies, *The Mind of God*, 24.

Thus far, I find Davies' basic line of reasoning persuasive. I shall be using it as the basis for further deliberation, and, for convenience, I shall give it a name. I shall refer to it as the *selection value dilemma*: scientists have a remarkable degree of success investigating phenomena unlike those for which the human psyche is adapted.[37] In the remainder of this section, I will give further arguments to support the validity of the selection value dilemma as something serious students of science need to address.

A possible weakness in Davies' selection value dilemma is that it relies on physicists' assessment of the challenges involved in doing their research. At face value, it seems reasonable enough to suppose that Davies and other physicists have a fairly realistic grasp of the challenges they face in their own work. One could argue, however, that physicists, like all professionals, may overestimate the intelligence required for their own profession. So it would help have a more objective measure of the degrees of difficulty and the levels of built-in SFI required to negotiate them.[38]

There are several ways to get a more objective measure of the situation. One way would be to describe the increasing degrees of difficulty in terms of a model based on actual historical stages in the history of science. We shall offer such a model in the following section. A model for the long-term history of a discipline can give some perspective on the experience and reflections of current practitioners.

Another way to assess the selection value argument would be to use psychological aptitude tests, following a procedure like that of Howard Gardner (described above).[39] If Davies' argument is correct, such tests should show that the prospect of pursuing scientific training to the point of doing original scientific research would be beyond

---

37   Another physicist-theologian who has clearly stated the selection value dilemma is John Polkinghorne, *Rochester Roundabout: The Story of High Energy Physics* (New York: Freeman, 1989), 175-6; idem, 'The Reason Within and the Reason Without', 179, and many other publications. The selection value dilemma is appropriately referred to as 'Wallace's paradox' because the first person to articulate it was the co-discoverer of biological evolution, Alfred Russel Wallace, *Darwinism* (London: Macmillan, 1890), 466-7 (seriously marred by racist ideas). Wallace had argued the point on the basis of Darwin's principle of utility for survival as early as 1869; see Martin Fichman, 'Science in Theistic Contexts: A Case Study of Alfred Russel Wallace on Human Evolution', in John Hedley Brooke, Margaret J. Osler and Jitse Van der Meer (ed.), *Science in Theistic Contexts: Cognitive Dimensions*, *Osiris* 16 (Chicago: University of Chicago Press, 2001), 227-50. The philosophical value of the paradox was explored by Charles S. Peirce (1839-1914), *Collected Papers*, ed. Arthur W. Burks et al., 8 vols (Cambridge, Mass: Harvard University Press, 1931-58), 7:507-8; see Steiner, *The Applicability of Mathematics*, 48-52 for a critical discussion. A more recent philosophical formulation has been given by Thomas Nagel, *The View from Nowhere* (New York: Oxford University Press, 1986), 78-82.

38   In the language of cultural anthropology, we are asking whether an 'etic' assessment by an outside observer would corroborate the 'emic' assessments of participants in a given discipline. On the need to balance the two approaches, see Nick Jardine, 'Etics and Emics (Not to Mention Anemics and Emetics) in the History of the Sciences', *History of Science* 42 (2004), 261-78.

39   For a review of personality and intelligence tests for SFI, see Gregory J. Feist, *The Psychology of Science and the Origins of the Scientific Mind* (New Haven, Conn.: Yale University Press, 2006), chap. 5.

the ability of many members of a representative test group. Only a few would have the built-in aptitude to complete such a course of study and go on to basic research in areas that require the development of novel concepts and methods. In ways like these, evidence could be offered to support Davies' contention that the ability to do science is indeed a mystery in need of explanation.[40]

A more common problem for sustaining the selection value dilemma is that modern educational curricula condition us to view continuous progress in science as a fundamental attribute of human nature. In order for us to recapture a sense of the wonder of human creativity in the sciences, it may be helpful to place it in the context of humanity's anthropoid origins. A species whose ancestors diverged from the lineage of the African apes less than ten million years ago and who still shares 98 per cent of its genetic makeup with chimpanzees might have little more capability for serious scientific endeavour than an inquisitive gorilla or a chimpanzee.[41]

A great deal has been learned about the special intelligence that African apes exhibit in the wild and the way in which it can be augmented under human tutelage. Let us think, however, about the capability of apes (and our common hominoid ancestors) for scientific endeavour in terms of experiences that are familiar in our own daily lives. Many hominoids could be taught how to operate an ATM machine in order to obtain a suitable reward (provided that paper money could be traded for food). But we would never conclude from such cleverness that such a hominoid might also be able to figure out how ATM machines work in order to design a new one to suit their own purposes. Nor would we expect them to work out the principles of the banking systems that underlie such machines. We are very far indeed from anything like built-in SFI, and genetic proximity between apes and humans makes the mystery of SFI all the greater.

We can bring the point a step closer to home by considering our own built-in intelligence. Most of us are quite capable of finding shortcuts. With a little experience we can usually even find the 'best shortcut' between two points. We do this every time we have to walk somewhere, even without thinking it through step by step. It is part of everyday life for us, and it must have been an everyday skill for our hominin ancestors as well.

As any student of calculus knows, shortcuts can also be diagrammed and computed mathematically. But a student will also realize that the intelligence required for solving the mathematical problem is entirely different from that needed to work

---

40   Paul Davies' version of the selection value dilemma is based on what we know about our own universe, but it can also be stated more generally. Any physical universe governed by laws that are complex enough to evolve metazoan species must be beyond the comprehension of any species that evolved by continuous adaptation to a natural environmental niche in that universe. To put it the other way around, no species that evolved to succeed at survival and reproduction in a particular natural environmental niche should be trusted to derive laws governing its broader environment, to say nothing of the laws of the entire universe.

41   The point was already made by Alfred Russel Wallace: natural selection in the prehistoric environment would have required an intellect only slightly greater than that of the apes; Fichman, 'Science in Theistic Contexts', 236. However, chimpanzees are smarter than humans in wilderness skills like the identification of plant species.

out shortcuts in practice.[42] In fact, individuals who can most easily figure out the best shortcuts in practice may have a very poor aptitude for calculus, and vice versa. Other examples could be developed for athletic skills like shooting a basketball. The point is that the practice of scientific research is quite different from the skills of needed for life in the natural world or in society.

Now apply the same reasoning to Paleolithic humans. The Paleolithic era in Europe or the Middle Stone Age in Africa is the critical period because the genetic base for human intelligence was stabilized between 40,000 and 400,000 years ago, at any rate within the last 500,000 years since the original divergence between *Homo sapiens* and Neandertals.[43] The developments of modern science and technology since the nineteenth century have improved our nutrition and health care enough to enhance the phenotypic expression of human genes, but it has had no significant effect on the human genome itself other than the re-distribution of pre-existing genetic traits (particularly those related to immunity) enabled by modern technologies of transport.[44]

We know that these Paleolithic hominins developed the ability to manipulate simple materials in order to gain a reward: they could make tools and use them to hunt or scavenge food and to sew garments. It is likely that these skills were programmed into early humans genetically for their survival value. But we would never conclude from such cleverness with tools that these hominins might also be able to figure out the atomic structure of those materials or the principles of the chemistry and quantum mechanics that underlie them. This brings us back to the mystery that haunts physicists like Davies. Why should humans have any built-in SFI at all? SFI seems to defy the laws of natural selection.

In contrast to Davies and others, however, I shall argue that natural selection can account for the origin of built-in SFI (as Mithen would also argue). Demonstrating this possibility will require us to explore the constraints that adaptation places on

---

42   Keith Devlin thus distinguishes 'abstract' or 'symbolic' mathematics from 'natural' or 'instinctive' mathematics; Devlin*, The Math Instinct: Why You're a Mathematical Genius* (New York: Thunder's Mouth Press, 2005), 249-51. Tim Pennings has shown that dogs (particularly Welsh Corgis) are remarkably good at minimizing the time needed to fetch a tennis ball even when the ball is thrown at an arbitrary angle into a lake. As the author points out, however, dogs do not actually do the calculus; Pennings, 'Do Dogs Know Calculus?', *The College Mathematics Journal* 34 (May 2003), 178-82; cf. Devlin, *The Math Instinct*, 17-28.

43   The 40,000 to 400,000-year range results from the diversity of ways for dating the stabilization of the human genome and 'modern' human behaviour, see Christopher Henshilwood and Curtis W. Marean, 'The Origin of Human Behaviour', *Current Anthropology* 44 (Dec. 2003), 629-31. This dating is consistent with the opinion of most anthropologists that the Neandertal capacity for symbols was much more limited than that of *Homo sapiens*; for example, Juan Luis Arsuaga, *The Neanderthal's Necklace: In Search of the First Thinkers* (New York: Four Walls Eight Windows, 2002), 307-8; idem, 'Requiem for a Heavyweight', *Natural History* 111 (Jan. 2003), 43-8; cf. Lewis-Williams, *Mind in the Cave*, 189-92. Accordingly, the development of SFI is likely to have occurred sometime after the original divergence of the two species approximately 465,000 years (with confidence limits of 317,000 and 741,000 years ago) ago as determined by DNA dating; Matthias Krings et al., 'DNA Sequence of the Mitochondrial Hypervariable Region II from the Nedandertal Type Specimen', *Proceedings of the National Academy of Sciences of the United States* 96 (11 May 1999), 5581-5.

44   Kate Douglas, 'Evolution and Us', *New Scientist* 189 (11 March 2006), 30-33.

our genetic heritage and to press the theory of evolution as far as we can in order to account for the origin of built-in SFI. The argument will lead us into spiritual and theological terrain. Such a development may not appeal to all natural scientists, but I can see no alternative. In any case, the line of argument will serve to demonstrate that it is possible to foster theological endeavour by defending the principles of natural selection rather than by opposing them.

*Where does Science-Fostering Intelligence come from? Paleolithic and modern environments*

In order to address the selection value dilemma as articulated by Paul Davies, I would like to refer to another of Eugene Wigner's observations about scientific endeavour. We have already stated that the development of science often requires the construction or discovery of new laws of nature. Wigner pointed out that the historical development of physics is progressive in the sense that the new laws required are 'more general and more encompassing' than those previously known.[45] He also provided a model for the long-term history of physics as a succession of layers that delve deeper and deeper into the physical nature of our world and move farther and farther away from everyday experience.

To give an example, Einstein's General Theory of Relativity represents a deeper and more comprehensive layer of description than classical Newtonian mechanics. Einstein's theory is also more abstract than Newton's in the sense that it is more remote from everyday experience.[46] Two such different layers of description are incommensurable, and the metaphoric use of concepts taken from classical, Newtonian physics is needed in order to compare them.[47] Similarly, Newtonian mechanics was more comprehensive and abstract than the mechanics of Galileo; the latter being based on relatively simple experiments involving gravitational acceleration. Galileo's mechanics was, in turn, more comprehensive and abstract than the more intuitive physics of Aristotle, which was based on generalizations from the everyday experience of heavy falling objects and rising fiery flames.[48]

Wigner developed this layered model of physics as a way of assessing the prospects for future scientific endeavour. The exploration of a succession of increasingly abstract layers and the prospect of even more remote layers to come led

---

45  Wigner, *Symmetries and Reflections*, 227.

46  The idea of increasing levels of abstraction was already stated by Albert Einstein, 'Physics and Reality' (1936), in idem, *Out Of My Later Years* (New York: Philosophical Library, 1950), 63-5; also in idem, *Ideas and Opinions* (London: Alvin Redman, 1954), 293-5. Following Alfred North Whitehead, *Science and the Modern World* (New York, Macmillan, 1925), 51, we may observe that the deeper, more abstract descriptions of natural science are less directly related to the complexities of life as explored, for example, by the social sciences and the arts.

47  The idea that the concepts of different paradigms are incommensurable was discussed by Thomas Kuhn, *The Structure of Scientific Revolutions*, 150, 198-200. The role of metaphor in relating incommensurable concepts was pointed out by Earl R. MacCormac, 'Meaning Variance and Metaphor', *British Journal for the Philosophy of Science* 22 (1971), 145-59.

48  Wigner, *Symmetries and Reflections*, 215-216, 227.

him to warn that even the most gifted and highly trained physicists might be limited in the number of new layers of science that they could master.[49] At some point, they would be literally 'out of their depth'.

In Figure 2.1, I have portrayed Wigner's description of the development of physics as a series of layers descending into an unknown depth.[50]

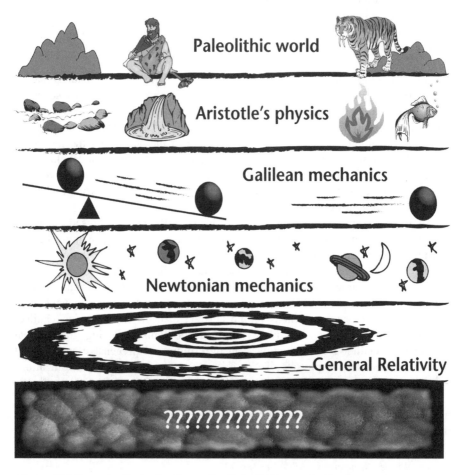

**Figure 2.1 Layers of physics from the Paleolithic era to the present (after Wigner)**

---

49    Wigner, *Symmetries and Reflections*, 216.

50    John Archibald Wheeler portrays physics as a staircase going upward, in which each step is a level of physical law and each riser transcends that law and leads to the next step; Wheeler, 'Beyond the Black Hole', in Harry Woolf (ed.), *Some Strangeness in the Proportion* (Reading, Mass: Addison-Wesley, 1980), 349-50. In Wheeler's formulation, the law of chemical valence, which is already rather abstract, is only the second of at least six steps.

The top layer in Figure 2.1 represents the natural world as it was experienced by our Paleolithic ancestors. Beneath that is the natural world as it was understood by ancient philosophers like Aristotle. Deeper layers of abstraction were achieved by Galileo, Newton and Einstein. Even deeper layers of a quantum vacuum are believed to exist, even though the physics has not yet been completely worked out. And there may be layers beyond that. Of course, this is a highly simplified portrayal of history. It does not do justice to all the twists and turns in the history of physical science. It is designed to convey the basic idea of increasing degrees of abstraction and levels of difficulty in dealing with new frontiers in physics.

Similar diagrams can be constructed for other natural sciences. In biology, for example: molecular biology represents a deeper level of description that Mendel's laws of inheritance; cladistics is a deeper level than systematics (taxonomy), and so forth. The exact number of layers is not as important as the fact that there is an unknown number of them.

Wigner's layered model of science allows us to rephrase the selection value dilemma as follows: hominins that are adapted to the everyday world of nature and society should be ill adapted for probing the deeper layers of the physical universe. The layer lying just beneath the surface (corresponding to Aristotle's physics) might be accounted for by the selective pressures occasioned by the need to track animals and anticipate the changing seasons of the year. However, its deeper, more general laws should forever remain beyond human comprehension. There might not be a problem if the concepts and principles needed for understanding all the layers were basically similar to those that apply to the empirical level of everyday experience (the work-a-day world of Paleolithic hominins). To the contrary, however, novel concepts and principles are generally needed at each new stage of scientific endeavour – concepts and principles quite unlike those that apply in everyday life. So why is the degree to which humans have exceeded their pre-human ancestors in the number and the depth of new layers of physics that they can master so much greater than what was required for survival and reproduction in the physical world in which they evolved?

With the help of Wigner's idea of layers of scientific endeavour, the selection value dilemma can be illustrated as shown in Figure 2.2. The paleohuman on the left-hand side of Figure 2.2 represents the limited range of the Paleolithic experience of the physical world (with very few layers in the primary environment) compared to that of modern scientific endeavour. The man with a shovel on the right represents the modern scientist digging into the deeper layers of the physical world. His culture is different from that of the paleohuman on the left, but his phenotype is essentially the same. The cartoon illustrates the basic feature of the mystery of built-in SFI. Brains that are only adapted to the everyday world of the Paleolithic era can hardly be expected to cope with the abstractions of modern physics or biology. This visible disparity shows the mystery of built-in SFI in graphic form.

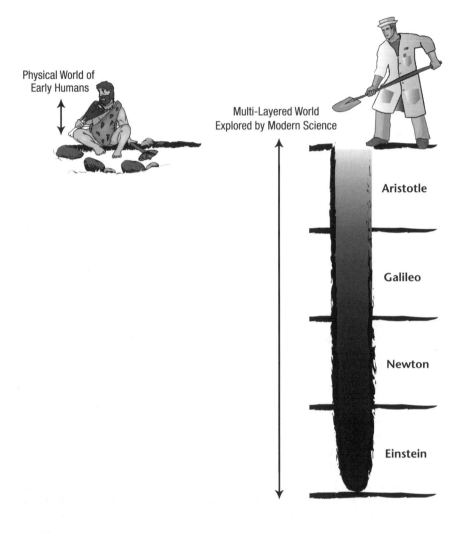

**Figure 2.2 The range of physics explored in the Paleolithic era and in modern science**

*Where does Science-Fostering Intelligence come from? The case for preadaptation*

On the basis of the selection value dilemma, Paul Davies concluded that natural selection by itself can not account for the emergence of built-in SFI. But one of Davies' statements of the paradox gives us an important clue that might help unravel the mystery. 'Our brains', he states, 'are remarkably fine-tuned to spot the patterns and order of Nature in domains that are quite irrelevant to biological evolution'.[51]

---

51    Davies, 'The Mind of God', 234.

The heuristic feature of this statement is the idea that the human brain is finely tuned for a particular cognitive skill. Davies' observation allows us to pinpoint a crucial aspect of built-in SFI: it involves the mental ability to discern and interpret patterns that are unlike all previously recognized patterns and orders. Davies concludes that natural selection by itself cannot account for such a human ability.

In effect, there is a double challenge here. Scientific endeavour is a phenomenon to be explained as well as a set of explanatory principles. Physicists like Paul Davies clearly see the difficulty explaining the phenomenon of SFI even though they offer no explanation in terms of natural selection. Anthropologists and archaeologists like Steven Mithen rightly insist on an evolutionary explanatory principle for human traits even though they fail to address the characteristic features of SFI.[52] The physicists have got the right question, but the anthropologists have the appropriate method.

Our contention is that both of these challenges can be met by a single, scientifically constructed scenario. In fact, they must be met by a single scenario if we are to demonstrate that scientific endeavour can be self-referential and avoid an epistemological gap between our knowledge of nature and the endeavour to extend that knowledge. The plausibility of the steps we shall take to explain the origin of SFI will depend on the sense of urgency involved in meeting the double challenge.[53]

---

52 A third option would be to view innate SFI merely as the accidental byproduct of other adaptations. Stephen Jay Gould referred to such byproducts as 'spandrels'; Stephen Jay Gould and R. Lewontin, 'The Spandrels of San Marco and the Panglossian Paradigm: A Critique of the Adaptationist Programmeme', *Proceedings of the Royal Society of London*, Series B 205 (1979), 581-98; Gould, *The Structure of Evolutionary Theory* (Cambridge, Mass: Belknap Press, 2002), concluding chapter. Other biologists are more optimistic about demonstrating the role of adaptation in evolution; for example, Ernst Mayr, 'How to Carry Out the Adaptationist Programme', *American Naturalist* 121 (1983), 324-34. In the absence of a detailed evolutionary history, a rule of thumb is that highly functional traits are likely to be adaptive (or exaptive); see Mary Jane West-Eberhard, 'Adaptation: Current Usages', in Evelyn Fox Keller and Elisabeth A. Lloyd (eds), *Keywords in Evolutionary* Biology (Cambridge, Mass: Harvard University Press, 1992), 13-18, reprinted in David L. Hull and Michael Ruse (eds), *The Philosophy of Biology* (Oxford: Oxford University Press, 1998), 8-14, along with references cited there; John Alcock, *Animal Behavior: An Evolutionary Approach*, 6th edn (Sunderland, Mass: Sinauer Associates, 1998), 266-8, 604-5. For example, the human eye is most sensitive to light at about 5,000 Angstrom units (colour green). Even though we have not yet constructed a detailed evolutionary history to explain this, we may infer that it is adaptive because 5,000 Angstrom units is the wavelength at which the spectrum of sunlight is most intense. The aptitude of human intelligence for exploring many layers of cosmic laws is very likely adaptive (or exaptive) for the same reasons. Such inferences can be confirmed in cases of convergent evolution, where more than one lineage of descent develops the same trait under similar environmental conditions. Since innate SFI is unique to *H. sapiens* here on earth, such a convergence could be demonstrated by comparison with scientific civilizations in other parts of the universe. So our inference is testable in principle.

53 Recognizing the challenge of meeting conflicting standards is essential to scientific endeavour: a scientist must tackle difficult problems using rigorous methodologies. Similar double challenges define most sports. Team sports, for example, require a team to achieve goals under the constraint of specific rules. A failure to appreciate either the goals or the rules would make the game pointless. The same is true for scientific endeavour.

Even though there was no direct precedent for scientific endeavour in early human experience, as Davies points out, the uncanny human ability to 'spot the patterns and order of Nature in domains that are quite irrelevant to biological evolution' must have an evolutionary explanation.

The only way to meet both of these challenges within the purview of evolutionary biology is view SFI as a preadaptation. A 'preadaptation' is any trait of an organism that functions well in a new environment but is largely based on the genetic adaptations to some earlier environment. Because the environment that originally conditions preadaptive traits can be quite different from that in which they eventually flourish, the idea of preadaptation could get us around the obstacle of the selection value dilemma. All we have to do is identify some survival-and-reproduction-skill that was adaptive in the Paleolithic era and may have preadapted the human brain for scientific endeavour.[54]

Looked at from the perspective of preadaptation, scientific endeavour was the foster-child rather than the natural child of the human psyche as it was formed in the Paleolithic era. That is why I have termed the intelligence required 'Science-Fostering Intelligence'. SFI was not adapted for scientific endeavour, but rather 'exapted' (co-opted) thousands of years after it was programmed into the human genome for other purposes.[55] We shall try to pinpoint the sort of prehistoric endeavour that would have required the emergence of built-in SFI. First, let us work through a few familiar examples of preadaptation in order to establish the investigative procedure. The critical scientific concept is that of an environmental niche.

We know one familiar example of preadaptation: mice are highly skilled at finding their way through artificial mazes in laboratory settings – all they need is a little incentive. The universality of this ability in mice indicates that it is genetically inherited. But neither laboratories nor mazes existed until modern times. So why should mice have built-in intelligence for something they never encountered in the wild? We have a 'mystery' or enigma.

Fortunately, the mystery of built-in maze intelligence in mice is fairly easy to resolve. We infer that the ancestors of present-day mice had to negotiate landscapes that were structurally similar to mazes in order to survive and reproduce. In other words, the psyche of the mouse assumed its present capabilities in terrains that presented the same mental and physical challenges that mazes do. So it is reasonable

---

54  Willem Drees has also argued that innate SFI might be a case of preadaptation similar to the human ability to read and write or the ability to play the piano, but, given his metaphysical naturalism, he was not willing or able to suggest any particular mechanism of preadaptation; Drees, 'Problems in debates about physics and religion', in Jan Hilgevoord (ed.) *Physics and Our View of the World* (Cambridge: Cambridge University Press, 1994), 202-3.

55  Some evolutionary biologists prefer to say that such traits are 'exaptations'. Exaptations are 'characters, evolved for other usages (or for no function at all), and later "co-opted" for their current role... and are *fit* (*aptus*) *by reason of* (*ex*) their form, or *ex aptus*'; Stephen Jay Gould and Elisabeth Vrba, 'Exaptation: A Missing Term in the Science of Form', *Paleobiology* 8 (1982), 4-15, reprinted in Hull and Ruse (eds), *The Philosophy of Biology*, 55, 64-5. See also Ian Tattersall, *Becoming Human: Evolution and Human Uniqueness* (New York: Harcourt Brace, 1998), 108.

to suppose that mice are preadapted for something that didn't exist during their evolutionary history.

Based on these simple inferences, we can say something about the environment in which mice evolved. There must have been lots of tunnels and thickets through which ancestral mice had to find their way quickly in order to survive and get back to their mates – a 'wild-terrain hypothesis'. This hypothesis could be tested in various ways. For example, one could try to monitor the regions of the brain that are activated in both wild terrain and laboratory maze. Alternatively, one could do topological studies of the two environments: the level of maze complexity that present-day mice can negotiate (a normal distribution) should match that of the wilderness landscape.

Many traits of humanity can also be understood as cases of preadaptation. For example, humans in a diversity of cultures can become accomplished pianists in spite of the fact that pianos were only invented a few hundred years ago in Europe. Naturally, no one would have tried to build a instrument that no human could play. Still, the level of digital dexterity required for piano playing calls for some sort of explanation. Other primates have remarkable dexterity for grasping branches, picking fruit, and manipulating simple tools, but none of these behaviours involves the kind of precision required for playing the piano. So we have another mystery.

The mystery of piano-playing dexterity is not as simple as that of built-in maze intelligence in mice, but it can be resolved in much the same way. We infer that early humans performed tasks that required the same digital dexterity as piano playing, though in a very different environment. The dexterity required for piano playing must have enabled some other manual task that contributed to survival and reproduction.[56] This preadaptation must date back before the dispersal of modern humans out of Africa. Recent studies of nested clades of genetic (DNA) haplogroups indicate that *Homo sapiens* originated in Africa and then spread into Asia sometime between 65,000 and 85,000 years ago.[57] Consequently, genetic traits of humans that are universal (not specific to one particular region or climate) are likely to date back at least 80,000 years. So we must look for evidence of some behaviour distinctive to human evolution during that timeframe that might have required significant advances in dexterity. It is reasonable to hypothesize that the ability to braid rope or to manufacture and haft arrowheads reinforced the development of neural structures that overlap those required for modern-day piano playing – a 'tool-use hypothesis'.

---

56 The piano preadaptation is discussed by Drees, 'Problems in Debates about Physics and Religion', 203; Tattersall, *Becoming Human*, 108.

57 Alan Templeton has used a nested clade-analysis to derive a DNA date of 80,000 to 115,000 years ago for the expansion-wave of modern humans out of Africa; see Templeton, 'Out of Africa Again and Again', *Nature* 416 (7 March 2002), 45-51. The L3 haplogroup associated with the first major migration of modern humans into Asia can be dated to around 85,000 years ago; Peter Forster and Shuichi Matsumura, 'Did Early Humans Go North or South?', *Science* 308 (13 May 2005), 965-6. This 'out of Africa' scenario allows for interbreeding with archaic populations in Asia and Europe; Vinayak Eswaran, Henry Harpending, and Alan R. Rogers, 'Genomics Refutes an Exclusively African Origin of Humans', *Journal of Human Evolution* 49 (2005), 1-18.

As anyone who braids or is handy with tools knows from experience, their use requires the coordination of all five fingers – an artisan can not be 'all thumbs'.

The tool-use hypothesis has to be tested. Like the wild-terrain hypothesis for mice in mazes, it could be tested by observing the activation of specialized regions of the brain. In addition, the tool-use hypothesis could be tested by designing aptitude tests and looking for correlations between the built-in abilities for the two skills involved. Either of these tests would require us to reconstruct the ways in which early humans handled their materials. Nonetheless, a variety of suitably designed experiments could determine the plausibility of the tool-use hypothesis. One should also compare it with the plausibility, similarly determined, of alternative hypotheses.

There are added dimensions to the case of early human tool use that make it rather more complex than that of mouse terrains. For one thing, the materials for rope or tool manufacture must be located and collected – they are not so prevalent in the environment as tunnels and thickets are for mice. In evolutionary terminology, a specific locus within the primary environment like that of stones suitable for tool manufacture is called a 'secondary environment' or 'environmental niche'.[58] Such niches must be discovered by a species as enclaves within the primary environment, but they are usually also restructured by the species that discovers and exploits them.[59] A niche becomes a nest.

Another dimension of early human tool use is the huge range in aptitude for making tools among humans. The variation in skill is far wider than in the case of mice. This variation is consistent with the multiple-intelligences theory we discussed earlier. While some degree of dexterity was required of all individuals, we may infer that the survival of the group required some of its members to be exceptionally adept at the manipulation of materials. These tool specialists were exceptional members of the group just as accomplished pianists are exceptional in our society today.[60] If so, the dexterity required for skilled tool-manufacture and piano-playing is like SFI in that it is a property of the entire gene pool, not just of particular individuals. Noting

---

58   An environmental niche is one special aspect of the primary environment, but it does not need to be small as the word 'niche' might seem to imply. An example would be the evolution of photosensitivity in early bacteria. Sunlight penetrated the entire ocean surface, but it had not been exploited by earlier forms of life.

59   Evolution in relation to niche-modification is often referred to as 'Baldwinian evolution'. An example is the development of lactose tolerance in early Near Eastern people, which was the result of the domestication of cattle and the consumption of dairy products. Such niches are cultural adaptations of pre-existing features of the environment; see Terrence W. Deacon, *The Symbolic Species: The Co-Evolution of Language and the Brain* (New York: Norton, 1997), 322-4, 344-6.

60   See Mayr, *What Evolution Is*, 131-2, for a brief defense of the idea of group selection. Jered Diamond appeals to the idea of the survival of the tribe in order to explain the extended lifespan of women past menopause, which is peculiar to *Homo sapiens*; Diamond, 'Why Women Change', *Discover* 16 (July 1996), 131-7. David S. Wilson has tried to explain the pervasiveness of religion as the result of large-group selection; Wilson *Darwin's Cathedral: Evolution, Religion, and the Nature of Society* (Chicago: University of Chicago Press, 2002). Nonetheless, the idea of group selection continues to be controversial.

these variations on the basic idea of preadaptation will be helpful in tackling the problem of built-in SFI that we have set before us.

Our immediate goal is to see what we can learn about the origin of SFI by viewing it as an adaptation to the Paleolithic environment, mediated perhaps by early human artifacts as in the example of piano-playing dexterity. Since prehistoric humans had no contact with the phenomena that modern science investigates, there must have been at least one environmental niche that provided challenges to the human psyche comparable to those that modern scientists face. Such a niche (or niches) could not simply have been part of the space-time world in which humans spent most of their lives. Like the deeper layers of modern physics and biology, this enclave of the Paleolithic environment must have been governed by principles quite unlike those of everyday life. It must have presented humans with successive layers of phenomena the exploitation of which would require brains capable of discerning the properties or laws governing those layers. In order to account for SFI, the exploitation of such a niche must have favored survival and reproduction and thereby altered the gene pool and favoured the development of neural structures that overlap those required for modern scientific endeavour. Figure 2.3 illustrates the idea using the same conventions as Figures 2.1 and 2.2.

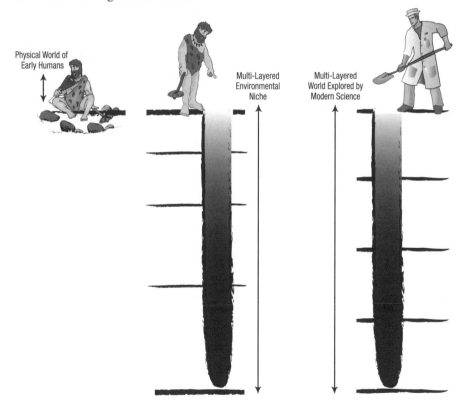

**Figure 2.3 Multilayered environments in the Paleolithic era and in modern science**

As in Figure 2.2, the left-hand side represents the limited range of Paleolithic experience of the space-time world compared to that of modern scientific endeavour, shown on the right. In some (unspecified) environmental niche, however, represented here by the second column from the left, Paleolithic humans were exposed to a much wider range of layers that are entirely different from those of everyday experience. As before, the exact number of layers of phenomena is not as important as the fact that they become increasingly remote from everyday experience. The visible parallel between the multilayered niche of the Paleolithic era and that of modern science is intended to suggest the idea of preadaptation. Adaptation of the Paleolithic psyche to the multilayered niche required an increased capacity for interpreting unfamiliar phenomena and could, therefore, have preadapted the human psyche for built-in SFI.

In order to make any further progress in resolving the mystery of built-in SFI, we must consider the various environmental niches known from the archaeological record and develop a hypothesis. Speculative hypotheses are an indispensable part of all scientific work (provided they are comparable and testable), so it is hardly out of place in an investigation of the very foundations of scientific endeavour. Our main purpose here is to call attention to a problem of built-in SFI and to demonstrate that at least one viable way of addressing it involves us in theological endeavour without demeaning science itself. If we can succeed in accomplishing these rather modest goals, other inquirers may be able to identify alternate solutions to the selection value dilemma and some sort of empirical testing will then be required in order to decide among such alternatives (as in the case of piano-playing dexterity and the 'tool-use hypothesis'). We shall consider some possible tests once we have developed the hypothesis.

Before engaging the more speculative part of our investigation, it may be helpful to restate the most important steps in our discussion so far. We have argued:

- That SFI is a distinct, definable form of human intelligence that has thus far defied scientific explanation (the selection value dilemma).
- That SFI has a genetic base and is adaptive–it can be discussed in terms of evolutionary biology without reducing it to an aspect of general human intelligence (the 'double challenge').
- That there was an environmental niche in which early humans developed survival-enhancing behaviours that might have preadapted the human psyche for the kind of creativity required in scientific endeavour (SFI).

Given these rather plausible assumptions we can try to reconstruct the sort of environmental niche that might have preadapted the human psyche for scientific endeavour.

*Where does Science-Fostering Intelligence come from? Reconstructing the Paleolithic context*

In order to address the mystery of the origin of built-in SFI, we must identify some survival-and-reproduction-enhancing behaviour(s) that might have preadapted the human psyche for scientific endeavour. The behaviour in question involved the recognition of patterns in novel phenomena, and it required the development of sufficient mental agility to interpret such patterns.

Unfortunately, we lack the knowledge needed to make a definitive identification of such behaviour. All that we know about the activities of Paleolithic humans is what they have left us in durable remains and artifacts. But we do have evidence for a fairly wide range of prehistoric human activities, and it is possible to suggest some reasonable candidates and test them against the double challenge described above. Future archaeological finds may supply further candidates to allow comparative testing.

We have argued that the distinctive feature of built-in SFI is the ability to detect patterns and develop appropriate concepts for novel domains of experience. In fact we know of several forms of Paleolithic behaviour that required the mastery of novel domains, and some of these behaviours may well have required special rewiring of the brain. I will consider just two that have been discussed before moving on to a new hypothesis. The first of these known forms of behaviour does not fit our criteria completely, but it will provide us with some clues for locating one that does. The second will provide a better fit and lead us into some interesting theological questions. A variety of other behaviours have been discussed in anthropological literature. Interested readers should be able to evaluate how well alternative proposals address the Survival Value Dilemma based on our treatment of the two below.[61]

Early humans certainly had to adapt to changing climatic conditions in order to survive and reproduce. Anthropologist Richard Potts has speculated on the effect of large periodic climate fluctuations over the last three million years. Potts argues that the need to survive the uncertainties caused by these fluctuations is largely responsible for the dramatic increase in both the size of the human brain and the density of its neural connections over that same extended period of time. Such changes in the size and structure of the human brain resulted in what Potts calls 'variability selection': selection for ingenuity in generating new survival strategies under widely varying conditions. Inter-continental migration and technological innovation are among the behaviours that Potts offers as examples of specific adaptations to these fluctuations.[62]

Potts' climate-variability hypothesis is an important contribution to the discussion about human origins in general, but it does not work very well with respect to the origin of SFI. There are at least two reasons for this. It is worthwhile thinking them through as an introduction to the issues involved and a preparation for an alternative suggestion.

---

61 For example, Marc D. Hauser and Haim Ofek have argued that the emergence of trade networks favoured individuals with enhanced computational skills; Hauser, 'What do Animals Think About Numbers?', 150-51; Ofek, *Second Nature: Economic Origins of Human Evolution* (Cambridge University Press, 2001). Peter Carruthers suggests that the development of pretend play among children facilitated the generation of novel hypotheses about causes of observed events; Carruthers, 'Human Creativity: Its Cognitive Basis, its Evolution, and Its Connections with Childhood Pretense', *British Journal for the Philosophy of Science*, 53 (2002), 225-49.

62 Richard Potts, *Humanity's Descent: The Consequences of Ecological Instability* (New York: Morrow Books, 1996), esp. pp. 231-2, 242-4; idem, 'Evolution and Climate Variability', *Science* 273 (16 Aug. 1996), 922-3. For another similar argument, see William H. Calvin, *A Brain for All Seasons: Human Evolution and Abrupt Climate Change* (Chicago: University of Chicago Press, 2002), esp. pp. 59-63.

One limitation of Potts' climate variability theory is that the periodic climate fluctuations it is based on are spread out over the entire history of human evolution. In fact, they go back to the very beginning the most recent Ice Age, 2,500,000 years ago.[63] So Potts' scenario is not well suited to explain specific forms of human intelligence that developed along the way. The origin of SFI is likely to have been within the last 500,000 years, as determined by comparing the DNA of *Homo sapiens* and Neandertals.[64]

An even more serious problem with Potts' scenario is that the capacity for adapting to climate change is much too general a trait to account for built-in SFI. Adapting to extreme climate change undoubtedly required the intelligence to develop new technologies, new migration and hunting strategies and new social flexibility (compare Steven Mithen's modules of technical intelligence, natural history intelligence and social intelligence). But climate adaptation by itself did not involve an ability to discern patterns and develop concepts appropriate to radically novel domains – the environment may become colder or drier, but it does not change in its underlying principles of geometry or causation.

Even though Potts' theory is too general for our purposes in its present form, it could be made more intelligence-specific by allowing for a diversity of enclaves within a given environment. For this we need to make use of the concept of a secondary environment or environmental niche discussed in the previous section. Humans may well have experimented with environmental niches as one strategy for dealing with the larger problem of climate change. In this case, the structures that conditioned human intelligence were those of the environmental niches rather than overall climatic conditions.

As a test case, consider the possibility that severe climactic variation forced early humans to explore novel terrains like deep cave systems. We know from archeological finds that cave exploration was a prominent feature of Upper Paleolithic hominins.[65] Extensive cave exploration required spelunking parties to reorient themselves to conditions entirely different from those to which they were previously adapted. Not only would the topography of caves be radically different from that of the outside world, but the absence of sunlight would accentuate the unpredictable strangeness of

---

63  Potts, *Humanity's Descent*, 113, 119, 124, 209, 243. A technical problem with Potts' climate variability theory is that there are thousands of generations (10,000 to 100,000 years) between major climate shifts, so the effects of Darwinian selection might cancel each other out rather than cumulate over many such shifts; so James M. Cheverud, reported in Bruce Bower, 'Humanity's Imprecision Vision', *Science News* 152 (21 July 1997), 27c.

64  Potts does focus on one particular period of intense climate variation around 130,000 years ago, approximately the time of the emergence of *Homo sapiens* in Africa; Potts, *Humanity's Descent*, 157-8, 201-2. But the adaptation to climate variation Potts discusses does not differentiate between SFI and the type of intelligence that developed in Neandertals.

65  Cave exploration has been observed in anthropoids like baboons and chimpanzees. According to L. Barrett et al., however, the use of caves as shelters (for temperature regulation) is a cultural innovation limited to particular groups of baboons; L. Barrett et al., 'Habitual Cave Use and Thermoregulation in Chacma Baboons', *Journal of Human Evolution* 46 (Feb. 2004), 215-22. So the skills needed for extensive spelunking have probably not been reinforced in baboons by genetic reprogramming.

the environment and might occasion unfamiliar experiences of the mind as well as the body. Therefore, the mental skills required for spelunking on a regular basis approximate the requirements for built-in SFI far more closely than a more general capacity for adapting to climate change. The degree of approximation could even be quantified by correlating test scores for aptitudes in spelunking and scientific research.

This extension of Potts' climate-variation theory shows that evolutionary change may involve conditioning by two or more environments at the same time. Greater difficulty of survival under a general environmental stress like climate variability may create an advantage for subgroups that explore some special secondary environment like deep cave systems. If the secondary environment has a multilayered structure, it might help account for the development of built-in SFI (Figure 2.3). The important feature is the cognitive ability to move back and forth between the two environments on a regular basis.

All things considered, we may conclude that variation in climate was not a sufficient cause for the origin of built-in SFI. Climate variation may account for the development of limited technological skills, but it is not specific enough to select for an ability to discern patterns or laws in a variety of novel forms. Our dual-environment extension of Potts' climate variability theory, on the other hand, opens up a range of new possibilities, particularly when we bring the need for symbol based behaviour into the picture.

The development of spelunking skills may be an approximation, but it is not adequate preadaptation for built-in SFI for various reasons. Cave exploration in itself is not mediated by symbol systems. Moreover, while the structure of caves is different from that of the outside world, it is not multilayered in the sense that we are looking for.

Even though spelunking intelligence does not entail the use of extensive symbolism, archeologists have discovered a rich treasure of art forms in caves frequented by Homo sapiens. Upper Paleolithic caves in northern Spain and southern France are the repository for some of the earliest known artistic symbolism dating back some 15 000 to 30 000 years. At some stage of development, it appears, exploration of the subterranean environment occasioned the exploration of a world of symbolic forms. While neither cave exploration nor artistic symbolism would provide a suitable niche for the development of SFI by themselves, the combination of the two can open our inquiry to a much wider range of human behaviour than we have considered thus far. So any attempt to discover behaviour that might have preadapted the human brain for scientific endeavour should take into account this early form of human creativity. We need to know more about it.

*The shamans of prehistory and the spirit-niche hypothesis*

There are various interpretations of Paleolithic cave art: we should not take any of them as a proven fact.[66] For our purposes, however, one particular interpretation, based on comparison with shamanic symbols and rituals, stands out because it

---

66    For a review of the various interpretations, see John E. Pfeiffer, *The Creative Explosion: An Enquiry into the Origin of Art and Religion* (New York: Harper & Row, 1982),

postulates cognitive abilities with remarkable similarities to our definition of SFI. Jean Clottes and David Lewis-Williams argue that these paintings originally functioned as symbolic windows into the spirit world. I shall briefly explain their findings and speculate on the neurological changes in the human brain that the shamanic journeys through the spirit world suggested by these paintings would have required. Soul journey required the mental agility to engage and interpret novel phenomena.[67] So it is possible that the interpretive skills required preadapted the human psyche for scientific endeavour.

The normal separation between space and spirit in modern Western thought might lead us to discount paranormal phenomena like soul journeys as unrelated to natural science. However, scientific creativity (as well as other forms of human creativity) does involve unconscious depths of the human psyche.[68] So given the fact that analysis of the anthropological foundation of scientific endeavour results in paradoxes like the selection value dilemma, it may be the very paranormality of this interpretation that qualifies it as a clue to the origin of built-in SFI. We can not insist on one particular interpretation of Paleolithic cave art, but the choice of a particular framework for investigation is legitimate provided it leads to a meaningful result and provided that the investigation of other options is not excluded. So let us review the evidence for the spirit world interpretation of the Paleolithic paintings.

According to Clottes and Lewis-Williams, Paleolithic cave art is best understood as a record of early human engagement with a spirit world. The record can be interpreted by means of comparison with the practice of shamanism in present-day hunter-gatherer and pastoral-agricultural societies (cultural anthropology). This comparison leads us into another controversy: disagreement on the validity of using the term 'shamanism' in cross-cultural comparisons. Many anthropologists believe that exotic forms of spirituality should not be invoked uncritically to explain ancient artifacts.[69] However, Clottes and Lewis-Williams have been careful in their definitions, and their basic argument does not depend on the terms used to describe the varying cultural expressions of 'shamanic' spirituality.[70] It concerns

---

102-118, 132-52; Jean Clottes and David Lewis-Williams, *The Shamans of Prehistory: Trance and Magic in the Painted Caves* (New York: Abrams, 1998), 63-79.

67  '...the shaman learns... first of all, how to orient himself in the unknown regions that he enters during his ecstasy. He learns to explore the new places of existence disclosed by his ecstatic experiences.' Mircea Eliade, 'Shamanism', in Lindsay Jones (ed.), *Encyclopedia of Religion*, 2nd edn, 15 vols (Detroit: Thomson Gale, 2005), 12:8272a.

68  This sentence reflects the turning point in my own shift from scientism to humanism when, as a college student, I first read Brewster Ghiselin's anthology, *The Creative Process: A Symposium* (Berkeley: University of California Press, 1985).

69  See, for example, Cecelia F. Klein et al., 'The Role of Shamanism in Mesoamerican Art: A Reassessment', *Current Anthropology* 43 (June 2002), 383-401, and Dale Guthrie's critique of the shamanistic interpretation of Paleolithic art, which he argues is a realistic portrayal of hunting practices and erotica; Guthrie, *The Nature of Paleolithic Art* (Chicago: University of Chicago Press, 2006). More than one interpretation may be needed to explain different galleries and various stages of Paleolithic cave art.

70  See Lewis-Williams, *Mind in the Cave*, 229, for the idea of diverse 'shamanisms' in the Upper Paleolithic. Cecelia F. Klein and Maya Stanfield-Mazzi judge that Lewis-

only the cognitive skills required for exploring altered states of consciousness and communicating their contents.[71] In order to get around the complex issue of semantics, I shall use the term 'paleoshamanism' when referring to the spirituality of Paleolithic humans as Clottes and Lewis-Williams define it.

According to this paleoshamanic interpretation, the reason that humans ventured so deeply into cave systems and practiced their artistic skills there was that they found a gateway into the spirit world. Specific evidence for this interpretation includes the following. First, the paintings have many surrealistic features that weigh against more this-worldly interpretations like the depiction of hunting scenes. The animal forms (theriomorphs) are not located in recognizable environments: they are often free-floating and out of proportion to each other. Modern viewers are likely to credit this surrealism to the absence of proper training in perspective. But Clottes and Lewis-Williams conclude that animal forms were drawn just as they appeared to the artists. They are animal-like spirits rather than ordinary natural species.[72]

In addition to the absence of modern, realistic conventions, the Paleolithic paintings have tell-tale conventions of their own. Many of the paintings are centred on natural protrusions or large cracks in the surface of the cave walls. As a result, the animal forms appear to be emerging from the other side of the wall. Paintings from Altamira Cave (northern Spain), for example, clearly suggest the appearance of animal spirits from within the rock.[73] The cave wall represents a membrane between human space and the world of the spirits.

Detailed examination of the paintings indicates that the traffic across the membrane was not all one way. There are places on the cave walls where the painters have pressed on the cave wall with their hands leaving the clear imprint of their fingers. Clottes and Lewis-Williams see these finger impressions as an indication that the artist was reaching through the wall to the side of the spirits.[74] In the case of present-day shamans, such an imaginary entry into the spirit world is generally termed 'soul-flight' or 'soul journeying'.[75] Such an identification is also consistent with the

Williams' definition of shamanism exemplifies the kind of precision that is called for; Klein and Stanfield-Mazzi, 'On Sharpness and Scholarship in the Debate on "Shamanism" – Reply', *Current Anthropology* 45 (June 2004), 405b.

71  See Lewis-Williams, *Mind in the Cave*, 13-3, 206n.2 for an able defense and definition of the category of shamanism as a 'universal' for hunter-gatherer cultures. For background, see Michael James Winkelman, 'Shamans and Other "Magico-Religious" Healers: A Cross Cultural Study of Their Origins, Nature, and Social Transformations', *Ethos* 18 (Sept. 1990), 308-52, especially the typology outlined in Table 2 (315-16). See also Jane Monnig Atkinson's criticism that cross-cultural, psychological interpretations of shamanism like Lewis-Williams' risk ignoring the varying historical and cultural contexts; Atkinson, 'Shamanisms Today', *Annual Review of Anthropology* 21 (1992), 310-13.

72  Clottes and Lewis-Williams, *Shamans of Prehistory*, 91-2; Lewis-Williams, *Mind in the Cave*, 193-6, 220.

73  Clottes and Lewis-Williams, *Shamans of Prehistory*, 86-91; David Lewis-Williams, *Mind in the Cave*, 199, 210-14, 253, 256-9, 266, and Plates 4, 5, 27.

74  Lewis-Williams, *Mind in the Cave*, 216-20.

75  As described by Michael Winkelman, 'entering ecstasy to interact with the spirit world on behalf of the community' is the core of hunter-gatherer shamanism; Winkelman,

common interpretation of pictures that show dancing 'therianthropes' – humans with animal characteristics like antlers who are thought to reflect the ritual behaviour of the people who depicted them.[76] Such ecstatic dancing, usually conducted in an animal costume, is also characteristic of present-day shamans. So these paintings may well give us a small window into the rituals of paleoshamans.

Within this general framework of interpretation, Clottes and Lewis-Williams use anthropological studies of present-day cultures to reconstruct the complex universe in which these Paleolithic humans apparently lived. Such a cosmos has had a number of levels extending both into the heavens and into the underworld (underground and sometimes underwater).[77] We are familiar with the idea of a 'three-storey universe' from classical mythology, but for shamans supramundane worlds are more than a literary topos. As mediated by symbols and rituals, they are actually tangible and visible to the imagination. Each new level that the shaman experiences requires a refocusing of awareness and a restructuring of the symbolic imagination.[78] The range of cognitive experience is far wider than that of empirically oriented pragmatists.

Later in this chapter we shall address the question of how much credence we can give to such beliefs today ('Challenges to theological endeavour: the ontological status of the spirit world'). For the present, it is sufficient to note that the paleoshamanic behaviour which Clottes and Lewis-Williams infer from the archaeological evidence satisfies the basic criteria we have established for the preadaptation needed to account for built-in SFI. Paleoshamanic soul journeys were a form of behaviour that required the detection and interpretation of patterns in what would otherwise have been just a chaotic, paranormal experience. As explained above, the caves and their symbol systems constituted the kind of environmental niche needed to explain the evolution of SFI. Early humans cultivated the experience of the paranormal and attempted to interpret its structures and dynamics as a means of coping with challenges from the

'Shamanism and Cognitive Evolution', *Cambridge Archaeological Journal* 12 (2002), 95b.

76   Clottes and Lewis-Williams, *Shamans of Prehistory*, 94-5. Miranda and Stephen Aldhouse-Green suggest that the Paleolithic theriomorphs may be shamanic spirit helpers rather than paleoshamans, Aldhouse-Green, *The Quest for the Shaman: Shape-Shifters, Sorcerers and Spirit-Healers in Ancient Europe* (London: Thames and Hudson, 2005), 60-64, 174.

77   Lewis-Williams, *Mind in the Cave*, Figure 29 on 145, Figure 61 on 267. For background on shamanic cosmology, see Åke Hultkrantz, 'A Definition of Shamanism', *Temenos* 9 (1973), 30-31. Lewis-Williams argues that, while the propensity for intracosmic journeys is a neurological inheritance, the beliefs and practices of each tribal group originate independently. The prominence of complex cosmologies in Upper Paleolithic cave art, for example, may have been due to religious-artistic specialization in conjunction with increasing social differentiation; Lewis-Williams, 'Harnessing the Brain: Vision and Shamanism in Upper Paleolithic Western Europe', in Margaret W. Conkey et al. (eds), *Beyond Art: Pleistocene Image and Symbol* (San Francisco: California Academy of Sciences, 1997), 324, 336-7.

78   Richard Noll, 'Mental Imagery Cultivation as a Cultural Phenomenon: The Role of Visions in Shamanism', *Current Anthropology* 26 (Aug.-Oct. 1985), 449b; Roger N. Walsh, 'Shamanic Cosmology: A Psychological Examination of the Shaman's Worldview', *ReVision* 13 (Fall 1990), 88-9. Later literary sources like the Book of Revelation gave dramatic expression to the succession of such refocusings on the part of a seer; cf. Rev. 4:1-2; 6:1-2, 7-8; 14:1-2, 14; 15:5; 19:11.

environment like those described by Richard Potts. On this reading of the evidence, a thick description of the foundations of natural science leads us to attribute a thick cosmology and epistemology to our prehistoric human ancestors.

This brief sketch of the evidence for Paleolithic behaviour places us in a position to formulate a working hypothesis, which I shall refer to as the 'spirit-niche hypothesis' (SNH). Since it forms a conceptual link between the categories of anthropological archaeology and those of evolutionary genetics, it can be stated in either of two ways. If we begin with archaeological categories, our hypothesis can be stated as follows:

> SNH 1: Symbols and rituals associated with the spirit world of Paleolithic humans were the principal environmental niche for the development of the genetic basis for SFI. The ability to negotiate this secondary environment required a rewiring of the human brain (through genetic variation, expression and selection) enabling it to discern and interpret novel patterns and thereby preadapted it for scientific endeavour.

If instead we begin with categories of genetics, the spirit-niche hypothesis takes a different form:

> SNH 2: Genetic mutations that underlie built-in SFI were selected for because they enhanced ability to explore a multilayered spirit world with the aid of symbolic forms and thereby contributed to group survival.

In short, the kind of interpretive intelligence needed for scientific endeavour (viz. discerning deeper patterns of order and unification in domains far removed from everyday experience) was required in order to negotiate the complex structure of the spirit world as experienced and symbolized by early humans. Alternative hypotheses are also possible. Our main concern is to call attention to a mystery that lies at the very foundation of scientific endeavour and to develop a research programme for resolving that mystery. Any such hypothesis must be testable.

*Evaluating the spirit-niche hypothesis*

According to the spirit-niche hypothesis, the specific form of intelligence that makes scientific endeavour possible originated in the context of the early human exploration of spirit worlds. This hypothesis may seem contradictory at first: what could be more antithetical than modern science and ancient (for us outdated) religion? Stick to math (mathematics); leave myth for the poets.

However, the constraints of evolutionary biology require us to invoke archaic behaviour of some sort, and that constraint limits the field of human behaviours that might have provided the required niche for SFI development. Math and science are not among them.

Moreover, scientific endeavour and soul journeys have more features in common than our assumptions about 'likes and opposites' would allow. Both science and soul journeying have thick epistemologies. They both require the cognitive skill to generate mental imagery independent of the senses and translate that imagery into empirical terms.[79] Both posit imaginary worlds that are radically different from everyday life in their structures and laws of operation. Both draw on the creative processes of the unconscious mind. Practitioners have to focus on indistinct elements at the 'fringes of consciousness' and give them shape so that they can be communicated to their peers.[80] Both become adept at shifting back and forth between the worlds of their imagination and the empirical world. Both rely on the use of metaphors and symbols in order to articulate their visions and to and revisit them for further exploration.[81]

Scientists habitually use geometrical and mathematical symbols as tools for mapping invisible codes and forces. The surfaces on which these symbols are drafted serve as membranes interfacing with imaginary worlds much like those found in Paleolithic caves (see Figure 2.4).

The experience of the scientist at the blackboard or computer screen is not as different from that of the Paleolithic artist at the cave wall as our modern ways of categorizing things might suggest.

Natural philosophers and mathematicians often describe their own mental processes using journeying metaphors similar to those of shamans.[82] Nearly two thousand years ago, the Roman statesman and philosopher, Seneca, described his own journey into the imagination as follows: 'Then the mind wanders among the very stars... until it goes around the entire universe and looks down upon the earth from above....'[83] Classical philosophers understood their pursuit as a kind of soul journey and bequeathed that imagery to later generations.

---

79   According to Michael Winkelman's review, the function of trance states in hunter-gatherer healing rituals is 'circumventing the normally employed cognitive processes to seek novel solutions to problems'; Winkelman, 'Shamans and Other "Magico-Religious" Healers', 323-4. The English word 'theory', which is so instrumental in scientific endeavour, derives from the Greek term, *theōría*, meaning an act of 'viewing' or 'contemplating' that is independent of the senses. Plato used this term in a contemplative sense not unlike descriptions of shamanic visions; Plato, *Republic* 517b-d; cf. Bernard McGinn, *The Foundations of Mysticism* (New York: Crossroad, 1991), 25, 29.

80   Anna-Leena Siikala, response to Richard Noll, 'Mental Imagery Cultivation as a Cultural Phenomenon', 455b. I owe the idea of 'fringes' or 'wings' of consciousness to Ghiselin, *Creative Process*, 11-12.

81   The role of metaphor and symbol in the development of Paleolithic intelligence is explored by Winkelman, who argues that this cognitive ability antedated the advent of spoken language; Winkelman, 'Shamanism and Cognitive Evolution', 84, 97b. On the use of metaphor in science, see especially Ian G. Barbour, *Myths, Models and Paradigms: The Nature of Scientific and Religious Language* (London: SCM Press, 1974), 42-5.

82   The shamanic use of journeying metaphors is well documented. For symbolic maps of such journeys, see Joan Halifax, *Shaman: The Wounded Healer* (New York: Crossroad, 1982), 66c, 68.

83   Seneca, *Naturales Quaestiones* I, Pref. 7-8, in Loeb Classical Library, *Seneca in Ten Volumes* (Cambridge, Mass: Harvard University Press, 1917-71), 7:7. Cf. Plato, Phaedrus 246b-247d for the cosmic imagery, and Philo, *De opificio mundi* 69-70, cited later in Chapter 3.

**Figure 2.4 Symbolism in science: Niels Bohr at the board with son, Aage[84]**

A more recent example is Andrew Wiles, the British mathematician who developed a long-sought proof of Fermat's Last Theorem in 1986. Wiles described his process of mental exploration in terms of a journey through a dark mansion:

> One enters the first room of a mansion and it's dark. Completely dark. One stumbles around bumping into the furniture, but gradually you learn where each piece of furniture is. Finally, after six months or so, you find the light switch, you turn it on, and suddenly it's all illuminated. You can see exactly where you were. Then you move into the next room. So each of these breakthroughs ... are the culmination of, and couldn't exist without, the many months of stumbling around in the dark that precede them.[85]

Wiles has forcefully described the mental adjustments that one must make in order to explore and map out unfamiliar terrain in the world of mathematics.

The cultural differences between the worlds of science and soul journeying are far too pronounced to allow a simple identification of the two phenomena. Scientists do not consciously project an image of their own bodies into their calculations

---

84   Photo from AIP Emilio Segre Visual Archives, Margrethe Bohr Collection. Used by permission.

85   Andrew Wiles quoted in Simon Singh, *Fermat's Enigma: The Epic Quest to Solve the World's Greatest Mathematical Problem* (New York: Anchor Books, 1997), 236-7.

or descriptions, whereas shamans are consciously aware of their own location in the spirit world.[86] Shamanic experience involves sensory deprivation, the use of psychotropic substances (in some but not all traditions), experience of death by a painful ordeal, travel through a psychedelic vortex, and rebirth from darkness into visible light.[87] Only in the most metaphoric or humorous of senses could such experiences be attributed to modern scientists.

For our purposes, the shaman's involvement in the spirit world and the scientist's engagement with mathematical symbols need not be any more similar than tool use and piano playing are the same. The point of our brief comparison is not that scientists are shamans in disguise (though I have known a few who made me wonder), but that the cognitive moves that Andrew Wiles described are analogous to those involved in soul journeying.[88] Our claim is that the Science-Fostering Intelligence required for scientific endeavour may be an exaptation of the soul-journeying intelligence developed in the Paleolithic.[89] That is the substance of the spirit-niche hypothesis.

*Four contingencies to be tested*

From a scientific standpoint the spirit-niche hypothesis should be evaluated like any other hypothesis. It can not be proven, but it can contribute to the overall unity of scientific knowledge by organizing a wide range of phenomena that might otherwise seem disconnected. It can also serve as a stimulus to further research in areas where our knowledge is still incomplete.

There are at least four contingencies that affect our argument: (1) whether shamanic soul journeying was actually practiced during the time period when the human brain achieved its modern form; (2) whether Paleolithic soul journeying was an 'adaptive' behaviour that required modification of the human genome; (3) whether individuals who are adept at soul journeying share a distinctive form of intelligence; and (4) whether the soul journeying type of intelligence could be

---

86   For cosmic maps that show successive locations and forms of the shaman, see Halifax, *Shaman*, 66c, 68, 71c.

87   Lewis-Williams, *Mind in the Cave*, 282. A helpful psychoanalytic model for the comparable experiences of apocalyptic visionaries has been developed by Daniel Merkur. Merkur's model involves an unconscious (but healthy) bipolar mechanism of the superego that processes visual imagery by alternating between mourning and elation; Merkur, 'The Visionary Practices of Jewish Apocalypticists', *The Psychoanalytic Study of Society* 14 (1989), 119-48, esp. 130-34, 144-5.

88   Among the writings of recent mathematicians, note particularly Barry Mazur's description of the process of concretizing relatively abstract mathematical entities like complex, higher dimensional spaces (for example, Hilbert space). In Mazur's words, mathematical intuition is 'not an inert, unchanging resource, but something that can expand when challenged' thereby making spaces of any number of dimensions accessible. Mathematicians' spatial intuition has an 'unexpected pliability' that allows them to overcome the limits of their normal sensory imagination and to 'reach out' with their intuitions and then to 'squash' as much as they can into them; Barry Mazur and Peter Pesic, 'On Mathematics, Imagination and the Beauty of Numbers', *Daedalus* 134 (Spring 2005), 128-9.

89   See note 55 on exaptation.

exapted for scientific endeavour. I shall briefly describe each of these contingencies and point to findings that might support or refute our hypothesis.

(1) Was shamanic soul journeying practiced during the time-period when the human brain achieved its modern form? In order to qualify as a behaviour that could have preadapted the human brain for scientific endeavour, soul journeying must have been practiced as early as the Middle Paleolithic (in Europe) or the Middle Stone Age (in Africa). The paleoshamanic interpretation of Jean Clottes and David Lewis-Williams, upon which I have relied, is most convincing for the cave art of the Magdalenian period in Western Europe, which began around 18,000 years ago, i.e., during the Late Upper Paleolithic rather than the Middle Paleolithic. The human brain, however, is thought to have reached its present neural capacity at least 40,000, and perhaps as much as 400,000, years ago.[90] Can the evidence for soul journeys be extrapolated back that far?

The archaeological evidence is not conclusive, but it suggests an origin of paleoshamanic behaviour in Old Stone Age Africa. The Bradshaw rock art of northwest Australia provides some evidence for shamanic practice 13,000 to 17,000 years ago, approximately the same time as the more famous cave art of Magdalenian Europe. If confirmed, this evidence would support the contention that such behaviour was not unique to Western European humans and that it probably had a much earlier origin.[91]

In support of this conclusion, there is evidence for the widespread use of red ochre at least 128,000 years ago. Red ochre was often used in ritual burials in prehistoric times, and it is still widely used today for ritual purposes, particularly by shamans to aid in their journeys to heaven.[92] So the 'cultural explosion' of visual art in Late Upper Paleolithic Europe should not be taken to imply that either shamanic practices or the cognitive ability involved in soul journey was a lately acquired trait. The origin of paleoshamanism may well have coincided with the evolution of the cognitive skills of *Homo sapiens* in Middle Stone Age Africa. Much more archaeological evidence will need to be found to clarify the issue.[93]

This fragmentary archaeological evidence can be supplemented by theoretical considerations based on genetics. Lewis-Williams argues that shamanic spirituality

---

90   Christopher Henshilwood and Curtis W. Marean, 'The Origin of Human Behaviour', *Current Anthropology* 44 (Dec. 2003), 629-31.

91   The research of Per Michaelsen and Noel Smith is reviewed by Allan Coukell, 'Spellbound (Could mysterious figures lurking in Australian rock art be the world's oldest shamans?)', *New Scientist* 169 (19 May 2001), 34-37. Note the accompanying reservations by Alan Watchman, Grahame Walsh, Paul Bahn and George Chaloupka.

92   Ian Watts, 'The Origin of Symbolic Culture', in Frans B. M. de Waal (ed.), *Tree of Origin: What Primate Behavior Can Tell Us about Human Social Evolution* (Cambridge, Mass: Harvard University Press, 2001), 121-37; but see also the critique of the evidence by Steven Mithen, 'Symbolism and the Supernatural', in de Waal (ed.), *Tree of Origin*, 151-3, 165.

93   It is not necessary to demonstrate continuity of either art work or shamanic activity over the entire Middle Paleolithic or Middle Stone Age. If soul journey behaviour was adaptive at some early stage in such a way as to alter the gene-pool of a small founder population (80,000 to 200,000 years ago), it would have been rediscovered and expressed periodically even if the original beliefs and practices were discontinued in the interim.

must already have been part of human experience millennia before the earliest surviving paintings were created.[94] In other words, the soul journeying rituals of Magdalenian Europeans were a new use of a much older practice, rather than a European innovation.

Genetic studies that indicate a Middle Stone Age origin of modern *Homo sapiens* lend some support to Lewis-Williams contention. Genetic traits of humans that are universal are likely to date back before the dispersal of modern humans out of Africa. Like the dexterity required for piano playing, the cognitive skill prerequisite for soul journeying must have originated at least 80,000 years ago and falls within the timeframe when the human brain was assuming its modern neural capacity. So there are both archaeological and genetic reasons for this conclusion. Again, this is an issue that can only be resolved by further evidence and debate.

(2) Was Paleolithic soul journeying an 'adaptive' behaviour? In order to qualify as a behaviour that could have preadapted the human psyche for scientific endeavour, soul journeying must have contributed in some important way to the survival and reproduction of early human groups. If soul journeying were irrelevant (or even deleterious) to human survival, it would not have been selected for as a trait, and the genetic basis for intelligence would not have been affected in a way that might explain the emergence of built-in SFI.

Soul journeying is a complex phenomenon. Any attempt to explain its adaptive value must be specific about the feature that was being selected for. In all likelihood, it was not the mere occurrence of altered states of consciousness like dreams and hallucinations. Many other mammals besides humans have dreams and hallucinations. However, most mammals do not cultivate such experiences as a way of promoting healing or providing leadership for social groups. What is unique to humans, Lewis-Williams points out, is the ability deliberately to induce altered states of consciousness and to translate them into symbolic forms for ritual and artistic purposes. In other words, humans can access an 'alternative reality' with 'parallel states of being' and can move back and forth between that alternative reality and everyday life at will (aided by ritual).[95]

Given the limits of our present knowledge, it is difficult to say just how such shamanic behaviour might have contributed to human survival and reproduction. The pervasiveness of healing and crisis management among shamans in present-day societies suggests that they contribute to the health and solidarity of social groups.[96]

---

94  Lewis-Williams explains the development of cave art as the projection of mental imagery onto plane surfaces as the natural result the social differentiation required by the interaction of *Homo sapiens* with the Neanderthals; *The Mind in the Cave*, 94-5, 193.

95  Lewis-Williams, *The Mind in the Cave*, 93, 134-5, 190-91. Cf. Richard Noll, 'Mental Imagery Cultivation as a Cultural Phenomenon', 445-9, on the cultivation of visions in present-day shamanism: 'The hallmark of the shaman is the ability to control his visions – to begin, manipulate, and end them at will' (ibid., 448b).

96  The role of healing (mostly by hypnosis) in the evolution of religious consciousness is discussed by James McClenon, *Wondrous Healing: Shamanism, Human Healing, and the Origin of Religion* (Dekalb, Ill.: Northern Illinois University Press, 2002), 21-45.

So soul journeying may also have fostered social cohesion and tribal solidarity in the Middle Paleolithic.

In all likelihood we are dealing with an instance of 'group selection' in which genes are propagated and expressed in varying degrees because of the contribution they make to the survival of the group.[97] However, other explanations are also possible. It may simply be the case that individuals who had contact with the spirit world had prestige and were more attractive to the opposite sex! As we noted in our discussion of human tool production, adaptation to a relatively small niche may have benefits for survival and reproduction in the larger context of the primary environment.

We may feel secure in our conclusion that the cultivation of soul-journeying intelligence played a significant role in the formation of the human psyche without trying to pin down the exact evolutionary advantage it afforded. Nonetheless, it would be interesting to know just how such behaviour contributed to the welfare of our distant ancestors. Further research and alternative suggestions in this area are certainly needed.

(3) Does soul journeying behaviour involve a distinctive form of intelligence? In order to qualify as a behaviour that could have preadapted the human psyche for built-in SFI, the development of soul journeying behaviour must have been a distinct new form of intelligence – call it soul-journeying intelligence – based on alterations of the human genome. In other words, early humans who were adept at soul journeying must have been distinctive both neurologically and genetically.

If soul journeying were itself just an exaptation (rather than a secondary adaptation)[98] of the neural processes underlying some prior trait like dreaming or hypnotic susceptibility,[99] the origin of built-in SFI would have to be sought in those earlier traits and would probably lead us to very different conclusions about the anthropological foundation of scientific endeavour. As explained above, however, we understand soul-journeying intelligence as the distinctive ability to cultivate altered states of consciousness and to translate them into symbolic forms for social purposes, an ability that appears to be unique to *Homo sapiens*.[100] But can it be measured?

---

97   See Mayr, *What Evolution Is*, 131-2, for a brief defense of the idea of group selection. Jered Diamond appeals to the idea of the survival of the tribe in order to explain the extended lifespan of women past menopause, which is peculiar to *Homo sapiens*; Diamond, 'Why Women Change', *Discover* 16 (July 1996), 131-7. David S. Wilson has even tried to explain the pervasiveness of religion as the result of large-group selection; Wilson *Darwin's Cathedral: Evolution, Religion, and the Nature of Society* (Chicago: University of Chicago Press, 2002). These ideas continue to be controversial.

98   See Gould and Vrba, 'Exaptation', 64-5 for the terminology.

99   James McClenon associates one aspect of the aptitude for shamanic healing with hypnotic susceptibility and shows that this susceptibility is present in a variety of primates and other animals; McClenon, *Wondrous Healing: Shamanism, Human Evolution, and the Origin of Religion* (Dekalb, Ill.: Northern Illinois University Press, 2000), cited in Winkelman, "Shamanism and Cognitive Evolution," 97ab.

100 Lewis-Williams, *The Mind in the Cave*, 93, 134-5, 190-91.

We have already discussed Howard Gardner's empirical differentiation of eight types of intelligence: linguistic, spatial, musical, logical-mathematical, kinesthetic, interpersonal, intrapersonal, and naturalist. Gardner also considered the possibility of including 'spiritual' (or 'existential') intelligence as a ninth type. He noted that distinctive states of the brain appear to be correlated with the altered states of consciousness achieved by those who practice meditation.[101]

Gardner's suggestion has received support in the work of Andrew Newberg and (the late) Eugene d'Aquili. Working with Tibetan monks and Franciscan nuns as representative subjects, these neuroscientists have located a center of 'unitive consciousness' in a region of the posterior superior parietal lobe which is called the 'orientation association area'.[102] Such empirical markers for the common mystical experience of unity with all things could be cited in support for our claim that soul journeying requires a distinctive type of intelligence.

There are problems with defining soul-journeying intelligence on the basis of patterns of brain activity. For one thing, Newberg and d'Aquili argue that the brain structures involved in experiences of self-transcendence originally evolved as a way of facilitating mating and sexual reproduction, not for symbol based religious experience like that associated with Paleolithic cave art.[103] The authors also point out that much of the brain structure that underlies religious experience is still unknown.[104] The description they give of 'unitive consciousness' does not include some basic elements of soul journeying: the ability to process mental imagery in detachment from the immediate empirical environment; the use of creative processes of the unconscious mind to generate such mental imagery; the ability to posit orders that are radically different from everyday life; the ability to focus on indistinct elements and develop them in ways that can be communicated to their peers and applied in practice; and the use of metaphors and symbols.[105] So ecstatic soul journeying may be somewhat different from unitive meditation, and areas of the brain other than the posterior superior parietal lobe may be involved.[106] Gardner actually gave up trying to define spiritual intelligence, partly because spirituality meant so many things to so many cultures and people.[107]

---

101 Gardner, *Intelligence Reframed*, 56-7.

102 Andrew Newberg and Eugene d'Aquili, *Why God Won't Go Away: Brain Science and the Biology of Belief* (New York: Ballantine Books, 2001), 4-7.

103 Newberg and d'Aquili, *Why God Won't Go Away*, 125.

104 Newberg and d'Aquili, *Why God Won't Go Away*, 185-6n.12.

105 In an earlier work, Newberg and d'Aquili described shamatic entry into the world of the spirits as a form of unitive mysticism that attempts to control the environment by entering the world of the spirits to verify personal sources of power; d'Aquili and Newberg, *The Mystical Mind: Probing the Biology of Religious Experience* (Minneapolis: Fortress Press, 1999), 160. But their primary concern in *Why God Won't Go Away* is with the religious experience of undifferentiated being (or non-being); *Why God Won't Go Away*, 147.

106 Newberg and d'Aquili describe the multiplicity of brain regions involved in various forms of intelligence: abstract-objective; intuitive problem-solving; artistic-creative; and social: d'Aquili and Newberg, *The Mystical Mind*, 69-75.

107 Gardner, *Intelligence Reframed*, 54, 59-60.

The form of intelligence involved in soul journeying is defined even more precisely than Gardner's 'spiritual intelligence' or Newberg and d'Aquili's 'unitive consciousness'.[108] Therefore, it should result in a characteristic intelligence profile for practitioners of soul journey around the world. Measuring this profile would require the use of specially designed psychometric surveys. If and when such surveys become available, our hypothesis about the origin of built-in SFI may need to be re-evaluated.

(4) Could soul-journeying intelligence be exapted for scientific endeavour? The spirit-niche hypothesis will not work unless soul-journeying intelligence and built-in SFI overlap significantly at the neurological level. I have already suggested some operational similarities between the two phenomena, but a more quantifiable way of comparing soul-journeying intelligence and built-in SFI is needed in order to sustain the claim that one is an exaptation of the other.

Sustaining the spirit-niche hypothesis in this way would involve measuring the complex intelligence profiles of both soul journey practitioners and research scientists. In view of the fact that not every one with the aptitude for soul journey is trained to be a practitioner, the comparison would be statistical. The thesis to be tested would be that built-in SFI is consistently over-represented among practitioners of soul journeying as compared with the general population.

Demonstrating such a statistical overlap might prove to be difficult. Aptitude tests would have to be designed in such a way that built-in SFI could be documented in all social groups. Ideally, the tests would show that aptitude for scientific endeavour is present in hunter-gatherer and pastoral societies just as much as it is in industrialized ones. So many of the values and assumptions that industrialized societies take for granted would have to be factored out in order to eliminate cultural bias. But such surveys are possible in principle. If and when the results become available, our hypothesis about the origin of built-in SFI will again need to be re-evaluated.

Clearly our way of accounting for built-in SFI is vulnerable at a number of points. The spirit-niche hypothesis could be proven false – or at least our argument for it could be proven false – at any one of these points. From the standpoint of scientific endeavour, however, such vulnerability is good because it generates reasons for further research and it provides added value to any research that is done. The effort to develop a research programme and to answer the question is more important than any particular answer we may eventually reach.

For the time being, we can accept a balance of simultaneous plausibility and uncertainty for the spirit-niche hypothesis. It is sufficient for our purposes that the question of the origin of SFI can be addressed using the tools of evolutionary biology and anthropology. We have demonstrated a way to address the origin of built-in SFI within the framework of natural selection while recognizing the distinctive character of SFI. It is not necessary either to abandon the principles of evolutionary anthropology or to reduce built-in SFI to a modification of general intelligence.

---

108 For some careful descriptions of shamanic spirituality, see, for example, Halifax, *Shaman: The Wounded Healer*, 65-73; Noll, 'Mental Imagery Cultivation as a Cultural Phenomenon', 443-51.

The process of accounting for the anthropological foundation of scientific endeavour has led us to take the spiritual side of human experience seriously and raises a number of issues of theological import. In the remainder of this chapter we shall explore some of them. As in Chapter 1, we show that theological issues are implicated in the investigation of the foundations of scientific endeavour and that the Judeo-Christian tradition has resources that can help address them.

## Theological challenges and resources

We have seen that examination of the anthropological foundation of scientific endeavour (built-in SFI) requires serious consideration of the spiritual life of early humans. Our discussion to this point has been restricted to scientific issues and empirically testable ideas. The spirit world experienced by early humans was introduced as an interpretation of archeological and anthropological evidence: the purpose was to help us understand the evolution of the human psyche. But a thick description of science like this involves us in theological questions just as it did in our examination of the cosmic foundation of scientific endeavour (Chapter 1). The scientific and theological aspects of the question are best treated separately, but there is no neat line of demarcation between them.[109]

At least four theological challenges arise here. First and foremost is the question of whether the spirit world experienced and symbolized by early humans was anything more than a psychological construct. There are also important questions regarding theological cosmology, the existence of a Creator, and the meaning of the divine image in humanity. In the following four sections, we will sharpen those challenges and explore resources in the Judeo-Christian tradition that might help address them. As in our discussion of the cosmic foundation of scientific endeavour, the challenges arising from our analysis of the foundations of scientific endeavour will serve as a lens to bring traditional theology into new focus.

### *The ontological status of the spirit world*

To this point we have only assigned an instrumental role to the experience of soul journeying in the emergence of human psyche, particularly in the case of built-in SFI. What are we to make of such experiences of the spirit world from a present-day perspective?

Modern anthropologists frequently report shamanistic behaviour in the societies they study. In their professional work, they normally bracket out the troublesome issue of the reality of the spirit worlds experienced by their subjects.[110] Such a bracketing

---

109 On the importance of 'transversal intersections' that soften the lines of demarcation between disciplines like science and theology, see Wentzel Van Huyssteen, *Alone in the World? Human Uniqueness in Science and Theology* (Grand Rapids, Eerdmans, 2006), 9, 19-20, 34, passim.

110 Technically speaking, the bracketing occurs in 'etic', or analytic discourse of the anthropologist. Tribal beliefs and experiences must be described in 'emic' terms as self-reported by the subjects.

or 'suspension of disbelief' is a necessary precaution against prejudgments based on the anthropologist's own cultural standards.

A similar bracketing is often done by cognitive psychologists and neuroscientists who describe 'altered states of consciousness' in laboratory settings. David Lewis-Williams based his interpretation of Upper Paleolithic cave art on the work of cognitive psychologists like Colin Martindale who study an entire spectrum of states of consciousness. At one end of this spectrum is waking, purposive thought, which is closely related to the external, empirical environment that we share with others. At the other end of the spectrum are autistic states that have little or no direct relevance to external, empirical reality. Lewis-Williams locates the hallucinations of shamanic experience at the autistic pole of the spectrum on a trajectory parallel to that of dreams.[111]

Lewis-Williams is careful to point out that from a scientific point of view all parts of the spectrum of consciousness are equally 'genuine'.[112] Yet, given our post-Enlightenment cultural biases concerning hallucinations, we tend to assume that there is no objective reality involved in such radically altered states of consciousness. They may play a role in some forms of artistic expression, but they do not hold anything of value for science. We shall have to address this challenge for our investigation of the foundations of scientific endeavour.

A similar sort of problem is raised by the work of Andrew Newberg and Eugene d'Aquili. If, as these neuroscientists argue, there is a region of the posterior superior parietal lobe that is programmed to generate unitive experiences, one is not likely to conclude that there is any actual basis for such experiences and images in the external world. Skeptical critics like Michael Shermer of the Skeptics Society and Ron Barrier of American Atheists insist that neurologically based religious experience has absolutely no external referent: 'The real common denominator here is brain activity, not anything else.'[113]

However, as Andrew Newberg has argued (in response to one of Barrier's comments), scientific endeavour is itself based on experiences and images that can be traced back to particular areas of the brain. So the validity of spirit experiences and images need not be regarded as any more imaginary than scientific ones are.[114] In fact, our 'normal' sense of separateness from the external world is also located in the 'orientation association area' of the brain studied by Newberg and d'Aquili. Neurologically speaking, the only thing that differentiates in-the-body experiences from out-of-the-body ones is the fact that one is normal and the other is not. An a priori

---

111 Lewis-Williams, *Mind in the Cave*, 123-30. For a critique of the 'three-stages' model used by Lewis-Williams, see Patricia Helvenston and Paul Bahn, 'Testing the "Three Stages of Trance" Model', *Cambridge Archaeological Journal* 13 (Oct. 2003), 213-16. Even if these criticisms were taken at face value, for Lewis-Williams the model still provides a heuristic schema for categorising altered states of consciousness; Lewis-Williams, 'Neuropsychology and Upper Paleolithic Art: Observations on the Progress of Altered States of Consciousness', *Cambridge Archaeological Journal* 14 (April 2004), 107-8.

112 Lewis-Williams, *Mind in the Cave*, 125.

113 Robert Holmes, 'In Search of God', *New Scientist* 170 (21 April 2001), 28c. See also Michael Shermer, 'Demon-Haunted Brain', *Scientific American* 288 (March 2003), 47.

114 Holmes, 'In Search of God', 28c; cf. Newberg and d'Aquili, *Why God Won't Go Away*, 142-4, 146-7.

rejection of the reality of spiritual experience risks undermining the credibility of science as well as that of mysticism.[115] The same considerations could be applied to the question that concerns us more directly here – what are we to make of a particular kind of mystical experience, that of soul journey?[116]

There are various ways of approaching this question. In the present study we restrict ourselves to what can be learned from examination of the anthropological foundation of scientific endeavour: what does the fact that humans actually have the cognitive capacity for pursuing natural science (SFI) tell us about the matter?

Our working hypothesis is that the spirit world experienced and symbolized by Paleolithic humans was the environmental niche required for the development of built-in SFI. There are two ways of developing this thesis: a weaker, psychological version and a stronger, ontological version. Both versions are dependent on the four contingencies described above and are equally speculative. The ontological version opens more avenues for dialogue with the theological traditions, and we will explore some of those avenues. But the psychological version may be more palatable to many working scientists. Both versions have their own distinctive strengths and weaknesses. We will briefly explore these in order to clarify the nature of the choice involved.

According to the psychological version of the spirit-niche hypothesis, the spirit world experienced by early humans had no existence outside their imaginations and their myths. The experiences themselves were generated randomly in special regions of the brain and given form by culturally conditioned categories and values. In short, the experience of soul journey for early humans was just a cultural adaptation of the capacity for dreams and hallucinations.

Psychological research shows that dreams are based on the neural activity of the limbic and thalamo-cortical systems of the brain associated with random eye movement (REM). Dream imagery is the brain's response to such neural activity much as if it were caused by sensory input. Such cerebral activity is not unique to humans. It occurs

---

115 A similar argument is made by Ian Barbour in relation to evolutionary explanations of the origin of religious practices; Barbour, *When Science Meets Religion*, 13.

116 Anthropologists and psychiatrists often tend to be more open minded on the issue because they have to deal with the spirit world more directly than most other scientists do. Anthropologist Victor Turner, for example, concluded from his studies among the Ndembu tribe of Zambia (then Northern Rhodesia) that ritual and symbolism have 'ontological value'; Turner, *Revelation and Divination in* Ndembu (Ithaca: Cornell University Press, 1975), 32. Psychiatrist Roger Walsh argues for 'ontological indeterminacy', which means that the ontological status of spirits may be undecidable based on scientific methods alone; Walsh, 'Shamanic Cosmology', 98a; idem, *The Spirit of Shamanism* (Los Angles: Tarcher, 1990), 135-7. Ronald Hutton points out that the native explanation of shamanic phenomena in terms of spirit-agents makes as much sense as the view of some Western anthropologists that they were merely projections of the shaman's psyche; Hutton, *Shamans: Siberian Spirituality and the Western Imagination* (London: Hambledon and London, 2001), 67. Philosopher Philip Wiebe argues that postulating the existence of finite spirits is a reasonable way of explaining certain cases of exorcism; Wiebe, 'Finite Spirits as Theoretical Entities', *Religious Studies* 40 (Sept. 2004), 241-50.

in most or all mammals and is thought to be adaptive, probably being beneficial for the production of brain protein.[117]

A psychological version of the spirit-niche hypothesis can accomplish many of the objectives of our quest for an explanation of the evolutionary emergence of built-in SFI. We know from firsthand accounts that new scientific theories are generated in the human unconscious and then refined in terms of appropriate mathematical formalisms. An important aspect of built-in SFI is the ability to cultivate and capture the inchoate intuitions of the unconscious mind and give them communicable form.[118] Therefore, SFI may well have originated in connection with the ability to remember and interpret altered states of consciousness like dreams and hallucinations. The imagery of soul journeying might be viewed as a metaphorical way of processing and interpreting such experiences. Many scientists will see it this way with good reason.

The psychological version of the spirit-niche hypothesis supports our contention that there is a deep connection between early human spirituality and modern scientific endeavour. Both are based on the brain's ability to articulate and process the suggestions of the unconscious mind. So both have thick epistemologies – epistemologies thick enough to make genuine creativity possible.

As a result of this connection, the psychological version overcomes one of the major dualities of the modern world, that between rational scientific thought and extrasensory experiences of the paranormal. Even though the actual symbol systems produced by soul journeying and scientific endeavour are entirely different, the thought processes that generate those systems are similar, if not identical. From a theological perspective, this unification is a significant result (still subject to the four contingencies and requiring further investigation).[119] So the psychological version of the spirit-niche hypothesis should not be viewed as being opposed to religion or even to theology.[120]

Finally, the psychological version of the spirit-niche hypothesis has the advantage of parsimony in explanation. It allows one to hold a personal faith that is agnostic or even skeptical concerning the existence of spirits. It provides a plausible answer to the question of the origin of built-in SFI without invoking the supernatural or otherwise pressing the limits of scientific method. All of its assertions can be tested, at least in principle, using standard techniques of archaeology, anthropology and psychology. There are plenty of good reasons to favour this option.

---

117 Lewis-Williams, *The Mind in the Cave*, 190-91.

118 Ghiselin, *Creative Process*, 1-21. On the role of intuition and imagination in the abstract world of theoretical physics, see Hideki Yukawa, *Creativity and Intuition: A Physicist Looks at East and West* (Tokyo: Kodansha, 1973), 56-8, 101-9, 118-21.

119 The psychological version of the spirit-niche hypothesis might also help make sense of widespread religious phenomena like belief that humans have souls, the sense of loss or estrangement from the spiritual world, and the attempt to reconnect with the spirit world through visions and prophecy. If soul journeying was instrumental in the origin of human intelligence, the potential for such experiences and the difficulties involved in cultivating them would likely have an impact on subsequent belief systems.

120 For example, Michael Winkelman interprets shamanism in purely psychological terms as the basis for a 'neurotheology'; Winkelman, 'Shamanism as the Original Neurotheology', *Zygon* 39 (March 2004), 193-217.

Useful as the psychological version of the spirit-niche hypothesis is, it does have one serious drawback with respect to the selection value dilemma. It does not account for the consonance between human creativity and cosmic creativity that we set out to explain in the first place. The fact that the human brain is adapted to interpret random patterns of its own making could account for heightened powers of imagination and creativity, but it would not account for the specialized intelligence needed for scientific endeavour. It would be fortuitous, an unimaginable stroke of luck, if the interpretive skills that resulted from dreams and hallucinations were also suited to the discovery and mathematical formulation of previously unknown layers of cosmic laws. We would have no more reason to expect the intelligence involved in soul journeying to be able to analyse the workings of the universe than we would expect the same of the human ability to read palms or to see patterns in the stars. The result is that the effectiveness of scientific endeavour would be purely coincidental and incapable of explaining its own effectiveness, hardly the scenario to give one confidence in science as a sustainable endeavour. Contrary to a common perception, denying ontological status to the world of spirits is not entirely consistent with a high view of scientific endeavour.

So in spite of all our efforts to this point, we are still left with the question of why any aspect of human creativity is capable (to a surprising degree) of discerning the laws of cosmic creativity. The same would be true of our efforts to explain the maze exploring intelligence of mice if we believed that the forest-terrain of their ancestors was purely hallucinatory, or to explain the facility of humans for piano-playing in terms of Paleolithic tool-use if we concluded that those tools only existed in their minds (parallel cases of preadaptation).

In order for the spirit-niche hypothesis to account for built-in SFI, we must posit some sort of analogy between the way soul journeying functions in the unknown regions of the spirit world and the way SFI functions in the unknown regions of the physical world. We must consider the possibility that the Paleolithic spirit world had a structure and laws of its own the exploration of which required mutations of the human brain. This possibility leads us to consider the strengths and weaknesses of the ontological version of the spirit-niche hypothesis.

The ontological version of the spirit-niche hypothesis affirms the existence of a spirit world with its own structure and laws. The structure of the spirit world is a layered structure something like that of the physical world (see Figure 2.3). It has layers of phenomena that can be explored only by discerning increasingly comprehensive principles of operation. In this view, the environment in which we live is not limited to the empirical world around us. The thick epistemology of the psychological version is matched by a thick ontology.

On the other hand, the spirit world need not resemble the physical universe (or multiverse) any more than stone tools resemble piano keys. All that our hypothesis requires is that the ability of Paleolithic humans to explore the spirit world required the development of neural networks that could later be exapted for the exploration of the heights and depths of the physical world.

Undoubtedly Paleolithic experiences of the spirit world were facilitated by culturally specific rituals and were processed by special regions of the brain. But the spirit world was just as much a part of the Paleolithic environment as stone materials and deep caves were. Due to genetic mutations, certain members of early tribal groups were able to experience this world in a rudimentary way and to negotiate its peculiar structures. Subsequently, these mutations were selected for and enhanced (contingency 2 above). As a result, a certain proportion of the species has the type of intelligence needed to negotiate entirely novel features of their empirical environment today.

How are we to evaluate the ontological version of the spirit-niche hypothesis? It has many of the same advantages as the psychological version. It is consistent with the known role of unconscious brain processes in processing strange new phenomena. It accounts for the ability of the human brain to process such phenomena and to devise new symbol systems in order to articulate their findings. It may therefore help account for the cultivation of media like art, poetry, music and dance as means for recalling what was experienced and informing the larger community.[121]

One nagging concern critically minded people might have with the ontological version of the spirit-niche hypothesis is that it appears to be more complex than the psychological version. Positing one or more spirit worlds would add to the list of unknowns in the world around us layers of phenomena that are not readily accessible to most humans in the modern world. On the other hand, researchers rarely make progress in tackling new problems without expanding the list of unknowns. High-energy physics posits a plethora of subatomic particles beyond the simple proton-neutron-electron picture of elementary textbooks – some have been discovered, but many so far have not. Present-day cosmology is based on the existence of an unknown inflationary force and two forms of matter-energy which together constitute 96 per cent of the mass-energy of the universe. And, as we explained in Chapter 1, the contingencies involved in the origin of our universe may require positing an infinite number of parallel universes. One always hopes that simplicity will be restored in the longer term, but one often cannot move forward without allowing greater complexity in the short term.

It could even be argued that the ontological version of the spirit-niche hypothesis is more parsimonious than the psychological version. For one thing, people for whom spirits are real (or who accept the testimony of others) might see the ontological version leading to a broader, more unified rationality that encompasses all of human experience. But even from a strictly scientific perspective one could argue that the ontological version of the spirit-niche hypothesis is the more parsimonious of the two.

There are several ways to make the case. First, in terms of methodology: if we assume that built-in SFI is an evolutionary adaptation like the others that we have discussed (contingencies 1 and 2), then we must posit some sort of environmental pressure outside the bounds of the organism in question. As argued above, it would make no more sense to insist that the phenomena to which intelligence was tuned were only hallucinatory for science-capable humans than it would for piano-playing humans or maze exploring mice. It would actually be more parsimonious to say that what counts as an explanation for evolutionary adaptation should be the same in all cases.

A second way to press the ontological version is based on the quest for unity of knowledge that underlies all scientific endeavour. The very definition of scientific

---

121 In keeping with Howard Gardner's theory of multiple intelligences, I view art, poetry, music and dance as distinct human endeavours. They are not the same as soul journeying intelligence even if they were instrumental in the ritual practices of paleoshamans.

endeavour requires that the tools of science be applied to all empirical aspects of the space-time world, including the phenomenon of scientific endeavour itself. The work of scientists is not supposed to be treated as something self-explanatory or self-existent like God. So it is more parsimonious to posit a spirit world in order to explain one of the foundations of science than it is to leave the foundations of science unexplained as a matter of blind faith.

Neither an appeal to people's spiritual experiences, nor the parallel to maze exploration and piano-playing, nor the ideal of scientific closure by themselves prove that the ontological version is true. But considerations like these do show how difficult it can be to draw firm conclusions on the basis of the simple criterion of parsimony.

Our purpose in this essay is to give an account of the remarkable degree of consonance that exists between human creativity and cosmic creativity. From this particular perspective, the ontological version of the spirit-niche hypothesis has a decided advantage. Based on what we know about our Paleolithic forbears, it is reasonable to suppose that some aspects of human creativity are an adaptation (over many generations) to an environmental niche with multiple layers of paranormal phenomena. The fact that such an adaptation has preadapted the human brain for scientific endeavour can then be explained quite simply on the basis of a structural similarity or homology between the multiple layers of the spirit world and the layers of laws that we find in the natural world (as in Wigner's description of scientific development portrayed in Figure 2.1).

The spirit world is the one niche of the environment evidenced in durable Paleolithic remains that could have required the development of an intelligence capable of exploring multilayered domains and thus have made possible the scientific exploration of new layers of laws in the natural world. If journeying through spirit worlds did in fact require the restructuring of the human psyche through the development of a new type of intelligence (contingency 3), the actual existence of such worlds would account for the overlap between the intelligence needed for soul journeying and built-in SFI (contingency 4). In short, the ontological version of the spirit-niche hypothesis replaces a mysterious coincidence at the foundation of science with a meaningful consonance.

Deciding the issue is not the aim of this essay. The argument given here is intended as an illustration of a general method of discerning theological issues at the foundations of scientific endeavour and a stimulus to further discussion. There are, however, three thoughts that I would like to leave with all of my readers whether they are persuaded of the spirit-niche hypothesis, or not. The first is that the mystery of the origin of built-in SFI constitutes a real lacuna in the fabric of modern science. It is an important problem, and a very interesting one. Scientific endeavour should make it possible to use the tools of science in order to address the necessary conditions or foundations of its own existence. One should not have to abandon the framework of evolutionary adaptation or to resort to panaceas like general intelligence in order to explain one of the greatest mysteries in modern science.

Second, if the solution offered here (the spirit-niche hypothesis) seems improbable to some of my readers, they may be motivated to come up with better ones. That would be the best possible result of this particular investigation.

Third and most importantly, this discussion has shown that spiritual and theological ideas can be explored in the context of scientific endeavour, including the ideas of Darwinian evolution.[122] They can even be formulated in such a way that scientific testing is possible. That conclusion alone is of considerable consequence. A thick description of scientific endeavour can lead to an enrichment of theological endeavour even if it does not provide sufficient grounds for establishing any particular theological dogma.

## *Developing an integrated thick cosmology*

The starting point for this chapter was the fact that the feasibility of scientific endeavour is based on a high degree of consonance between the laws of cosmic creativity and the capabilities of human creativity (SFI). From an evolutionary point of view, this consonance is an unresolved mystery. However, we have argued that the consonance needs to be explained as a special case of preadaptation (or exaptation) and that it calls for serious consideration of the spiritual life of Paleolithic humans (the spirit-niche hypothesis). We have further argued that, in order to succeed, any effort along these lines must consider a thick ontology that allows for a complex spirit world with a multiplicity of layers of phenomena, not unlike the physical universe (or multiverse) studied by modern cosmology (Figure 2.3).

Such an ontological claim leads to additional theological questions and invites comparison with several traditional ideas, particularly those from the Judeo-Christian tradition. Our purpose here is not to defend the ideas of a particular tradition: theological traditions have their own foundations and their own criteria for assessment. Our aim is to select and highlight some of the ideas in the Judeo-Christian tradition that stand out in relation to the spirit-niche hypothesis and thereby relate to the anthropological foundation of scientific endeavour. The fruitfulness of this approach to theological endeavour is validated by the range of such ideas that emerge in the process. In this and the following sections we shall examine the implications of our argument for theological cosmology, the existence of a Creator, and theological anthropology and soteriology. The results are cumulative, each section building on the results of the previous one.

The most direct implications of the spirit-niche hypothesis concern theological cosmology. To begin it is sufficient to harvest the implications of the argument about the ontological status of the spirit world given above. The reason we have taken the existence of the spirit world of Paleolithic shamans seriously within a scientific context is to provide a multilayered niche suited to the preadaptation of the human psyche for the exploration and comprehension of the multilayered physical world. As stated earlier, the force of this argument depends on a homology or consonance between the two worlds – adaptive experience of the one preadapting the human psyche for the other. The entire argument can be stated quite compactly: the degree of consonance that exists between human ingenuity and cosmic creativity is best

---

122 I do not regard postulating a spirit niche as a violation of the principles of natural selection. What is proposed here is an enhancement of the environment in which natural selection takes place. It is not antievolution, but enhanced evolution.

explained by a prior consonance between the physical universe and the spirit world – a consonance of consonances. If there were no consonance of spiritual and physical worlds, adaptation of the human creativity to the spirit world would not explain its preadaptation for scientific exploration of the physical cosmos.[123]

Positing such a consonance implies the existence of a metacosmos or metaverse that embraces one or more physical universes (a multiverse) and one or more spirit worlds in a larger psychophysical unity.[124] The result may be viewed in one of two ways: either as an extension of the material universe known to natural science or as a unification of material and the spiritual universes.

From the perspective of strict empiricism, this metacosmic ontology is a further instance of the proposed generalizations of our concept of the 'universe' that have become common in recent cosmology. As discussed in Chapter 1, some cosmologists have posited parallel physical universes in an all-encompassing multiverse. The validity of such speculative extensions is always contingent on testing – in fact, the value of such extensions is often the fact that they generate new kinds of testing and thereby stimulate new ways of exploring the space-time world. We have considered some ways of testing the spirit-niche hypothesis in the previous section. The result, if sustained, would be a significant thickening of our understanding of the cosmos. The entire argument of this chapter can be summarized by the statement that a thicker view of scientific endeavour leads to a thicker cosmology.

The difference between the generalization to a multiverse and the proposed generalization to a metaverse is that the latter is a metaphysical (or psychophysical) extension. Many scientists and philosophers would invoke the limits of naturalism or empiricism to rule out such an extension – it is a transgression of the empirical limits of scientific cosmology. Such restrictions on cosmology are quite recent in its history. Reasons for such limitations on scientific discourse will be discussed in Chapter 4. Here it will suffice to set the entire issue in historical perspective.

The cosmologies that predominated before the time of Kant and Laplace (the late eighteenth century) were much thicker spiritually than the ones we are familiar with today.[125] In the high Middle Ages and the Renaissance, for example, Aristotelian cosmology surrounded the earth by a series of spherical shells – elemental and celestial – surrounded by a heaven called the 'empyrean', the habitation of God and

---

123 At this stage it is best to describe the consonance of spiritual and physical worlds in rather general terms. There are too many uncertainties on both sides of the equation to be more specific. The main idea is that the exploration of deeper layers of the physical world (after Wigner) is analogous to ascending into 'higher' heavens. On the ancient tradition of spiritual ascent through a sequence of heavens, see, for example, Moshe Idel, *Kabbalah: New Perspectives* (New Haven: Yale University Press, 1988), 88-96; Martha Himmelfarb, *Ascent to Heaven in Jewish and Christian Apocalypses* (New York: Oxford, 1993).

124 The term, 'metaverse', is intended to build on the idea of the 'multiverse' discussed in Chapter 1. The relation of the multiverse to the spiritual worlds is considered in the following section.

125 For the impact of the mechanical philosophy on cosmology in the late eighteenth century, see Kaiser, *Creational Theology*, 335-51.

the elect angels that extended to infinity.[126] In the context of the long-term history of science, the absence of a spirit world in modern cosmology appears to be more a reflection (or even a projection) of the empirical constraints of technological society than it is of any philosophical or scientific necessity.

Even after the demise of the Aristotelian cosmos in the seventeenth century, major scientists posited entities that transcended the limits of the empirical (as it was then understood). Major advances such as Isaac Newton's positing active (supramechanical) principles and James Clerk Maxwell's theorizing about electromagnetic fields would not have been possible without such generalizations of the empirical.[127] As long as extensions of our cosmology are carried out in the interest of scientific explanation rather than introducing miraculous intervention, there is room for the suspension of disbelief.

On the other hand, not everyone works with a strictly naturalist cosmology even today. At the other end of the ideological spectrum, there are people who believe in the existence of separate realms – one material and the other spiritual. From the perspective of such a matter-spirit dualism, the ontology proposed here is not so much a thickening as a unification in cosmology. The material universe and the spiritual compose a single psychophysical metaverse.

Such unification is an objective of all scientific endeavour. It is often assumed that the nature and dynamics of the spiritual world are entirely different from those of the physical cosmos. The Aristotelian cosmology described above was based on a similar dualism: that between the celestial (superlunary) realm governed by perpetual circular motion (motivated by the love of God) and the terrestrial (sublunary) realm governed by transitory linear motions toward or away from the centre of the earth.[128] The birth of modern physical science was based on the work of natural philosophers like Descartes and Newton who postulated universal laws that applied on earth as they did in heaven.

In competition with Aristotelian dualism, there were also Neoplatonist cosmologies that integrated the spirit and physical worlds. In Plato's philosophy the exemplars for all parts of the visible world were located in an invisible world of ideas.[129] In the Jewish and Christian Neoplatonism of the Renaissance, the exemplars were located in a celestial world of angels that mediated between the divine and the mundane. In Aristotelian cosmology, the spirit world or 'empyrean' was just a quasi-spatial extension of the visible heavens. The Neoplatonic world of angels and exemplars, however, was structured in layers parallel to those of the celestial and terrestrial worlds. The significant point, from our perspective, is that the spiritual, celestial and terrestrial levels were homologous: the structures and laws of one paralleled the

---

126 See the illustration from Peter Apian's *Cosmographicus liber* (Cosmographical Book, 1524), in S.K. Heninger, Jr, *The Cosmographical Glass: Renaissance Diagrams of the Universe* (San Marino, Cal.: Huntington Library, 1977), 38, Fig. 28.

127 On Newton and Maxwell's efforts to generalize the mechanical philosophy, see Kaiser, *Creational Theology*, 240-44, 379-88.

128 See Kaiser, *Creational Theology*, 102-6.

129 For a Jewish adaptation of this cosmology, see Philo, *De Confusione Linguarum* 171-2, cited below.

others, even though they operated on different levels. These parallels can clearly be seen in the sixteenth-century diagram, a reproduction of which is shown in Figure 2.5.

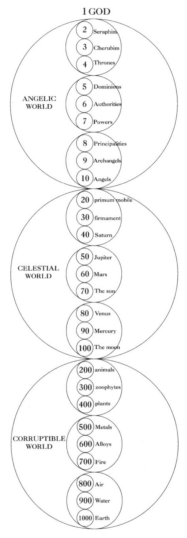

**Figure 2.5 A Neoplatonic cosmos with parallel layered worlds**[130]

This diagram originally illustrated a French translation (1579) of Pico della Mirandola's *Heptaplus*. It portrays the terrestrial (corruptible), celestial and angelic worlds as large contiguous circles, each with a set of three smaller circles in it and three even smaller

130 Adapted from a plate in Nicolas LeFévre de la Boderie's French translation (1579) of Pico della Mirandola's *Heptaplus*, ('Commentary on the Seven Days of Creation', 1488-9), as reprinted in Heninger, *The Cosmographical Glass*, Figure 55.

circles within each of them. It nicely illustrates the idea of a thick cosmology – a metaverse. It also shows a striking consonance between the layered structure of the Angelic World and that of the other two worlds. The message to the sixteenth-century reader was that, even though humans only have immediate access to the lowest of the three worlds (Corruptible World), perfection in that humble sphere prepares them for the angelic world to which they are destined.

The Renaissance diagram is highly schematic: for example, the elements of earth, water and air are represented by three separate small circles at the very bottom. It is also based on several simplifying assumptions about the structure of the metaverse – for example, perfect circles and repeated triads. In order to make it suit our purposes, we would have to replace the series of circles, for instance, with the layers of phenomena and laws like those shown in Figure 2.3.

With this substitution in mind, we can use Pico's multilayered cosmology to illustrate the spirit-niche hypothesis. Early humans were primarily adapted to the everyday world of the elements (Corruptible World), but they also had direct access to the spirit world (Angelic World) through soul travel as evidenced in Paleolithic cave art. As the human psyche developed, it was reprogrammed to explore and interpret successive layers of phenomena in this secondary environment. As a result, humans were preadapted to explore (given the appropriate technologies) and interpret successive layers of phenomena in the intermediate world of physics and cosmology (Celestial World). The message we can read in the diagram is that adaptation to the world of seraphim and cherubim is preadaptation to the cosmos of genetic codes and quantum foam.

To sum up the results of this section on theological cosmology, our quest for a thicker description of scientific endeavour has led us to a thicker, more unified cosmology. To some extent, this shift is a return to the rich philosophical cosmologies of the Middle Ages and the Renaissance. The Renaissance picture needs to be updated with the ideas of present-day science, particularly those of modern cosmology and evolutionary theory. However, the ideas of modern cosmology and anthropology are incomplete. Their specialized methodologies result in the lack of a larger framework that can do justice to the foundations of scientific endeavour; so they need to be integrated in the context of a cosmology like that of Renaissance Neoplatonism. This line of investigation provides us with a second illustration of the transition from the anthropological foundation of scientific endeavour to theological discourse.

*Evidence for a governing Spirit*

What are the implications of the spirit-niche hypothesis for the nature of the spiritual world itself? What are the implications and challenges for our view of the deity? If we postulate the existence of a world of spirits, do we end up with a plurality of gods?

As we saw in the previous section, the spirit-niche hypothesis can be thought of as a consonance of consonances: the degree of consonance between human creativity and cosmic creativity that makes scientific endeavour possible can be explained by a prior consonance between the spiritual and physical worlds. In this approach to theological endeavour, our view of the world of spirits to which the human psyche is adapted must mirror the complex universe (or multiverse) to which the human psyche is preadapted.

Thus far, we have focused on one particular aspect of this consonance – the diversity of layers of the physical world (Figure 2.1). Our conclusion was that there must be a comparable diversity of layers in the environmental niche that preadapted the human psyche for scientific endeavour (Figure 2.3). The question to which we must now turn is whether the deep unity of the physical world is also reflected in a comparable unification of the spirit world.

In order to pursue the idea of unity, let us go back to the model of scientific endeavour proposed by Eugene Wigner that we took as our starting point. As Wigner pointed out, major advances in science involve the construction or discovery of increasingly 'more general and more encompassing' laws of nature.[131] One of the hallmarks of progress in science is the achievement of higher degrees of unification in our description of phenomena.

One of the classic statements of the ideal of unification was made by Niels Bohr in his 1954 lecture on the 'Unity of Knowledge':

> This attitude [of physical science] may be summarized by the endeavour to achieve a harmonious comprehension of ever wider aspects of our situation, recognizing that… any apparent disharmony can be removed only by an appropriate widening of the conceptual framework.[132]

According to Bohr, the pursuit of scientific endeavour depends on our ability to broaden our conceptual tools in order to apprehend the unity underlying disparate phenomena in the natural world. This description is clearly based on Bohr's personal experience of breaking new ground in quantum theory in the early twentieth century. It is a general and inescapable feature of scientific endeavour.[133]

If our explanation of the preadaptation of the human psyche for such an endeavour is to succeed, it must account for the human aptitude for discerning increasingly 'more general and more encompassing' laws of nature (Wigner) or 'ever wider aspects of our situation' (Bohr). If this skill is to be explained by the adaptation of the human psyche to the exploration of successive layers of the spirit world (the spirit-niche hypothesis), then the multifarious phenomena of that spirit world must themselves have a high degree of underlying unity, the discernment of which could have preadapted us for this aspect of built-in SFI.

We have already described the way in which human encounter with the spirit world involves layers of experience similar to the layers of laws in the physical world (Figure 2.3). The further point we need here is that these successive layers of experience must involve cognitive skills of progressive integration based on layers of increasing

---

131 Wigner, *Symmetries and Reflections*, 227.

132 Niels Bohr, 'Unity of Knowledge' (1954), in idem, *Essays 1932-1957 on Atomic Physics and Human Knowledge* (New York: Wiley, 1958), 81-2.

133 Other examples can be culled from the literature, for example, Yukawa, *Creativity and Intuition*, 130-31.

unification in the spirit world itself. Such an underlying unity must be there if the spirit-niche hypothesis is to explain the emergence of built-in SFI as it is intended.[134]

What are the theological implications? We can affirm on the basis of the principles of evolutionary adaptation that any spirit world capable of preadapting the human psyche for scientific endeavour must have a principle of unification that governs it analogous to the unifying principles we have discovered in physics. We are not compelled on logical grounds to identify this governing principle with a personal God. An impersonal principle of unification would work just as well and would provide a closer parallel to the unified field of energies and particles that underlies all physical phenomena. However, two observations can be made to demonstrate the overlap between scientific endeavour (thickly conceived) and theological endeavour.

The first observation is that postulating a unified field of spiritual energies is itself a valid and interesting theological idea. Theologians have often regarded personal language and the more impersonal idea of a *plērōma* (Greek for 'fullness' or 'field') of energies as alternative ways of speaking about God. One example is the early first-century Jewish philosopher, Philo of Alexandria, whose ideas we discussed in Chapter 1. An additional quotation from the same writing of Philo cited earlier will serve to illustrate the idea:

> God is one, but he has around him numberless potencies [Greek, *dynámeis*] which all assist and protect created being…. Through these potencies the incorporeal and intelligible world was framed, the archetype of this phenomenal world, that [intelligible world] being a system of invisible ideal forms [*idéais*], as this [phenomenal world] is of visible material bodies.[135]

Philo was commenting on biblical texts like Genesis 11:5-7 that describe the divine council of God and his angels. The way Philo recast these texts shows that the spirit world could be conceived in the relatively impersonal terms of 'ideal forms' and 'potencies' (or 'powers') that converge in a higher unity ('God is one').

Convergence in a higher unity is precisely the sort of structure in the spirit world that is required in order for the spirit-niche hypothesis to work.[136] Philo's 'ideal forms' were the archetypes for the structures and forces of the phenomenal world we

---

134 The spirit world of Paleolithic humans includes netherworlds as well various heavens. Early Mesopotamian sources like the 'Descent of Inanna' deal with the experience of chthonic realms associated with death and disintegration as much as with the experience of any heavens; for example; Thorkild Jacobsen, *The Treasures of Darkness: A History of Mesopotamian Religion* (New Haven: Yale University Press, 1976), 55-61. Our inference of underlying unity only requires that the Paleolithic soul-travellers found their way beyond the chthonic into a more integrated layer of the spirit world. For example, Clottes and Lewis-Williams view the netherworld as the first of several tiers of the Paleolithic spirit world; Clottes and Lewis-Williams, *Shamans of Prehistory*, 29, 85-6.

135 Philo, *De Confusione Linguarum* 171-2; ET in Loeb Classical Library, *Philo*, 4:103-5. The texts commented on are Gen. 1:26; 3:22; 11:7, and Deut. 10:17.

136 In other texts like *Questions on Exodus* 68, Philo maps out the hierarchy of unifying principles. To begin with there is an 'intelligible world' of many ideal forms (symbolized by the Ark in the Temple); above that there are just two complementary powers (symbolized by the two cherubim – theriomorphs from the Bible); above that there are two superior powers; at the next level there is just one (the Logos); and ultimately there is the 'Existent One' (Loeb

live in. Therefore, adaptation of the human psyche to the world of divine potencies could conceivably preadapt it for the phenomenal world (cf. the cosmology of Pico della Mirandola in Figure 2.5). Philo was quite capable of moving back and forth between the personal language of Scripture and the more impersonal language of Platonic philosophy and demonstrates that the two are equally valid options from a biblical-theological perspective. Though many Jews and Christians may prefer to use personal God-language, one does not have to restrict oneself to personal language about the spirit world in order to work within the Judeo-Christian tradition.

That being said, a second observation to be made is that there are good reasons for the use of personal or at least animate language about the spirit world (in addition to the reasons for viewing God as interpersonal Lord given in Chapter 1). Good reasons, that is, provided that we do not limit the 'personal' to the personality exhibited by humans, particularly humans as conceived in modern Western individualism. The plausibility of a personal God follows from what we have already suggested about the Paleolithic formation of the human psyche. Our explanation of the anthropological foundation of science (built-in SFI) indicates that the unified field of spiritual energies was experienced by Paleolithic humans in the form of spirits with the characteristics of wild animals (theriomorphs). These spirits were apparently more than simple, impersonal forces – they could be conjured, and they could be interrogated concerning the needs of the tribal community.[137] In order to participate in such communication, the human visionary was him or herself transformed into a spirit. According to the prevalent interpretation of the composite, therianthropic (animal-human) forms found in Paleolithic caves, the visionary was transformed into an animal on the same footing (literally) as the other spirits.[138] The paleoshamanic experience was predicated on the interaction and the inter-convertibility of spirits and humans. If there had been no such transformation and interaction on an equal footing, soul travel would probably not have feasible for hunter-gatherers. This much we learn from paleoanthropology.

We may conclude that a spirit world capable of preadapting the human psyche for scientific endeavour must have the capability of taking on quasipersonal, animate forms. Therefore the principle of unification (already posited) must also be a source of animation.[139] One of the more credible interpretations of the symbolic world of

---

Classical Library, *Philo*, Suppl. vol. 2:113-17). This hierarchy extends all the way from the multiplicity of the phenomenal world to the unity of God.

137 Clottes and Lewis-Williams, *Shamans of Prehistory*, 23, 33, 92.

138 See Clottes and Lewis-Williams, *Shamans of Prehistory*, 45-6 (Figures 41, 42, 45), 69 (Figure 64), 94-5 (Figure 96); Lewis-Williams, *Mind in the Cave*, 195 (Figure 44), 202 (Figure 46), 224, 231 (Figure 54), 235-6.

139 In this respect, the spirit world may be different from the physical world as portrayed by modern science, the preponderance of which is understood to be impersonal and inanimate. However, the structures and laws that govern the world of spirits (to which the Paleolithic psyche adapted) would still be impersonal. From a cultural anthropological perspective, what needs to be explained is not the animate, personal character of the spirit world as experienced in pre-modern cultures, but rather the complete deanimation of the physical cosmos in industrialized ones – a topic that we shall take up in Chapter 4 (societal foundation).

Paleolithic humans helps us identify the environmental niche to which SFI is an adaptation as a spirit world with structure, layers of complexity and the capacity for manifesting itself in personal, animate form.

To affirm the existence of a spirit world that is both animated and highly unified does not logically entail the existence of a personal God. Neither the constraints of explaining the emergence of SFI nor the symbolic world of Paleolithic humans requires such a conclusion. Our explanation for the emergence of SFI only requires an environmental niche that exposed early humans to the challenge of negotiating increasing degrees of unification. While Paleolithic humans may well have experienced such a niche in the form of spirits, there is no evidence that they had any experience or concept of a unique God.[140]

For those who expect a proof of the existence of God, there will likely always seem to be a gap in the argument – we can not provide a natural theology in the classic sense of the term (as stated in the Introduction). What we have demonstrated, however, is something – actually two things – just as significant. We have demonstrated the plausibility of a principle of unification and a source of animation for the spiritual aspect of the metaverse. And we have supported the basic point of our entire study, the inevitability of theological discourse and endeavour as part of any attempt to examine the foundations of scientific endeavour.

Our examination of the anthropological foundation of scientific endeavour does not by itself justify a particular theological tradition. However, it does involve us in theological discourse, and it makes an appeal to traditional ideas of God plausible, at least, in certain respects. If there really is a governing principle in the spirit world, then the existence of a God who is capable of self-disclosure as Spirit is a viable option. One may or may not accept such a proposition about a personal God, but it is at least compatible with a thick description of scientific endeavour.

In this respect, our approach to the God question in this chapter closely parallels the one we developed in relation to the cosmic foundation of scientific endeavour in Chapter 1. In the context of the anthropological foundation of scientific endeavour, however, the appropriate term for God would be a governing principle of unity in the spirit world or an animating Spirit, rather than a cosmic Lawgiver. God is animating Governor and governing Spirit.

There are two further steps that we can take in considering the possible existence of a Creator as seen from the perspective of the foundations of scientific endeavour. The first is to search for theological resources that might fit our description of the animating Governor of the spirit world. The other is to return to our quest for a sufficient cause of the emergence of SFI and consider what further steps might be needed there.

---

140 The fact that spirits would sometimes appear unbidden to paleoshamans could have been understood in the context of a tribal society to imply that the spirits were commissioned by a higher authority. But we do not have enough information about the beliefs of Paleolithic humans.

*The Lord of spirits*

If we search the Judeo-Christian tradition for something like a Governor of the spirit world, we need look no farther than the ancient (Near-Eastern) idea of the divine council already discussed in Chapter 1. In the standard model, the sovereign Lord presided at a council of divine beings ('gods' or angels) in heaven as illustrated in texts like Psalm 82:1-2.[141] In the previous discussion, we focused on the 'inter-personal' character of this sovereign Lord. The idea of the divine council provided a conceptual link between transcendence and relational personality. In our present context, however, the feature of the idea of the divine council that is most helpful is its link between unity and multiplicity.

The Old Testament allowed a multiplicity of divine energies, but it also resolved that multiplicity in the sovereignty of a unique 'Lord of hosts' or 'Lord of spirits' who was the sole source of their existence and energy.[142] These subordinate gods were the 'children' of God and served as God's messengers (or angels); they were both animated and commissioned by their Sovereign Lord.[143]

This ancient idea of the divine being is a surprisingly good match for the comprehensive animating Governor we have inferred from the spirit-niche hypothesis. Once again, this does not constitute a proof. For our purposes, it is sufficient to have demonstrated coherence between scientific and theological discourse along these lines. There have been a number of steps in the argument (reviewed in the following section), but most of those steps occurred within the realm of discourse about the foundations of scientific endeavour, not in some neutral domain that is needed to bridge between science and theology. Epistemologically, we have not crossed a bridge, but rather passed through a tunnel. At their foundations, scientific and theological endeavours are entangled in ways that are not evident from their institutional manifestations.

*A sufficient rationale for Science-Fostering Intelligence?*

Our search for a sufficient rationale for the emergence of SFI has led us to posit the existence of a spirit world that parallels the physical universe (or multiverse). The two worlds must have analogously layered structures of successively 'more general and more encompassing' laws (Wigner), and they must have analogous forms of energy (if not animation).

The simplest way to account for such similarities is to carry the principle of unification a step further and posit a common origin for both worlds. The origin of the multilayered spirit world to which Science-Fostering Intelligence is adapted must be the same as that of the multilayered physical world explored by modern

---

141 Psalm 82:1-2 was discussed in Chapter 1, Theological challenges and resources: God as inter-personal Lord.

142 'Lord of hosts' is a common title in the Hebrew Bible (for example, Isa. 6:3). The 'Lord of spirits' is a prominent title of the deity in 1 Enoch 38:2, 4, 6; 39:7-14; passim. 1Enoch is in the Ethiopic canon of the Old Testament and is quoted in the New Testament (Jude 14-15).

143 Cf. 1 Kgs. 22:19-22 ; Job 1:6-12; Ps. 29:1-2; 82:6-7; 103:19-21; 148:1-6; Zech. 1:8-13.

science. The animating Governor must be the same as the Lawgiver of the multiverse discussed in Chapter 1. Though short of being proven, this identification of origins offers an attractive economy of explanation.[144] From a theological standpoint, it also has the merit of matching the first article of biblical faith – belief in a single Creator of 'heaven and earth'.[145] To use the familiar wording of the Nicene Creed, the one God is 'Creator of heaven and earth and of all things visible and invisible'.[146]

Within the constraints of our discussion of scientific endeavour, the existence of a personal Creator like that spoken of in Scripture and Creed is at most a logical possibility. As we saw in Chapter 1, many cosmologists argue that physical universes like our own may have been generated by natural, lawful processes that antecede our universe. In view of the deep consonance between the physical and spiritual worlds that we have postulated to account for SFI, we must consider the possibility that a spirit world like that of Paleolithic humans could also have been generated by lawful processes. Or, if we return to the idea of an overall unity of the physical and spiritual, the two worlds constitute a psychophysical 'metaverse' that was generated in accordance with laws or symmetries comprehensive enough to combine physical and spiritual properties.[147]

This move returns us to the issue of the contingency of lawfulness that we discussed in Chapter 1 (the 'nomistic turn'). Whenever we try to account for the totality of things in terms of pre-existing laws, we are forced to ask about the origin of those laws. Who created them? (James Trefil). What is it that breathes fire into the equations and makes a universe for them to describe? (Stephen Hawking).[148]

The very same questions arise in an exploration of both the cosmic and anthropological foundations of scientific endeavour, and they lead us well inside the terrain of theological endeavour. Given a thick description of these two foundations of scientific endeavour, the existence of a Lawgiver/Governor who created the metaverse is a distinct possibility. The 'Lord of spirits' who presides over the divine council can be thought of as a self-projection of this transcendent Lawgiver into the forms of the spirit world (Ps. 82:1). And a sufficient ground for such projections can again be found in an inter-personal Lord as confessed in the creeds of the Church.

To summarize this extended discussion: Our journey from the anthropological foundation of scientific endeavour to discourse about God has taken several major steps. We have argued:

---

144 The alternative would be to postulate an animating Governor who organized and energized the spirit world along the lines of a pre-existing physical world, or else a Lawgiver of the physical world who organized and energized it as an imitation of a pre-existing spirit world. The latter idea is basically the Demiurge (Yaldabaoth) of Sethian Gnostic texts like the Apocryphon of John and the Gospel of Judas.

145 Pss. 33:6-9; 148:1-6.

146 The Nicene Creed was formulated at the first two ecumenical councils of the Church: Nicea (325) and Constantinople (381). It is the one creed still used in all confessional churches.

147 The genesis of a psychophysical metaverse is a macrocosmic equivalent of the doctrine of Traducianism, according to which each human being originates (from its parents) as a psychophysical whole according to the laws of heredity.

148 James S. Trefil, *Moment of Creation*, 222-3; Stephen Hawking, *Brief History of Time*, 174, both discussed in Chapter 1.

- That Science-Fostering Intelligence (SFI) is a distinct form of human intelligence that calls for scientific explanation (the selection value dilemma).
- That SFI has a genetic base and is adaptive–its origin can be discussed in terms of evolutionary biology without reducing it to a byproduct of general human intelligence (the 'double challenge').
- That SFI was naturally selected for the social benefits of exploring a spirit world (the Spirit Niche Hypothesis and a 'thick epistemology').
- That the spirit world required early humans to negotiate a succession of layers of increasing unification comparable to those in the physical world of modern science (a 'thick ontology').
- That the principle of unification in the spirit world is also its source of animation.
- That the necessary consonance of spiritual and space-time worlds indicates a larger psychophysical 'metaverse' with its own laws and its own Lawgiver, which, for consistency, must be the same as the Lawgiver of the multiverse discussed in Chapter 1.

Each of these steps can be debated, so our result falls short of the kind of proof sought by traditional natural theology. But these steps demonstrate a linkage between the technical issues of natural science and the categories of confessional theology.

It is not our intention to use scientific ideas to demonstrate the existence of God or the existence of angels. We investigate the theological implications of scientific work as a way of generating interest in both science and theology as human endeavours. For those who love theology, I hope to have stimulated greater respect for the amazing development of natural science. For those who are already science-minded, I hope to have generated some interest in theological discourse. For all interested readers, I hope to have highlighted the value of some aspects of the biblical tradition that have been neglected in recent theology.

*Humanity in the image of God?*

In discussing of the anthropological foundation of scientific endeavour, we have developed a scenario for the origin of SFI in the Paleolithic era (African Stone Age). Our assumption all along was that all human attributes may be treated as evolutionary adaptations to environmental constraints. In fact, we have insisted on the idea that SFI is an adaptive trait in order to reconstruct the kind of behaviour that might have fostered early human survival and reproduction and thereby coded SFI into the human genome.

This evolutionary approach to the origin of human intelligence creates a huge challenge for theological endeavour. On the basis of texts like Genesis 1:26-27, Jews and Christians have believed humanity to be specially created by God as a reflection of the divine image and likeness. But just what does it mean to be created in the divine image? It means that humanity is unique among the forms of life on earth, but there has never been a consensus among students of Scripture about the nature (or even the degree) of that uniqueness. Interpretations have ranged from the idea that the human body is analogous to the visible form of the divine being (Exod. 24:10; Isa. 6:1; Ezek. 1:26) to the claim that human capacity for relationships and self-giving love reflects the intra-trinitarian relations (John 17:26).[149] Nor is there any consensus on how the story of creation in Genesis 1 relates to an evolutionary approach to human origins. Is the origin the result of continuous natural selection, or is it the result of divine intervention? Here we shall address this issue by drawing out the implications of the spirit-niche hypothesis.

One fairly broad interpretation of human origins would be to view the adaptive process itself as an aspect of the divine image. In Chapter 1, we cited the ancient idea of God's attributes being diffracted in space and time. The very first instance of adaptation to a new environment was the divine self-projection into the realm of finite form. In this sense, the image of God's adaptation can be seen in all life on earth (and possibly elsewhere in the universe) – wherever the laws of biological evolution pertain.[150] The strength of this option is its universality – the image is not restricted to any particular species. The weakness is that it is too general to help us with the focus of this chapter, the anthropological foundation of scientific endeavour, which is unique to *Homo sapiens* on this earth. We need, therefore, to ask what is distinctive about the evolution and adaptation of humanity and how that might relate to the divine image.

In the reconstruction of the development of early humanity that we have proposed, the spirit-niche hypothesis, the truly unique feature of human evolution was the practice of soul journey. The human psyche was formed and reformed by the cultivation of journeys into a spirit world and the symbolic articulation of the novel patterns of that world. As far as we know, no other species on earth engages in this sort of behaviour (though some do experience hallucinations). So one aspect of the divine image that is unique to humanity might best be exemplified in the ecstatic visions of early *Homo sapiens* as evidenced in Paleolithic cave art.

Viewing the capacity for soul journey as the image of God (or one aspect of the divine image) is a direct result of the methodology we have followed in this study. It has significant implications for the relation between humanity and God, for the reading of Scripture, for our assessment of patterns of religious behaviour and liturgy today (primal and Pentecostal), and for a theological assessment of modern scientific endeavour.

(1) What are the implications for the relation between humanity and God? According to the scenario that we have developed for the origin of SFI, an important aspect of the image of God resides in the ability of humans to detach their attention from their immediate surroundings and ecstatically engage an alien world.[151] This result raises a

---

149 For a concise summary of the options, see H. D. McDonald, *The Christian View of Man* (London: Marshall, Morgan & Scott, 1981), 33-41.

150 The image of the self-diffracting God (*Lógos prophorikós*) may also be seen in the fundamental laws of the universe, multiverse, or metaverse, particularly in the symmetries embedded in those laws and the breaking of those symmetries.

151 The ability to discern invisible realities and commune with the angels was described by Athanasius as part of the divine image humanity; *Contra gentes* 2, 33.

theological difficulty in that 'self-detachment' is not normally placed among the divine attributes. So how could this human trait reflect the image or likeness of the divine?

One way of answering this question would be to return to one of the theological traditions we discussed in relation to the cosmic foundation of scientific endeavour. The biblical and patristic understanding of primal creation involves God's self-projection into the alien realm of finite form. Creation for God is an ecstatic act of self-transcendence or detachment that could meaningfully be compared to the flight of the shaman's soul into the spirit world.[152] In both cases, the subject in question must take on a new form and adapt to structures and limitations that are alien to its proper frame of reference.

The result of this interpretation of primal creation is an unforeseen homology between the creation of the cosmos and the creation of humanity (understood here as an evolutionary process). The formation of the human psyche through soul-travel mirrors the divine ecstasy in primal creation. Human soul journey into the spirit world is actually a microcosm of divine self-projection into the realm of finite form. One is the mirror image of the other.

(2) What are the implications for our reading of Scripture? Since we have related the idea of the divine image to that of soul journey, several possibilities arise for the interpretation of the Bible. Our point of contact with the Paleolithic symbolic world was the reciprocity between humans and spirits. As shown on the painted cave walls, spirits could project themselves into the life-world of humans. Conversely, humans could project themselves into the spirit world. If so, the human attribute of self-projection mirrors the ecstatic character of the spirits as well as that of the 'Lord of the spirits'. Self-projection characterizes all the members of the divine council (in differing degrees), not just God.

From this anthropological perspective, we can address the primary text describing the creation of humanity, Genesis 1:26, *Then God said, "Let us make humankind in our image, according to our likeness....* It has often been recognized that the royal 'we' in this passage introduces a divine decree in the council of God and the angels.[153] In other words, the divine image in humans is a reflection of the life of the angels as well as of God. Viewing the formation of the human psyche in relation to soul journey gives us one way of seeing how that might have been understood in the ancient world. Both God and the angels are capable of leaving their heavenly domains in order to converse with humans. Humans formed in their image and likeness can leave earth temporarily in order to enter heaven and join the divine council. So we may expect the image of God to involve human participation on the divine council. Such participation is one of the roles of the prophet, as shown by both the Hebrew Bible and the New Testament:

---

152 The ecstatic self-projection of the Creator is nicely illustrated in Michelangelo's 'The Creation of Adam', painted on the ceiling of the Sistine Chapel in 1508-1512.

153 On the divine council in the Hebrew Bible, see the discussion of Psalm 82:1-2 in Chapter 1.

I saw the Lord sitting on his throne, with all the host of heaven standing beside him to the right and to the left of him. And the Lord said, 'Who will entice Ahab....?' (1 Kings 22:19-20)

In the year that King Uzziah died, I saw the Lord sitting on a throne, high and lofty.... Then I heard the voice of the Lord saying, 'Whom shall I send and who will go for us?' (Isaiah 6:1-8)

But, if they [the false prophets] had stood in my council, then they would have proclaimed my word to my people.... (Jeremiah 23:18-22)

I know a person in Christ who fourteen years ago was caught up to the third heaven. ... And I know that such a person ...was caught up into Paradise and heard things that are not to be told, that no mortal is permitted to repeat.... (2 Corinthians 12:2-4)

After this I looked, and there in heaven a door stood open! And the first voice ... said, 'Come up here, and I will show you what must take place after this.' At once I was in the spirit, and in heaven stood a throne with one seated on the throne! (Revelation 4:1-8, 5:8-10)

Micaiah, Isaiah, Jeremiah, the apostle Paul, and the apocalypticist John were all Jewish prophets. Many features of their prophetic experiences are the same as those of soul journeys as we have described them: detachment from the empirical world; visions of the spirit world; conversation with God and the angels; symbolic accounts of these experiences; learnings of benefit to their communities.[154] If so, the function of the divine image in humans can be understood in terms the capacity for participation in the divine council as in the narratives of the prophets and apostles.[155]

(3) What are the implications for our assessment of patterns of religious behaviour and liturgy today? Theologians have traditionally located the divine image in human sovereignty over nature, or in human reason, or in male-female parity (all based on Gen. 1:27-28).[156] Generally they have seen in these attributes something pristine that has since been damaged or lost. As early as the Book of Genesis, spiritual decline has been associated with the founding of cities and the development of technologies of power. The implication seems to be that humans fell from an ideal state into civilization with all of its discontents.[157] Much theological interest in the divine image relates to the sense of loss and the possibility of restoration: the primal innocence of the relationship between humans and God has been lost, but it can be recovered through various religious beliefs and practices.

---

154 According to Johannes Lindblom and Yochanan Muffs, the ancient Arabian shaman or *kahin* was a predecessor of the Hebrew prophet; Lindblom, *Prophecy in Ancient Israel* (Oxford: Blackwell, 1973), 7-8, 33; Muffs, *Love and Joy: Law, Language and Religion in Ancient Israel* (New York: Jewish Theological Seminary of America, 1992), 25, 38-9.

155 H. Wheeler Robinson pointed out that the image in which humans were created in Gen. 1:26 was that of the 'sons of God" who were members of the divine council; Robinson, 'The Council of Yahweh', *Journal of Theological Studies* 45 (1944), 154.

156 McDonald, *The Christian View of Man*, 33-41.

157 Gen. 4:17-24. A typical modern expression can be found in Jacques Ellul, *The Meaning of the City*, trans. Dennis Pardee (Grand Rapids, Eerdmans, 1970).

Although we have located it in the kind of ecstatic soul journeying normally associated with primal religions, the divine image suggested by our examination of the foundations of scientific endeavour fits in with the traditional picture rather well. In the dominant societies of Asia and Europe, ecstatic spirituality has largely been marginalized and replaced by reliance on text-based rituals.[158] In this sense, the divine image may have been limited, if not lost, for vast numbers of people living in industrialized societies, thus substantiating the traditional view of the image and its loss.[159]

The practice of soul journey continues to thrive in many hunter-gatherer and pastoral peoples, whose technologies have continued to evolve in a more symbiotic relationship with their natural surroundings. Soul journey has also continued to be prominent in African, Asian and Native American civilizations that have resisted or protested industrial technologies in various ways.[160] And spiritual ecstasy is practiced in the charismatic churches of Latin America and the independent prophet-centered

---

158 Careful historians like Douglas Winiarski have noted that heavenly journeys were repeatedly experienced by laypeople right up into the nineteenth century. Written expressions of such journeys were often based on literary conventions and so may not directly reflect an engagement with previously unknown aspects of the spirit world; Winiarski, 'Souls Filled with Ravishing Transport: Heavenly Visions and the Radical Awakening in New England', *William & Mary Quarterly* 61 (Jan. 2004), 3-45 (34-5). Carol Zaleski finds that European Christian otherworld journeys among elites were more literary than actively experiential after the twelfth to thirteenth centuries; Zaleski, *Otherworld Journeys: Accounts of Near-Death Experience in Medieval and Modern Times* (New York: Oxford University Press, 1987), 6. However, night soul journeys are still well documented among the peasants and artisans of sixteenth-century Europe, particularly prior to the climax of the witch craze; see, for example, Wolfgang Behringer, *Shaman of Oberstdorf: Chonrad Soelckhlin and the Phantoms of the Night*, trans. H.C, Erik Midelfort (Charlottesville: University of Virginia Press, 1998), 24-5, 70-71, 92-3, 144, passim. Jewish mystical journeys have been documented well into the twentieth century; see, for example, Louis Jacobs, *Jewish Mystical Testimonies* (New York: Schocken Books, 1977[1], 1996[2]).

159 The ideal of ecstatic soul journey was preserved by poets and sages of many nations, particularly ancient China; David Hawkes, trans. *The Songs of the South: An Ancient Chinese Anthology of poems by Qu Yuan and Other Poets* (London: Penguin Books, 1985), 42-51, 73-8 (on the *Li sao*); Jordan Paper, *The Spirits Are Drunk: Comparative Approaches to Chinese Religion* (Albany: SUNY Press, 1995), 55-7, 133-6 (on the *Zhuang zi*). There are also vestiges of soul journey among institutional religions. Christian rituals like the Eucharistic prayers were viewed as an elevation of the soul into the presence of the Lord Christ as late as John Calvin and Jonathan Edwards; Kaiser, 'Climbing Jacob's Ladder: John Calvin and the Early Church on Our Eucharistic Ascent to Heaven', *Scottish Journal of Theology* 56 (2003), 247-67.

160 For example, shamanism continues to be practiced in social niches of industrialized societies like China, Korea and Japan; see Clark Chilson and Peter Knecht, *Shamans in Asia* (London: RoutledgeCurzon, 2003). On the use of ecstatic states in resistance to industrial life, see Aihwa Ong, *Spirits of Resistance and Capitalist Discipline: Factory Women in Malaysia* (Albany: SUNY Press, 1987).

churches of Africa, in both of which a recent historian has seen the beginnings of a new 'Christendom'.[161]

The results of this part of our investigation suggest a fresh way of looking at the much needed reformation of religious practices in Western Judaism and Christianity. For cultural reasons, it is neither necessary nor feasible for us to practice shamanic rituals, but we do need to restore the ecstatic aspect of the divine image so severely limited by the development of nature-dominating technologies. We shall return to this topic in our analysis of technological society in Chapter 4.

(4) What are the implications for a theological assessment of modern scientific endeavour? One of the more interesting results of our investigation is the idea that scientific endeavour is the foster child of a form of intelligence adapted to a very different environment from that of modern technoscience. Science-Fostering Intelligence was the natural parent of an older child, paleoshamanic soul journey. Scientific endeavour is an unanticipated exaptation of this ancient human trait.

Many of the basic features of soul journeying – the capacity for detachment from the immediate empirical environment, engagement in a world of symbolic forms and abstract entities, intuition of solutions to unsolved problems, articulation in community based language – characterize scientific, as much as it does shamanistic, endeavour. In fact, we took this underlying similarity between these two endeavours as the heuristic basis for developing the spirit-niche hypothesis and thereby explaining the emergence of SFI.

If such is the case, then the divine image that was formed in humanity through adaptation to the heights and depths of the spirit world can also be seen in the imaginative engagement of modern scientists in the heights and depths of the physical world. In other words, the divine image can take different seemingly incompatible forms in different cultural contexts.

Science and spirituality are both complex phenomena, each with many expressions and applications that are alien to the other. At their very centre, however, science and spirituality are kinsfolk. In spite of their differing and sometimes antagonistic cultural manifestations, science and spirituality are of the same parentage as far as genetic intelligence is concerned. Both are rooted in the divine image or, at least, in that aspect of the divine image that accounts for the emergence of SFI.

## Summary

In this chapter we have taken the existence of a species with Science-Fostering Intelligence (SFI) as another precondition, an anthropological foundation, for scientific endeavour. We have shared the wonder and puzzlement of practicing scientists in their realization that the intellectual gifts they rely on had no survival

---

161 Philip Jenkins, *The Next Christendom: The Coming of Global Christianity* (Oxford: Oxford University Press, 2002); see esp. pp. 47-51, 119-21. The title Jenkins gives to the first of these two sections is 'Out of Africa' – an oblique reference to the current theory about the origin of *H. sapiens* in Africa.

(or reproduction) value in the Paleolithic era, when the human psyche evolved in its modern form. In spite of this scientific paradox (the Survival Value Dilemma), we have insisted on using the principles of evolutionary adaptation for understanding the emergence of SFI in the Paleolithic period. The explanations offered in current scientific literature fail to meet this double challenge. We have formulated a working hypothesis by taking the spirit world with which early humans apparently interacted as an environmental niche within which such adaptation could have occurred. Once again our attempt to press scientific enterprise to account for its own foundations involves us in theological discourse and leads to further theological questions. Scientific endeavour blends into theological endeavour without any gap between them. What we have constructed are more like tunnels than bridges.

These theological questions raise important challenges for the contemporary theological traditions, and we have mined the Judeo-Christian tradition for resources to address these challenges. The theological concepts we have explored include biblical and Renaissance cosmologies that were thick enough to include spirit worlds, belief in a God who is the animating Governor of the spirit world as well as the Lawgiver of the psychophysical metaverse, and the formation of the human psyche in the image of the ecstatic Creator – an image reflected in scientific endeavour as well as in ecstatic religion.

As in Chapter 1, our investigation does not attempt to prove any given theological doctrine. Warrant for belief in a personal God would still require support on other grounds such as those of personal disclosure. But our investigation continues to demonstrate the viability of disciplined theological endeavour in the context of a thick description of scientific endeavour, this time with a special focus on its anthropological foundation.

In the following chapter we shall examine another precondition, a cultural foundation, for scientific endeavour. We shall explore how the emergence of modern science was facilitated and sustained a culture of Science-Fostering Belief – a culture that encoded the very ideas we have been discussing in Chapters 1 and 2: the lawfulness of the physical world and the capacity of the human mind for discerning those laws.

# CHAPTER THREE

# Cultural Foundation: The Challenge of Science-Fostering Beliefs

**Abstract** (with brief definitions of technical terms for reference)
The viability of scientific endeavour requires special conditions of the traditions of belief in which scientists are nurtured. Science-Fostering Beliefs (SFB) are needed to enable people to devote their lives to scientific endeavour with confidence that they will be successful. Among these is the belief that humans are capable of understanding the heights and depths of a cosmos they have never experienced directly. The prescientific cultural traditions from which modern science emerged must have portrayed the cosmos as sufficiently intelligible and the human psyche as adequately intelligent. Historians of science have documented such traditions in medieval and early modern European cultures, where they are found to be based on the idea of divine creation. We further trace the roots of this historic 'creationist' tradition back to the ancient Near East, Israel and Greece. Unfortunately, historical treatments of theology have largely neglected these aspects of the idea of creation, thereby reinforcing the erroneous impression that natural science is a nontheological endeavour. The challenge to theology is to bring into focus the role of creational beliefs in the history of secular disciplines like the sciences. A thick description of scientific endeavour, therefore, leads to a thicker view of historical theology.

**Keywords**: Albert Einstein, ancient Near East, apocalyptic, Cappadocian fathers, Greek philosophers, historical theology, history of science, image of God, Johannes Kepler, Paul Davies, Philo of Alexandria, wisdom tradition.

In this chapter we examine the *cultural foundation* of scientific endeavour and its implications for theological endeavour. We begin with a description of the cultural foundation and the mystery that scientists find embedded within it – a mystery that arises largely from a deficient view of the history of culture. We then use tools from the history of ideas to address this deficiency and to explore the possible implications for theological endeavour – in this case, biblical and historical theology. Although we are still examining the foundations of scientific endeavour, our discussion will be more historical and less scientific or philosophical.

We have defined natural science as the endeavour to explore and understand all accessible features of the space-time world. In Chapters 1 and 2, we examined the existence of a lawful universe and of a species with the intelligence required for discerning the laws of that universe as prerequisites for scientific endeavour. The focus of this chapter is another implication of our definition: the endeavour to explore all accessible features of the space-time world implies that the possibility of discerning law-like features of the universe is accepted by many people as a matter of belief, which I shall refer to as Science-Fostering Belief (or beliefs).[1]

All of the foundations of scientific endeavour are forward contingent. The mere existence of a lawful universe does not guarantee that it produce a species capable of investigating its laws. By the same logic, the mere existence of a species with the prerequisite intelligence (SFI) does not guarantee that members of that species will want to do scientific research or that any society will value and support their efforts.

Scientific endeavour does not exist in a world of its own. It requires an entire culture of Science-Fostering Belief in order for significant numbers of people to be motivated to pursue scientific work and for adequate resources to be directed toward scientific endeavour rather than toward more immediate goals. SFB is therefore a third, cultural, foundation – that underlies all science education and research. This cultural foundation is a layer that further thickens our view of scientific endeavour and that calls for investigation in its own right.[2]

Present-day scientists are not generally in the habit of articulating these beliefs in their daily work. SFB is a property of the culture in which new young scientists are trained and sustained. It may only be a tacit belief in the daily work of most scientists, but it is very real nonetheless.[3] If a lawful universe and Science-Fostering Intelligence (SFI) can together be thought of as the natural hardware required for scientific endeavour, such Science-Fostering Beliefs (SFB) constitute the necessary software that motivates scientists and sustains them in their endeavours.[4]

As always, we must be alert to the element of contingency and ask 'why?' Why should any people be so audacious as to think that they could use their meagre brains to investigate the heights and depths of the universe? The question is still why any culture or subculture that ever existed should have cultivated and sustained such an audacious belief.

Exploring the cultural roots of SFB will lead us to an examination of the historic 'creationist tradition' and to rethink the relationship between scientific and theological endeavour. In spite of the fact that the interests of science and theology have at times

---

1    I use the term 'belief' to describe the working assumptions that sustain scientific endeavour. As shown below, these beliefs originated in religious 'beliefs', but to avoid confusion I shall refer to the latter as ideas or convictions or religious faith. I intend to show that scientists are 'believers' even if they do not practice a religion.

2    The analysis here is restricted to finding conditions for the possibility of scientific endeavour. Historical conditions that may have impelled particular people to pursue science within the context of those conditions are likely to vary from individual to individual. Here we focus on the common cultural frame that made scientific endeavour possible – a necessary though not sufficient condition for such endeavour.

3    Tacit knowledge (or awareness) is knowledge upon which people rely without necessarily thinking about it; see Michael Polanyi, *The Tacit Dimension* (New York: Doubleday-Anchor, 1966), 9-10, passim.

4    Belief in the possibility of doing science is actually only part of the software needed. It must be supplemented and reinforced by years of training in mathematics and other disciplines. Here we are concerned with the beliefs that motivate people to undergo such training and to devote their lives to advancing their discipline.

conflicted, the two are much more closely related than we often assume. As recent studies have shown, the history of science overlaps significantly with the history of theology.[5] The tendency to treat them as two separate phenomena like skepticism and faith is a peculiar result of modern secularization – a historical process of societal differentiation that we shall examine in the following chapter.[6]

## The contingency of belief: four clarifications

Before trying to account for the cultural foundation, it will be helpful to clarify the nature of our inquiry in four ways.

We have first to reckon with the fact that those who laid the foundations of modern science in the sixteenth and seventeenth centuries were Europeans who were all raised as Christians and who approached their work within an intellectual framework strongly influenced by biblical teachings. The result is that one particular religious tradition is singled out for examination. It is not exclusively a Christian tradition. The 'creationist tradition' can be thought of more like a tree with roots going back to the ancient Near East, Israel and Greece and branches reaching out to medieval Islam and Judaism.[7] It was in the process of formation centuries before Christianity became a distinct religion, and its values have spread across all cultures in modern times. However, our methodology for investigating the various foundations of scientific endeavour leads us to focus on Christian theology as an integral part of the foundation discussed in this chapter, and not just as a particular confession to be challenged by our findings about those foundations as in previous chapters. Here Christian faith is singled out by historical fact, not just by confessional choice.

Our focus on the history of European science should not be misinterpreted to imply that non-Western theological traditions can not be science-fostering. It is true that our discussions in Chapters 1 and 2 might suggest an implication along such lines. In considering the cosmic foundation of scientific endeavour, we explored the possibility that there might a plurality of universes, the vast majority of which would not be lawful enough to allow scientific investigation. In discussing the anthropological foundation, we considered the anthropoid forbears of *Homo sapiens* and their various descendents, of which *Homo sapiens* appears to be the only one that ever had the capacity for scientific endeavour – the marvel is that even humans have this capacity. So it might be inferred by analogy that, of all the historic cultures of the world, the vast majority could not have had the inclinations or beliefs needed to develop modern science on their own. However, such analogies between natural evolution and cultural developments are extremely hazardous. It does not follow that non-Western cultures

---

5    See, for example, Kaiser, *Creational Theology*.

6    As noted already in Chapter 1, I take issue with Chet Raymo's characterization of good scientists as natural skeptics even though they 'trust the ability of the human mind to make sense of the world'; Raymo, *Skeptics and True Believers*, 2-4.

7    I have borrowed the term 'creationist tradition' from Richard C. Dales, 'A Twelfth-Century Concept of the Natural Order', *Viator* 9 (1978), 191-2. This historic 'creationist tradition' is a composite of beliefs that supports scientific endeavour and is not to be confused with 'creation science'.

lack the capability of sustaining scientific endeavour or even that progressive science might not have originated independently outside of Western Europe.

The point that other cultures can embody SFB can best be made by citing a few examples. Ancient Chinese texts like *Master Lü's Springs and Autumns* (c. 240 BCE) affirmed belief in the symmetry and lawfulness of the complementary forces that emerge from the Supreme Oneness.[8] Such beliefs are very similar to those we shall discover at the foundation of modern Western science. Similarly, the Holy Qur'an portrayed the sun, moon and heavens as subject to the irrevocable ordinances of Allah – a tradition that sustained the development of Islamic science.[9] In a matter of centuries, Islamic science developed mathematical and experimental techniques that would not appear among early Western scientists until centuries later.[10] Even given the limits of human nature, cultures are capable of adapting to new challenges much more readily than biological species can. So any analogy to the treatment of Science-Fostering Intelligence breaks down at this point. In this chapter, we are focusing on the cultural frame that lies at the foundation of modern Western science, so we have to deal with the Judeo-Christian tradition from which our culture inherited its Science-Fostering Beliefs.

On the other hand, there are definite constraints on any culture that would promote scientific endeavour. While the kind of beliefs needed to foster science are not exclusively based on the Judeo-Christian tradition, they are not universal either. A culture that can promote scientific research must inculcate the belief that the universe is intelligible in principle, and that humans have the ability to learn more and more about it. Humans also need to be made aware of their limitations, and most religious traditions do a good job at that. But forms of nihilism or fundamentalism (Confucianist, Islamic or Christian) that undermine confidence in the lawfulness of

---

8    *Lü shi chun qiu* V.2; ET in *The Annals of Lü Buwei*, trans. John Knoblock and Jeffrey Riegel (Stanford: Stanford University Press, 2000), 136-9; cf. Derk Bodde, *Chinese Thought, Society, and Science: The Intellectual and Social Background of Science and Technology in Pre-Modern China* (Honolulu: University of Hawaii Press, 1991), 335-6, for a variety of similar texts from ancient China. Other ancient Chinese texts like the famous Chuang Tzu (*Zhuang zi*, chaps 2, 5) tend rather to emphasize the difference between conventional human understanding and the laws of Heaven. On the debate concerning the limits of human knowledge (and power) in the Late Warring States and Han periods, see Michael J. Puett, *To Become a God: Cosmology, Sacrifice, and Self-Divinization in Early China* (Cambridge, Mass: Harvard University Press, 2004), 109-112, 212-13, 257-8.

9    Qur'an Sûrah 13:2 ('each running to an appointed term'); 36:37-8 ('each in an orbit'); 41:12 ('in each heaven its mandate'); ET in *The Meaning of the Glorious Koran*, trans. Mohammed Marmaduke Pickthall (New York: New American Library, 1953), 182, 316, 341.

10   The thirteenth-century Syrian physician, Ibn al-Nafîs, developed a theory of the circulation of blood very similar to the later ideas of William Harvey. His treatise was preserved by a Cairo hospital, but remained unknown until its modern rediscovery. In the 16th century, Taqî al Dîn wrote books on astronomy, optics and mechanical clocks. As court astronomer to the Sultan, al Dîn built an observatory in Istanbul (1577) comparable to that of Tycho Brahe in Denmark (begun 1576). Al Dîn's observatory was later destroyed on the recommendation of the chief Mufti and was never rebuilt; see Bernard Lewis, *What Went Wrong? The Clash Between Islam and Modernity in the Middle East* (New York: Oxford University Press, 2002), 79-81.

the universe or the Science-Fostering Intelligence of humanity will not be able to sustain scientific endeavour over the long term.

A second preliminary point to be made is that no set of beliefs – science-fostering or otherwise – has ever predetermined the course of human culture. Today we often take public support for the sciences for granted. We know that a career in science is possible for anyone with the ability and the inclination to pursue the subject. Universities and research institutes provide the resources to make such careers possible and profitable. Without such support and the institutions that sustain it, scientific endeavour as we know it would not be possible.

Cross-cultural travel (or reading) reveals that such institutions are neither universal nor inevitable. At present, they are becoming more prevalent as industrial society globalizes, but there are still many areas of the world where people have more pressing – and to them more important – things to attend to than the balance of matter and anti-matter or the circulation of the mantle in the Earth's interior. Even within industrial culture the inevitability of scientific developments must be questioned. The research institutes and universities we take for granted have only originated within the last few hundred years.[11] Prior to that time civic leaders were more likely to support the building of cathedrals or the quest for the philosopher's stone than they were to support scientific endeavour as we know it today. Historically speaking, therefore, the emergence of modern science was far from inevitable in Western Europe, to say nothing of other parts of the world.

Third, there is no need to suppose that every individual will value or support the work of scientists even in a culture that on the whole does support scientific endeavour. Western Europe and North America are highly scientific cultures, yet there has been and continues to be skepticism, if not downright opposition, with regard to basic forms of scientific research. Cultures of belief establish certain propensities, but they are far too complex and conflicted to have exactly the same effect on all of their members.[12]

Human cultures differ enormously in the kinds of occupations they encourage, or even allow. The cultures of India traditionally have provided a way for many (if not most) individuals to graduate from the demands of socioeconomic life and seek enlightenment. Even if only a minority of people is inclined or even allowed to pursue such a life trajectory, it is a distinct option in everyone's mind. The same is true of many industrialized cultures in regard to the development of careers in science. So a science-sustaining culture need not be totally committed to scientific endeavour any more than the cosmos in which we live is readily intelligible or the human brain is ideally suited for scientific research.

A fourth preliminary point is that I hope to reverse the common perception of the science-theology relationship as one of conflict or incommensurability. Historically,

---

11 It is difficult to adjudicate competing claims for the earliest sustainable research institutes, but the idea was first advocated by seventeenth-century Europeans such as Francis Bacon, Jan Comenius and Samuel Hartlib. The origin of research universities will be discussed in Chapter 4.

12 See Kaiser, *Creational Theology*, 47-59, on the genesis of conflicts within the creationist tradition itself.

there have been instances in which religiously motivated authorities have felt threatened enough to oppose particular scientific ideas. The Congregation of the Holy Office's pressuring Galileo to renounce his Copernican convictions and the prosecution of John Thomas Scopes for teaching the evolution of humanity in an American public school are two of the best known examples.[13] The publicity that has grown up around instances like these has sometimes been generalized into the dogma that religious faith is inherently opposed to scientific endeavour.

In order to counteract this impression, I shall refer to scientists who have been sustained by the creational teachings of the Church.[14] I shall also give some examples of recent scientists who are not committed to a particular creed or institution, but who recognize the importance of biblical teachings for their profession. Historians of science have tried to set the record straight on this matter,[15] but historians of theology and religion still tend to ignore the role of the theological doctrines in the history of science. Accordingly, I shall make a case for broadening and thickening our teaching of biblical and historical theology in order to exhibit its implications for secular disciplines like the natural sciences.

## The origin of Science-Fostering Belief (SFB)

With these four clarifications in mind, we can now focus on the main question of this chapter: what was the source of the conviction of early modern scientists that they could probe beneath the surface phenomena and discover the underlying laws of nature? What made them think that the enormous amount of time they spent investigating seemingly intractable problems would lead to improved understanding? Why did anyone ever dream that questions as abstruse as those scientists investigate could ever be answered?

### An appropriate method of accounting for Science Fostering Beliefs

As in earlier chapters, we need to select a method that is appropriate to the question at hand. In Chapter 1 we used some of the ideas of current cosmology in order to explain why our universe is lawful enough to allow scientific endeavour. In Chapter 2 we used the principles of evolutionary biology, supplemented by cognitive psychology and current interpretations of archaeological artifacts, to investigate the origin of the intelligence needed to pursue scientific endeavour (SFI).

---

13  See the excellent studies by David Lindberg and Edward Larsen in *When Science and Christianity Meet*, ed. David C. Lindberg and Ronald L. Numbers (Chicago: University of Chicago Press, 2003).

14  The word 'scientist' did not come into use until the nineteenth century when various sciences became professionalized. Before that time, most scientists thought of themselves as natural philosophers or simply 'philosophers'. Using a term like 'scientist' for the earlier centuries is technically anachronistic but necessary in order to allow comparison and critique.

15  For example, David C. Lindberg and Ronald L. Numbers, 'Beyond War and Peace: A Reappraisal of the Encounter between Christianity and Science', *Perspectives on Science and Christian Faith* 39 (Sept. 1987), 140-49.

The question before us now – the origin of Science-Fostering Beliefs – has to do with a historically conditioned culture and so can not be addressed with the tools of natural science. The pursuit of natural science is the subject of our study, but any method for addressing the cultural foundation that supports natural science must be based on the human or social sciences – the application of which to science is sometimes lumped together under the rubric of 'science studies'. Science studies and their methodologies must be included if scientific endeavour is to be self-explanatory. But which social scientific methodology is appropriate here? There are several possibilities to consider.

One possibility would be to turn to the psychologists. Cognitive psychologists have hypothesized, for example, that humans are programmed to posit meaning even in the most accidental of situations. In this perspective, the belief that there is meaning even in the events of the natural world is a universal trait of *Homo sapiens* rather than a characteristic of a peculiar culture. If such a trait could be well defined and substantiated, it might be considered as a further precondition for scientific endeavour: any species that did not persistently look for meaning in events would not be likely to pursue scientific endeavour. This universal precondition of belief in meaning is therefore more fundamental than the culturally contingent beliefs we are concerned with in our present investigation.

In order to illustrate the point and support our preliminary assessment, let us consider one rather plausible psychological explanation of the human propensity for meaning. Extensive research has been done with split-brain patients – people whose *corpus callosum* has been severed so that the cerebral hemispheres operate independently of each other. In studying such patients, cognitive neuroscientists learn that the world can appear differentl to each of the two hemispheres. Yet split-brain patients are like everyone else in that they normally experience the world as a consistent picture. Michael Gazzaniga and his associates have found that our picture of the world around us is automatically constructed in a unified way from the bits of information gathered by the modules of our brains. An 'interpreter', located in the left hemisphere, provides an integrated picture that makes sense of these disparate inputs.

In one of their experiments, Gazzaniga's team used a standard procedure to project different visual images into the two cerebral hemispheres (using different sides of the retina) and then asked the patients to select pictures that might match what they saw. When the image of a chicken claw was flashed into the left cerebral hemisphere, one patient picked out the picture of a chicken (using the right hand). When the image of a snow scene was flashed into the right hemisphere, he picked out a picture of a snow shovel (using the left hand). Each of these associations was meaningful in its own terms, but had no connection to each other. The right hand literally did not know what the left hand was doing. But, when asked why the pictures of the chicken and the shovel were selected, the patient replied that picture of chicken went with image of the chicken claw and the shovel was needed to clean out the chicken shed! Apparently, the left-brain of the patient constructed a higher order meaning that made sense of the shovel in the context of what it knew about chickens (being ignorant of the snow scene flashed into the right hemisphere). Generalizing from these results, Gazzaniga concludes that the left-brain 'interpreter' is a built-in system that automatically constructs theories about our experiences and actions and 'tries to bring order to our conscious lives'.[16]

Although the field of cognitive psychology is developing rapidly, it seems reasonable to agree with Gazzaniga's hypothesis that something in the human psyche compels us to search for answers to life's puzzles. It is likely that this compulsion (like SFI) was programmed into the brain for its survival value – individuals who noticed conflicting signals and tried to resolve them had a better chance of finding game, avoiding predators and pairing up with mates.[17]

An innate compulsion to resolve apparent contradictions is a very basic precondition for the motivation to do scientific research. However, it would not adequately explain why members of some cultures (particularly China, the Islamic world and Western Europe) have pursued investigations into hidden dimensions of the natural world far beyond the impressions that actually strike the eye. Nor would it explain why members of some cultures consistently test the received solutions to scientific problems and continue the investigation even when those solutions fail the test. The split-brain patient's explanation for the picture of a snow shovel was clever, but it only obscured the fact that something more was happening at deeper layers of the environment. The viability of sustained research requires something more than the universal left-brain 'interpreter'. It requires the support and discipline of a culture with beliefs that will sustain scientific endeavour and hold it accountable for the validity of its findings.

The fact that SFB is so highly conditioned by culture requires us to consider social-scientific disciplines other than cognitive psychology. Cultural anthropology, for example, describes ways in which the lives of people in a given culture are ordered by the meanings embedded in language and symbol systems. Sociology studies the social structures of a culture, its segmentation into various classes and subcultures, and the way those structures support and are sustained by ideologies.

Disciplines like cultural anthropology and sociology can be helpful in understanding how science-sustaining systems function. A good example would be the education-research loop that is so instrumental in present-day scientific endeavour. Primary and secondary schools and liberal arts colleges are the primary agents for inculcating SFB: they teach science as a perennial subject; they provide the necessary training in mathematics and logic; and they disseminate a general sense of ongoing progress in science and medicine. They generate a steady supply of candidates for further training who eventually go into scientific research as a profession. Some of these professionals, in turn, train teachers and develop curricular materials for schools and universities (given appropriate incentives). Cultural anthropology and sociology can explain this education-research loop in detail. For example, they can clarify the role that SFB plays in the present-day structure (rather different from its historical roles)

---

16   Michael S. Gazzaniga, 'Organization of the Human Brain', *Science* 245 (1 Sept. 1989), 947b, 951; idem, *The Mind's Past* (Berkeley: University of California Press, 1998), 24-7.

17   Another version of the same idea is d'Aquili and Newberg's idea of a 'cognitive imperative' that results from evolutionary adaptation and impels humans to organize their perceptions of the world in meaningful patterns; d'Aquili and Newberg, *The Mystical Mind*, 80, 164.

– two of the primary social functions are to enhance national prestige and to promote industrial development through advances in science.

Our particular interest here is not how the education-research loop functions (a synchronic question), however, but what made such a structure possible in the first place (a diachronic question). While the concepts of cultural anthropology and sociology can be helpful is showing how SFB is inculcated and legitimated, the primary question we have to address is a historical one: what is the origin of the belief structure that undergirds scientific endeavour at the cultural level? And, if our method of explanation is to be historical, we must also be more explicit about the nature of the beliefs of scientists that we are trying to explain. In short, there are two topics that we need to address in the following pages: what basic beliefs are operative in the work of modern scientists, and the historical roots of those beliefs.

Three scientists we shall look at are Albert Einstein, Henry Margenau and Paul Davies. Even though these writers differ in many ways, they all have reflected on the epistemology and values of their disciplines. Their beliefs are characteristic of their scientific subculture and will give a good sense of the SFB that provides the cultural foundation of scientific endeavour.

We shall review these three physicists in reverse chronological order, beginning with Paul Davies in order to illustrate the role of belief in present-day physics. Then we shall turn to Margenau and Einstein in order to illustrate the kind of belief that lay at the foundations of modern physics (especially relativity and quantum theory). Following a historical insight of Einstein's about the cultural foundation of early modern science, we shall turn to a representative early modern scientist, Johannes Kepler, in order to examine the theological roots of those beliefs. Kepler's beliefs will demonstrate the role of creational beliefs in early modern science and will raise the question why such beliefs have not been given more prominence in the discipline of historical theology. Later we shall briefly review the historic creationist tradition and suggest ways of revising biblical and historical theology.

*Paul Davies on the importance of Science-Fostering Beliefs*

My first example is the 1995 Templeton laureate, Paul Davies (b. 1946).[18] In several seminal articles and most eloquently in his 1992 book, *The Mind of God: The Scientific Basis for a Rational World*, Davies drew attention to what he calls the 'great miracle of science':

> The success of the scientific method at unlocking the secrets of nature is so dazzling [that] it can blind us to the greatest scientific miracle of all: *science works*. Scientists themselves normally take it for granted that we live in a rational, ordered cosmos subject to precise laws that can be uncovered by human reasoning. Yet why this is so remains a tantalizing mystery.[19]

---

18   Paul Davies is currently visiting professor of physics at Imperial College London, adjunct professor of physics at the University of Queensland and adjunct professor of natural philosophy in the Australian Centre for Astrobiology at Macquarie University, Sydney; www. abc.net.au/science/morebigquestions/davies.htm.

19   Paul Davies, *The Mind of* God, 20.

Davies articulates the basic point of this chapter – that the pursuit of science is based on belief. In fact, he is quite specific in spelling out that belief. All scientific endeavour rests on two foundational beliefs. Scientists believe that the cosmos is rationally ordered – that it is governed by precise laws of some sort. This belief is an irreducible article of faith, since scientific cosmology does not tell us where those precise laws ultimately come from (as discussed in Chapter 1). Secondly, scientists believe that humans are fortunate enough to be capable of understanding that rational order – they have the built-in intelligence (SFI) needed to develop mathematical formalisms and models and that can be tested against data gathered by experiments, even data from the heights and depths of space-time. In this case, evolutionary biology and anthropology can help us locate the origin of this intelligence (as discussed in Chapter 2), but the belief of modern scientists is independent of such explanations. It is socially conditioned and historically mediated.

The substance of these two beliefs – rational ordering and human understanding – corresponds to the two foundations of scientific endeavour discussed in previous chapters. The burden of Davies' argument, however, is not just that this double foundation exists – a matter of cosmology and evolutionary biology – but that modern scientists 'normally take it for granted' – a matter of scientific culture. It has become almost self-evident to working scientists today in spite of the fact that neither the rationality of the universe nor the possibility of human understanding it is at all obvious in itself.

For Davies, the double foundation of rational order and human understanding is a 'tantalizing mystery', or a double-mystery. But a third mystery is implied in Davies' statement about the 'miracle' of science. In addition to the mysteries of rational order and human understanding, there is the mystery of why scientists believe the universe to be intelligible. This belief is the cultural foundation of scientific endeavour that we are investigating. In pursuit of this goal, we next work our way back to earlier examples.

*Henry Margenau on the role of Science-Fostering Beliefs*

The realization that scientific endeavour is motivated and sustained by beliefs did not begin with Paul Davies. Any number of scientists could be cited on this topic. One of the clearest of the previous generation was Henry Margenau (1901-1997), professor of physics and natural philosophy at Yale University in the 1950s and '60s. In his major philosophical study, Margenau spelled out what he called 'the new faith of science', by which he meant the set of beliefs to which all working scientists are personally committed even though they are 'not subject to logical and empirical proof' and are often even contradicted by the difficulties encountered in scientific research.[20] Such faith clearly matches our definition of Science-Fostering Belief.

---

20  Henry Margenau, *Open Vistas: Philosophical Perspectives of Modern Science* (New Haven: Yale University Press, 1961), 73, 75. For Margenau, the 'newness' of this faith was relative to the prior ideology of logical positivism, which held that science was independent of metaphysics and dealt only with the empirically verifiable. As we shall argue, the 'new faith' of which Margenau spoke had deep historical roots.

Margenau was troubled by the possibility that scientists might regard their efforts as futile. He described eloquently the difficulties that nuclear physicists were experiencing in constructing a unified theory for nuclear forces. In the 1950s, high-energy experiments were leading to the discovery of many new 'elementary particles' seemingly unrelated to each other. There were also problems with the theoretical calculations governing particle interactions: obviously finite parameters seemed to become infinite. Scientists who had to work on such problems for years and who saw 'little but chaos' (Margenau's phrase) often became pessimistic about the long-term prospects of their discipline. What actually prevented scientists from giving up under such conditions was an 'over-arching faith'. As Margenau described it:

> [The scientist] holds with the fervor of a religious conviction that his task is meaningful, that the history of science does converge in the limit upon a set of knowledge, laws and principles that are unique, categorical, and all inclusive.[21]

Margenau's point here corresponds to the first article of faith we found in Davies' writings: 'that we live in a rational, ordered cosmos subject to precise laws'. But Margenau saw this belief as something more than an assumption that scientists take for granted. It was a personal commitment made with the 'fervor of religious conviction'.

Margenau's analysis of the 'faith of science' focuses on the belief that the cosmos is rationally ordered. The complementary belief that humans are capable of discerning that order is implicit in his optimism about the prospects of eventually reaching a final theory. It is also expressed in the 'catechism' that Margenau developed to express the faith that sustained scientific research. This catechism had a total of six articles, three of which relate closely to our discussion:

> I believe that the search for truth is a never-ending quest, yet I pledge myself to seek it.

> I recognize no subjects and no facts which are alleged to be forever closed to inquiry or understanding; a mystery is but a challenge.

> I believe in the convergence of the scientific laws upon principles that are all embracive, though they may never be completely within our reach.[22]

According to Margenau's catechism, the search for the ultimate laws of the cosmos is a 'never-ending quest', yet those laws do exist and there is no obstacle that need prevent scientists from getting successively closer approximations. Scientific endeavour is a process of 'continual self-correction toward an ideal limit of understanding which

---

21 Margenau, *Open Vistas*, 75. Another physicist-philosopher, William G. Pollard, also wrote in 1961 about the importance of 'a firm and unshakable faith in the ultimate intelligibility of the chaotic torrent of phenomena in terms of underlying laws and universal principles'; Pollard, *Physicist and Christian: A Dialogue between Two Communities* (New York: Seabury Press, 1961), 14-16. Pollard and Margenau were two writers who influenced me in my studies as a student of science in the 1960s.

22 Margenau, *Open Vistas*, 76. The three articles I have cited are the first, third and fifth of the six Margenau lists.

is forever approached and yet never fully attained.'[23] As Margenau stated, every mystery should be viewed as a new challenge.

Henry Margenau was a physicist and a philosopher. We might even call him a 'theologian of scientific endeavour' in that he articulated the beliefs that motivate scientists and showed the religious dimensions of science as a human endeavour.

### *Albert Einstein on the religious origin of Science-Fostering Beliefs*

In the 1910s, while he was working on his General Theory of Relativity and in the early years of quantum theory, Albert Einstein began a series of epistemological writings in which he described the role that beliefs played in scientific research. We find the same basic points here that were made by Davies and Margenau.[24] Einstein stressed, to begin with, the necessity of presupposing the intelligibility of nature itself. As he stated in 1929: 'Certain it is that a conviction, akin to religious feeling, of the rationality or intelligibility of the world lies behind all scientific work of a higher order.'[25] The devotion scientists must have to their work, particularly in dealing with the more remote aspects of nature, requires that they be entirely convinced of the intelligibility of the object of their study.[26]

But research scientists must also presuppose some proportion between the object of their study and their own capabilities. Here Einstein reflected on his own work in physics, particularly in relativity theory. He observed that he had always approached his work assuming as given that there is a deep connection between the human mind and nature. There could be no logical bridge between the phenomena themselves and the principles that explain them. So the only way to explain how valid concepts could arise in the scientist's mind was to assume some primordial harmony between the object and subject.[27]

Using a well-known phrase from Leibniz, Einstein argued for a 'pre-established harmony' between the human mind and nature that could not be explained in terms of any underlying mechanism, whether logical or natural.[28] He also borrowed a striking phrase from Immanuel Kant to formulate one of his most cogent statements of the problem ever made: 'the eternal mystery of the world is its comprehensibility'. As

---

23   Margenau, *Open Vistas*, 74.

24   The following is largely based on Kaiser, 'Humanity in an Intelligible Cosmos' (2001).

25   Einstein, 'Scientific Truth' (1929), in idem, *The World As I See It* (London: John Lane, 1935), 131; also in idem, *Ideas and Opinions*, 262.

26   Einstein did not view quantum theory as 'rational' in this sense due to the seemingly contradictory properties of photons; see Marcus Chown, 'Einstein's Rio Requiem', *New Scientist* 181 (6 March 2004), 50-51.

27   Einstein, 'Principles of Scientific Research' (1918); 'Inaugural Address to the Prussian Academy of Sciences' (1914); 'The Method of Theoretical Physics' (1933), in idem, *World As I See It*, 125-6, 128, 136; also in idem, *Ideas and Opinions*, 221, 226-7, 274.

28   Einstein, 'Principles of Scientific Research' (1918), in idem, *World As I See It*, 125-6; also in idem, *Ideas and Opinions*, 226-7.

Einstein paraphrased the point: '…the world of our sense experiences is comprehensible. The fact that it is comprehensible is a miracle'.[29]

Einstein described this philosophical idea of 'pre-established harmony' or 'comprehensibility' in religious terms as a matter of 'belief' or 'faith'.[30] He also confessed his own faith in 'a superior mind' that revealed itself in the laws of nature[31] and stressed the necessity of intellectual humility in the face of 'reason incarnate' in the world – incarnate yet inaccessible to the human mind in its profoundest depths.[32]

Like Davies and Margenau, Einstein pinpointed two beliefs that underlie scientific endeavour: (1) that the world is governed by mathematical laws; and (2) that human reason is capable of grasping those laws. The consistency with which philosophically minded physicists return to these two convictions reassures us of their role in scientific endeavour.

More than our previous two writers, Einstein reflected on the historical and religious origins of the beliefs he had inherited.[33] Here is the way he put it in 1941:

> Science can only be created by those who are thoroughly imbued with the aspiration toward truth and understanding. This source of feeling, however, springs from the sphere of religion. To this [sphere] there also belongs the faith in the possibility that the regulations valid for the world of existence are rational, that is, comprehensible to [human] reason.[34]

Einstein pointed repeatedly to this larger 'sphere of religion' as the source of scientist's belief in the comprehensibility of the natural world. In the essay cited,

---

29   Einstein, 'Physics and Reality' (1936), in idem, *Out Of My Later Years*, 61; also in idem, *Ideas and Opinions*, 292. The 'world of our sense experiences' refers to the empirical world of scientific discovery; cf. 'The Method of Theoretical Physics' (1933), in idem, *World As I See It*, 133; also in idem, *Ideas and Opinions*, 271.

30   For example, Einstein, 'The Fundaments of Theoretical Physics' (1940); 'Message to the Italian Society for the Advancement of Science' (1950), in idem, *Ideas and Opinions*, 324, 357; idem, 'Autobiographical Notes', in Paul Arthur Schilpp (ed.), *Albert Einstein: Philosopher-Scientist* (LaSalle, Ill.: Open Court, 1949), 63.

31   Einstein, 'The Religiousness of Science' (1934 or earlier); 'Scientific Truth' (1929), in idem, *World As I See It*, 28, 131; idem, *Ideas and Opinions*, 40, 262.

32   Einstein, 'Science and Religion II' (1941), in idem, *Out Of My Later Years*, 29; also in idem, *Ideas and Opinions*, 49. Cf. Einstein's 1952 letter to Beatrice F. of San Francisco from the Einstein Archive, quoted in Max Jammer, *Einstein and Religion: Physics and Theology* (Princeton: Princeton University Press, 1999), 121-2. That same year he spoke of 'the theorist's hope of grasping the real in all its depth'; Einstein, 'The Method of Theoretical Physics' (1933), in idem, *World As I See It*, 138; also in idem, *Ideas and Opinions*, 275.

33   Davies also states that the quest of modern science has historical roots in a theological world view; Davies, *Are We Alone? Philosophical Implications of the Discovery of Extraterrestrial Life* (Harmondsworth: Penguin, 1995), 138. I owe this reference to Professor Del Ratzsch of Calvin College.

34   Einstein, 'Science and Religion II' (1941), in idem, *Out of My Later Years* (New York: Philosophical Library, 1950), 26; idem, *Ideas and Opinions*, 46. Cf. Einstein's reference to 'the truly religious conviction that this universe of ours is something perfect and susceptible to the rational striving for knowledge'; 'Religion and Science: Irreconcilable?', in idem, *Ideas and Opinions*, 52.

he gave one example of such religious conviction, physicist James Clerk Maxwell (1831-79), who had had been the mentor of some of Einstein's own teachers.[35]

Reflecting back even further, Einstein pointed out the debt of science to the seventeenth-century natural philosophers, who were also people of profound religious conviction.

> What a deep conviction of the rationality of the universe and what a yearning to understand, were it but a feeble reflection of the Mind revealed in this world, Kepler and Newton must have had to enable them to spend years of solitary labour in disentangling the principles of celestial mechanics! .... Only one who has devoted his life to similar ends can have a vivid realization of what has inspired these men and given them the strength to remain true to their purpose in spite of countless failures.[36]

According to Einstein, a prior belief in the intelligibility of the cosmos convinced early scientists like Kepler and Newton that technical scientific problems were soluble long before such advances became the everyday occurrence they are today. That belief also sustained them in the disappointments they experienced in their efforts. For himself, Einstein disavowed any notion of a 'personal' God who answers individual prayers and who judges people according to their individual choices.[37] At the same time, he recognized that the beliefs of early scientists had deep roots in the theistic teachings of the Psalms and the Prophets.[38] Einstein's overview of the tradition he inherited was almost as comprehensive as his survey of physics itself. It points us back to a time when belief in the comprehensibility of the natural world depended on the doctrine of creation rather than the other way around.[39]

Einstein, Margenau and Davies all came to the conclusion that scientific endeavour depends on the twin beliefs in universal laws of nature and human intelligence to match those laws. And if Einstein's historical overview is to be trusted, those beliefs were engendered by a theological heritage reaching from early modern scientists all the way back to Hebrew Scripture. If so, we should be able to find examples of that belief in the writings of Johannes Kepler, and we should be able to identify the theological tradition that he, Newton and Einstein inherited.

---

35   On Maxwell's creational beliefs and its impact on Einstein, see Kaiser, *Creational Theology*, 379-99.

36   Einstein, 'Religion and Science' (1930), in idem, *World As I See It*, 27; also in idem, *Ideas and Opinions*, 39-40.

37   For example, Einstein, *World As I See It*, 25, 28; cf. Jammer, *Einstein and Religion*, 47-50, 74-5.

38   Einstein, 'Religion and Science' (1930); 'Johannes Kepler'; 'Religion and Science: Irreconcilable?' (1948), in idem, *World As I See It*, 25-27, 141-2; also in idem, *Ideas and Opinions*, 38-40, 52. Here Einstein also cited Spinoza's and Schopenhauer's descriptions of unspecified Buddhist ideas.

39   The historical shift from reliance on creational theology as a legitimation for science to reliance on science as a legitimation for creational theology (natural theology) is usually dated to the late seventeenth or eighteenth century, but it has roots that go back to medieval theologians like Aquinas; Kaiser, *Creational Theology*, 92-8, 252-5, 264-6.

*Johannes Kepler on the theological basis of Science-Fostering Beliefs*

In the late sixteenth century, Johannes Kepler (1571-1630) studied theology and astronomy at the University of Tübingen. There he became convinced that the traditional (Ptolemaic) idea that the earth was the centre of the universe was wrong, and Copernicus' was right – the earth moved through space, revolving around a point very near the centre of the sun. As Kepler's personal correspondence indicates, questioning the received wisdom of the ages took considerable intellectual courage.[40] His courage was based on his belief that a better understanding of things was possible, which in turn was based in his Christian faith.

Kepler was fascinated with the spacing of the intervals between the orbits of the six known planets – the six planets visible to the naked eye. As he stated in the 'Greeting to the Reader' of his first publication (1596),[41] there ought to be a good reason for this arrangement, and yet neither the treatises of the ancients nor Copernicus' own work gave an adequate answer. He tried to solve the problem using solid geometry.[42] One of the basic constructions of solid geometry is the regular polyhedron – any solid with plane faces that all have the same shape and size (tetrahedron, cube, etc.). It so happens that there are only five of these solids, the same as the number of intervals between the orbits of the six known planets (Mercury, Venus, Earth, Mars, Jupiter and Saturn). A mere coincidence? Not if you hold, as Kepler and his contemporaries all did, that God created the world using the principles of geometry. To test this hypothesis, Kepler constructed a model for the orbits of the six planets by inscribing them on a set of spheres with the five regular solids nested between them to determine the spacing.[43]

The idea of building a mathematical model for a natural system is standard procedure today. For Kepler the procedure was based on the idea of divine creation, which he inherited from a longstanding theological tradition (to be surveyed later in this chapter). Kepler expressed this conviction at the outset of his 1596 treatise:

> It is my intention, reader, to show in this little book that the most great and good Creator, in the creation of this moving universe and the arrangement of the heavens, looked to those five regular bodies…and that God fitted to the nature of those solids the number of the heavens, their proportions, and the law of their motions.[44]

---

40   For example, Kepler's letter to Galileo, Aug. 1597; Carola Baumgardt, *Johannes Kepler: Life and Letters* (New York: Philosophical Library, 1951), 40-42.

41   Johannes Kepler, *Mysterium cosmographicum: The Secret of the Universe*, trans. A.M. Duncan (New York: Abaris Books, 1981), 48-9. The full Latin title was *Prodromus dissertationum cosmographicarum continens mysterium cosmographicum* ('A Preview of Cosmographical Dissertations Containing the Secret of the Cosmos'). A second, annotated edition was published in 1621.

42   For Kepler's other attempts to explain the arrangement of the planets, see Fernand Hallyn, *The Poetic Structure of the World: Copernicus and Kepler* (trans. from French by D. M. Leslie, New York: Zone Books, 1990), 187-9.

43   Johannes Kepler, *Mysterium cosmographicum*, trans. A.M. Duncan, frontpiece and Plate 3, drawn by Christopher Leibfried. See p. 228 for a listing of all the planets and the matching regular solids.

44   Johannes Kepler, *Mysterium cosmographicum*, Preface to the Reader; trans. A.M. Duncan, 63.

In the very beginning, God had constructed the planetary system according to the laws of solid geometry – the first of two beliefs identified by modern physicists like Einstein and Davies as the foundation of all scientific work. The other, complementary belief that humans are capable of imitating God and constructing a miniature model of the planetary system will be discussed shortly.

Even if by some fluke Kepler's geometrical model had worked, it would not have revealed God's plan in creation. For one thing, it was based on incomplete data: there were at least three other planets and vast numbers of asteroids to account for that could not be seen prior to the invention of the telescope. So there are aspects of Kepler's thinking that would be bypassed in the subsequent development of astronomical science. What was enduring was the belief he modeled. Kepler was convinced that there must be a discernible reason for the arrangement and motions of the planets. That conviction continued to motivate his research even though he never completely solved the problem that he started with. Kepler's beliefs were good, but the assumptions he made were based on limited knowledge.[45]

In view of present-day assumptions about scientific endeavour, I must emphasize the fact that Kepler's belief was not based on his (limited) success. Rather it preceded his work and motivated it. In Chapter 1 we discussed the implications of the existence of laws of nature for the possible existence of a wise Creator. Our starting point was the reliance of present-day cosmology on the fundamental laws of physics. On that basis we demonstrated the necessity of the God question even in a culture for which it is supposed to be strictly optional. But Kepler's approach was precisely the opposite. He was a pious Lutheran who immersed his life and work in prayer and theological study. So he started with faith in God as a wise Creator and argued on this basis that the planets God created must follow simple laws.[46] Creational theology was the source of Kepler's belief in the possibility of doing science.

The rest of Kepler's story is well known. He eventually gained access to the latest observational data on one of the planets – those made by Tycho Brahe and his associates for the changing position of Mars in the night sky. It was already known that the orbit of Mars was not exactly circular even when viewed from the sun. Kepler believed it possible to explain the data in terms of a simple geometric pattern. But proving it was a long, laborious process. Today the entire problem can be solved using a simple computer algorithm. But Kepler had to rely on his beliefs to sustain his work for years using the rudimentary mathematical methods of his time.[47] As Einstein later observed, his work is an early illustration of the way Science-Fostering Belief enables scientists to 'remain true to their purpose in spite of countless failures'.

---

45   As it turns out, there is no simple answer to the question of planetary orbits as Kepler formulated it. As in all of life, beliefs do not guarantee an answer to any particular question. All they do is motivate us to keep reformulating our questions until we understand the phenomena.

46   Kepler did express the hope that his discoveries would convince some philosophers that the world was created and ordered by God, but his own belief was rooted in his religious heritage; cf. Kepler's letter to Baron von Herberstein, 15 May 1596; in Baumgardt, *Johannes Kepler: Life and Letters*, 33-5.

47   Calculus was not invented until Newton and Leibniz. Kepler did his calculations using old-fashioned logarithms.

By 1605, Kepler had finally demonstrated a solution for the changing position of Mars. It could best be explained as an ellipse rather than any combination of circles.[48] With the advantage of scientific hindsight, this may seem like a trivial step. However, the shift from circles to ellipses was more daring than just picking a different equation. Kepler was taking a huge risk in assigning a fundamental role in nature to a geometric shape that had not previously played any role in everyday life.[49] Most astronomers played it safe and stayed with the simpler idea of circular orbits for years until Isaac Newton demonstrated that elliptical orbits result from the inverse square law of gravitation.[50]

**Figure 3.1 Kepler's innovative idea[51]**

Another difficulty was the fact that the data Kepler had to work with did not neatly fit his geometrical constructions. The ellipse was at best an approximation, but that was

---

48    Kepler's *Astronomia nova*, written in 1605-6 and published in 1609. For a brief description of Kepler's long process of discovery, see. A. C. Crombie, *Augustine to Galileo: The History of Science AD 400-1650*, 2nd edn, 2 vols (Oxford: Heinemann, 1959), 2:188-90.

49    Howard Margolis coins the term 'around-the-corner inquiry' for insights like Kepler's in order to differentiate it from direct inference; Margolis, *It Started with Copernicus: How Turning the World Inside Out Led to the Scientific Revolution* (New York: McGraw-Hill, 2002), 126-7, 160-61.

50    Isaac Newton, *Philosophiae naturalis principia mathematica* ('Mathematical Principles of Natural Philosophy'), published in 1687.

51    Sydney Harris cartoon from www.ScienceCartoonsplus.com. Used by permission.

good enough for Kepler because he recognized the hand of the Creator who must have used basic geometrical constructions like conic sections in creating the solar system.

Extending his search for mathematical patterns in Tycho's data, Kepler discovered a formula that governed the varying motion of a planet along its elliptical orbit (the law of 'equal areas in equal times'). Ten years later he devised a third formula that related the period of revolution to the size of the orbit for each of the planets.[52] These three equations, since known as 'Kepler's laws', provided the groundwork for subsequent advances in natural philosophy.

Kepler synthesized his hard-earned results in a treatise entitled, *Harmonics of the Universe*,[53] published twenty-three years after his first effort. As always, he was forthright about the basic convictions that had sustained him in his efforts:

> Geometry, which before the origin of things was coeternal with the divine mind... supplied God with patterns for the creation of the world and passed over to human nature along with the image of God....[54]

Here Kepler restated his long-standing conviction that God had created the heavens according to the principles of basic geometry. But the passage quoted adds a second belief – the idea that humanity was created in the image of God, based on Genesis 1:26-27. Besides Scripture, Kepler cited Plato and Proclus to show that geometry was not derived from human experience: it was present in the mind of each human from birth and only needed to be elicited by a good teacher.[55] As a Neoplatonist, Kepler believed that geometry was an innate form of knowledge. As a Christian Platonist, he reasoned that it must have been part of the divine image in humanity – a ray of the

---

52   For details, see Crombie, loc. cit., and Arthur Koestler, *The Sleepwalkers: A History of Man's Changing Vision of the Universe* (New York: Macmillan, 1959), 213-22.

53   The Latin title is *Harmonice mundi* (1619), which is sometimes translated 'Harmony of the World'.

54   Kepler, *Harmonice mundi* IV.1; Johannes Kepler, *Gesammelte Werke*, 20 vols., ed. Walther von Dyck, Max Caspar, et al. (Munich: Becksche Verlagsbuchhandlung, 1937-88), 6:223, lines 32-4; ET from Johannes Kepler, *The Harmony of the World*, trans. E.J. Aiton, A.M. Duncan, and J.V. Field (Philadelphia: American Philosophical Society, 1997), 304 (slightly modified). The same idea is found in Kepler's defense of Galileo, *Dissertatio cum Nuncio Sidereo*; *Gesammelte Werke*, 4:308. In *Harmonice mundi* IV.1, Kepler identified geometry as one of the attributes of the divine being (*quid enim in Deo quod not sit Ipse Deus*, 'for what is in God that was not God himself?'). This idea was already found in Augustine (for example, *On Genesis Literally* IV.3.7), but Kepler was commenting here on the (recently read) Neoplatonic ideas of Proclus, which he had interpreted in accordance with what is 'known to Christians' like Augustine concerning the doctrine of creation; cf. Kepler, *Harmony of the World,* 299, 303, 493. See the marginal note in *Harmonice mundi* I, Proposition 45, and the discussion of Axiom 7 in Book III; *Gesammelte Werke*, 6:47-9; ET in Kepler, *Harmony of the World*, 74, 146-7.

55   Proclus was a sixth-century Neoplatonist who taught that geometrical structures like the sphere were inscribed on the human soul by the cosmic Mind or Intellect (Nous); Proclus, *A Commentary on the First Book of Euclid's Elements*, trans. Glenn R. Morrow (Princeton: Princeton University Press, 1970), 14. The relation of Platonist and biblical teachings is discussed below under 'Theological challenges and resources'.

divine that was infused into the human soul at birth.[56] The idea of the divine image sustained his belief, not only that there was a solution to the longstanding enigma of planetary orbits, but that human beings had the ability – in fact the obligation – to discover that solution.[57]

In this passage from *Harmonics of the Universe*, we can see two complementary features in Kepler's belief structure. The belief that the universe is ordered by mathematical laws is one of these – Kepler thought of it largely in terms of geometry as the pattern of creation. Second is the belief that mortals have the intelligence needed to discover those laws because they are created in the divine image – again Kepler thought in terms of geometry implanted in the human mind. These two beliefs correspond to the dual-belief identified by modern physicists like Einstein and Paul Davies as the foundation of their scientific work. There is a correspondence between the depths of the human psyche and the deep structures of the universe, between deep subject and deep object – not a perfect correspondence, perhaps, but more than one might infer from observing humans in everyday life.

Kepler frequently noted the importance of this subject-object correspondence for scientific endeavour. A leading historian has called this conviction the 'mainspring of his life's work'.[58] Mainspring is a good term here, because Kepler's belief was operative from the very start of his endeavours. It was stated most clearly in correspondence of the late 1590s, years before his major breakthrough. In a letter addressed to his astronomy professor, Michael Mästlin, Kepler (1597) explained that:

> ...God, who founded everything in the world according to the norm of quantity, also has endowed humanity with a mind which can comprehend these norms. For, as the eye for color, the ear for musical sounds, so is the human mind created for the perception not of any arbitrary entities, but rather of quantities....[59]

Kepler's letter portrays the human mind as being specially adapted to discern the mathematical structures of creation in the same way that the eye is adapted to perceive color.[60] Although Kepler does not refer here to the divine image in humanity, he does base his belief on the idea that humans are special creations. God ensured that humans

---

56  As Kepler explained in a letter to Johann Georg Brengger, 5 April 1608, the human soul was formed out of celestial (spiritual) substance and then 'illuminated and instructed by a ray out of God's image'; Baumgardt, *Johannes Kepler: Life and Letters*, 79; cf. Philo, *De opificio mund.* 146 ('a copy or fragment or ray of that blessed nature'). The interpretation of the 'heavens' in Genesis 1:1 as unformed spiritual substance goes back as far as Augustine, *Confessions*, XII.17.25; XIII.2.2-3.

57  In this chapter the idea of the divine image is cited as a biblical, theological construct. An attempt to define it in anthropological terms was made in Chapter 2, 'Theological challenges and resources'.

58  Gerald Holton, *Thematic Origins of Scientific Thought: Kepler to Einstein* (Cambridge, Mass: Harvard University Press, 1973), 84; revised edn (1988), 68.

59  Letter to Michael Mästlin, 9 April 1597; *Gesammelte Werke*, 13:27; ET from Holton, *Thematic Origins of Scientific Thought*, 84; revised edn, 68 (modified). Mästlin had helped arrange the publication of Kepler's *Mysterium cosmographicum* (1596), for which he also provided a preface and an appendix.

60  In Chapter 2, I argued for an evolutionary explanation for both kinds of adaptation.

would have what we have called Science Fostering Intelligence – the innate ability to discover the norms according to which the world and everything in it were created.[61]

Kepler does refer to the divine image in humanity in another of his letters, written just two years later (1599):

> Those [laws which govern the material world] are within the grasp of the human mind. God wanted us to recognize them by creating us after his own image so that we could share in his own thoughts...and, if piety allows us to say so, our understanding is in this respect of the same kind as the divine, at least as far as we are able to grasp something of it in our mortal life.[62]

As the context of the passage indicates, Kepler beleived he sometimes needed to justify his efforts to improve on the science of the ancients. Some of his critics evidently thought that matters as recondite as planetary orbits would forever be beyond the ken of beings who were confined to live on earth. So Kepler's reference to a well-known biblical text like Genesis 1:26 provided needed theological support.

Kepler questioned received knowledge not as a skeptic, but as a believer. His efforts toward a deeper understanding of nature were generated by religiously convictions, as Einstein was later to observe. For some of Kepler's contemporaries, scientific understanding and religious belief apparently seemed contradictory, but for Kepler himself they were not only consistent, but mutually affirming. The theological background for his conviction is to be found in his theological training at the University of Tübingen based on the theology of Luther and Melanchthon.

*Background of Kepler's Science-Fostering Beliefs in creational theology*

The example of Kepler shows that our investigation of the cultural foundation of scientific endeavour leads us into theological terrain, just as our earlier investigations of the Cosmic and Anthropological Foundations did. In the previous cases, however, we could only infer the need for discussing the possibility of a Creator or the plausibility of a spirit world presided over by a governing Spirit. In this case, we immediately enter the world of biblical theology because we are dealing with a culture of belief that was deeply informed by biblical teachings.

Kepler is most often associated with scientific developments abstracted from his theological training. In order to locate him in his own thought world, where

---

61 Gerald Holton suggests that Kepler had two different gods: one biblical and the other Pythagorean; Holton, *Thematic Origins of Scientific Thought*, 86; revised edn, 70. However, the idea that God had created everything 'according to the norm of quantity' was already in Kepler's Bible in texts like Wisdom 11:20 as will be shown below.

62 Letter to Johannes Georg Herwart von Hohenburg, 9/10 April 1599; *Gesammelte Werke*, 13:309, letter no. 117, lines 174-9; ET in Baumgardt, *Johannes Kepler: Life and Letters*, 50. As Chancellor of Bavaria, von Hohenburg was able to help Kepler establish connections at the imperial court in Prague. Like Kepler, he was a mathematician, and had also studied under Mästlin; Baumgardt, *Johannes Kepler: Life and Letters*, 57-9. The way Kepler shares his ideas about God and creation with Herwart suggests that he expected the latter to remember them from Mästlin's teachings.

science and theology more were closely interrelated, we turn to the primary written sources of his beliefs about the cosmos and humanity: Luther's 'Lectures on Genesis' (published in 1544); and Melanchthon's treatise, 'On Christian Doctrine' (*Loci communes*, 1521-1555). The two treatises are best considered together because they were written and revised over the same period of time and because Luther's lectures were strongly influenced (if not partly written) by Melanchthon.[63]

Luther's 'Lectures on Genesis' naturally discussed the first human pair and their creation in the image and likeness of God. Among other aspects of this primeval endowment was 'the most dependable knowledge of the stars and of the whole of astronomy'.[64] Even though such perfect knowledge was largely lost due to human rebellion against God, a spark of that original life is still evidenced in human efforts to 'understand the motion of the heaven or measure the heavenly bodies'.[65] Melanchthon's *Loci communes* was equally optimistic. The gifts of God may still be observed in humans, and among them are 'understanding about number and order'.[66]

Although these beliefs make their first appearance in most histories of science with Kepler, they were not at all new. They were ensconced in the writings of Luther and Melanchthon and mediated by the lectures of Tübingen professors like Michael Mästlin and Jakob Heerbrand.[67] They were not unique to the Lutheran Reformation either. Among natural philosophers and educators with the same affirmations, one finds Lefèvre d'Étaples, Paracelsus, George Bauer Agricola, John Dee, Giordano Bruno, Francis Bacon, Thomas Tymme, Alsted, d'Espagnat, Beeckman, Descartes and Comenius. Our extended examination of Kepler will suffice, however, to establish the theological origin of the Science-Fostering Beliefs that were passed on to the founders of modern science from Johannes Kepler to Albert Einstein.

Scientists are believers and their beliefs are theological in origin. A suitably thick description of scientific endeavour must include the cultural foundation that has provided the motivation (Kepler), conviction (Einstein), and persistence (Margenau) needed for sustained endeavour. The history of that foundation must include a theological dimension. In following section, we will argue that historical theology must also be thickened to include a scientific dimension.

---

63   For a detailed treatment of Kepler's Lutheran background, see Peter Barker and Bernard R. Goldstein, 'Theological Foundations of Kepler's Astronomy', in John Hedley Brooke, Margaret J. Osler, and Jitse Van der Meer (eds), *Science in Theistic Contexts: Cognitive Dimensions* (*Osiris* 16, Chicago: University of Chicago Press, 2001), 88-113.

64   Martin Luther, *Lectures on Genesis, Chapters 1-5*, in *Luther's Works: American Edition*, ed. Jaroslav Pelikan and Helmut T. Lehmann, 55 vols (St Louis and Philadelphia: Concordia and Fortress Press, 1955-76), 1:66.

65   *Luther's Works*, 1:45-6.

66   Melanchthon, *On Christian Doctrine: Loci communes 1555*, ed. Clyde L. Manschrek (New York: Oxford University Press, 1965), 71.

67   Robert S. Westman, 'The Melanchthon Circle, Rheticus, and the Wittenberg Interpretation of the Copernican Theory', *Isis* 66 (June 1975), 165-93; E.J. Aiton, Introduction to *Johannes Kepler, Mysterium cosmographicum: The Secret of the Universe*, trans. A.M. Duncan (New York: Abaris Books, 1981), 23.

**Theological challenges and resources**

The role that creational theology has played in the cultural foundation of scientific endeavour provides a healthy challenge to historical treatments of theology and to theological education in particular. Historians of science have written extensively on the role of religious faith in the lives and work of many scientists. They have described the historic 'creationist tradition' that informed the beliefs of natural philosophers from the twelfth-century renaissance of classical learning to the late nineteenth-century professionalization of science.[68] The discipline of the history of science has long since outgrown the 'internalist' strictures of positivist historiography and described scientific endeavour as a convergence of many cultural dimensions, including that of theology.

In spite of such progress, the historical picture is still far from complete. The problem is that historians of theology have not reciprocated by exploring the various creational and scientific dimensions of their subject. Most histories of the development of Christian theology deal exclusively with the ideas of professional theologians and the confessions of various denominations – also written by theologians. Very few make reference to the impact of biblical and theological doctrines on secular disciplines like the sciences.[69] Fortunately, there are several fine theological studies that focus on some aspect of creational belief in relation to the development of modern science.[70] But very few seminarians or students of religion will be exposed to these ideas in their more accessible textbooks. They will learn about the professional theologians who debated biblical teachings, but few will learn about scientists like Kepler, Newton, Maxwell and Einstein whose articulations and applications of those teachings helped restructure the world in which we live.

For most historians of theology, the natural sciences are 'secular' subjects that lie outside the bounds of their discipline. The work of scientists may challenge theological beliefs from the outside, but it does not have any theological value in its own right. At the level of ideas, our theology may be challenged, perhaps even modified, in the light of scientific discoveries, but the historiography remains the same and the impression is given that science and theology are separate phenomena with only occasional points of contact.

Historical theology is the study of the origins, controversies, alterations and practical applications of theological teachings. It traces faith-laden practices and life-sustaining doctrines from generation to generation with an eye toward lines of

---

68   For example, Richard C. Dales, 'A Twelfth-Century Concept of the Natural Order', *Viator* 9 (1978), 191-2; Paul Theerman, 'James Clerk Maxwell and Religion', *American Journal of Physics* 54 (April 1986), 312-17.

69   One exception is the late Colin Gunton, *The Triune Creator: A Historical and Systematic Study* (Grand Rapids: Eerdmans, 1998), 102-111.

70   Examples are N. Max Wildiers, *The Theologian and His Universe: Theology and Cosmology from the Middle Ages to the Present* (New York: Seabury Press, 1982); Harold Nebelsick, *The Circles of God: Theology and Science from the Greeks to Copernicus* (Edinburgh: Scottish Academic Press, 1985); Olaf Pedersen, *The Book of Nature* (Vatican City: Vatican Observatory Publications, 1992); and Botond Gaál, *The Faith of a Scientist: James Clerk Maxwell* (Debrecen: István Hatvani Theological Research Centre, 2003).

continuity and stages of transformation. It is usually narrative in style. The difficulty in writing such history is that lines of such development are rarely straight. They converge from many directions and then diverge again. Real history is nonlinear and multidimensional. As a result, the significance of scientific endeavour is bound to be missed unless the relevant lines of creational theology are included and traced into secular areas like the sciences. Therefore, the historian of theology must look beyond the boundaries of confessional theology and institutional religion in order to do justice to the pervasiveness of theology in culture as a whole.

In the remainder of this chapter, I shall give an overview of the role of biblical ideas that provided the background for the origin of modern science in the time of Johannes Kepler.[71] In other words, recognition of the role creational theology played in forming a cultural foundation for scientific endeavour will serve as a lens for refocusing the history of early beliefs about the created order. It is not possible to be exhaustive here. Many other lines of convergence and divergence could also be traced. But it is important to highlight some of the major themes that biblical and historical theology must incorporate if they are to address the wider dimensions of a scientific culture.

From the writings of Kepler, Einstein. Margenau and Davies, we have identified two basic beliefs for which historical precedent needs to be traced: the belief that the world is governed by mathematical laws and the belief that humans have the ability to discern and describe those laws. Beginning with their ancient Near Eastern roots, we shall trace the appearance of these beliefs in the Hebrew Bible and Greek natural philosophy and follow their development through Hellenistic Judaism, early Christian theology, and the medieval and Renaissance thought that provided the framework for the Lutheran Reformation and Johannes Kepler. The origin of modern science has a thick cultural foundation: its many layers go back as far as the time of the early Babylonians and Egyptians. And its theological texture turns out to be far richer than a traditional approach to historical theology might suggest.

*Belief about mathematical laws in the ancient Babylon, Greece and Israel*

As stated above, the origin of belief in the intelligibility of the natural world is an inheritance from the cultures of the ancient Near East, Greece and Israel. In other words, it goes back to the beginnings of history, as far as written records allow us to probe. As we shall see, this belief could be expressed in different ways: as the result of decrees made by the Deity to govern the lower world; as the adherence of all creatures to laws and bounds set by the Creator; or as the outward manifestation of mathematical formulas used by the Deity in designing creation. Some of the examples given here may seem repetitive: the same basic ideas recur over and over again. There is continual change, however, in the conceptual form and the ideological function of the ideas from one cultural context to another. In view of the huge chronological and cultural gap between the ancient world and that of early modern science, the

---

71 The idea of the 'comprehensibility of the world' is just one of at least four themes in the historic 'creationist tradition'; Kaiser, *Creational Theology*, 18-21.

element of repetition is necessary to establish the depth and solidity of the creationist tradition upon which early modern scientists based their endeavours.

The cultural foundation of modern science has layers going back as far as the time of the early Babylonians and Egyptians. That is as far as historical methods will carry us. There may be a prehistoric foundation lying beneath this cultural foundation of scientific endeavour, but we lack a good methodology for pursuing it. If such a methodology could be developed, a further thickening of the description of scientific endeavour might well occur in the future.[72]

One of our earliest sources of ancient creational ideas is the *Enūma elish*, a Babylonian creation epic whose name is taken from the opening words of the text:

> When on high [*Enūma elish*] the heaven had not (yet) been named,
> And below the firm ground had not (yet) been called by a name....[73]

The *Enūma elish* originated during or soon after the First Babylonian Dynasty (between the nineteenth and sixteenth centuries BCE). So it antedates even the earliest strata of the Hebrew Bible and provides a helpful comparison for the creation account in the Book of Genesis (whose Hebrew name, *Běre'shît*, is likewise taken from the opening word of the text).

The *Enūma elish* assigns the role of Creator to the Babylonian god Marduk. Marduk established the present world order by assigning laws for everything that exists in the heavens and the atmosphere:

> He [Marduk] created the heavenly residence for the great gods;
> the stars, their manifestations, the 'likenesses' [constellations?], he fixed in it;
> he determined the year, and gave (it) its zones;
> he assigned three stars to each of the twelve months.
> When he had set up the marks for the year
> he determined the station of the pole star, in order to establish their [the stars'] spheres [of influence],
> and so that there should be no deviation and no falling short. (Tablet V, lines 1-7)[74]

What is so impressive about this three thousand-year old poem is the cosmic scope of the rule of its reigning deity. Rules laid down by Marduk govern the heavenly luminaries (here viewed as subordinate gods), their daily and annual rotations around the pole, and even their influences on the world below. The narrative goes on

---

72    Ancient Near Eastern accounts of creation reflect (or project) the royal court proceedings of ancient city states. So a sociological explanation for the creational ideas we are discussing is a distinct possibility even though it would be difficult to demonstrate it with any rigour. It is likely that these ideas have ideological roots going back to pre-urban traditions. There may even be a connection with the paleoshamanic spirituality described in Chapter 2.

73    *Enūma elish*, Tablet I, lines 1-2; ET from Walter Beyerlin (ed.), *Near Eastern Religious Texts Relating to the Old Testament* (London: SCM Press, 1978), 82. Biblical parallels can be found in Genesis 1:1-2; 2:4-5.

74    Beyerlin (ed.), *Near Eastern Religious Texts*, 83.

to include the phases of the moon, which mark the passing of each month of the year (Tablet V, lines 13-14).[75]

The judicial flavor of these pronouncements is reflected in the insistence on strict adherence: 'no deviation and no falling short...without ceasing' – a theme that we shall see developed in later Greek, Jewish and Christian literature. The ideological function of all this cosmic legislation was evidently to establish a common calendar to govern daily life. The cosmos is envisioned as a macrocosm of the ideal state, and the legislation of the divine council as the celestial counterpart of similar deliberations on earth.

Counterexamples to cosmic order could of course be offered to challenge the ideology of the text. Perhaps for this reason, the *Enūma elish* does not limit the ordering of creation to the heavens whose order is evident to the senses. The rule of Marduk extends even to the seemingly chaotic phenomena of the atmosphere below:

> He joined the clouds together and made them overflow with water.
> To unleash the wind, to make the rain, to bring cold,
> to draw the clouds (and) to put their vapour in layers,
> all this he planned himself and took it in hand. (Tablet V, lines 49-51)[76]

Although rather impressionistic by modern scientific standards, this ancient text already contains the belief that the gathering of the clouds, the outpouring of rain, and even stormy gusts of wind were subject to some deeper order established by the reigning deity. Its affirmation of cosmic order clearly goes beyond empirical observation. Even though the *Enūma elish* does not use the term 'law' to describe the cosmic order, the concept of cosmic law is clearly implied and given nearly universal scope.[77]

The belief in the existence of cosmic laws was developed more explicitly by younger cultures like the Greeks and Hebrews that inherited much of their ideology from Babylonian sources.[78] In order to illustrate the historical background for modern belief in cosmic law, I shall cite a few examples from each of these cultures before moving on to describe the synthesis of Hebrew and Greek ideas in Hellenistic Judaism and early Christianity.

Contrary to a common assumption, classical Greek literature rarely refers to the basic principles inherent in nature as a 'universal natural law' as distinct from human

---

75   Beyerlin (ed.), *Near Eastern Religious Texts*, 83

76   Beyerlin (ed.), *Near Eastern Religious Texts*, 84.

77   Needham claimed that Marduk 'prescribed laws' for the star gods in *Enuma elish* V.8; Needham and Ling, *Science and Civilization in China*, 2:533. More recent scholars translate this line as 'he set up stations'; Beyerlin, ed., *Near Eastern Religious Texts*, 83.

78   For the Babylonian origin of early Greek culture, see Walter Burkert and Margaret E. Pinder, *The Orientalizing Revolution: Near Eastern Influence on Greek Culture in the Early Archaic Age* (Cambridge, Mass: Harvard University Press, 1992); Burkert, *Babylon, Memphis, Persepolis: Eastern Contexts of Greek Culture* (Cambridge, Mass: Harvard University Press, 2004).

laws.[79] Among the early Greeks, the idea of cosmic law (*nómos*) was implicit in the writings of Anaximander (c. 600 BCE), Heraclitus (c. 500) and Anaxagoras (c. 470), which only survive in fragments.[80] These fragments may well indicate the existence of a wider oral tradition analogous to the Babylonian creation epic.

Evidence of such an oral tradition is seen in a fragment from the fourth-century orator, Demosthenes. According to the Athenian statesman: 'the whole world, things divine [celestial] and what we call the seasons, appear, if we may trust what we see, to be regulated by law and order'.[81] Demosthenes relied here on the vocabulary of Greek civic law to describe the processes of nature. But his statement was a purely empirical one, based on everyday observation (for example, changing seasons). It does not reflect a fundamental belief like the one we found in the *Enūma elish* and later in Kepler.

Demosthenes' contemporary, the Pythagorean philosopher Archytas (early fourth cent. BCE) is credited with having developed a more coherent set of metaphysical principles and to have anticipated the cosmological ideas of Plato. According to fragments ascribed to him, Archytas divided all beings and all phenomena into two distinct categories: those that are organized and subject to verbal analysis; and others that are beyond all reason.[82] Such 'irrational' processes may have included the meteorological phenomena so carefully included in the Babylonian *Enūma elish*. Unlike Demosthenes, 'Archytas' does not seem to have used the idea of natural law even to describe the 'rational' processes of his cosmology.

In the philosophy of Plato (d. 347 BCE), who was a personal friend of the historical Archytas, there were two very similar ultimate principles: mathematical forms or eternal ideas that give order to the world; and formless matter which by itself chaotic and unpredictable. According to the *Dialogue with Timaeus*, Plato's principle discussion of cosmic origins, only the eternal ideas are truly intelligible. The material world is only intelligible as far as it exhibits the mathematical forms, so any propositions about nature could only be probable at best.[83] Plato attributed this partial ordering of the material world to a creator God (the Demiurge), who

---

79    Helmut Koester, 'Nomos Physeōs: The Concept of Natural Law in Greek Thought', in Jacob Neusner (ed.), *Religions in Antiquity: Essays in Memory of Erwin Ramsdell Goodenough* (Leiden: Brill, 1968), 522; Joan R. Kung, 'Review Essay on *Magic, Reason and Experience*, by G.E.R. Lloyd', *Nature and System* 4 (1982), 101-5.

80    Helpful overviews of these early Greek texts can be found in Joseph Needham and Wang Ling, *Science and Civilization in China, Volume 2: History of Scientific Thought* (Cambridge: Cambridge University Press, 1956), 533-9; Cornelius Loew, *Myth, Sacred History, and Philosophy: The Pre-Christian Heritage of the West* (New York: Harcourt, Brace & World, 1967), 215-20, 225-9.

81    Demosthenes, *Adv. Aristog.* B; Greek text and ET in Thomas Erskine Holland, *The Elements of Jurisprudence* (St Paul, Minnesota: West, 1896), 17; cited in Needham and Ling, *Science and Civilization in China*, 2:533.

82    Archytas, frag 1; ET in Robert Navon (ed.), *The Pythagorean Writings* (Key Gardens, N.Y.: Selene Books, 1986), 142. Most of these fragments are thought to be pseudepigraphal.

83    Plato, *Timaeus* 29a-c, in *The Collected Dialogues of Plato*, ed. Edith Hamilton and Huntington Cairns (Princeton: Princeton University Press, 1961), 1162.

had imposed geometric measure, form and number on the primordial substratum of chaotic matter.[84] Far from being an apologist for political order (his mentor Socrates was silenced as a threat), Plato intended his philosophy to draw students and direct them to the invisible world of ideas.[85]

Plato's theistic cosmogony was of great interest to later Jewish and Christian philosophers. They saw strong similarities to the biblical tradition they inherited, which had developed the Babylonian belief in divine ordering in a remarkably similar way but with greater emphasis on the idea of prescribed laws for created beings.[86] One of the earliest sources we have is the second collection of prophecies attributed to Isaiah, which dates slightly before the time of Heraclitus (c. 500). In Second Isaiah, we find the idea of an intelligible, mathematical order for the material world expressed in the form of a taunt against other members of the divine council:

Who [among the gods] has measured [*madad*] the waters in the hollow of his hand
and marked off the heavens with a span,
enclosed the dust of the earth in a measure,
and weighed [*wᵉshaqal*] the mountains in scales
and the hills in a balance? (Isa. 40:12-13)

In making his claim for the LORD God of Israel, the prophet portrayed creation as a cosmic construction project in terms comparable to those later used by Plato (geometric measure and form).[87] Unlike Plato, however, Isaiah included chaotic elements like the waters and specified the weight of matter in the mountains in the list of things that the LORD God had measured out. This prophetic text reflects aspects of the cosmopolitan wisdom tradition, but its purpose is to instill a sense of ethnic identity and the hope of rebuilding a theocratic state.

Another important example of mathematical ordering in the Hebrew Bible is found in the Book of Job. While Job in its present form is somewhat later than Isaiah, it reflects the same underlying traditions of ancient wisdom. Like Isaiah, Job included both measure weight and geometric measure in the divinely appointed order:

---

84  Plato, *Timaeus* 53a-b, in *Collected Dialogues of Plato*, 1179. Plato's omission of the parameter of weight is striking, particularly in contrast to the work of a human craftsman in *Philebus* 55d-e and to Hebrew writings to be examined below. In *Timaeus* 83e, Plato describes the progress of a particular disease as being 'contrary to the laws of nature' (*parà toùs tēs phýseōs... nómous*); in *Collected Dialogues of Plato*, 1204.

85  The idea that God (or the gods) measured out the materials of creation also appears in ancient Indian and Chinese texts; see Rg Veda I.152:1-3 (habitations on earth); X.121:5 (atmosphere); *Huainan-zi* (c. 139 BCE) III.6; IV.15 (the four seasons and four quarters of heaven and earth); V.10 (sun, moon and stars, seasons, wind).

86  Philip S. Alexander, 'Enoch and the Beginnings of Jewish Interest in Natural Science', in C. Hempel, A. Lange, and H. Lichtenberger (eds), *The Wisdom Texts from Qumran and the Development of Sapiential Thought* (Leuven: Leuven University Press, 2002), 240-42.

87  Isaiah 40:29 also uses the category of number, in this case for the nightly appearance of the stars.

He gave to the wind its weight [*mishqal*],
  and apportioned out the waters by measure [$b^e$*middah*];
when he made a decree [*hoq*] for the rain,
  and a way for the thunderbolt.... (Job 28:25-6).

In the narrative frame of this book, Job and his family suffer one calamity after another and are brought down very low. In this context, Job's affirmation of the divine ordering of these chaotic phenomena is truly remarkable. This was not just an observation of the pristine order in the heavens, but an affirmation of personal faith.

Our text in Job uses the Hebrew word *hoq* for 'decree' or 'law' in order to describe this ordering. The idea is similar to that of 'law and order' we found in Demosthenes, dating from approximately the same time.[88] One major difference is that the decrees of the LORD are set in the context of the divine council, where all such decisions are made (Job 1:6; 2:1; 5:8). Demosthenes could only read the idea of law and order out of the more orderly aspects of the material world like the changing seasons, whereas Job affirmed a belief in the operation of law even in the midst of evident calamity and injustice,[89] and in the face of widespread pessimism about human ability to understand those laws (Job 38-39).[90] This priority of belief over personal experience was to have a profound influence on early Christian scientists like Kepler. Like Job, Kepler refused to isolate his personal convictions from his beliefs about the cosmos in which he lived. This background also helps us understand how modern physicists like Einstein and Margenau could affirm their belief in the rationality of the cosmos in the face of massive evidence to the contrary.

*Belief about mathematical laws in Jewish apocalypses*

The ancient Greek and Hebrew traditions about the intelligibility of the material world were parallel developments of the mythic ideas of the Babylonians. The parallel developments were compatible enough to be synthesized in the apocalyptic and wisdom traditions of Hellenistic Judaism.[91] These traditions codified the creational

---

88   The Hebrew word *hoq* is used again for the creation of the heavens in Job 38:33. The early Greek translation of the Hebrew Bible, the Septuagint, paraphrased both Job 28:26 and Job 38:33 without using the Greek term *nómos*. Jerome's Latin translation, the Vulgate, used the Latin word *lex* in Job 38:33, however, thus restoring the force of the Hebrew.

89   Similar affirmations of divinely appointed laws of nature in the face of tragedy is reflected in Jer. 31:35-6; 33:25 (the 'Book of Consolation'), which use the Hebrew term *hoq*; see Chapter 1, 'Theological challenges and resources', under 'God as Lawgiver'. In this case, the function was to sustain faithfulness on the part of Israel to match the covenant faithfulness of their God.

90   On the epistemological skepticism expressed in Job 38, see Ithamar Gruenwald, *Apocalyptic and Merkavah Mysticism* (Leiden: Brill, 1980), 8; Alexander, 'Enoch and the Beginnings of Jewish Interest in Natural Science', 236-7. There is a strong note of epistemological optimism in Job 32:8 ('it is the spirit in a mortal, the breath of the Almighty, that makes for understanding'), but it is ascribed to the enigmatic character, Elihu, rather than Job.

91   The phrase 'Hellenistic Judaism' is not as contradictory as it sounds. The term, 'Judaism' (Greek, *Ioudaïsmos*), was first used in 2 Macc. 2:21 to describe adherence to the

beliefs that the world is governed by immutable laws and that it is quantitatively ordered in accordance with measure, weight and number. Both of these beliefs imply a degree of intelligibility to the natural world.

We shall look at a few historic expressions of each of these related beliefs in the apocalyptic and wisdom traditions before moving on to their appropriation by early Christian writers.[92] The ongoing transmission of these ideas demonstrates the extent and continuity of the creationist tradition that early modern scientists like Kepler inherited. The many variations on these beliefs also demonstrate the ferment of the tradition. It was not just an inert dogma, but an energetic conversation that continued to meet an intellectual and emotional need in the lives of its proponents in varying contexts. The texts cited below all reflect on ways these creational beliefs affected the life and self-understanding of ordinary people.

The word 'apocalypse' that appears in the titles of many early Jewish and Christian texts simply means 'revelation'.[93] The popular image of apocalyptic literature is one of religious fanaticism rather than rational scientific discourse. To the contrary, most ancient Jewish apocalypses placed a high value on understanding the natural world and included lengthy descriptions of cosmic structures and operations. Assuming an antithesis between mystic practices and scientific research the way we do today makes it difficult either to appreciate ancient texts like these or to understand the traditions underlying the development of modern Western science.

Apocalyptic texts included dramatic accounts of people who were elevated through the heavens to explore the psychophysical 'metaverse'.[94] These visions were usually attributed to great biblical heroes like Enoch or Moses, whose names go back hundreds of years before these texts were written. As a result of their voyages,

---

city of Jerusalem and to Jewish, as distinct from Greek, customs. Hellenistic culture (after the late fourth century BCE) was not just Greek ('Hellenic') culture. It was an eclectic synthesis of many Near Eastern cultures including the Persian, Babylonian, Egyptian and Jewish, as well as Greek, with many regional variations.

92   Qumran texts form another group that cited the idea of cosmic law, for example, 1QS 3:15-17; 10:1, 6-8; 1QH 9 (1):10-14; 20 (12):4-9; 1QpHab. 7:13.

93   The English word 'apocalypse' comes from the Greek term *apokálypsis*, which is found in the New Testament (for example, Rom. 16:25) and is best known from the first verse of the Book of Revelation.

94   Literary descriptions of these archaic soul journeys may distantly reflect paleoshamanic rituals like those described in Chapter 2. The similarity between Jewish mystical experience and shamanic ecstasy has often been pointed out: Phillip S. Alexander, 'The Historical Setting of the Hebrew Book of Enoch,' *Journal of Jewish Studies* 28 (Autumn 1977), 170-72; James Davila, 'The Hekhalot Literature and Shamanism,' in Eugene H. Lovering, Jr (ed.), *SBL Seminar Papers 1994* (Atlanta: Scholars Press, 1994), 767-89. Even so, the cosmological ideas in apocalyptic visions were probably derived from the culture of the apocalypticists. A comparable recasting of shamanic soul journeying images into cosmologically informed literature appears to have occurred in both ancient China and ancient Greece; David Hawkes, 'The Quest of the Goddess', in Cyril Birch (ed.), *Studies in Chinese Literary Genres* (Berkeley: University of California Press, 1974), 42-68; M.L. West, *The Orphic Poems* (Oxford: Clarendon Press, 1983), 5-7, 146-50. Moreover, if the propensity for soul journey is pre-wired in the human psyche (as argued in Chapter 2), shamanistic practices could emerge in new contexts without any historical continuity at all.

these ancient heroes were able to observe the underpinnings of the cosmos firsthand (anticipating the modern practice of viewing the heavens through astronomical instruments). They examined the celestial movements and atmospheric phenomena already described in earlier texts, and they were able to discern for themselves the laws that governed them – a powerful witness in an era when injustice was widespread and social structures were breaking down. These descriptions were purely imaginary by modern standards, but they illustrate the point at hand – belief in the lawfulness of even the most complex natural phenomena then known – and they transmitted that belief to later generations of believers. A few examples will illustrate the depth of Jewish belief in the intelligibility of God's creation. We shall turn to the complementary question of the human discovery and understanding these laws in the following section.

One of the earliest apocalypses is known as the First (Ethiopic Apocalypse of) Enoch.[95] In one of the earliest portions of this work (third century BCE or earlier), the patriarch Enoch traveled through the heavens to observe the sun and the moon and found that their daily and annual movements were completely regular and consistent.[96] As in the Babylonian *Enūma elish*, cosmic order was cited as justification for regulating human life by a calendar based on celestial phenomena. What is important for our historical survey is the dramatic expression of belief in the lawfulness of the astronomical phenomena involved.[97]

A collection of parables found in later parts of First Enoch describes a divine decree (or oath) that maintains the order of the universe. Every known aspect of the natural world obeyed this decree: the earth, the sea, the movements of sun, moon and stars, and even the winds, and thunder and lightning. None of these creatures ever deviates from the laws that God made for them (1 Enoch 69:13-26).[98] In a culture for which temporary disruptions of solar and lunar orbits were described in ancient

---

95   The First Apocalypse of Enoch was originally written in Hebrew and Aramaic, but it only survives in Ethiopic and Greek, with some fragments in Aramaic (Qumran) and Latin. Relevant information and an English translation on this and other apocalyptic texts are available in James H. Charlesworth, ed., *The Old Testament Pseudepigrapha*, 2 vols (Garden City, N.Y.: Doubleday, 1983), 1:5-89.

96   1 Enoch 72:1-3, 35-7; 73:1; 79:1-2, all part of what is called the 'Book of the Heavenly Luminaries' or 'Astronomical Book' (1 Enoch 72-82); Charlesworth, ed., *Old Testament Pseudepigrapha*, 1:50-53, 58.

97   Enoch's descriptions of the heavens are based on personal observation under the guidance of angels like Uriel; cf. Jeremy Corley, 'Wisdom versus Apocalyptic and Science in Sirach 1,1-10', in F. García Martínez (ed.), *Wisdom and Apocalypticism in the Dead Sea Scrolls and in the Biblical Tradition* (Leuven: Leuven University Press, 2003), 278. For details on 1 Enoch 72-82, see Otto Neugebauer, trans., *The 'Astronomical' Chapters of the Ethiopic Book of Enoch* (København: Munksgaard, 1981); James C. VanderKam, *Enoch and the Growth of an Apocalyptic* Tradition (Washington, DC: Catholic Biblical Association of America, 1984), 89-104. Alexander, 'Enoch and the Beginnings of Jewish Interest in Natural Science', 231-2, neatly summarizes the laws for the heavenly luminaries in a chart on p. 243. See also the helpful illustrations in Daniel C. Olson, *Enoch, A New Translation* (North Richland Hills, Texas: Bibal Press, 2004), 146, 152, 158.

98   1 Enoch 69 is part of the 'Book of the Parables' or 'Similitudes' of Enoch (1 Enoch, chaps 37-71); Charlesworth, ed., *Old Testament Pseudepigrapha*, 1:7, 48-9. Cf. Jubilees 36:7

lore (for example, Joshua 10:12-14; Joel 2:31), this was a revolutionary affirmation of belief in the lawfulness and intelligibility of the natural world. The new emphasis on cosmic law reflects similar emphases in Babylonian and Greek texts described above.[99] Its rediscovery by apocalypticists was evidently a response to the social disorder and perceived lawlessness of Hellenistic times.[100] The affirmation of such belief in the face of apparent disorder would be critical for early modern scientists like Johannes Kepler.

In the somewhat later Second (Syriac Apocalypse of) Baruch (early second century CE), it was Moses' turn to journey through the heavens. In the biblical account from the Book of Exodus, Moses ascended Mount Sinai to receive the Torah (Mosaic Law) that would order the life and worship of Israel (Exod. 19-20). In Second Baruch, Moses' education was expanded to include a complete course in cosmology:

> He [the Most High] also showed him the measures of fire, the depths of the abyss, the weight of the winds, the number of the raindrops... the height of the air... the treasuries of light, the changes of the times, and the inquiries into the Law. (2 Baruch 59:5-11)[101]

This list of Moses' findings is a fairly extensive inventory of the elements of ancient cosmology: fire, watery abyss, wind, rain, air, light – all of them subject to measure, weight and number as in Job 28 and Isaiah 40. Moses' journey through the heavens was imaginary, even by biblical standards, but its articulation of the mathematical character of creation was fundamental to biblical thought.

According to Second Baruch, all of these elements could be studied and interpreted in the same way that Scripture was studied by Torah scholars. Here we have an early version of what later became known as the 'two books of God': Scripture and nature are both written in code.[102] Any one of Moses' calibre should be able to discover the code embedded in creation.[103] I postpone the question of whether ordinary humans were believed to be capable of such understanding to a later section of this chapter.

---

(*Old Testament Pseudepigrapha*, 2:124) on the use of the divine Name that created all things as an oath.

99 There are particularly close parallels in Plato, *Republic* 500c; *Timaeus* 47bc, 90d, although these lack the concept of cosmic law as pointed out earlier.

100 See 1 Enoch 5:4; Charlesworth, ed., *Old Testament Pseudepigrapha*, 1:15.

101 Charlesworth (ed.), *Old Testament Pseudepigrapha*, 1:642. 2 Baruch was written in Hebrew in the early second century CE, but it survives only in Syriac and Arabic, plus a few fragments from an earlier Greek version (ibid., 615-16).

102 Philip Alexander has argued that the ideal of cosmic knowledge was taken from Enoch and transferred to Moses in a rivalry between two schools of Jewish thought; Alexander, 'From Son of Adam to Second God: Transformations of the Biblical Enoch', in Michael E. Stone and Theodore A. Bergren, ed., *Biblical Figures Outside the Bible* (Harrisburg, Penn.: Trinity Press, 1998), 109-110. There was ample precedent for the ascription of cosmic knowledge to Moses. The Torah already assigned a cosmic dimension to Moses' plan for the Tabernacle (Exod. 25:8-9; 40:16-33; cf. Sir. 24:23; Ezekiel the Tragedian, *Exagoge* 77-80). In the synagogue lectionary, the Torah-portion describing the giving of the Torah through Moses (Exod. 21-24) is followed by a Haftorah (reading from the Book of the Prophets) that included Jer. 33:25-6, describing the 'ordinances [or laws, *huqqôt*] of heaven and earth'.

103 Such a possibility is further evidenced by Rabbinic strictures against such speculation, for example, in Mishnah Hagigah 2:1 (c. 200 CE); Tosefta Hagigah 2:1 (c. 300).

*Belief about quantitative measure from the Hellenistic era to the Renaissance*

During Hellenistic times, several Jewish wisdom texts were written that were to be included in the early Christian Bible and become foundational for early and medieval theology. One of the most influential of these books was the Wisdom of Solomon (probably early first century CE), one of the most influential books in the history of the Church.

Wisdom's major contribution to our history was its reformulation of the belief in creation by quantitative measure. In explaining the power of God to redeem Israel from Egypt, the author first described how God created the world out of 'formless matter' (Wis. 11:17), very likely using the terminology of Greek cosmologists like Plato.[104] The way creation exhibits God's redeeming power is supported by an exclamation: 'But you [Lord] have arranged all things by measure and number and weight' (Wis. 11:20). These words distilled the ideas we have already seen in Plato's *Timaeus*, the Old Testament, and apocalyptic literature in a single pithy credo.

The Wisdom of Solomon was included in the Greek Bible (the Septuagint) and was widely cited in the early Church. Christians regarded it as 'inspired Scripture' up to the time of the Protestant Reformation, when the apocryphal books were separated from the preferred Hebrew canon of the Old Testament (the Hebrew Bible). Even after the Reformation, Wisdom was usually included in Protestant Bibles in a separate section of apocryphal writings located between the canonical Old and New Testaments. It continued to be widely read and much loved, and its depiction of the mathematical structure of creation became a prooftext for the importance of mathematical disciplines for the understanding of both God's word and God's world.

One early Latin writer who frequently quoted Wisdom 11:20 was Augustine of Hippo. He often cited our text in order to uphold the rationality of the natural world against detractors of creation like the Manicheans. In one of his best known writings, *The City of God*, Augustine also brought in Plato's *Timaeus* for support:

> Plato emphasizes that God constructed the world by the use of numbers, while we have the authority of Scripture where God is thus addressed, 'You have set in order all things by measure, number, and weight.' (*City of God* XII.19)[105]

Augustine cited the *Timaeus* to get the attention of his Platonist readers, but he used a biblical wisdom text to make his point authoritative. The phenomena of our world are the result of an underlying mathematical structure even if that order is hidden from our view.[106] Even though Plato's writings did not extend that order

---

104 For example, Plato, *Sophist* 265c. Wisdom's spin on the language of Plato was based on the Septuagint (Greek) version of Genesis 1. Here creation takes place in two stages: first primordial earth and water are created in an unformed state (Gen. 1:2); subsequently they are given form and appear as firmament, earth and seas as we know them. It was not the same as Plato's original notion of an eternally pre-existing material substratum.

105 Henry Bettenson, trans., *Augustine, City of God* (Harmondsworth: Penguin Books, 1967), 496. In the context, Augustine was actually arguing against the followers of Origen; see Kaiser, *Creational Theology*, 25n.54 for details.

106 See, for example, *On Genesis Literally* III.16.25.

to the weightiness of the material world, Augustine and later Christians saw their compatibility with biblical thought on this essential point.

The attention Augustine drew to Wisdom 11:20 ensured its place as one of the biblical texts most often cited in discussions of the natural world. It was quoted as a mandate for the use of mathematics by virtually all of the natural philosophers of medieval and Renaissance Europe: Adelard of Bath, Nicolas of Cusa, Agrippa of Nettesheim, Paracelsus, John Dee, Thomas Tymme, Francis Bacon, René Descartes, de Rhetia, and Comenius to cite just a few.[107] Figures like these are rarely included in histories of Christian thought, but all of them were important for the development of early modern science, and all of them were profoundly theological in their thinking about natural philosophy. Kepler's belief that God had created the world according to geometry and measurable quantities was part of a longstanding tradition.[108]

*Beliefs about laws of nature from the Hellenistic era to the Renaissance*

We circle back to the Hellenistic Era to follow a similar trajectory for the doctrine that God had given laws to all creatures. We have already noted this idea in Babylonian, Greek, and Hebrew Bible texts. Here we sketch the history of this important theological teaching down to the time of Kepler.

Perhaps the most influential vehicle for the idea of cosmic laws was another of the Hellenistic wisdom texts later included in the Christian, the Wisdom of Jesus Son of Sirach (Hebrew orig. 190-175 BCE). Like earlier writers, Sirach cited the regularity of the cycles of nature as an indication of God's creation. What was new in this context was the role he assigned to the power of God's spoken word:[109]

> The Lord... arranged his works in an eternal order,
>  and their dominion for all generations.
> They neither hunger nor grow weary,
>  and they do not abandon their tasks.
> They do not crowd one another,
>  and they will never disobey God's word. (Sir. 16:26-28)

---

107 For references, see Allen G. Debus, 'Mathematics and Nature in the Chemical Texts of the Renaissance', *Ambix* 15 (Feb. 1968), 3, 12-15, 20; Kaiser, *Creational Theology*, 54-7, 114-17, 190-99. In 1645, de Rhetia cited Wis. 11:20 to show that one should be able to figure out the distance from earth to the firmament and even to the empyrean; W.G.L. Randles, *The Unmaking of the Medieval Christian Cosmos, 1500-1760* (Aldershot, Hants.: Ashgate, 1999), 144.

108 For Kepler's thinking on God as an architect who created the universe in accordance with preconceived quantitative measurements, see, in addition to the 1597 letter to Mästlin, cited above, his Dedicatory Letter to Lord Sigismund Frederick, Baron von Herberstein, dated 15 May 1596, in *Mysterium cosmographicum*; ET in Baumgardt, *Johannes Kepler: Life and Letters*, 33. Like Plato, Kepler ignored the parameter of weight, which was not needed for his work in either astronomy or optics.

109 Aside from the idea of cosmic laws (found in Job, Isaiah and Jeremiah), the biblical background for the role of God's word or command in creation is found in Pss. 33:6; 148:5; Prov. 8:29.

Sirach's poetry recalls the Babylonian idea that the god Marduk gave tasks and rules to all creatures. The similarity is an indicator in itself of the persistence of theological ideas, particularly when they are expressed in such memorable poetry or prose. In Sirach, however, as in First Enoch, the idea of cosmic law has taken on universal scope ('his works', 'all generations').[110] Equally striking is the image of inexorable regularity – not an impersonal momentum, as we tend to think in a culture of machinery, but an ordered faithfulness in creation that manifests the intelligence of a caring God.

Along with the Wisdom of Solomon, Sirach was included in the major Greek translation of the Old Testament (the Septuagint) and was part of the early Christian Bible. In the Latin West, it was referred to as *Liber ecclesiasticus*, or the 'Church Book', (Ecclesiasticus, not to be confused with the Ecclesiastes). The assimilation of Sirach's idea of laws of nature into Christian theology can be seen as early Christian apologists like Athenagoras, who wrote a *Plea on Behalf of Christians* in the 170s:

> God's particular providence [over heaven and earth] is directed toward the deserving, while everything else is subject to [God's] providential law of Reason [*nómō lógou*] according to the common nature of things…. Each part has its origin in Reason [*gegonòs lógō*], and hence none of them violates its appointed order. (*Plea* 25.2-3)[111]

Athenagoras used the Greek term *lógos*, here translated as 'reason'. He subscribed to the idea of the Logos as God's agent in creation that we discussed in Chapter 1. Athenagoras also echoed Sirach's contention that God's creatures could keep their appointed order because each of them was subject to the Logos. As in Sirach, one gets a sense of the regularity and predictability of this order – not a merely mechanical regularity, but one that manifests the intelligence of a caring God. In following centuries, this idea matured in the hands of writers like Eusebius and Basil, and it was transmitted (like the idea of quantitative measure) to the Western world through the writings of Augustine.

Writing in the early fourth century, Eusebius of Caesarea (Palestine) compiled a rich variety of Greek and Jewish sources in his treatise on *The Preparation for the Gospel* (c. 315 CE). This massive work contains the first instance of the idea of 'laws of universal nature' in Christian literature. Like Second Baruch, Eusebius cited the tradition that Moses had ascended to receive the laws of nature as well as laws for human conduct, but he phrased it in a new way:

> He [Moses] teaches us therefore at the outset to regard God as the real Author and Ruler not only of the laws [of conduct]…but also of the laws of universal nature [*tōn nómōn en tē phýsei tōn hólōn*]." (*Prep.* VII.9)[112]

---

110 Several scholars have suggested Sirach's dependence on early strata of 1 Enoch; see the review in Corley, 'Wisdom versus Apocalyptic and Science in Sirach', 270-71.

111 Richardson (ed.), *Early Christian Fathers*, 328 (with reason capitalized due to its identity with Logos Christ). Athenagoras is traditionally associated with the city of Athens, but he may just as well have taught in Alexandria.

112 Eusebius of Caesarea, *Preparation for the Gospel*, Greek text in Jacques Paul Migne (ed.), *Patrologiae Cursus Completus… Series Graeca*, 162 vols (Paris: Garnier Fratres, 1857-66), 21:532; ET in Edwin Hamilton Gifford, 2 vols (Oxford: Clarendon Press, 1903), 1:314a. A

Grammatically speaking, the phrase 'laws of nature' was borrowed from earlier Jewish writers like Philo, but Eusebius was probably the first writer to apply it explicitly to the regularities of the natural world.[113] The parallel between the laws of Moses and the laws of nature implies that nature is a second book that can be read like the Torah.

Eusebius followed up this parallel by describing how God's 'word and law' established and continually regulates the phenomena of nature: day and night; the courses of sun, moon and stars; the seasons of the year; the depths of the ocean; rain showers and snowstorms; plants and animals. As in earlier writers like Sirach and Athenagoras, none of these creatures transgress the appointed laws.[114] For biblical support, Eusebius brought in the divine edicts of Genesis 1 to show that all natural phenomena were subject to natural laws: earth's regular production of vegetation (Gen. 1:11); the waters' production of fish and fowl (Gen. 1:14); and the seasonal orbits of the luminaries (Gen. 1:20).[115] Early Christians never denied the possibility of miraculous divine interventions, but following Genesis 1, they gave priority to God's operation through laws of nature.

The early Christian view of creation was most thoroughly discussed in exegetical treatments of Genesis 1 that go by the name of *hexaemera*. In Greek, *hexaemeron* literally means 'six days' work'. In Christian literature, the term refers to commentaries on the description of creation in the first chapter of Genesis.[116] One of the most influential statements of belief in cosmic law occurs in the *Hexaemeron*, composed by Basil of Caesarea (Cappadocia) around 360 CE.

Basil's *Hexaemeon* was actually a series of sermons for Holy Week (the week before Easter). Basil preached them to people who came to church on their way to work and again on their way home (but only one on Wednesday for a total of nine sermons). Like Eusebius, he used the idea of laws of nature to describe the edicts of Genesis 1, for example, *Let the earth put forth vegetation: plants yielding seed, and fruit trees of every kind....* (Gen. 1:11). In its biblical context, this verse describes God as a farmer supernaturally seeding the ground and waiting for things to grow, but Basil also understood it as describing a regular natural cycle. Here is the way he explained it:

---

similar phrase in used in *Prep.* VII.10: 'laws which concern the nature of the universe'; trans. Gifford, 315a.

113 Philo had used the phrase *phýseōs nómois* to describe the Pythagorean numerical pattern of the six days of creation; *De opificio mundi* 13. In *De specialibus legibus* IV.232-3, Philo described the regularities of nature in terms of unchangeable laws, though he did not use the phrase 'laws of nature' in this particular context. Christian writers had understood 'laws of nature' only in the moral sense; Robert M. Grant, *Miracle and Natural Law in Graeco-Roman and Early Christian Thought* (Amsterdam: North Holland, 1952), 26. See the discussion in Koester, 'Nomos Physeōs', 533-40 (focusing on the moral laws of nature); and Kaiser, *Creational Theology*, 36.

114 Eusebius, *Preparation* VII.10, trans. Gifford, 314b-d. As in much of the Jewish literature he relies on, Eusebius' point is that humans ought to obey the (Mosaic) laws prescribed for them. The ideological function is apologetic.

115 Eusebius, *Preparation* VII.10, trans. Gifford, 315b-d.

116 *Hexameron* is roughly equivalent to the Hebrew *ma'aseh be-re'shit* ('work of creation'), which developed esoteric overtones in continuing Judaism (Mishnah Hagigah 2:1); J.H. Laenen, *Jewish Mysticism: An Introduction* (Louisville: Westminster John Knox Press, 2001), 23-4.

It was deep wisdom that commanded the earth...first to bring forth grass, then wood [trees], as we see it doing still at this time. For the voice that was then heard and this command were as a natural and permanent law [*nómos tis egéneto phýseōs*] for it [the earth]; it gave fertility and the power to produce fruit for all ages to come.... (*Hexaemeron* V.1)

This short command was in a moment a vast nature [*phýsis*], an elaborate system [*lógos*].... It is this command which, still at this day, is imposed on the earth, and in the course of each year displays all the strength of its power to produce herbs, seeds, and trees. Like tops, which after the first impulse, continue their evolutions; thus nature, receiving the impulse of this first command, follows without interruption the course of ages until the consummation of all things. (*Hexaemeron* V.10) [117]

As Basil exegeted the text, God's command to the primordial elements was not a supernatural intervention aimed at a one-time result. It became a permanent law that would govern nature 'for all ages to come'. God's act of creation gave us a lawful cosmos. The laws are natural and permanent, but not impersonal. They imbue nature with a deep regularity and a degree of predictability (grass, then trees) that enables human understanding and cultivation. Basil's Holy Week listeners must have included lots of farmers.

Basil's *Hexaemeon* was influential throughout the Middle Ages and Renaissance. In the West, it was first paraphrased by Ambrose (c. 387) and then translated into Latin (c. 400). When Robert Grosseteste wrote his own *Hexaemeon* in the twelfth century, he made extensive use of Basil and quoted the passage cited above word for word.[118] Basil's *Hexaemeon* was republished in the sixteenth century and was used by Protestant Reformers like Melanchthon and Calvin.[119] But there was also another, even more effective, vehicle for the idea of laws of nature in the Latin West.

Basil's ideas about cosmic law were incorporated by Augustine into his final Commentary on Genesis (*On Genesis Word for Word*), which also became a major source of cosmological ideas for medieval theologians and Protestant Reformers. Like Basil, Augustine combined the biblical idea of laws for all of God's creatures with the idea of seeding the earth:

For through Wisdom all things were made [cf. Ps. 104:24], and the motion we now see in creatures, measured by the lapse of time, as each one fulfills its proper function, comes to creatures from those causal reasons implanted in them, which God scattered as seeds at the moment of creation. ... Time brings about the development of these creatures according to the laws of their numbers... (*On Genesis Word for Word* IV.51-2)[120]

---

117 *Nicene and Post-Nicene Fathers*, Second Series, ed. Philip Schaff and Henry Wace (14 vols, Buffalo and New York, 1890-1900), 8:76a, 81.

118 Grosseteste, *Hexaemeon* IV.17.2; ET in C.F.H. Martin, trans., *Robert Grosseteste: On the Six Days of Creation* (Oxford: Oxford University Press, 1996), 144.

119 Kaiser, 'Calvin's Understanding of Aristotelian Natural Philosophy: Its Extent and Possible Origins', in Robert V. Schnucker (ed.), *Calviniana: Ideas and Influence of Jean Calvin* (Kirksville: Sixteenth Century Journal Publishers, 1988), 91-2.

120 *Ancient Christian Writers*, 41:141 (modified). The words 'causal' and 'laws of' are part of the meaning, but they do not occur in the Latin: *ex illis rationibus insitis... numeros*; see Jacques Paul Migne (ed.), *Patrologiae Cursus Completus... Series Latina*, 221 vols (Paris: Garnier Fratres, 1844-79), 34:318b.

In this passage Augustine makes explicit (as a commentary should) what Basil had only hinted at. Mathematical instructions ('causal reasons') are embedded in nature in such a way that their effects occur naturally in their proper time according to a predetermined sequence. In stating that these laws have a mathematical form, Augustine was combining the idea of laws in nature with the idea we traced earlier, that of creation in accordance with quantitative measure (based on Wisdom 11:20).

The result of this Latin synthesis was a prescientific concept of mathematical law that gave early modern scientists like Kepler confidence that the phenomena of nature obeyed fixed laws even if they did not conform to any known laws. The point was made most memorable by Augustine in his reflections on a verse of Psalm 148:8 *fire and hail, snow and frost, stormy wind fulfilling God's command*:

> Nothing seems to be so much driven by chance as the turbulence and storms by which these lower regions of the heavens...are assaulted and buffeted. But when the Psalmist added the phrase, *fulfilling his command* [Ps. 148:8], he made it quite clear that the plan in · these phenomena subject to God's command is hidden from us rather than that it is lacking to universal nature. (*On Genesis Word for Word* V.42)[121]

The basic idea here goes all the way back to the Babylonian *Enūma elish* as we have seen: even the most chaotic elements in nature have laws prescribed by the Creator. Reformulations by Greek, Hebrew and early Christian writers strengthened this idea by affirming the universality and mathematical nature of those laws. The belief in the intelligibility of nature that we have found to be an article of faith in early modern astronomers like Kepler and later physicists like Einstein had a long history behind it.

Like Augustine, Kepler and Einstein were keenly aware that the laws of nature are rarely obvious on the surface of phenomena. God has implanted them in nature in such a way that they are only discerned with great difficulty. If so, why would any of our natural philosophers have believed that they themselves would be able to discover those laws? That is the next topic we must examine in our review of the implications of belief in divine creation for the cultural foundation of scientific endeavour.

*Belief in human intelligence from Dynastic Egypt to Hellenistic Judaism*

We began with a review of representative modern physicists, in whose writings we found two primary Science-Fostering Beliefs. One was the belief that we have just traced in different forms from ancient Babylon to the time of Kepler – the belief that the universe is ordered in accordance with mathematical laws. The second is the belief that human beings have sufficient intelligence to discover and understand those laws. Together these beliefs imply that there is some affinity or proportion between the mathematical structure of the universe and the capabilities of human intelligence. Human science will eventually fall short of the complexities of the natural world if the needed resources and technologies are lacking, but in principle there are no barriers to human discovery and understanding. The following sections will trace the origin of this belief in the ancient Near East, and its development by the Hebrews, Greeks and Christians down to the time of Kepler.

---

121 *Ancient Christian Writers*, 41:172-3.

The earliest known evidence of this belief is found in ancient inscriptions describing the Egyptian pharaoh. Here are two examples:

> You [Pharaoh] are the living likeness of your father, Atum of Heliopolis [the sun-god, Re], for authoritative utterance is in your mouth, understanding is in your heart, [and] your speech is the shrine of Truth [*Ma'at*]. (Kubban Stela, lines 17-18)

> I [Pharaoh] have made bright *Ma'at*, which he [Re] loves. I know that he lives by it. [Likewise] it is my bread; I eat of its brightness; I am a likeness from his limbs, one with him. (Hatshepsut inscription)[122]

The Pharaoh is portrayed here as a son or an image of the sun god Re. This father-son affinity had largely to do with their roles of legislation and rule, but it also implied commensurate attributes of wisdom and judgment. The two potentates share the attribute of *Ma'at* ('truth', 'justice' or 'right order'), who was Pharaoh's inspiration ('bread' or 'brightness'). The knowledge Pharaoh received included all the secrets of the cosmos because *Ma'at* was also a personification of the order of the universe.[123]

The coupling of the idea of human likeness to God with the function of rule over creation is more familiar to most of us from Genesis, chapter 1:

> Then God said, 'Let us make humankind in our image, according to our likeness, and let them have dominion over the fish of the sea, and over the birds of the air, and...over all the wild animals of the earth.... (Gen. 1:26)

The wording here may well have been influenced by the ideology of kingship in neighbouring Egypt.[124] If so, the divine image in humanity in Genesis 1, like that in the Egyptian prototype, was understood to include the wisdom to enable dominion over the phenomena of nature. A notable difference from the Egyptian texts we just examined is that the biblical account regarded all humans as possessing the divine image and thereby extended wisdom and dominion (ideally) to all.[125]

---

122 Henri Frankfort, *Kingship and the Gods: A Study of Ancient Near Eastern Religion as the Integration of Society and Nature* (Chicago: University of Chicago Press, 1948), 149, 157-8 (modified).

123 On *Ma'at* as the order of creation, see Frankfort, *Kingship and the Gods*, 51, 157; idem, *Ancient Egyptian Religion* (New York: Columbia University Press, 1948), 53-4. The potentially cosmic attributes of the Pharaoh are also described in Pyramid Texts; James H. Breasted, *Development of Religion and Thought in Ancient Egypt* (New York: Harper, 1959), 123-6. The king's intimacy with an auxiliary spirit like *Ma'at* is one of the most striking parallels between Near Eastern ideals and shamanism; cf. Hultkrantz, 'A Definition of Shamanism', 32-3.

124 So James E. Atwell, 'An Egyptian Source for Genesis 1', *Journal of Theological Studies* 51 (Oct. 2000), 462-4.

125 Atwell finds precedent for the democratization of the divine likeness in the Tenth Dynasty *Instructions for King Merikare* (late twenty-second century BCE): 'They are his images, who came forth from his body' (verse 132); Atwell, 'An Egyptian Source for Genesis 1', 464; cf. Beyerlin (ed.), *Near Eastern Religious Texts*, 46.

Elsewhere in the Old Testament, the attributes of wisdom and protoscientific knowledge were associated with the kings of Israel. Something very similar to the Egyptian prototype is found in the following tradition about King Solomon:

> God gave Solomon very great wisdom, discernment, and breadth of understanding as vast as the sand of the seashore, so that Solomon's wisdom surpassed the wisdom of all the people of the east, and all the wisdom of Egypt.... He would speak of trees... he would speak of animals, and birds, and reptiles, and fish. (1 Kgs. 4:29-30, 33)

The understanding of Solomon was boundless, according to this Deuteronomistic tradition – even greater than the fabled wisdom of the Egyptians![126] The breadth of Solomon's understanding included all of earth's creatures and thereby matched the scope of sovereignty promised to humankind in Genesis 1:26-28.

The only limitation on Solomon's wisdom was the fact that it was granted as a special gift (1 Kgs. 3:12). In the wisdom tradition of the Hebrew Bible, however, the same protoscientific intelligence was ascribed to royalty in general (Prov. 25:2-3), and, by the Hellenistic era, the idea of divine wisdom had been democratized to the point that was promised to all those who would seek it from God (as Solomon had done).

The results of this democratization can be seen in the Wisdom of Solomon (early first century CE), the same apocryphal text in which we earlier found the idea of the mathematical measures in creation. Solomon now speaks as a model for all those who seek wisdom:[127]

> For God is the guide even of wisdom
>  and the corrector of the wise.
> For both we and our words are in his hand, as are all understanding and skill in crafts. (Wis. 7:15-16)

Wisdom is not limited here to royalty as it was in Pharaonic inscriptions and the Deuteronomistic traditions. It is extended to all 'the wise', including all Israelites and potentially all humans.[128] The greater generality of this important wisdom text applies to the range of its applicability in nature as well as among humans. In contrast to the earlier tradition about King Solomon, the breadth of protoscientific knowledge is also no longer limited to commonly observable creatures like animals and plants:

---

126 On the influence of Egyptian models on Solomon's administration, as described in Deuteronomistic tradition, see E.W. Heaton, *Solomon's New Men: The Emergence of Ancient Israel as a National State* (London: Thames and Hudson, 1974), esp. 27-8 on 1 Kgs. 4:29.

127 A similar democratization can be found in Dan. 2:21-3; Job 32:8 and Sir. 17:3-11, the latter two of which follow Genesis (2:7 and 1:26-8, respectively) in portraying human wisdom as a universal endowment by virtue of creation rather than a response to individual piety. The two notions of wisdom are finely balanced in Sir. 1:9-10, 'he poured her out … upon all the living … he lavished her upon those who love him'; cf. Corley, Wisdom versus Apocalyptic'.

128 Judith H. Newman, 'The Democratization of Kingship in Wisdom of Solomon', in Hindy Najman and Judith H. Newman (eds), *The Idea of Biblical Interpretation* (Leiden: Brill, 2004), 310-11, 327-8.

For it is God who gave me unerring knowledge of what exists,
to know the structure of the world and the activity of the elements,
the beginning and end and middle of times,
the alterations of the solstices and the changes of the seasons,
the cycles of the year and the constellations of the stars…
the varieties of plants and the virtues of roots.
I learned both what is secret and what is manifest,
for Wisdom, the fashioner of all things, taught me. (Wis. 7:17-22)

The applicability of human intelligence is here extended to include the activity of the elements and the constellations – reflecting the growing interest in physics and cosmology in the Hellenistic period – and even to hidden, theoretical entities like the solstices and the inner virtues of plants that could only be surmised by inference. Here we have a clear articulation of belief in scientific intelligence in what later became the sacred scriptures of the Christian Church.

Our remaining task is to sketch the appropriation of this tradition down to the time of Kepler. Before we do so, it is worth noting some other developments of the Hellenistic era that led to an even more robust form of belief in scientific intelligence than we see here in the Wisdom of Solomon. We can readily identify two major influences here: Jewish apocalyptic visions; and Greek natural philosophy. These traditions were to be synthesized by the Jewish philosopher, Philo of Alexandria, and passed on to early Christian theology.

*Belief in cosmological intelligence in Jewish apocalypses*

We have already seen how First Enoch and Second Baruch affirm that the universe is governed by natural laws and quantitative measures. There was no antithesis between mystic journeys and cosmological inquiry. In this section, we review the belief that humans have the capacity to understand the structures and laws of the cosmos providing further evidence against any such antithesis in apocalyptic literature.

Modern-day science gains access to the deep structure of the natural world through advanced technologies (the topic of Chapter 4). Today we take it for granted that new technologies will be developed and give us access to new data. When we revisit the thoughts of the ancients, however, we enter a world in which such technologies had not even been imagined. Most early people accepted the fact that their knowledge was limited to what they could perceive with their five senses.[129]

Nonetheless, our spiritual forbears affirmed their belief that in special cases where the heights and depths of the cosmos could be directly observed, suitably trained explorers would be able to understand them even in their most alien aspects. Apocalyptic literature provides some of the most memorable evidence of this belief. The range of the five senses was extended, not by telescopes, but by soul journeys.[130]

---

129 See 4 Ezra 4:7-11, 21-23 on the limits of unaided human perception.

130 One of the earliest studies of this epistemological optimism was Michael E. Stone, 'Lists of Revealed Things in the Apocalyptic Literature', in Frank Moore Cross (ed.), *Magnalia Dei, The Mighty Acts of God* (Garden City, New York: Doubleday, 1976), 414-52; note the

In another of the early sections of First Enoch (third century BCE or earlier), the patriarch Enoch recounted his travels through the heavens. As in our previous reading, Enoch was able to observe the motions of the sun and the moon, evidently for calendrical purposes. Once again he found that the daily and annual movements of the luminaries were lawful and mathematical, but this time emphasis was placed on Enoch's own ability to decipher those laws:

> And the gates of heaven were open, and I saw how the stars of heaven come out, and I counted the gates out of which they exit and wrote down all their exits for each one according to their numbers, their names, their ranks, their seats, their periods, their months, as Uriel, the holy angel who was with me, showed me. (1 Enoch 33:2-3)[131]

Enoch was granted two things that were not available to everyone: personal access to the heavens and the guidance of an angelic teacher (Uriel).[132] The mythic figure of Enoch represents a conventicle of initiates. These apocalypticists were among the educated elites of their time not unlike university-trained scientists today who have access to instrumentation and technical training that others do not have.[133] The significant point for our history is that such people were believed to benefit from the privileges of access and training. Enoch and those who studied under him could understand remote phenomena in terms of the conceptual tools and rudimentary mathematics at their disposal.

A more democratized version of this belief is found in the Second (Slavonic Apocalypse of) Enoch (probably late first cent. CE). Here Enoch describes his accumulated knowledge of the cosmos to his children, who very likely stand in for the disciples. Most of what he learned, he says, was based on his personal observation (2 Enoch 40:1). Enoch claimed to have learned the dimensions of the heavens, to have counted the stars, and to have measured all the movements of the sun and moon – recondite topics that are said to exceed the understanding of ordinary people and even that of the angels (2 Enoch 40:2-5). He also investigated the source of the clouds and how they carry the rain, the routes of lightning, the sources of snow and ice, and the winds (2 Enoch 40:8-11). Enoch's point is not just that these phenomena

---

association of speculative investigation and ecstatic experience on 435-6. On the influence of Hellenistic literature about soul journeys of mythic figures like Hermes, see Martin Hengel, *Judaism and Hellenism: Studies in their Encounter in Palestine during the Early Hellenistic Period*, trans. John Bowden, 2 vols (London: SCM Press, 1974), 1:210-18.

131 1 Enoch 33 is part of the 'Book of the Watchers' (1 Enoch 1-16); Charlesworth, ed., *Old Testament Pseudepigrapha*, 1:28-9.

132 Uriel ('Light of God') is associated with knowledge and the administration of cosmic phenomena in 1Enoch 20:2 (Greek text); 72:1; 74:2; 75:3; 82:7-8; 4 Ezra 4:1-11.

133 1 Enoch 19:3 limits direct knowledge of the cosmos to Enoch. According to Jonathan Z. Smith, however, the 'objective narrative' of apocalyptic texts like 1 Enoch had a 'subjective correlative' in the experience of their readers; J.Z. Smith, 'The Prayer of Joseph', in Jacob Neusner (ed.), *Religions in Antiquity: Essays in Memory of Erwin Ramsdell Goodenough* (Leiden: Brill, 1968), 288-92. The representative character of Enoch is stated in Wis. 4:10.

have a mathematical structure, but that the human psyche is capable of grasping that structure in its fullness.[134]

Second Enoch went decisively further than earlier Enochic literature in emphasizing the capabilities of the human psyche – rivaling that of the angels. In support of this belief, the writer retold the story of the creation of humanity in Genesis 1 and thereby extended its claims for cosmos-penetrating powers of the psyche to all humans (2 Enoch 30:8-12).[135]

In Enoch's version of the creation story, humanity is portrayed as a microcosm: each attribute of human nature was derived from one of the domains of the psychophysical metaverse. Each of them was thought to be necessary to human life. On the visible side, human flesh was derived from the earth; human blood from the dew and the sun; human bones from stone, and so forth. There were also two invisible attributes. The human spirit was derived from God's own spirit and from the wind (cf. Gen. 1:2; 2:7). Human reason (intelligence) was derived from the mobility of the angels and from clouds (2 Enoch 30:8).[136] The faculty of reason, being derived from the 'mobility of the angels', enabled humans to gain access to the heavens and to comprehend the dynamics of the luminaries. As a result, all humans reflect the divine: they are capable of ruling on earth and of sharing God's own wisdom (2 Enoch 30:12; cf. Gen. 1:26-30).

This emphasis on human ability to understand an immense and bewildering universe supports our earlier findings about the science-fostering potential of apocalyptic literature. A culture informed by this literature would always remember the dream of pursuing recondite topics like the laws that govern the heavens.

*Belief in mathematical intelligence among Pythagoreans and Platonists*

Parallel to the development of Jewish apocalyptic traditions was the development of belief in the possibility of a mathematical understanding of the cosmos among the Pythagoreans. The early thinking of this movement has survived only in fragments among the writings of later authors. Particularly important are the fragments attributed to Philolaus, a Pythagorean, who taught in the late fifth and early fourth centuries BCE and who is best known for the innovative idea that the earth revolves around a central fire. For Philolaus' belief in the role of reason in mathematical science, we must rely on a tradition cited by a later writer (c. 200 CE):

> The Pythagoreans declare that it [the way to truth] is not reason [*tòn lógon*] in general, but the reason which is obtained from the sciences [lit. 'from mathematics'], even as Philolaus

---

134 Charlesworth (ed.), *Old Testament Pseudepigrapha*, 1:164-77 for the long (J) and short (A) recensions. Second Enoch was written in Hebrew in the late first century CE, but it survives only in Slavonic (ibid., 94).

135 Charlesworth (ed.), *Old Testament Pseudepigrapha*, 1:150-52. The complete passage survives only in the longer (J) recension.

136 On the combination of terrestrial and angelic attributes in humanity, see Gen. Rab. 14:3. Cf. Wis. 7:24 on the mobility of Wisdom that enables her to penetrate all things. On the parallels to other Greek texts like Wis. 7:24 that describe the human mind, see David Winston, *The Wisdom of Solomon, A New Translation*, Anchor Bible 43 (New York: Doubleday, 1979), 182.

said that 'It, being conversant with the nature of all things [*tês tôn hólôn phýseôs*], possesses a certain kinship thereto, since it is in the nature of like to be apprehended by like.'[137]

Viewed from the background of the Egyptian and Hebrew traditions, this formulation of the idea is distinctive. Human intelligence is explicitly stated to be mathematical in character, particularly as it applies to the natural world. As a result there is a direct relationship ('a certain kinship') between human intelligence and the nature [*phýsis*] of the universe – the latter also being mathematical.[138] Similar ideas could (and later would) be inferred directly from the Jewish scriptures: the Wisdom that structured the cosmos mathematically was also reflected in the psyche of people like Solomon. But this tiny fragment of Philolaus states the point explicitly: the human mind can develop a deep affinity with the structures of the universe.

The ideas of the Pythagoreans had a major influence on Plato and his followers in the fourth century BCE. Subsequently, it permeated a wide range of popular works in natural philosophy and religion. Before we look at Philo, one example will illustrate the influence of the Pythagoreans on the popular (Middle) Platonism of Hellenistic Alexandria.

The dialogue known as the *Axiochus*, an imitation of Plato's Socratic dialogues, was written in the second or first century BCE. The writer describes Socrates speculating on the seemingly supernatural capabilities of human intelligence as follows:

> ...a mortal nature would certainly not have arisen to such lofty attempts... to cross seas, to build cities, to establish governments, to look up at the heavens and to see the revolutions of the stars, the courses of the sun and moon, their risings and settings, their eclipses, their swift periodic returns, the equinoxes and the double tropics [solstices], the storms of the Pleiades, the summer winds and falls of rains and the sudden fury of hurricanes, and to chart for eternity the conditions of the universe, unless there were really some divine spirit in the soul by which it has comprehension and knowledge of such important matters. (*Axiochus* 370BC)[139]

This anonymous writer evidently had a high view of the intelligence required for government and manufacture. His main focus, however, was on human ability to understand celestial and atmospheric phenomena – an ability he attributed to a 'divine spirit' residing in the human soul.[140] Although there is no reference to the

---

137 Philolaus cited in Sextus Empiricus, *Adversus Mathematicos* VII.92 = *Adversus Dogmaticos* II.92, ET in Loeb Classical Library, *Sextus Empiricus*, 4 vols (Cambridge, Mass: Harvard University Press, 1933-49), 2:49. The Greek text reads *apò tōn mathēmátikōn*. The authenticity of the quotation is debated, but the idea is undoubtedly much earlier than Sextus Empiricus (c. 200 CE).

138 The idea that the universe is based on principles of 'measures, weights, and numbers' is attested in frag. 8 of Philolaus; see Navon (ed.), *Pythagorean Writings*, 133. Fragments of the Pythagorean philosopher, Archytas, refer to aspects of intelligence being engraved on humans by the deity; for example, frag. 6 in Navon, ed., *Pythagorean Writings*, 147.

139 Jackson P. Hershbell, *Pseudo-Plato, Axiochus* (Chico, Calif.: Scholars Press, 1981), 45. See pp. 1-3, 20-21 for the Pythagorean orientation and the date.

140 The idea that humans are endowed with a divine spirit (*pneûma*) reflects the Stoic influence on Middle Platonism as it does in Philo of Alexandria; see David Runia, 'God and Man in Philo of Alexandria', *Journal of Theological Studies* 39 (April 1988), 67-8.

mathematical nature of these phenomena, the human psyche is said to have a deep affinity with the structures of the universe.

The belief that a spiritual endowment enabled humans to understand the world in which they lived was well known from Scripture as evidenced in the passages cited earlier. But the Pythagorean-Platonic version of this belief became a virtual second revelation for Jewish and Christian authors from Philo and his Christian followers all the way down to Johannes Kepler. Tracing this line of influence will complete our review of the early history of the creationist tradition.

*Belief in mathematical intelligence in Philo of Alexandria*

Philo's commentaries on the Mosaic Torah were based on Jewish exegetical traditions (wisdom and apocalyptic), but they also incorporated insights from the Hellenistic schools that proliferated in Alexandria, particularly those of the Pythagoreans and the Platonists. As a result, Philo was able to reformulate earlier Jewish ideas about human understanding of the natural world in terms of a direct relationship between the rational nature of humanity and the structures of the cosmos.

Belief in the human capability for comprehending the laws of the cosmos appears in many of these commentaries. I shall cite two examples, both based on the belief that humans are created in God's image. The first refers explicitly to Genesis 1:26.

> ...Moses tells us that humanity was created after the image and likeness of God [Gen. 1:26-27]... For the human mind evidently occupies a position in humans precisely answering to that which the great Ruler occupies in all the world.... And, while it opens by arts and sciences roads branching in many directions...it comes through land and sea investigating what either element contains. Again, when on soaring wing it has contemplated the atmosphere and all its phases, it is borne yet higher to the ether and the circuit of the heaven and is whirled round with the dances of the planets and fixed stars in accordance with the laws of perfect music, following that love of Wisdom which guides its steps. (*On the Creation of the World* 69-70)[141]

The literary conceit of the philosopher's mind journeying through the heavens reflects the apocalyptic visions attributed to archetypal figures like Enoch and Moses.[142] Philo's ascription to the human mind of both seeing (contemplating) and comprehending is similar to that found in Middle Platonic texts like the *Axiochus*. As in both apocalyptic and Middle Platonic speculations, the realms to be investigated are the circuits of the stars and phenomena of the atmosphere. The motif of love for Wisdom was also a common theme from Pharaoh's love for *Ma'at* (discussed

---

141 Philo, *De opificio mundi* 69-70; ET in Loeb Classical Library, *Philo*, 1:55; cf. the passage from Seneca, *Naturales Quaestiones* I, Pref. 7-8, cited in Chapter 2. Philo also used the idea of humanity as a microcosm as a way of affirming the quasi-divine nature of the human intellect; *De opificio mundi*; ET in Loeb Classical Library, *Philo*, 1:115).

142 On Philo's awareness of apocalyptic traditions about the ascensions of Enoch and Moses is seen in *De confusione linguarum* 95; *Questions on Genesis* I.86; cf. Peder Borgen, 'Moses, Jesus, and the Roman Emperor: Observations in Philo's Writings and the Revelation of John', *Novum Testamentum* 38 (April 1996), 151-2.

above)[143] to the Wisdom of Solomon (Wis. 8:2). The idea of Wisdom as a guide for humans is also found in the Wisdom of Solomon, particularly in the passage quoted above (Wis. 7:22; 8:9; 9:11; 10:10, 17). Presently, we shall see these beliefs deeply influenced the Alexandrian tradition of Christian thought.

Philo's second treatment of God's image as the source of cosmos-investigating intelligence occurs in one of his commentaries on Genesis:

> The invisible Deity stamped on the invisible soul the impress of itself...the image of God [cf. Gen. 1:26-27].... For how could a mortal nature at one and the same time have stayed at home [in the body] and been abroad [in mind].... How again would it have been possible for it to fly up from the earth through the air into the sky and to examine the condition and movement of the heavenly bodies, discovering how the beginning of their movement and its cessation is determined, in what manner they are, in accordance with some law of congruity adjusted both to one another and to the universe.... How then was it likely that the mind of humans being so small, contained in such small bulks as a brain or a heart, should have room for all the vastness of sky and universe, had it not been an inseparable portion of that divine and blessed soul? (*That the Worse Attacks the Better* 86-90)[144]

According to Philo, the capacity of the human mind was literally boundless in spite of the limitations of the human body – a theme we have also come across in the Middle Platonic *Axiochus*.[145] As in the previous passage quoted, Philo describes all the phenomena and laws of the universe as being intelligible to the human mind. His epistemological optimism was somewhat exaggerated given the rather limited technologies available in his time. But it clearly reinforced belief in the capabilities of the human mind, extending beyond normal human experience to the remotest parts of the universe.

It is remarkable how this passage in Philo anticipates the present-day discussion about the mystery of Science-Fostering Intelligence. In current discussions (reviewed in Chapter 2), the source of concern about human capacity for scientific endeavour stems from the apparent limits of the evolutionary origins of the human brain. For Philo similar concerns derive from consideration of the small size of the brain (or heart). But like Einstein, Margenau and Davies, Philo took the possibility of scientific investigation as an article of belief.

## Belief in scientific intelligence in early Christian theology

Like belief in an intelligible universe, belief in a human intelligence capable of exploring that universe was transmitted to later generations by the Church. From the Hebrew Bible and its commentators, Christians inherited the belief that humans

---

143 See the Egyptian Hatshepsut inscription cited above. On the ancient Egyptian background for Philo's thinking, see A. Broadie and J. MacDonald, 'The Concept of Cosmic Order in Ancient Egypt in Dynastic and Roman Times', *L'Antiquité classique* 47 (1978), 106-128.

144*Quod deterius potiori insidiari soleat.* 86-90; ET in Loeb Classical Library, *Philo*, 2:261-3.

145 The fact that Philo is following a literary topos is confirmed by the fact that elsewhere he seems to deny the immortality of the rational soul; *Quaestiones et Solutiones in Genesin* I.16; II.62.

are created in God's image and thereby related to divine Wisdom. From apocalyptic literature they learned that human mental capabilities rivaled those of the angels in cosmos-exploring potential. From Greco-Roman traditions they absorbed the idea that the human psyche is specially tuned to the structures of the cosmos. The epistemological optimism of Philo was developed along Christian lines by early philosopher-theologians of Alexandria like Clement, Origen and Athanasius.[146] The long-range concern of these theologians was how one is to gain knowledge of God, but the possibility of understanding the cosmos God created was an integral part of their argument.

The primary vehicles that transmitted these beliefs to Western Europe were the Cappadocian Fathers and Augustine, all of whom followed the Alexandrian tradition. These theologians thought of creation as an imprinting of divine reason or word (*lógos*). In fact, there were two such imprintings: first on the universe, then on the human psyche.[147] This idea of imprinting occurs, for example, in one of Gregory Nazianzen's *Theological Orations* (380 CE). The orator begins with a rhetorical question:

> Is it not the Artificer [of heaven, the elements, and all moving things] who implanted reason [*lógon*] in them all, in accordance with which the universe is moved and controlled?... Thus reason [*lógos*] that proceeds from God that is implanted in all from the beginning, and is the first law in us, and is bound up in all leads us up to God through visible things. (*Oration* 28.16)[148]

Nazianzen's pairing of the reason [*lógos*] imprinted in all things with that imprinted on the human mind is reminiscent of the teachings of Philolaus and Philo in that it implied a close relationship between the rational capacities of humans and the structures of the cosmos.[149] He was more explicit, however, in attributing both of these imprintings to divine creation.[150]

For Gregory Nazianzen, the human mind transcended the limits of the body. However, Gregory was far less positive than Philo about the possibilities of human science in his orations. The reason for this apparent inconsistency is that Nazianzen was anxious not to give encouragement to local Arians (Eunomians), who prided themselves in their ability to uyse dialectic logic in opposition to Nicene orthodoxy.

---

146 For example, Clement, *Stromateis* VI.8; Origen, *Peri archōn* II.11.6-7; Athanasius, *Contra gentes* 2.

147 Precedent for the idea of imprinting on the universe is found in Philo, *De specialibus Legibus* I.47-8. Precedent for the idea of imprinting on the human psyche is found in Philo, *Quis rerum divinarum heres sit* 230-33; cf. Athanasius, *Orationes contra Arianos* II.78.

148 Gregory of Nazianzus, *Oration* 28.16; ET in Nicene and Post-Nicene Fathers, Second Series, 7:294b; Hardy and Richardson, *Christology of the Later Fathers*, 147. Orations 27-31 are known as the five 'Theological Orations'.

149 See Gregory of Nazianzus, *Oration* 28:22, on the ability of the human mind to travel over the universe in swift motion and enter all things. Cf. 2 Enoch 30:8 (cited above) on humans being created to approxime the 'the mobility of the angels'.

150 Biblical texts frequently drew parallels between God's creating the universe and the creation of humanity; see Sir. 16:26-17:14; 2 Macc. 7:28. Philo was primarily concerned with the creation of the ideal world as the pattern for the empirical creation; *De opificio mundi* 78; *De vita Mosis* II.127; *De specialibus legibus* I.48.

The Arians argued that God must be unbegotten by definition. Since all agreed that Christ was a 'begotten Son', not unbegotten, it followed that he could only be 'god' in a metaphorical sense of the term.

At the same time, Nazianzen was chastising supporters of orthodox Christology who relied on the same kind of logic to argue against the Arians.[151] Under these circumstances, he felt it necessary to stress the limits of human reason in defining the nature of God while, at the same time, arguing for the existence of a Creator.[152] The strategy Nazianzen developed to support this delicate balance was to cite numerous aspects of the natural order that defied scientific understanding: for example, the occult properties of medicines and the causes of thunder and lightning.[153] Even for the more orderly movements of the sun, moon and stars, where astronomers had mapped the patterns of motion, Nazianzen denied that they understood their real causes.[154]

Gregory Nazianzen's emphasis on human limits was largely the result of his polemical contexts. A more optimistic epistemology like that of Philo can found in the catechetical writing of his close associate, Gregory of Nyssa.[155] Nyssa's optimism was primarily directed against pagans who deprecated human nature – just the opposite of Nazianzen's situation with the Arians. In other words, the teachings of the early theologians about scientific intelligence could take different forms in different contexts.

Of all the voices that have echoed down the centuries of Western Europe into the Middle Ages and Renaissance, none was stronger or clearer than that of Saint Augustine. Augustine synthesized the ideas of the Alexandrians and the Cappadocians and reformulated them in crisp Latin texts that became the required reading of subsequent Western scholars. We shall look at two of these passages before turning to later writers who will illustrate the medieval and Renaissance background of Johannes Kepler.

When we discussed Augustine's belief about laws and mathematical norms in nature, we were left with some doubt about the ability of humans to understand those laws. In his discussion of chaotic phenomena like turbulent storms in his major Genesis commentary, Augustine suggested that 'the plan in these phenomena subject to God's command is hidden from us'.[156] Then how would Augustine deal with the Church's tradition about the capabilities of the human mind created in God's image?

Like Gregory Nazianzen, Augustine was often critical of what he saw as arrogance in pagan philosophers who opposed Christian teachings. His point was different, however. Augustine valued the efforts of natural philosophers to measure the universe and trace the paths of the stars, but he pointed out that these scientific skills were really divine gifts. Instead of pointing at the limits of human reason,

---

151 Gregory of Nazianzus, *Oration* 27.6, 8, 9; 28:6-7.

152 On the incomprehensibility of God, see Gregory of Nazianzus, *Oration* 28.10-11, 17.

153 On the inaccessibility of many phenomena of nature, see Gregory of Nazianzus, *Oration* 28.23-30.

154 Gregory of Nazianzus, *Oration* 28.29, which echoes texts like Job 38:33 and Sir. 3:21-4 that stress the limits of human understanding.

155 Gregory of Nyssa, *Catechetical Oration* 10. The wording clearly follows that of Philo, *Quod deterius potiori insidiari soleat* 90, cited above.

156 *On Genesis Word for Word* V.42. Cf. *City of God* XXI.5, where Augustine affirms that miracles also have causes even though the human mind can not explain them.

Augustine celebrated its strengths and stressed the importance of acknowledging reason's source in divine creation:

> They can foresee a future eclipse of the sun, but do not perceive their own eclipse in the present. For they do not in a religious spirit investigate the source of the intelligence with which they research into these matters. ... They have not known the way, your Word [*verbum*] through whom you made the things that they count ... the senses thanks to which they observe what they count, and the mind they employ to calculate. (*Confessions* V.4-5)[157]

In addition to the five senses, according to Augustine, humans have a kind of sixth sense by which they can understand the mathematical patterns of creation.[158]

Augustine's argument relied on two foundational ideas that we have seen in earlier literature. One idea is that humans are created in the divine image – the image itself being understood by Augustine and other Christian theologians as the Word or Son of God. The other idea is that the basic structures of the cosmos are all mathematical ones – they can be measured, numbered and sometimes weighed (based on Wis. 11:20).[159]

To these traditional ideas, Augustine added the Cappadocian concept of a double imprinting of the Word of God: the Word has imprinted number in the universe and the ability to recognize and interpret number in the human mind. As he stated in his *On Genesis Word for Word*, the main way in which humans differ from other animals is in their ability discern the numerical codes embodied in material things by first contemplating the nature of number within itself.[160] This portrayal of mathematics as an intrinsic part of human nature is the belief that Kepler later inherited and applied to the case of geometry.[161]

### Belief in scientific intelligence in the Middle Ages and Renaissance

Contrary to a common misunderstanding, the centuries between Augustine and the fourteenth-century Renaissance were not exceptionally dark or uninformed. The writings of Basil and Augustine continued to be read, and their ideas were supplemented by a variety of other sources. I offer a few examples from the Middle Ages and the Renaissance in order to round out our revision of historical theology with an emphasis on the emergence of Science-Fostering Beliefs.

---

157 Augustine, *Confessions*, trans. Henry Chadwick (Oxford: Oxford University Press, 1991), 74. Like the Greek *lógos*, the Latin *verbum* means 'word'. The usual Latin term for reason is *ratio*.

158 Along the same lines, the numerical powers that regulate the development of living beings are invisible to the human eye but can be discerned by the intellect; Augustine, *De Genesi ad litteram* VIII.8.16; X.21.37.

159 Cf. Augustine, *Confessions*, V.7 on the use of Wis. 11:20.

160 Augustine, *De Genesi ad litteram* IV.7.13; ET in *Ancient Christian Writers*, 41:112. Augustine here touched on the dual aspect of mathematics: encoded in nature and constructed in the human mind. Faith in God as Creator of both nature and mind ensured that the two aspects matched each other and provided the cultural foundation of scientific endeavour.

161 Kepler, *Harmonice mundi* IV.1, discussed above.

Although the Church was the primary conduit for transmitting ancient Jewish and Greek ideas to the early modern Europe, we should not overlook three important non-Christian sources for these beliefs: continuing Platonism, continuing Judaism, and Arabic natural philosophy.

The most important Platonist influence on Renaissance philosophers was Proclus Diadochus (d. c. 485). Like the Cappadocian theologians, Proclus taught that the human soul was a tablet on which cosmic Mind (*Nous*) engraved the forms of geometry enabling it to comprehend all things discursively.[162] As mentioned above, Kepler often quoted Proclus' ideas to support his argument for the importance of geometry in mathematical philosophy.

Continuing Judaism was another important source of Science-Fostering Belief in early modern Europe. The Rabbis debated human ability to understand phenomena like thunder, and the famous Jewish philosopher, Maimonides (c. 1190), was guarded about the possibility of demonstrating truths like the sphericity of the earth.[163] But the Babylonian Talmud preserved an older a tradition that gifted people like Moses' construction manager, Bezalel (the 'Shade of God'), knew how to combine the letters with which heaven and earth had been created.[164] In effect, the structure of the world could be represented by a simple set of numbers. The Rabbis also encouraged the calculation of orbital periods and constellations as a form of Torah observance.[165] Strong optimism about the possibilities of human science and control of nature continued to be expressed by medieval Jewish scholars like Nahmanides (1194-1270), Abulafia (fl. 1270-91), and Gikatilla (1248-c.1325).[166]

Arabic natural philosophy was another important influence at the early stages of Western science in the twelfth and thirteenth centuries. Arab astronomers, alchemists and physicians synthesized material from China and India as well as from the ancient Greeks, Syrian Christians and Sephardic Jews.[167] One of the most popular Arab sources was the *Ghâyat al-Hakîm* ('Aim of the Sage'), a text of Neoplatonic philosophy, astrology and magic that was probably composed in eleventh-century Spain. The *Ghâyat* was translated into Castilian Spanish during the reign of the Christian king, Alfonso X of Castile (r. 1252-82), and later known to the Latin world as the *Picatrix*. Like 2 Enoch and Philo of Alexandria, the *Picatrix* portrayed humanity as a microcosm capable of participating in all aspects of the metaverse:

> ...he is a complete, animated and rational body with a rational spirit... and rational means capable of knowledge.... God has made him the maker and inventor of all science and knowledge, able to explain all qualities, to accept everything in the world, to understand

---

162 Proclus, *A Commentary on the First Book of Euclid's Elements*, 14.

163 Genesis Rabbah 12:1; Maimonides, *Guide for the Perplexed* 31.

164 Babylonian Talmud, tractate Berakhot 55a. The reasoning is based on a comparison of Exod. 35:31 with Prov. 3:19, 20. Hebrew letters also represent numbers.

165 Babylonian Talmud, tractate Shabbat 75a.

166 See Moshe Idel, *Absorbing Perfections: Kabbalah and Interpretation* (New Haven: Yale University. Press, 2002), 321-2; idem, *Language, Torah and Hermeneutics in Abraham Abulafia* (Albany: SUNY Press, 1989), 49, 105, 109.

167 See Kaiser, *Creational Theology*, 73-6, on the role of Syrian Christians in transmitting Greek medicine to the Islamic world and its eventual influence on medieval Western Europe.

the treasures within everything with a prophetic spirit.... He understands all intelligent forms and everything in the world. ...with his words he numbers, narrates, and explains their natures and actions....[168]

These influential philosophical texts helped revive the epistemological optimism that the West had inherited from early Platonic, Jewish and Christian writers.

Twelfth-century Europe experienced a renaissance of interest in both natural philosophy and the mechanical arts. One of the challenges that apologists for such endeavours had to address was the argument that all such capacities had been vitiated by the fall of humanity described in Genesis 3. However, belief in the continued presence of the divine image and its possible restoration provided a strong counterbalance that allowed the defense of traditional belief in scientific intelligence. Here are two writers who argued the case for science.

One important source was the popular early twelfth-century manual of the arts like painting, glassmaking and metalwork that were needed for the construction of churches. The author, known as 'Theophilus the Presbyter', grappled with the apparent contradiction between the Bible's positive portrayal of artisans like Bezalel and the idea that humans had been deprived of their godlike skills after the Fall.[169] 'Theophilus' found an apparent resolution to the problem by noting that there are, in fact, two creation narratives in Genesis. The account in Genesis 2 describes the animation of the first humans with divine breath, which is followed by their loss of immortality in Genesis 3. The earlier account in Genesis 1, however, described the creation of the first humans in the image of God (Gen. 1:26-27). According to 'Theophilus', the human fall into mortality only affected the gift of eternal life, and did not affect the divine image. As a result the skills needed for science and technology could still be relied upon:

> But, although they lost the privilege of immortality through the sin of disobedience... nevertheless they transmitted to the generations of posterity their distinction of knowledge and intelligence.[170]

This belief in the role of the divine image provides some background for the epistemological optimism of later writers like Philip Melanchthon and Johannes Kepler.

---

168 *Liber Picatrix* I.6; Latin text in David Pingree, ed., *Picatrix: The Latin Version of the Ghâyat Al-Hakîm* (London: Warburg Institute, 1986), 26-7; ET adapted from Eugenio Garin, *Astrology in the Renaissance: The Zodiac of Life*, trans. Carolyn Jackson and June Allen (London: Routledge & Kegan Paul, 1983), 50.

169 'Theophilus' is thought to have been a pseudonym of the Benedictine monk, Roger of Helmarshausen, who was himself a goldsmith. He was evidently familiar with puritanical criticisms of the use of the arts for the adornment of churches; see 'Theophilus' in Charles Coulston Gillispie (ed.), *Dictionary of Scientific Biography*, 16 vols (New York: Scribner's, 1970-80), 13:327a.

170 Theophilus Presbyter, *De diversis artibus*, Book I, Prologue; ET, *Theophilus, On Divers Arts: The Foremost Medieval Treatise on Painting, Glassmaking and Metalwork*, trans. John G. Hawthorne and Cyril Stanley Smith (London: Constable, 1963), 11. Like Philo and Augustine, 'Theophilus' located the image of God in the human intellect.

Another approach to the problem of the Fall was developed at about the same time by the English natural philosopher, Adelard of Bath. Adelard was one of the first Western Europeans to translate advanced Arabic scientific texts into Latin. He is often regarded by historians as the first scientific thinker on the Latin West.[171] Like 'Theophilus', Adelard focused on the formation of the human soul in the divine likeness. As a result of this divine endowment, humans were not limited to describing the patterns of nature; they could actually investigate the underlying causes. The effect of the Fall was to confine human souls to the confines of the their bodies and thereby limit their range of knowledge. Nonetheless, the original splendour of the soul was not obliterated and scientific questions could be pursued with due care.[172] Adelard was the first Western philosopher to attempt a rational account of everyday phenomena of nature.[173]

So neither craftsman nor philosopher felt that the biblical narrative disallowed the serious pursuit of natural philosophy. Their epistemological optimism was nicely summed up a mid-twelfth-century overview of the metacosmos written by Bernard of Tours (Bernardus Silvesteris):

> [Humanity] shall behold clearly principles shrouded in darkness, so that Nature may keep nothing undisclosed. He will survey the aerial realms, the shadowy stillness of Dis [the underworld], the vault of heaven, the breadth of the earth, [and] the depths of the sea. He will perceive whence things change, why the summer swelters, autumn blights the land, spring is balmy, winter cold. He will see why the sun in radiant, and the moon, why the earth trembles, and the ocean swells. Why the summer day draws out its long hours, and night is reduced to a brief interval.... (*Cosmographia, Micrcosmos* 10)[174]

Bernard's text distils the essence of Science-Fostering Belief: humans have the ability not only to recognize patterns of natural phenomena, but to discern the laws or principles that are hidden beneath those patterns.

Although none of these twelfth-century texts specified use of the mathematics in scientific investigation, they did establish the possibility of humans understanding natural phenomena including the most remote aspects of the universe. Moreover, they encouraged an investigation of causes as well as well as the phenomena themselves.

These beliefs were further developed in the European Renaissance that provided the context for the origin of early modern science. The field of knowledge was not compartmentalized as it is today, and it was quite common for these Renaissance figures to be expert in astronomy or medicine as well as theology.

---

171 Adelard of Bath (not to be confused with Peter Abelard) is the first figure discussed in standard texts of medieval science like A. C. Crombie, *Augustine to Galileo*.

172 Adelard of Bath, *De eodem et diverso* ('On Sameness and Diversity'); ET by Winthrop Wetherbee, 'Philosophy, Cosmology, and the Twelfth-Century Renaissance', in Peter Dronke (ed.), *A History of Twelfth-Century Western Philosophy* (Cambridge: Cambridge University Press, 1988), 26.

173 Adelard of Bath, *Quaestiones Naturales* 4; see Richard C. Dales, *The Scientific Achievement of the Middle Ages* (Philadelphia: University of Pennsylvania Press, 1973), 40.

174 *The Cosmographia of Bernardus Silvestris*, trans. Winthrop Wetherbee (New York: Columbia University Press, 1973), 113-14.

A good example is Jacques Lefèvre d'Étaples (d. 1536). In traditional church history, Lefèvre is best known for his translations of the Old and New Testaments and his commentaries on the Book of Psalms and the Epistles of Paul. In many ways he foreshadowed the work of Protestant Reformers like Philip Melanchthon. But Lefèvre also had other interests. He published two editions of Marsilio Ficino's translation of the Hermetic corpus, another ancient source of belief in the ability of the human mind to investigate the heavens.[175] He was also admired for his introductory treatise on astronomy, published in 1503, which was as deeply theological as his commentaries were. Here, for example, is the way Lefèvre described the task of the astronomer:

> The good and wise Artisan of all things, by an act of his divine intelligence, produced the real heavens and their real movements. Similarly, our intelligence, which seeks to imitate the Intelligence to which it owes its existence... composes within itself some fictive heavens and fictive motions; these are images of the true heavens and true motions. And in these images, as if they were traces left by the divine intelligence of the Creator, the human intelligence seizes hold of the truth. (*Introductory Astronomy*)[176]

According to Lefèvre, God created the heavens and their movements in accordance with a preconceived lawful plan, and then created the intelligence of humans with the ability to imitate the divine creation. Humans, therefore, are capable of creating imaginary mathematical or geometrical structures – what today we would call 'models' – that mimic the pattern of the heavens and their movements. This passage summarizes beautifully the idea of a double imprinting that goes back to Nazianzus and Augustine. It also anticipates the reasoning that Kepler used to justify his early efforts to determine the correct orbits of the planets.

By the time of the Renaissance, the basic beliefs that sustain modern scientific endeavour had been well established. Since humans image the life of God, the imaginary worlds humans create can image the world that God created. This is precisely what Kepler set out to do in his first major treatise on astronomy – to create a geometric model of 'the heavens, their proportions, and the law of their motions' that would mimic God's creation. Like Lefèvre, Kepler believed that humans had the ability to do this because they were created in the image of the Creator.

The creational beliefs that we have traced here should have a place in any treatment of biblical or historical theology. We have sketched the history of those beliefs from the ancient Near East up to the time of early modern scientists like Johannes Kepler and beyond to Einstein, Margenau and Davies. While we have

---

175 *Corpus Hermeticum* IV.5; V.5; X.25; cf. Kaiser, *Creational Theology*, 140-46. The Hermetica originated in second or third century Egypt. Since Lefèvre was primarily interested in astronomy, he could safely ignore the Hermetic idea that the sub-lunar, 'material' world was completely devoid of reason as stated in *Corpus Hermeticum* I.10.

176 Lefèvre d'Étaples, *Introductorium astronomicum*; ET in Pierre Duhem, *To Save the Phenomena: An Essay on the Idea of Physical Theory from Plato to Galileo*, trans. Edmund Doland and Chaninah Maschler (Chicago: University of Chicago Press, 1969), 56. Duhem points out the influence of Proclus and Nicolas of Cusa. Cusanus had viewed the mathematical arts of the classical *quadrivium* (including geometry) as the tools God had used in creating the world, based on Wis. 11:20; Nicolas of Cusa, *Of Learned Ignorance*, trans. Germain Heron (London: Kegan Paul, 1954), 118-19.

focused on the Christian tradition, similar reviews could be done from continuing Judaism and Islam. Our knowledge of the history of Western faith traditions needs to be deepened by exploring the implications of creational faith, and it needs to be broadened by including the beliefs of laypeople in secular disciplines like the sciences. Such a broadening and thickening of historical theology would allow students to see the foundational connections between theological and scientific endeavour and would thereby help us overcome the opposition of faith and science that we so often take for granted.

## Summary

At face value, religious faith and scientific research appear to be entirely separate, if not incompatible, endeavours within Western culture. The first aim of this chapter was to show that the picture looks quite different when you probe the cultural foundation of scientific endeavour – the beliefs and values we imbibe from our educational and research institutions. In pursuing their work, scientists rely on belief in the lawfulness of the natural world and belief in the human capacity for understanding that lawfulness. In short, science is a belief-based enterprise.

Our second aim was to show that these beliefs were inherited by modern scientists from a longstanding tradition with roots in the ancient Near East, ancient Israel and ancient Greece. The two central doctrines in this tradition were (a) the creation of the world in accordance with quantitative measures and natural laws, and (b) the creation of humanity in the image of God. The beliefs embedded in these doctrines were mediated to early modern scientists by the Church. This observation led to a challenge for traditional theology: historical treatments of the Judeo-Christian tradition need to be broadened and thickened in order for this cultural foundation to be more widely recognized. A thick description of science leads to a thick description of biblical and historical theology.

Crediting a particular religious tradition with an important role in the history of science does not require the exclusion of other traditions. An adequate historical sketch must take account of contributions from ancient Babylon and Egypt, parallel developments in the sibling Greek and Hebrew cultures, and the ongoing interaction of continuing Jewish, Neoplatonic and Arabic (Muslim), as well as Christian, lines of development. The exploration of any one of these faith traditions will inevitably reveal debts to all of the others. Even though the presentation here is still somewhat simplified, it should convey a sense of the durability and scope of a tradition that has been largely forgotten in modern historiography.

The present situation is paradoxical. The Christian churches emphasize salvation and ethics and do not place the same emphasis on creational beliefs that they once did. Many conservative Christians are more interested in supernatural interventions and revelations than they are in the laws of nature or the capabilities of the human intellect. Equally paradoxical is the fact that working scientists rely on deep beliefs in the intrinsic intelligibility of the natural world and in the human capacity for scientific endeavour, yet most scientists have lost interest in the larger historical and theological traditions that once sustained and transmitted those beliefs.

These inconsistencies are not simply matters of individual preference. They are part of the specialization and secularization that have fragmented all aspects of human life into separate enclaves – bound together by economic necessity, but lacking a set of beliefs comprehensive enough to engage the endeavours of all sides. The paradoxes of secularization will be the topic for our next chapter where we examine the societal foundation of scientific endeavour.

# CHAPTER FOUR

# Societal Foundation: The Paradox of Science-Fostering Social Systems

**Abstract** (with brief definitions of technical terms for reference)
Sustained scientific endeavour places special conditions on the social systems on which scientists rely. Such Science-Fostering Social Systems (SFSS) must include an industrial base to provide the technologies scientists need to probe the heights and depths of the cosmos. The availability of such technologies depends on corporate industries that are sustained by the demand for consumer goods and services. A market-driven system of production depends in turn on economic structures and legal codes that minimize the public role of spiritual practices and marginalize indigenous 'peoples of spirit'. This secularizing of the technical professions may be judged to be good or evil, or a mixture of both. In any case, it results in a seemingly intractable paradox: the continued progress of scientific endeavour requires the sequestration of all spiritual experience and theological traditions from the infrastructures of industrial societies at the same time that it strengthens the case for the role of the spirit in the evolution of humanity (Chapter 2) and likewise for the role of creational beliefs in the history of science (Chapter 3). This 'SFSS paradox' calls for an eschatology of scientific endeavour. The resulting challenge to a theology of history is to explain how secularizing developments can be understood in terms of the attributes of God. A thick description of scientific endeavour, therefore, leads to a thicker, more dialectical view of history and the attributes of God.

**Keywords**: attributes of God, commodification, de-animation of the cosmos, eschatology, ethics, First Nations, history of technology, industrialization, Midrash, New Testament parables, science and society, secularization theory, sociology of knowledge, technoscience, theology of history, unity of scientific knowledge.

In the present chapter, we discuss the *societal foundation* of scientific endeavour and its implications for theology. We begin with a description of experimental science and its dependence on the availability of complex, multilayered technologies. Then, using tools of the sociology of science and the history of technology, we demonstrate the necessity of social structures with a high degree of commodification and other secularizing developments and explore the possible implications for theological endeavour – in this case, the theology of history and eschatology.

We have defined natural science as the endeavour to explore and understand all accessible features of the space-time world. In chapters 1, 2 and 3, we examined the basic preconditions for such an endeavour: the existence of a lawful universe; a species with the intelligence to discern cosmic laws; and the culturally conditioned belief that humans are capable of discerning those laws. Early modern scientists like Kepler, Galileo and Newton already relied on these three foundations. These early scientists investigated fairly accessible natural phenomena, for example, the motions of planets visible to the naked eye and atmospheric air pressure. They required only relatively simple technologies like the telescope, balance, crucible and barometer, all of which could be manufactured by the scientists themselves or by their assistants.

This chapter will focus on one further precondition that had to be fulfilled if science was to progress beyond such readily accessible phenomena and investigate even deeper structures of the cosmos. Exploration of more remote features of the space-time world requires the development of multilayered technologies through which scientists can make observations far beyond the normal reach of the human senses and develop theories that exploit the full range of their built-in Science-Fostering Intelligence.[1] The development and maintenance of such complex technologies in turn requires social systems that place a high priority on industrial production. If Science-Fostering Beliefs provide the ideology or superstructure required for scientific endeavour, Science-Fostering Social Systems (SFSS) supply the instrumental infrastructure required for the continued progress of scientific research.[2] Investigation of this societal foundation will further thicken our understanding of scientific endeavour. It will also raise paradoxes that should stimulate further theological endeavour.

## Technoscience: the linkage of scientific knowledge to advanced technologies

The depth of the dependence of scientific endeavour on industrial technology is not always appreciated by those who are not actively engaged in it. Popular media usually treat scientific developments simply as new discoveries or theories or the questioning of old ones. Typically scientists are pictured standing at a blackboard or gazing at a computer monitor. Science education backs up the theories with mathematical formalisms and prepackaged laboratory exercises. Popular science books and periodicals also describe important new experiments like the Hubble space telescope or the 27-kilometer Large Hadron Collider. However, the general impression given is that such instruments are simply larger and more expensive versions of earlier technologies. The notion persists that basic scientific research is the pursuit of 'pure knowledge' and is only incidentally related to developments in technology: the latter being primarily known in the form of consumer goods like

---

1    As philosopher of technology Don Ihde has stated succinctly: 'technology, particularly in its more recent developments, is the *condition of the possibility of science*'; Ihde, 'The Historical-Ontological Priority of Technology Over Science', in Paul T. Durbin and Friedrich Rapp (eds), *Philosophy and Technology* (Dordrecht: Reidel, 1983), 243 (italics in original).

2    The idea of science having a societal foundation could be expanded to include government agencies for funding and regulation, professional societies and journals, institutions of higher education, research complexes, background technologies (transportation, communications, etc.), and so on; Joseph C. Pitt, *Thinking About Technology: Foundations of the Philosophy of Technology* (New York: Seven Bridges Press, 1999), 8-9, 132-4.

PCs and iPods. When viewed in terms of SFSS, however, 'what's new' in science is rather closely coordinated with 'what's hot' in marketing.

This misperception of scientific endeavour is not just the fault of popular media, however. It is also endemic in university curricula, where the history of science is rarely integrated with the history of technology. The two are separate disciplines, each with its own professional journals and societies. The participants usually only cross paths at annual meetings when those societies happen to meet jointly. For pedagogical purposes, historians of science generally focus on the work of scientists and ignore the stories of the technicians on whom scientists rely, to say nothing of the industrial suppliers of all the components and maintenance of the apparatus. As we shall see in this chapter, the societal reality is rather different: scientific endeavour is deeply embedded in industrial society.

In order to thicken our understanding of the science-industry connection, we need to examine the dependence of science on technology in two basic dimensions: its immediacy and its depth. First we shall review recent progress in observational astronomy, high-energy physics, and molecular biology to demonstrate the immediacy of its linkage to technology, constituting a complex that scholars have termed 'technoscience'.[3] With that linkage in mind, we shall look at the longer term history of technoscience to show the long-range persistence and depth of this dependence on the infrastructures of industrial society.

## The linkage of astronomy to advanced technology

Scientific research projects require years of planning and are normally written up as formal grant proposals. Occasionally someone comes up with an idea for a project that could have been done years earlier, but the majority of proposals are occasioned by technologies that only recently become available or, having been available, only recently became affordable. The pace of discovery and the competition among research teams pretty much guarantees this tight linkage.

New technologies make it possible for experimental astronomers to discover new astronomical phenomena by detecting electromagnetic radiation at previously inaccessible wavelengths and by resolving features that could not previously have been differentiated (in location, in time or in wavelength). As a result, astronomers are able to make entirely new kinds of observation and not just elaborate on older ones.

Just how closely advances in science are linked to those in technology can readily be documented. One way is to study the recent progress of observational astronomy as historian Martin Harwit has done. In an extensive review, Harwit found that most recent discoveries were made within five years of the introduction the requisite instrumentation. Some took longer, but not a single major recent discovery could have been made with the instruments that were available twenty-five years earlier.[4]

---

3   On the relatively new discipline of 'technoscience', see Ursula Klein, 'Introduction: Technoscientific Productivity', *Perspectives on Science* 13 (Summer 2005), 139-41.

4   Martin Harwit, *Cosmic Discovery: The Search, Scope, and Heritage of Astronomy* (Cambridge, Mass: MIT Press, 1984), 18-19 (esp. Figure 1.3), 169-76 (Figures 3.6-3.9), 242.

A current example will illustrate this technoscience linkage. It will soon be possible directly to observe planets that orbit other stars beside the sun. To date these exoplanets could only be detected indirectly (using spectroscopy) by the wobble that their orbital motions cause in the motion of their central stars. Telescopic images of these planetary systems are blurred by turbulence in the earth's atmosphere, so the image of the planet can not be differentiated from the much brighter image of its central star. However, new forms of adaptive optics like 'nulling interferometry' should make it possible for the first time not only to observe these planets directly but even to analyse the chemistry of their atmospheres. As these fresh results are celebrated in the press, it will be helpful to recall the many technological dimensions of the project.

In one particular case, that of the MMT telescope on Mt. Hopkins, Arizona, these technologies include a deformable mirror 6.5 metres in size, 336 radially polarized magnets, an equal number of voice-coil actuators, and half that number (168) of digital signal processors – all developed by industries that specialize in developing such instrumentation.[5] This example supports Harwit's findings and illustrates how tightly astronomical research is linked to contemporary developments in technology.

*The linkage of high-energy physics to advanced technology*

Harwit's conclusions about observational astronomy can be extended readily to other forms of scientific research: the ongoing quest for the most basic constituents of matter being a great example.

The situation in particle physics is just the reverse of what we usually experience. In everyday life, the smallest units are usually the easiest to find. Single issues of a journal are more common than bound volumes; you find pence and pennies more often than pounds and dollars. What makes the quest for the ultimate constituents of matter so difficult is that the smaller the particle, the higher the energy required to isolate and study it. Huge accelerators and banks of computers are needed for the task.

The earliest event in the history of such 'big science' took place at the Cavendish Laboratory at Cambridge University in the early 1930s. The recently developed theory of quantum mechanics suggested that it would be possible to split a lithium nucleus by hitting it with an accelerated alpha particle (a helium nucleus). In order to test these ideas, however, physicists John Cockroft and Ernest Walton needed much higher voltages and more intense magnetic fields than scientists had ever before been able to achieve. The apparatus needed to accomplish the task was well beyond the resources of a university lab like the Cavendish. They needed a 350 kilovolt generator, transformers, metre-long glass bulbs for the rectifier, and state-of-the-art Apiezon (oil) pumps. Equipment like that could only be developed economically by a large, profitable electrical engineering company like Metropolitan-Vickers of

---

For an update, see Harwit, 'The Growth of Astrophysical Understanding', *Physics Today* 56 (Nov. 2003), 38-43 (Figure 1).

5    Michael Lloyd-Hart, 'Taking the Twinkle out of Starlight', *IEEE Spectrum* 40 (Dec. 2003), 22-29.

Manchester.[6] In fact, they had only been developed in the previous few years as part of an ambitious program to develop and supply the first nationwide electrical grid in England – once again illustrating how tightly linked scientific research is to developments in technology and society.

Particle accelerators have gone through several 'generations' of development since Cockroft and Walton's pioneering experiment. Voltages have gone up by more than six orders of magnitude: the Large Hadron Collider now being built at CERN in southeast France and Switzerland will be 27 kilometers in circumference and is designed to achieve energies of 14 trillion electron volts (14 teravolts). For experiments of this magnitude, industrial technology is needed not only to provide immense pieces of hardware like the 5,000 superconducting magnets that weigh 35 tonnes each, but also to provide the computers to process the massive output of experimental data – on the order of 15,000,000 gigabytes a year. The only feasible way to process that much information at present is to distribute it to hundreds of high-speed computing centers around the world.[7] The linkage to industrial technology gets tighter as scientific endeavour progresses.

*The linkage of molecular biology to advanced technology*

This tight linkage to developing technology is not limited to the physical sciences: it applies to all experimental sciences in general, and that other main branch of natural science, the life sciences, in particular.

For most of us the mention of biology still conjures up images of boxes of butterflies and the dissection of frogs. However, experimental biology has become much more technical than the biology most of us learned in school. Rapidly developing techniques like 'high-throughput' genomic (DNA) analysis have become standard tools in disciplines like morphology, medicine or in paleontology. The complete sequencing of the human genome was just one of the more spectacular developments that new technologies have made possible. Just a few years ago, complete genomic analysis seemed like an impossible dream. Now it is not only an accomplished fact, but the standard for sequencing dozens of other species and performing numerous comparative analyses. Much of data discussed in Chapter 2 concerning the separation of *Homo sapiens* from other hominids and its intercontinental dispersal was achieved with the help of this new method of DNA sequencing.

In its initial stages, DNA sequencing of an entire genome has required the coordinated use of hundreds of high-speed sequencers that could separate chromosomes into fragments to produce a chromatogram that shows the exact order of their chemical bases. The basic technology (gel-based sequencers) has been available for decades, but the complexity of the process has made progress extremely slow.

---

6    Brian Cathcart, *The Fly in the Cathedral* (New York: Farrar, Straus and Giroux, 2004), 50-54, 102-7, 110-11, 204. The liaisons between university and industry were Cockroft himself and Thomas Allibone, both of whom had also been trained as industrial scientists at Metro-Vick; ibid., 59, 61-2.

7    Hazel Muir, 'Particle Smasher Gets a Super-Brain', *New Scientist* 186 (21 May 2005), 10-11.

The higher speed needed to make the completion of a genome project feasible and affordable required the development of micro-capillaries, new polymerase enzymes (Taq), CentriVacFuges, and ThermalCyclers – all done under the auspices of huge pharmaceutical corporations like Perkin-Elmer LAS and Hoffman-LaRoche, Inc.[8]

As in the case of high energy physics, analysis of the data requires the use of high-speed computers. All of the data that result from DNA sequencing must be synthesized and scanned for reading errors. The minimum standard for the Human Genome Project (HGP) was no more than a single error in every ten thousand bases recorded.[9] Computers are also needed for searching the data, zooming in on regions of special interest and comparing sequences from different genomes.[10]

These three brief reviews of current scientific research show that the sustainable development in both physical and life sciences depends on a tight linkage with concurrent developments in technology. The vast majority of these developments occur in research-oriented, profit-driven industries. Some historical analysis will show the depth of this dependence and bring us to terms with the societal foundation of current scientific endeavour.

## The industrial infrastructure of technoscience

The examples just given show how tightly linked current scientific research is to technologies that are embedded in the infrastructures of industrial society. Without the electrical and computer industries, for example, we would never have had the major breakthroughs that have so enriched our understanding of the universe, the constituents of matter and the human genome. In order to see the implications of this linkage for SFSS, it will help if we examine a few cases in deeper historical perspective. Looking at a few cases of long-term developments in the sciences will enable us to see how research industries are grounded in the structures of commerce and development that have characterized Western societies in the modern era.

We will begin by looking at a well-known example of recent scientific discovery and noting the various layers of industrial and social conditions that made that discovery possible. This (synchronic) description will further thicken our view of scientific endeavour and will also enable us to identify deeper layers of the societal foundation of scientific endeavour that date back to the foundations of industrial civilization. In a later section, we shall trace the historical background

---

8    The Roche Group employs more than 65,000 people and had around $30 billion in sales in 2004. In 2004 Perkin-Elmer had 10,000 employees and an annual budget of $1.7 billion. Perkin-Elmer describe their objective as follows: 'Our total application-driven laboratory solutions help our customers speed drug discovery, enhance research productivity, meet strict regulatory requirements, improve time-to-market, and increase manufacturing efficiencies'; http://perkinelmer.com/about/index.html (2005). Refined, more efficient methods of DNA sequencing can now be developed by smaller companies like 454 Life Sciences Corp. in Branford Connecticut.

9    Information on the Human Genome Project accessed at www.ornl.gov/sci/techresources/Human_Genome/faq/seqfacts.shtml (2005).

10    Declan Butler, 'Are You Ready for the Revolution?' *Nature* 409 (15 Feb. 2001), 758-60.

(diachronically) of our example in order to show how technoscience depends on a social system that sequesters spirit activity from the dominant industrial culture and marginalizes indigenous, spirit-oriented people. Thickening our view of scientific endeavour along these lines will raise a dilemma for the unity of science as well as serious issues of social justice. As in earlier chapters, such paradoxes lead to challenges for theological reflection.

*The discovery of the Cosmic Microwave Background (CMB)*

We begin with a brief tour through the recent history of scientific cosmology and its connections to industry and economic development going back to the early nineteenth century. The linchpin of present-day cosmology is the idea of an expanding universe, popularly known as the 'Big Bang' theory. The idea that our space-time universe is expanding was originally based on systematic redshifts in the spectra of distant galaxies discovered in 1929 by Edwin Hubble and Milton Humason at Mount Wilson in California (using two telescopes, incidentally, funded by the Carnegie foundation).[11] Theoretical models that could describe such expansion were developed by Alexander Friedmann, Georges Lemaître and George Gamow. In spite of this support from both experiment and theory, the Big Bang was just one possible explanation for the cosmic redshifts of distant galaxies. There was no definitive evidence for this particular theory until the 1964 discovery of the Cosmic Microwave Background (CMB) radiation. The story has been written up and told many times: anyone with an interest in astronomy knows most of it by heart. Here we shall retell the story with a view to identifying the deeper linkage of the discovery to industrial technology.[12]

Based on the early theoretical models, the existence of CMB radiation had been predicted by several physicists. The reason it took 25 years to find it was that the predicted radiation temperature was far too low (just a few kelvins above absolute zero) to be observed with existing radio antennas. In the early 1960s, physicist Robert Dicke and his coworkers at Princeton University were the only scientists actively investigating the possibility of detecting the CMB radiation. During his years at the Massachusetts Institute of Technology, Dicke had developed a radiometer that was good down to 20 kelvins, and the Princeton team was in the process of improving that instrument, hoping to get down as far as ten kelvins.

These university scientists were still making plans when they heard about the work of two men who worked for Bell Telephone Laboratories, a subsidiary of American Telephone and Telegraph (AT&T). Arno Penzias and Robert Wilson were experimenting with a 20-foot radio antenna at an observing station near Holmdel, New Jersey. The antenna had been developed just four years earlier in order to

---

11  Trinh Xuan Thuan, *The Secret Melody: And Man Created the Universe* (New York: Oxford University Press, 1995), 36, 56.

12  I base my abbreviated account on Harwit, *Cosmic Discovery*, 14, 147-51; John Gribbin, *In Search of the Big Bang: Quantum Physics and Cosmology* (Toronto: Bantam Books, 1986), 185-9; Stephen G. Brush, 'How Cosmology Became a Science', *Scientific American* 267 (Aug. 1992), 62-70.

detect signals coming from the first communications satellites (the Echo series). Penzias and Wilson had hoped to use the instrument for astronomical research – it would pick up signals down to a few kelvins – but first they had to identify all the extraneous sources of radio noise in the sky. To their dismay, after subtracting out all the identifiable sources, they were left with a steady excess that was the equivalent a 'black-body' (a 100 per cent efficient radiator) at three degrees kelvin (we return to the idea of 'black-body' thermodynamics below).

Subsequent communication between the two groups of physicists resulted in the 'discovery' of the Cosmic Microwave Background predicted by models of the expanding universe. The discovery required contributions from both groups: the theory-rich but technology-challenged university scientists, and the experiment-driven but theory-challenged industrial scientists. Their work, as supplemented by more sophisticated models and more detailed observations of the CMB, is the foundation of current scientific cosmology.

*The societal foundation of the CMB discovery*

In addition to providing further evidence for the tightness of technoscience linkage, the story of the CMB discovery also shows how this linkage is embedded in commercial developments. Looking back over the details of the story, we see that it is rather more complex than a simple textbook image of superstructure and infrastructure. The story moves back and forth among eight distinct layers of the societal foundation of scientific endeavour, ranging from 'pure' science to society.[13] Taking it from the top down: (1) the discovery of CMB radiation was a collaborative interpretation of (2) an observation (the excess antenna-temperature) made while two scientists were running (3) a standard experimental procedure (testing for sources of radio noise), using (4) a relatively new piece of equipment (the 20-foot radar antenna), which was made possible by (5) recent technological innovations (improved spectral resolution, transistors, etc.), which were developed (along with the observing station itself) by (6) a commercial enterprise (AT&T) that had the needed resources and that could afford the costs of development (estimated at $500 million) due to (7) profits from the expanding market for telephones together with the prospect of further profits from the development of communication satellites (the Echo series soon followed by Telstar), all of which depended on (8) the long-term globalization of commerce and communications.[14]

Viewed synchronically, these layers form a science-society pyramid with individual names and places near the top and larger, more impersonal structures and processes below. Actually, the deeper layers are just as personal and particular as

---

13   The top five layers were noted by Harwit, *Cosmic Discovery*, 18, 23, 24.

14   The long-range goal of the communications satellite program was direct television transmission between the United States, Europe and Japan; 'History of Telstar' at http://roland.lerc.nasa.gov/~dglover/sat/telstar.html (2005). See below on the earlier development of transistors at Bell Labs.

the top ones, but they involve so many people in such large networks that a simple description like ours makes them more abstract.[15]

The exact count of layers in the science-society pyramid can be revised, but the upshot of the analysis is clear in any case. The discovery that lies at the foundation of modern cosmology is grounded in the communications industry and, beyond that, in the long-range process of globalized commerce. Later in this chapter, we shall tackle some of the paradoxes that result from this linkage of science and society. In order to do that we need to know something about the history and origin of technoscience linkage. So first we shall look into the longer-range history behind the story of the CMB discovery.

*The historical background of the CMB discovery*

Taking the CMB discovery as our starting point we can explore the societal underpinnings of scientific endeavour. We shall tour our way back in time to the origin of the idea of black-body radiation in the mid-nineteenth century and then work our way forward again to the origin of quantum theory and the physics of semiconductors (transistors) in the early twentieth century. The result of this diachronic analysis will be greater historical depth in our understanding of the origin of modern cosmology and a clearer focus on the long-term linkage between developments in technoscience and society.

Our focus has been the dependence of scientific endeavour on the development of advanced technologies. The reverse is also true: most experimental apparatus is designed with the help of scientific theories that define the phenomena they are designed to detect. Those theories were, in turn, developed with the use of earlier developments in technology, and so on back.

In the case of the CMB discovery, success depended on the collaboration of two groups of scientists: theoreticians and experimentalists. In spite of their differences, the two groups could communicate with each other using common scientific concepts, particularly the idea of black-body radiation and its characteristic temperature (in kelvins). The method of calculating the 'radiation temperature' of a black-body was developed in the late nineteenth century by two German physicists, Wilhelm Wien (1896) and Max Planck (1897-1901): Planck's work provided the first evidence for the quantization of atomic energies at the turn of the century.

The underlying idea of black-body (100 per cent efficient) radiation began four decades earlier (1859-60) with Heidelberg physicist Gustav Kirchoff's spectroscopic research on the relation between the absorption and emission of light.[16]

---

15   Christian Smith has criticized the tendency of sociologists to invoke impersonal structures and processes as explanatory devices; C. Smith, ed., *The Secular Revolution: Power, Interests and Conflict in the Secularization of American Public Life* (Berkeley: University of California Press, 2004), 12-25. Our approach works at both levels – including several layers in between. The interpersonal nature of the lower layers can also be demonstrated using the idea of the 'deployment and experience of technological systems'; Kaiser, 'Holistic Ministry in a Technological Society', *Reformed Review* 41 (Spring 1988), 175-88.

16   Max Jammer, *The Conceptual Development of Quantum Mechanics* (New York: McGraw-Hill, 1966), 2-22; Helge Kragh, *Quantum Generations: A History of Physics in the*

Kirchoff's ideas developed out of the experimental work he and Robert Bunsen did on the spectrum of sunlight – together they designed the 'recording spectroscope' that has been the fundamental tool for the identification of chemical elements in modern chemistry and astronomy. For any luminescent object, they could use the spectroscope to observe and measure the characteristic spectral lines produced by its elements. Heating samples of known materials in the lab allowed them to observe and measure the patterns of their spectral lines. This information then allowed them to recognize similar patterns in the spectra of any star thereby determining its chemical composition. With the benefit of his new instrument, Kirchoff showed that some of the sun's spectral lines were produced by the element sodium whose characteristic yellow doublet of lines could be reproduced in the lab for detailed comparison.

The detection of chemical elements in distant stars was a major breakthrough philosophically as well as technologically. The importance of this historic shift bears some reflection. In our present stage of technological development, we take it for granted that every scientific challenge will have a solution. If there is no way at present to get the information needed to answer a given question, we assume that new technologies can and will be developed to make it available. It is just a matter of time and effort. This assumption, as much as anything, is what separates us from our medieval ancestors.

As far as observational science and technology are concerned, the early nineteenth century was still 'medieval' in this sense. Existing technologies merely extended the human senses to greater distances (navigation, telescopes) or finer detail (barometers, microscopes). No one realized that new instruments could also provide access to entirely new, qualitatively different, kinds of information about the natural world: not just new stars, but the chemical composition of a star; not just new species, but the genetic code of a species.

The writings of nineteenth-century philosophers show that they lived on the other side of the mid-nineteenth-century divide. In the 1830s, Auguste Comte argued that there was a limit to our knowledge of the sun and stars. We could determine their location, size and proper motion, but speculating about their chemical composition and inner structure was entirely 'unscientific'.[17] Comte and his positivistic philosophy have often been maligned, but he was quite right given his historical context. In a world where new technologies merely enhanced information that had been available to the human senses for millennia, his judgment made perfect sense. Writing at the same time as Comte and in no way a positivist, mathematician Charles Babbage made such limitations on science into a general principle. He affirmed the view of the ancients that the qualitative enhancement of human senses would never be possible in this life. In order to transcend those limitations, humans must wait for a future life in which we are no longer limited by the material body.[18] The issue

---

*Twentieth Century* (Princeton: Princeton University Press, 1999), 58-63.

17   Comte, *Cours de philosophie positive* (1830-42), cited in Gillispie (ed.), *Dictionary of Scientific Biography*, 3:377.

18   Babbage hoped that 'in a future state... with increased powers [we could] apply our minds to the discovery of nature's laws, and to the invention of new methods by which our faculties might be aided in that research...'; Charles Babbage, *The Ninth Bridgewater*

here was not personal belief in the capabilities of human intelligence (the cultural foundation dating back to ancient times), but the resources needed to gain new kinds of information about the cosmos. Babbage differed from Comte in believing that spiritual powers could transcend the five senses, but neither of them believed that technological innovations could do so.

All of this was to change with the spectroscopic methodologies developed by Kirchoff and Bunsen, which was done just over a century before the CMB discovery described earlier. From this convenient turning point in our history, we may look even farther back into the emerging technologies that made spectroscopy possible and then look forward again to the consequent development of quantum theory and the technologies that it made possible. The resulting picture is a long-term weave from technology to physics to new technologies, and so on toward the emergence of scientific cosmology.

*The societal foundation of nineteenth-century spectroscopy*

There were several technical innovations that made spectroscopic research possible in the mid-nineteenth century. In addition to the handy 'burner' that Bunsen developed (still used in chem-labs), Kirchoff made use of achromatic lenses. These state-of-the-art lenses were needed to scan the spectrum of sunlight with enough precision to differentiate and identify dark absorption features known as 'Fraunhofer lines'. These dark lines turned out to be the key to gaining qualitatively new information about the sun and the stars. They were named 'Fraunhofer lines' after the German artisan who first developed achromatic lenses (1813-14) and discovered that dark features in the solar spectrum were too numerous to be the boundaries between the familiar colours of the rainbow.[19]

If we look back over the story of the nineteenth-century discovery of solar chemistry, we find a pyramid of layers similar to the one we found in the case of the CMB discovery: (1) Kirchoff's discovery of chemical elements in the sun was based on (2) precise measurement of lines in the solar spectrum, while performing (3) experiments with chemical samples using (4) new equipment like the spectroscope, the development of which was made possible by (5) a technological innovation (achromatic lenses) that were first developed by Joseph von Fraunhofer.

This layered series is basically the same as the first five layers we found in our discussion of the work of Penzias and Wilson. Were there also deeper corporate, market and social layers like the infrastructure (layers 6-8) of the CMB discovery?

---

*Treatise: A Fragment*, 2nd edn (London: John Murray, 1838), 92-3, 165; cf. David F. Noble, *The Religion of Technology: The Divinity of Man and the Spirit of Invention* (Harmondsworth: Penguin Books, 1997), 72. Noble traces technological optimism back to the seventeenth-century English 'improvers', but it would not be until the nineteenth century that such visionary ideals became an indisputable (socially accepted) fact.

19   The first major steps toward overcoming chromatic aberration were made in 1758 by the Huguenot exile, John Dollond, in England. William Wollaston was able to detect seven dark lines in refracted sunlight already in 1802. Reasonably enough, however, Wollaston only thought they were the borders between the traditional rainbow colours (Occam's razor).

Prior to the work of Fraunhofer, optical lenses and prisms gave blurred images because each colour came into focus at a different point (chromatic aberration). Fraunhofer was probably no more skilled in crafting fine lenses than a number of other early nineteenth-century artisans. But Fraunhofer had an advantage in working for an upstart company willing to provide the staffing and resources he needed for his work. The situation was a lot like that of Penzias and Wilson at Bell Labs in the 1960s, only on a smaller scale. The CMB discovery had industrial roots in the emerging market for satellite communications; Fraunhofer's work had its roots in the booming business of ordnance surveying.[20] Land surveys were a major political and economic objective for developing nations like France, England and America, and progressive German states were catching up with the leaders in the early nineteenth century. Ordnance surveys were crucial to the definition of national borders and the control of international commerce. They were also necessary for internal improvements like the precise recording of land ownership and the development of natural resources that would replace the earlier feudal system of land use.[21]

Surveying techniques had been developed in the eighteenth century, but the increase in accuracy needed for determining the fair market (read taxable) value of land required major improvements. The basic tool used in such surveys was the theodolite: a small telescope mounted on a pivot. The theodolite allowed surveyors to determine the angle of a line of sight to any distant landmark. Using basic trigonometry, surveyors could then determine the distance to the landmark by triangulation. But the accuracy of the maps depended on two things: the optical resolution of the telescope used and calibration of the circular disk (a circumferentor) on which the telescope was mounted. There was plenty of room for improvement in both of these areas. Enter Joseph von Fraunhofer and the Optical Institute.

The immediate corporate context for Fraunhofer's innovations (his AT&T) was the Optical Institute, located in the newly secularized Benediktbeuern near Kochel.[22] The Optical Institute was part of the Mathematico-Mechanical Institute in the nearby city of Munich. The source of income that allowed the Munich Institute to develop such a research program came mostly from the sale of theodolites to the joint Franco-Bavarian Bureau of Topography and the Bavarian Bureau of Land Registry. One of the co-owners of the Munich Institute, Georg von Reichenbach, had already crafted a 'dividing machine' (*Teilmaschine*) that could calibrate a circular disk (the

---

20   I am indebted to Myles W. Jackson, *Spectrum of Belief: Joseph von Fraunhofer and the Craft of Precision Optics* (Cambridge, Mass: MIT Press, 2000), 43-84; idem, 'From Theodolite to Spectral Apparatus: Joseph von Fraunhofer and the Invention of a German Optical Research-Technology', in Bernward Joerges and Terry Shinn (eds), *Instrumentation Between Science, State and Industry* (Dordrecht: Kluwer Academic, 2001), 17-28.

21   The original motivation for land surveys in France was partly scientific – to enable the coordination of astronomical observations between London and Paris – but their continuance and expansion served the imperialist interests of Napoleon and his allies in Germany. Pressure for land surveys in England came more from landowners and industrialists; Andro Linklater, *Measuring America: How the United States Was Shaped by the Greatest Land Sale in History* (London: Penguin Books, 2002), 98-101.

22   For current information and pictures of the Benediktbeuern, log on to www.kloster-benediktbeuern.de.

circumferentor) into degrees, minutes, seconds, and even fractions of a second of ark. That was one of the two innovations needed to develop a spectroscope. The company still needed to devise a telescope with greatly reduced chromatic aberration and better optical resolution in order to determine the angle of the line of sight to a distant object. That was a task for Fraunhofer and a team of four dozen artisans,[23] and it was a good reason for his interest in the dark spectral lines that would later be named after him.

Fraunhofer's first task was to improve his techniques for stirring molten glass, producing homogeneous glass blanks, and polishing the blanks into lenses. Once improved, achromatic lenses were in hand, he used von Reichenbach's dividing machine to produce a modified version of the theodolite. With this new 'spectral apparatus' Fraunhofer found hundreds of dark lines in the solar spectrum that were seen with equipment developed by independent artisans.

A professional artisan like Fraunhofer had the resources needed to investigate these mysterious lines – later to prove so important for the progress of astrophysics – because he was supported by a profitable, research-oriented corporation. Fraunhofer's own interest was more commercial than scientific. The solar lines he meticulously measured were used as reference standards for the accurate calibration of prisms – accurate to six decimal places – and for testing and correcting lenses for chromatic aberration.

The basic technology needed to go beyond the human senses and probe the chemistry of the sun and stars was too complex and far too expensive to be developed by independent scientists or scientific laboratories. In this respect the situation was very much like that of Penzias and Wilson's work with microwave signals at Bell Labs a century and a half later. As in the case of their discovery of CMB radiation, we find a multilayered infrastructure that includes (6) a company (the Munich Institute) that had the needed resources, based on funding from (7) government and developmental agencies (French and Bavarian), all of which depended on (8) the commodification and development of real estate and the long-range development of nation states (European and American). The only real difference between our two cases is that this multilayered science-society pyramid was something of a novelty in 1814, whereas by 1964 it had become the unremarkable norm.[24]

---

23   In 1811, Fraunhofer had 48 people working under him, including polishers, tube drawers, a heater, turners, a glass pourer, and an assistant optician; Jackson, *Spectrum of Belief*, 58. The job descriptions of these assistants indicate a high degree of specialization in early nineteenth-century industry.

24   In the 1820s, 1830s and 1840s Italian botanist Jean Baptista Amici periodically devoted years of his career to improving his microscopes before returning to his own research on plant reproduction once he had a better instrument in hand. Scientists like Amici were still able to make contributions to both instrumentation and science. However, this kind of independence was already becoming the exception in the nineteenth century. The development of microscopes otherwise paralleled that of post-Fraunhofer telescopes rather closely; Aaron E. Klein, *Threads of Life: Genetics from Aristotle to DNA* (Garden City, N.Y.: Natural History Press, 1970), 69-77.

*A diachronic web of technoscience linkages*

The line we have traced from the CMB discovery back to Fraunhofer's work at the Optical Institute documents one case of the long-range dependence of technoscience on earlier industrial innovations. It is just one of many such lines that could be traced in either direction between the nineteenth century and the present. In order to appreciate the extent of linkage between science and society, one would have to imagine an entire web of such lines weaving back and forth between industrial enterprise and scientific endeavour – diverging at one point, converging at another. We can not possibly trace all of these lines of interdependence, but our case will be strengthened if we take a quick glance at some of the other ways in which Fraunhofer's innovations affected subsequent scientific endeavour.

In the short term, we may note several other lines of influence besides the one leading to the spectroscopic discoveries of Kirchoff. Fraunhofer designed a large solar telescope (a heliometer) for Friedrich Wilhelm Bessel, which was installed in his observatory at Königsberg (Prussia). The new instrument enabled Bessel to determine the positions of stars to within one-twentieth of a second of arc. As a result, he could for the first time in history measure the parallax of a star (61 Cygni, 1838) – providing long-sought direct support for the idea that the earth revolves around the sun.[25] In another major advance, Bessel was able to detect slight periodic oscillations in the positions of stars like Sirius and Procyon (1834-44) – the first evidence for the existence of double star systems. These experimental procedures proved to be foundational for modern astronomy. But neither experiment would have been technically feasible prior to the work of Fraunhofer. Again we can see how industrial enterprise was beginning to play an integral role in the development of science in the mid-nineteenth century. Many other examples could be detailed.[26]

To bring our web of linkage up to the present, we should note two of the long-term developments that lead from early spectroscopy to the more recent developments in technoscience that we examined earlier: 'high-throughput' genomic analysis; and the Large Hadron Collider now in production at CERN. The fact that these and most other research programmes rely heavily on the use of high-speed computers – both for running experiments and for analyzing the data – points to another weaving line between science and industry, which we now briefly trace.

Kirchoff had demonstrated that sets of Fraunhofer lines in the solar spectrum were the result of different chemical elements (1859-60) – they were like fingerprints revealing the identity of the otherwise invisible elements. Kirchoff identified the

---

25  The stellar parallax of Alpha Centauri was measured by two other astronomers within a few months. One, Wilhelm Struve, used a telescope (at Pulkovo, just south of St Petersburg) that had also been built by Fraunhofer at the Optical Institute; Harwit, *Cosmic Discovery*, 75, 84-5, 184-5.

26  Kirchoff's spectroscopic methods were also used by William Huggins, enabling him in 1868 to determine the radial motion of Sirius by measuring its Doppler shift. This method of determining radial motions was later used by Edwin Hubble (1929) to demonstrate the expansion of the universe, the point at which we began our discussion in modern cosmology. It is also the basis for the recent discovery of extra-solar planets – an indication of further weaving lines that could be traced.

Fraunhofer lines of several of the sun's elements himself, and the lines of other elements were also soon identified. Scientists began to notice patterns in the spacing of the Fraunhofer lines, which were thought to result from the inner dynamics of the atoms of the corresponding elements. In 1885, a Swiss mathematician named Johann Jakob Balmer came up with a formula that described the positions of all the Fraunhofer lines in the hydrogen spectrum, but there was no known mechanical process that would account for discrete series like these. Then, a generation later, Niels Bohr developed a new model of the hydrogen atom that could explain the entire Balmer series (1912-13).[27]

What Bohr proposed in order to explain the Balmer series was unprecedented. He concluded that the inner workings of the atom were not continuous as in classical mechanics. Electrons could only exist in particular rings or shells around the nucleus whose measurements (quantum numbers) fit given rules. The state of the atomic system was quantized.

Bohr's rules of quantization were designed to yield results that would match the observed spacing of the Balmer series. Just as important for our story is the fact that they also enabled physicists to explain many of the chemical properties of the elements. For example, they could explain the electrical conductivity of a material in terms of the number of electrons in the atoms' outermost shells (Felix Bloch, 1928). Of immediate interest was a particular kind of material – like silicon or germanium – in which the outer shell of electrons was normally half full. These 'semiconductors', as they were called, could be altered ('doped') in various ways to make them slightly more or less conductive. Producing very slight changes like this allowed engineers to design and control patterns of electric current on a miniature scale (Alan Wilson, 1931).

At this point our weaving story comes full circle. Fraunhofer's industrial innovations made possible spectroscopic observations that gave rise to a new (quantum) theory that led to another industrial innovation. In the 1930s and '40s, semiconductors were exploited with revolutionary results by the electronics industry. Bell Telephone Laboratories took the lead when William Shockley, Walter Brattain and John Bardeen demonstrated how semiconducting materials like silicon could be used to build a miniature amplifier, called a transfer resistor, soon abbreviated to 'transistor' (1946-48). By the 1950s, transistors were used as switching devices in telephones and in new electronic devices like miniature hearing aids and computers. Quantum theory thereby paid back to its industrial base what it had borrowed with interest. Not only was the telephone industry revolutionized, but the electronic computer as we know it was born.[28] Present-day computers use hundreds of millions of transistors. Their high-speed data processing has made it possible to develop information-loaded disciplines like radio astronomy, high-energy physics, and DNA sequencing.

Our findings can be summarized as follows. Advanced scientific research depends (synchronically) on advanced technologies that require the resources of corporate

---

27  Jammer, *Conceptual Development of Quantum Mechanics*, 62-80.

28  Earlier electronic computers had use less flexible technologies like vacuum tubes. T.R. Reid, *The Chip: How Two Americans Invented the Microchip and Launched a Revolution* (New York: Simon and Schuster, 1984), 15, 40-52; Kragh, *Quantum Generations*, 367-75.

industry. The scientific theories that we celebrate are tightly linked to cumulative results of industrial and commercial enterprise with historical roots in the early nineteenth century (diachronically), when the modern nation state and modern industry were just emerging. National-industrial society is an essential foundation of modern scientific endeavour. As we shall see in the following sections, however, this technoscience linkage entails secularizing forces seemingly at odds with the theological and spiritual orientation of the cosmic, anthropological and cultural foundations that we examined in earlier chapters.

## The linkage of technoscience to secularizing developments

The societal foundation of scientific endeavour confronts us with a major paradox. The industrial base of scientific endeavour participates in secularizing tendencies that make it difficult to address the foundations of science in a consistent way. From the standpoint of the quest for the unity of scientific knowledge, the paradox turns into a dilemma.

*Industrialization and secularization: some clarifications of terminology*

Discussions of industrialization and the secularization are plagued with controversy over terminology. Basic semantic difficulties are even greater than in previous chapters because we are discussing processes that directly affect our own lives and commitments. I shall try to allay suspicion by disavowing grand claims about either the inevitability of secularization or the nature of its effects.

This study uses the term 'industrialization' to describe changes in the legal, commercial and economic structures that characterize industrial societies. Even in a rapidly globalizing world, there are hundreds of nationalities, each with its own social structure and, consequently, its own distinctive way of negotiating the trade-offs involved in industrialization. Here we must restrict our discussion to societies in which industrial structures have become the matrix of social life, including western and central Europe, the United Sates, Canada and Japan.[29] For our purposes, the situation in nations like Egypt, India and China that are still moving toward full industrialization is still indeterminate.

It is best to avoid the broad generalizations of older 'secularization theories' and confine our comments to secularizing trends in nonreligious, technical professions. From a sociology of knowledge perspective, 'secularization' refers to a centuries-long reconfiguration of the relationship between the empirical and the supernatural.[30] The process did not have a goal, but its long-term result was social delimitation of the action of spirits and of discourse about the supernatural to finite provinces of meaning like institutional religious settings. Even if sometimes encouraged in private

---

29 According to one leading analyst, the matrix of industrial society includes the modern nation state, the military-industrial complex, and capitalist production; Anthony Giddens, *The Consequences of Modernity* (Stanford: Stanford University Press, 1990), 55-63.

30 Secularization in the West has taken place in successive stages from the twelfth to the nineteenth century; Kaiser, 'From Biblical Secularity to Modern Secularism', 8-12.

worship, consulting with spirits is regarded as illegitimate in the legal, commercial and technoscientific settings that dominate the base-world of the dominant culture.[31] Spirit influences may still occur in such settings (who can stop them?), but such occurrences are not regarded as legitimate. As a consequence, the contents of such encounters are not readily communicated in public settings.[32] The same process holds true for the confession of specific theological beliefs. In legal, economic and industrial settings, people who regularly make such assertions are stigmatized as 'proselytizing' and 'sectarian'. An uncharacteristic event of this sort would be regarded as the sign of a mental 'breakdown'. Systematic differentiation between language about the supernatural and the professional structures of industrial societies is accepted as a historical fact by proponents and critics of the 'secularization thesis' alike.[33]

Secularizing developments do not have to result in a lack of religiosity on the part of individuals or a decline of church attendance or a weakening of confessional traditions. It does, however, entail the marginalization of peoples of spirit, like the Native Americans and the First Nations of Canada, for whom traditional spiritual practices and beliefs are integral parts of subsistence practices and communal life. This marginalization is due partly to racial and religious bias, but there is also a genuine conflict of social systems. Many spirit peoples have elected not to adapt to the dominant European and Asian cultures, particularly in their industrialized forms. For their part, industrial societies have been unwilling or unable to adapt themselves to native spiritualities. The recognition of official tribes and the granting of reservations is an effective way of quarantining spirit peoples and the values embedded in their cultures.

The use of phrases like 'consulting with spirits' and the 'supernatural' is rather imprecise and needs further specification.[34] In order to illustrate the needed distinctions, consider a particular practice that is basic to Western religions – that of prayer. Secularizing developments do not necessarily mean that people spend less time in prayer or even pray less often in public. It does mean that people who have been trained for the legal, financial and technoscientific professions are extremely unlikely

---

31   The sociological ideas of 'finite provinces of meaning' and 'base-world' go back to Alfred Schutz via Peter L. Berger and Thomas Luckmann, *The Social Construction of Reality: A Treatise in the Sociology of Knowledge* (Harmondsworth: Penguin Books, 1967, 1971), 39-40 ('finite provinces'), 142 ('core universe'), 158 ('base-world').

32   The process of secularization is closely tied historically to the professionalization of secular disciplines; Frank M. Turner, 'The Victorian Conflict between Science and Religion: A Professional Dimension', *Isis*, 69 (Sept. 1978), 356-76. The disciplines in question are those of law, public commerce, industrial production and natural science.

33   See respectively, Karel Dobbelaere, 'Towards an Integrated Perspective of the Processes Related to the Descriptive Concept of Secularization', *Sociology of Religion* 60 (Fall 1999), 230-34, 241; Rodney Stark, 'Secularization, R.I.P.', *Sociology of Religion* 60 (Fall 1999), 252, expanded in Rodney Stark and Roger Fink, *Acts of Faith: Explaining the Human Side of Religion* (Berkeley: University of California Press, 2000), 60. Stark prefers to term the subsequent differentiation 'de-sacralization' rather than 'secularization'; ibid., 199-200.

34   I use the term 'supernatural' here in its earlier meaning of the world of spirits existing alongside the visible, empirical world (sometimes called the 'supra-normal'), not in the sense of violations of the laws of nature.

to offer prayers as part of their work. Conversely, they are not likely to discuss their professional disciplines in the context of their houses of worship. The issue here is not simply one of statistics or surveys about personal beliefs. Modern secularism is a distinctive mentality. Our social conditioning imbues us with the sense that some situations are quite natural and normal, while others are unnatural or unreal.

Finally, the rather simplistic view of antiquity and the Middle Ages as an 'Age of faith' needs revision.[35] People in ancient times were perhaps not as intentional about choosing their beliefs as people are today. However, the natural and social worlds in which they lived interfaced at nearly all points with the supernatural. For example, scientists of the Middle Ages and Renaissance – who would rather have been referred to as 'philosophers' than 'scientists' – pursued their research within a theological framework of meaning and immersed their efforts in urgent prayer, as we saw in Chapter 3.[36]

Preindustrial technologies like metallurgy and alchemy were also permeated with spiritualist practices.[37] Economic life in towns was organized by guilds and religious fraternities in which devotion to patron saints and adherence to specific religious beliefs were an integral part of professional identity and daily work,[38] the same saints and beliefs that were celebrated in the established religion.

With these clarifications in mind, we can proceed to investigate the secularizing aspects of the societal foundation of scientific endeavour.

*Non post hoc, non propter hoc!*

The next step of our investigation will be to show that the emergence of technoscience is related historically to secularizing developments. This is not a simple cause-effect relationship: modern secularism is not a result of either technology or science (*non propter hoc*, 'not on account of that'). In fact, secularizing developments began in the West long before the industrializing changes of the 18th and 19th centuries (*non post hoc*, 'not after that'). The point to be made here is that SFSS are inextricably

---

35   On the golden 'age of faith' pitfall, see, for example, Roy Wallis and Steve Bruce, 'Secularization: The Orthodox Model', in Steve Bruce (ed.), *Religion and Modernization: Sociologists and Historians Debate the Secularization Thesis* (Oxford: Clarendon Press, 1992), 24-5; Andrew M. Greeley, 'The Persistence of Religion', *Cross Currents* 45 (Spring 1995), 30-32; Stark and Fink, *Acts of Faith*, 63-8, 78.

36   Johannes Kepler included many personal prayers in his magnum opus, *Harmonice mundi*, published in 1619, and publicly claimed direct inspiration from God for his insights in his writing; Kepler, *The Harmony of the World*, 279, 389, 391, 491, 498. Even in the early eighteenth century, iatrochemist Herman Boerhaave stated publicly that every medical prescription should be accompanied by a prayer for healing; Rina Knoeff, *Herman Boerhaave (1668-1738): Calvinist Chemist and Physician* (Amsterdam: Edita KNAW, 2002), 196-7, 208.

37   Paula M. McNutt, *The Forging of Israel: Iron Technology, Symbolism, and Tradition in Ancient Society* (Sheffield: Almond Press, 1990), 45-6, 87-9, 208. On the role of spiritual disciplines in Renaissance alchemy, see Allen G. Debus, *Man and Nature in the Renaissance* (Cambridge: Cambridge University Press, 1978), 21-33.

38   Sylvia L. Thrupp, *The Merchant Class of Medieval London* (Ann Arbor: University of Michigan Press, 1948, 1989), 30-38.

linked to secularizing tendencies. A study of this linkage will raise a serious paradox for our understanding of scientific endeavour and thereby stimulate further theological endeavour, particularly with respect to the theology of history and the attributes of God.

Secularizing developments are deeply embedded in societal changes that have restructured all the professions. Professional language has been largely desacralized: religious confessions and language about supernatural phenomena, for example, have been sequestered out from professional discourse and relegated to finite provinces of meaning. This delimitation could be done quite consciously, for example, in reforming university education (the third example discussed below), but often it was the unintended consequence of other secularizing developments: the replacement of feudal demesnes by territorial nation states; the abstraction (or exorcism) of spirit-influences from the shared everyday world; the de-animation of the cosmos; the commodification of land and resources; and the emergence of life-patterns that transcend local traditions and local communities.[39]

In preindustrial societies, contact with spirits was facilitated by the sanctification of numinous places, portentous natural phenomena, and the performance of rituals in the shared space of the community.[40] Locations, phenomena, rituals and art forms provided a stable infrastructure for the supernatural, giving it real, interpersonal objectivity.[41] This kind of infrastructure dates all the way back to the Palaeolithic era, as discussed in Chapter 2, and it still provided a firm foundation for the supernatural as late as the eighteenth century.

The effect of secularizing forces was not overtly to suppress spirit encounters, but rather to deprive them of their empirical, societal infrastructure. Socially agreed-on, interpersonal objectivity shifted from the world of spirits, formerly reified in terms of myth and ritual, to the networks of science and industry, now reified in terms of production, finance, transportation and the distribution of goods. In short, a ritual-based ability to explore the heights and depths of the spirit world was traded for an industry-based ability to explore the heights and depths of the natural world.[42]

---

39   See Kaiser, 'From Biblical Secularity to Modern Secularism', 4-26, for descriptions and long-term histories of each of these aspects of secularization. Below we shall argue that humanly 'unintended consequences' are related to divine providence.

40   Gerardus Van der Leeuw, *Religion in Essence and Manifestation* (London: Allen & Unwin, 1938, 1964), 393-402; (London: Allen & Unwin, 1938, 1964), 393-402; Roland de Vaux, *Ancient Israel, Its Life and Institutions* (London: Darton, Longman & Todd, 1961, 1965), 274-8.

41   To cite one fascinating case: in 1562 the Duke of Württemberg consulted with his (Lutheran) court preachers to determine whether recent hailstorms that had devastated crops were divine punishment for his own failings as a ruler; Robert W. Scribner, 'Reformation and Desacralisation: From Sacramental World to Moralised Universe', in R. Po-Chia Hsia and Robert W. Scribner (eds), *Problems in the Historical Anthropology of Early Modern Europe* (Wiesbaden: Harrassowitz, 1997), 81.

42   The idea of socially agreed on objectivity comes from the sociology of knowledge; Berger and Luckmann, *The Social Construction of Reality*, 106-9, 142, 158. Here I use the term 'infrastructure' instead of Berger's phrase, 'plausibility structure'; cf. Berger, *The Sacred Canopy: Elements of a Sociological Theory of Religion* (Garden City, N.Y.: Doubleday, 1967), 45-8; *The Social Reality of Religion* (Harmondsworth: Penguin, 1973), 53-6; Peter

In our earlier discussion of the linkage of science to industrial technologies there were at least three distinct secularizing developments: (1) the legal definition of property that accompanied the development of European nation states; (2) the minimization of contingency in industrial processes; and (3) the bracketing of confessional distinctives in institutions that referee professional discourse.

## Nation states and the legal definition of property

The emergence of European nation states dates back as far as the fourteenth century. Prior to the Thirty Years' War (1618-48), Europeans still saw themselves primarily as inhabitants of a particular city or town or manor. Personal identities were defined by family, trades and religious confraternities. Social obligations and privileges were based on personal ties to territorial lords, bishops and abbeys. Beyond that, many Europeans identified themselves with the religion into which they were born, particularly its sacraments and sacred places. These determinants of identity were often celebrated and reinforced. Even when people rebelled against them, there was no doubt about their social reality.

The political upheavals of the late sixteenth and early seventeenth centuries are usually associated with 'wars of religion'. The causes of conflict were actually far more complex than simple confessional differences, yet they were certainly exacerbated by the emergence of state-sanctioned religions (Catholic, Lutheran, Reformed, Anglican) based on confessional identities that completely transcended earlier loyalties to territorial lords. One result of destabilizing religious conflicts was that nation states (England, France, The Netherlands, Spain) began to treat issues of religious conformity as a strictly internal affair.[43]

During the eighteenth and nineteenth centuries, individual identity was redefined in terms of citizenship – a social construct that required bureaucratic innovations like birth records, passports and periodic censuses.[44] Social privileges and obligations were based on nationality and civic responsibilities (mostly for male adults). Along with citizenship came the right to own land in one's own name ('fee-simple') and the obligation to pay taxes to the state.

In other words, secularization was not a single, all-encompassing wave of change, but rather a conglomerate of interweaving developments. The development that concerns us most is the codification of property rights. The institution of 'private property' was essential both to the development of legal systems and for economic

---

Berger, Brigitte Berger and Hansfried Kellner, *The Homeless Mind: Modernization and Consciousness* (New York: Random House, 1973), 16; British edn (Harmondsworth: Penguin Books, 1974), 21-2.

43   See, for example, Gerald R. Cragg, *The Church and the Age of Reason, 1648-1789* (Harmondsworth: Penguin Books, 1962), 9-12, 21-5. The term, 'state', started being used as a translation of the Latin *res publica* in the late sixteenth and seventeenth centuries; Diarmain MacCulloch, *The Reformation* (New York: Viking, 2004), 43-4, 649-50.

44   On the bureaucratic processes involved in the formation of state power, see, for example, Mara Loveman, 'The Modern State and the Primitive Accumulation of Symbolic Power,' *American Journal of Sociology* 110 (May 2005), 1651-83, esp. pp. 1679-80.

development.[45] Owning large tracts of land for grazing and agriculture paid huge dividends. Particularly in Britain, the government appropriated lands, particularly from churches and monasteries (Henry VIII, 1538), and redistributed them to private landlords. Common fields were gradually 'enclosed' to consolidate holdings and augment their agricultural and grazing capacities.[46]

Today we recognize private property as a fact of life, but in the seventeenth century it was a controversial innovation, and its legitimation required extensive land surveys and the recording of legal titles. The resulting dis-employment of villains and free peasants in Europe, most of whom had no legal title to land they had worked for centuries, was soon matched by the dispossession of native tribes in the New World, for whom the idea of land as an ownable commodity was entirely foreign.[47]

The relationship between mapping land and the control of natural resources is clear enough. The significance of this relationship for our inquiry stems from our earlier discussion of the multilayered societal foundation for scientific endeavour. We saw how the development of technoscience depended on the industrialization of electricity and communications. These industries depended, in turn, on the availability of detailed land maps, in order to deploy their networks and to access resources. As stated earlier, one of the very first producers of specialized precision scientific equipment, the Optical Institute of Bavaria, owed its existence to the growing demand for ordnance surveys from the state and from commercial enterprise.

Recognizing this multilayered linkage between science and society makes it impossible for us to dissociate the development of technoscience from the enclosure of land and the dispossession of spirit peoples. Advanced science and technology ultimately depend on the legal definition of property and the commodification of natural resources and hence the elimination of one of the principal supports for encounters with the spirit world. The natural world has ceased to provide the infrastructure of the sacred. Socially agreed-upon 'objectivity' has shifted from the world of spirits to the world of business. The emergence of technoscience as we know it would not have been possible otherwise. We shall take up the resulting paradox after examining two further secularizing developments that underlie technoscience.

*The elimination of contingency from natural processes*

The convenience of controlling a wide range of material phenomena is now taken for granted in industrial societies. We expect our automobiles, computers and cell phones to work as soon as we turn them on, and work consistently. If they do not

---

45   See Linklater, *Measuring America*, 8-13, 30-47, 78, 210-11, on the necessity of accurate mapping for establishing legal (fee-simple) ownership.

46   John Goodacre traces the shift (1570-1680) from an economy based on common-field agriculture to a fully commercial and capitalist economy based on land enclosure and pastoral husbandry; Goodacre, *The Transformation of a Peasant Economy: Townspeople and Villagers in the Lutterworth Area, 1500-1700* (Aldershot, UK: Scolar Press, 1994).

47   From a European perspective, the natives 'inclose no Land, neither haue [have] any settled habitation, nor any tame Cattle to proue [improve] the Land by'; The Journal of John Winthrop, first governor of the Massachusetts Bay Colony (1633), quoted in Linklater, *Measuring America*, 27-8.

work, it means something must (and normally can) be fixed. The contingencies that still remain in the technologies are defined as 'noise' and are generally hidden from view (all three technologies now rely on quantum mechanical processes).[48] Our technologies are packaged and marketed in ways that confirm our sense of clear-cut alternatives ('click here') and reproducible results (hit 'redial'). The fact that we routinely expect reproducibility from such complex technologies is the result of decades of conditioning.[49] Once the first recourse of people in trouble, prayer and ritual have become the least certain of ways of addressing our problems.

In premodern societies, numinous phenomena and contingent processes constituted another of the infrastructures for contact with the spirit world. Light-transmitting substances like gemstones and bodies of water connected people to the invisible world. Natural phenomena like rainbows and comets were long viewed as portentous.[50] The supernatural could be discerned in the behaviour of domestic animals and in the unpredictable results of cooking and childbearing, even in manufactured materials like glass and (al)chemical products.[51] Since the eighteenth century, such ideas have been dismissed as 'unscientific' superstitions. Eventually, they were collected as folklore from an imagined 'age of faith'. Even the supernatural could be commodified![52]

This bracketing of the spirit world was not the result of science (though scientific ideas could be invoked to support it). Many early scientists were quite interested in the role of spirits in nature even while it was being banned from professional discourse. Even as the 'mechanical philosophy' was being formulated during the seventeenth century, leading natural philosophers conceived the natural world in terms of spirit-forces (van Helmont, Boyle) and divine impetus (Barrow, Newton).[53]

---

48   The precise behaviour of computer microprocessors is highly unpredictable due to irreducibly stochastic ('chaotic') phenomena like aperiodic oscillations. The time taken to complete a specific task varies widely from one run to the next, but we do not concern ourselves as long as the task is completed in a reasonable time; Hugues Berry, Daniel Gracia Pérez and Olivier Temam, 'Chaos in Computer Performance', posted 13 June 2005 at http://arxiv.org/abs/nlin.AO/0506030.

49   The banishment of contingency was evident to an astute observer like Ludwig Feuerbach as early as 1841-3; Feuerbach, *The Essence of Christianity*, trans. George Eliot (New York: Harper and Row, 1957), xliv (industrial systems), 190-92 (the 'mechanical thinker').

50   For example, Carl B. Boyer, *The Rainbow: From Myth to Mathematics* (Princeton: Princeton University Press, 1987), 26-31, 130.

51   Theophilus Presbyter, *De diversis artibus*, Book III, Prologue; ET, *Theophilus, On Divers Arts*, 79; cf. Jackson, *Spectrum of Belief*, 45, on the monastic production of glass as a medium of divine light.

52   The term 'folklore' was introduced to the English-speaking public in 1846 by William John Toms (or Thoms) as the British equivalent for the work of the Brothers Grimm in Germany (1809-15); David L. Sills, ed., *International Encyclopedia of the Social Sciences*, 17 vols (New York: Macmillan, 1968), 5:497.

53   Kaiser, *Creational*, 203-4, 232-3, 239-40, 245-7. Alfred North Whitehead has argued that the mechanical philosophy contributed to the deanimation or disenchantment of the natural world through the differentiation of primary and secondary qualities; Whitehead, *Science and the Modern World* (New York: Macmillan, 1925), 46-55. We are not concerned here with the

Even in the nineteenth century, a scientific case for the role of an unseen, spiritual world could still being made by leading physicists (Tait and Stewart, 1875) and the codiscoverer of biological evolution (Wallace, 1890).[54] In Chapter 2 we argued that the explanatory power of both may be required in order to account for the origin of Science-Fostering Intelligence itself. In Chapter 3 we showed how modern belief in the intelligibility of the natural world originated in the historic creationist tradition. In short, scientists' belief in natural causation and scientific explanation has never required them to deny an instrumental role for the spiritual in natural processes.

Although there are plenty of scientists who have opposed vehemently the notion of the supernatural on methodological grounds, the eclipse of the spirit world in professional circles was due neither to scientific procedures nor to philosophic necessity. It was largely the unintended consequence of the harnessing of natural elements and material processes with industrial technology.[55] Since the mid-twentieth century, clean water and artificial light have been almost universally available as public utilities. Basic mechanical and chemical processes have been harnessed in ways that are both marketable and readily distributable.

Reducing contingency has been a human objective ever since the first controlled use of fire, at least 400,000 years ago. In that respect, nothing has changed. But the techniques of control developed by preindustrial humans were tiny islands of order in a largely unpredictable world. What makes industrial society radically different is that technology has become the matrix of everyday life. We 'live and move and have our being' in technological systems.[56]

The industrializing process that most contributed to commodification was the electrification of the infrastructure of modern life and industry. A reliable supply of electricity makes it possible for industrial society to run smoothly and relatively safely.[57] We depend on the electrical industry for everything from communications

influence of scientific or philosophical ideas, but rather with their societal foundation and the way its construction participated in secularizing trends.

54    Peter Guthrie Tait and Balfour Stewart (anon.), *The Unseen Universe or Physical Speculations on a Future State* (New York: Macmillan, 1875); Alfred Russell Wallace, *Darwinism* (London: Macmillan, 1890); cf. P. M. Harman (Heimann), 'The Unseen Universe: Physics and the Philosophy of Nature in Victorian Britain', *British Journal for the History of Science*, 6 (June 1972), 73-9.

55    This point was made by Rudolf Bultmann as long ago as 1941: 'It is impossible to use electric light and the wireless and to avail ourselves of modern medical and surgical discoveries and at the same time to believe in the New Testament world of demons and spirits'; Bultmann, 'The New Testament and Mythology', in Hans Werner Bartsch (ed.), *Kerygma and Myth: A Theological Debate*, trans. Reginald H. Fuller (London: SPCK, 1953), 5. As Bultmann explained in the following sentence, this 'impossibility' was a practical one. It is not a matter of philosophical inference, but of industrialized behavior and its influence on personal expectations and beliefs.

56    Kaiser, 'Holistic Ministry in a Technological Society', 176-80.

57    Inanimate energy sources had already been harnessed for machinery and lighting in the late eighteenth and nineteenth centuries. The alternating-current systems that were developed in the 1890s were safer, more energy-efficient, and more serviceable. They allowed a complex series of machines to be linked by automatic feeding devices, scanners and moving belts, and other electrical control devices. Still, it was not until the late 1920s that the majority

and manufacture to entertainment and worship. Everything comes to a halt with a power blackout in a way that would have been inconceivable in preindustrial society.

Even before the advent of electricity, secularizing processes of control and commodification played an instrumental role in the early technoscience developments described above. Fraunhofer's success required minimizing the contingencies in the production process to the point that his lenses and prisms would conform to exact standards. Even though the technique he developed for stirring molten glass was far from completely controllable, the glass blanks he produced could be standardized by a refined polishing process and then checked for quality using the newly developed spectral apparatus.[58] Regardless of how religious Fraunhofer and his associates might have been, no room could be allowed for spirits in measured processes that were accurate to six decimal places, nor any value attributed to the way refracted light might manifest the divine presence. Interest in the 'spectral' had been displaced from spirits that appear with the help of rituals to dark lines that appear with the help of a precisely designed ('spectral') apparatus.[59]

The mass production of electrical equipment was the crucial innovation needed for the splitting of the lithium nucleus by John Cockroft and Ernest Walton in the 1930s. The experiment that founded the new field of high-energy physics required the production of high voltages that would not have been possible before large-scale corporations built national grids and supplied nationwide areas with electrical power.[60] More recent experimental apparatus we looked at like the Large Hadron Collider, adaptive optics, and 'high-throughput' DNA sequencing all require massive electronic computation and ever greater control of the natural processes that computers rely on.

The experimental research that sustains scientific endeavour would be impossible without the cooptation of phenomena that traditionally provided the infrastructure for human engagement with the spirit world. Interpersonal, socially agreed-on 'objectivity' has to be shifted from the world of spirits to that of science and industry. After examining one last secularizing development that underlies technoscience, we shall turn to the paradox this secularization entails for the foundations of scientific endeavour.

---

of all locomotive power in England and America had switched to electricity; David E. Nye, *Electrifying America: Social Meanings of a New Technology, 1880-1940* (Cambridge, Mass., MIT Press, 1990), 13-15, 193-6. I have also drawn from Wolfgang Schivelbusch, *Disenchanted Night: The Industrialization of Light in the Nineteenth Century* (Berkeley: University of California Press, 1988); Jean-Pierre Goubert, *The Conquest of Water: The Advent of Health in the Industrial Age* (Princeton: Princeton University Press, 1989).

58   Jackson, *Spectrum of Belief*, 74; idem, 'From Theodolite to Spectral Apparatus', 19-20.

59   A sign of the times, the Benediktbeuern, where the Optical Institute was housed, was a secularized (Benedictine) monastery; Jackson, *Spectrum of Belief*, 44, 53-6. According to Jackson, some of the Institute's values of labor and privacy may have derived from the Benedictine legacy; ibid., 77-84.

60   Cathcart stresses the need for the unprecedented control of high-voltage electricity; Cathcart, *The Fly in the Cathedral*, 50-51, 54, 102-4.

*Bracketing confessional theology in research universities*

The two previous cases of secularizing forces changed basic consciousness – our everyday understanding of property, resources, materials and natural processes. Most people, however, tend to think of secularization in terms of public institutions. Institutions are a far more complex subject because they vary greatly in the ways in which they adjudicate between the public and private spheres. In the American public school system, for example, the demands for achievement in science and public health have to be balanced with diverse regional and sectarian values.[61] For our purposes, the problem is greatly simplified by the fact that the public institution that most directly contributes to the social structures that underlie scientific endeavour, the research university, is not so tied to local interests.

The first universities in Western Europe were founded in the 12th and 13th centuries. From the start they provided an arena for the consolidation and promotion of work in the natural sciences.[62] But the sciences in those days were mostly just parts of the liberal arts curriculum, along with rhetoric and literature (grammar), all leading to graduate study in medicine, law or theology. In Britain and America, chairs were specifically designated for natural philosophy and chemistry in the 17th and 18th centuries, but the classics continued to be the basis and major focus for education well into the nineteenth century. Throughout this period, religious affiliations and ecclesiastical professions were very much a part of the university world as they also were in many smaller, independent colleges.

The main secularizing shifts in higher education occurred in the late nineteenth century in conjunction with the professionalization of the sciences and the concurrent growth of the engineering professions. The new emphasis on rigorous technical training was necessitated by the growing demand for graduates trained in the latest experimental methods, the importance of which we have already discussed. Classrooms and labs needed to be equipped with up-to-date experimental apparatus, the complexity and sophistication of which was steadily increasing. The traditional approach to science education as a theology-and-ethics oriented (Baconian) collecting of specimens was no longer adequate to meet the demands for specialized training.

The process and timing of the secularization varied from nation to nation. In Britain, the shift spanned the decades around the middle of the nineteenth century. The major impetus, in this case, came from two quarters: positivistically minded scientists who worked to restrict membership in the scientific societies to professional scientists; and liberally minded churchmen and politicians, who legislated the reform of universities (the removal religious 'tests') and advocated the founding of new

---

61 Kaiser, 'Wearing Different Hats: Christian Living in a Fragmented World', in Craig E. Van Gelder (ed.), *Confident Witness, Changing World: Rediscovering the Gospel in North America* (Grand Rapids: Eerdmans, 1999), pp. 19-23.

62 David C. Lindberg, *The Beginnings of Western Science: The European Scientific Tradition in Philosophical, Religious and Institutional Context* (Chicago: University of Chicago Press, 1992), 206-13.

civic universities. The common overall rationale was one of national efficiency and industrial progress.[63]

In the United States, the trend toward professionalization was driven by pragmatic financiers in alliance with progressive churchmen and educators – a different dynamic leading to a similar result. The staffing and equipment of industry-oriented educational programmes were far beyond the financial means of smaller universities and colleges. However, plentiful funding became available in the late nineteenth century, not from the traditional sources of church and government, but from the new corporate-business tycoons, many of whom devoted huge sums of accumulated wealth to philanthropic causes. These American 'titans' were nothing like the reforming radicals of Britain. Many of them had strong religious affiliations, and gave generously to their churches as well as to philanthropy. But, when it came to education for the future workforce, they were concerned primarily about practical results. As several historians have explained in depth, the stipulations that went along with big money were oriented toward material productivity and economic growth rather than toward spiritual development or confessional perspectives.[64]

The theology-based worldview of traditional education had produced capable leaders for the relatively simple needs of early America. A more instrumental form of rationality that marginalized discourse about theological doctrine and the supernatural was needed for progress in more technical subjects, particularly at the post-graduate level. The models to which American educators looked were the departmentalized universities of Germany, the rational administrative principles of big business, and the natural sciences themselves.[65] Young adults were trained to be

---

63 Turner, 'The Victorian Conflict between Science and Religion', 361-75. In France, Hanover and Prussia, the shift toward professionalization and secularization spanned the first half of the 19th century. In each of these cases, most of the impetus came from the bureaucratic demands of the states; see Robert Fox, 'Science, the University, and the State in Nineteenth-Century France', in Gerald L Geison (ed.), *Professions and the French State, 1700-1900* (Philadelphia: University of Pennsylvania Press, 1984), esp. 72-5; R. Steven Turner, 'The Growth of Professional Research in Prussia, 1818 to 1848', *Historical Studies in the Physical Sciences* 3 (1971), esp. 142-55.

64 George M. Marsden, 'The Soul of the American University: An Historical Overview', in George M. Marsden and Bradley J. Longfield (eds), *The Secularization of the Academy* (New York: Oxford University Press, 1992), 13-21; idem, *The Soul of the American University from Protestant Establishment to Established Nonbelief* (New York: Oxford University Press, 1994), 150-58, 265-6; Christian Smith, 'Introduction: Rethinking the Secularization of American Public Life', 74-6. Historians have also pointed to a secularizing impetus from the religious side, particularly in America. Even though revivalistic movements led to the founding of many small colleges, their objectives were primarily to insulate Christian youth from secularizing influences like those in the universities. Paradoxically, revivalists and their institutions also eschewed theological confessions and adopted an anti-intellectual outlook, thereby furthering the very process they sought to oppose; C. Smith, 'Introduction: Rethinking the Secularization of American Public Life', 51-2; George M. Thomas, Lisa R. Peck and Channin G. De Haan, 'Reforming Education, Transforming Religion, 1876-1931', in C. Smith (ed.), *The Secular Revolution*, 362.

65 Thomas et al., 'Reforming Education', 355-8 on 'functional rationality', 367-9 on 'epistemological dualism'. Christian Smith defines 'procedural rationality' in terms of

inquiring minds able to meet the technical challenges of industrial enterprise rather than souls in search of a spiritual home or a moral way of life. The development of an industrial and educational infrastructure for scientific endeavour required a frame of mind radically different from those that had originally produced Science-Fostering Intelligence and Science-Fostering Beliefs. Therein lies the paradox we are about to explore.

## The paradox of Science-Fostering Social Systems

We have seen in previous chapters that a thick description of scientific endeavour reveals three primary conditions or foundations: (1) a universe (or multiverse) governed at all levels by immaterial laws; (2) a species that is preadapted for the investigation of counterintuitive domains beyond the everyday world; and (3) a cultural of belief, contrary to all appearances, in the lawfulness of the world around us and in human ability to understand those laws. As far as science is concerned, these conditions can not be brushed aside as outdated concepts that only applied in the Paleolithic or in an imagined 'age of faith'. Scientists embody all three of them in their daily work. They are essential to sustained scientific endeavour.

We also found that using basic tools of analysis like science and history to describe these foundations leads to important theological questions. Neither the existence of a Creator nor the reality of a spirit world can be proved, but it is difficult to ignore such possibilities once the paradoxes embedded in the deep structures of scientific endeavour are uncovered. These paradoxes did not entail any particular theological doctrines, but they did engage us in theological discourse, and they allowed us to draw on traditional theological ideas in order to meet the challenges they raise. Without all three of these theology-fostering conditions, modern science could never have emerged as it did in seventeenth- and eighteenth-century Europe. Such were the results of our earlier chapters.

In this chapter we have shown that natural science would not have progressed beyond its seventeenth- and eighteenth-century beginnings, unless the social structures on which it depended were secularized in such a way that the reality of the spirit world and the creational teachings of the Judeo-Christian tradition were bracketed from industrial processes and from technoscientific discourse. The possible existence of a cosmic Lawgiver is often allowed by scientists in their personal musings (which we have taken seriously), but it does not play a role in professional scientific discourse the way it did for the early natural philosophers like Kepler. Serious consideration of the spirit world to which early humans devoted their explorations (and to which the intelligence we inherit from them may be partly adapted) is largely confined to the disciplines of anthropology and psychiatry, which often deal with supernatural phenomena directly. The role that creational beliefs played in medieval and early modern science is left to the historians.

Now placing the results of this chapter alongside those of the three previous chapters, we are forced to conclude that the foundations of scientific endeavour are in

---

universality, (theological) neutrality, and the public/private partitioning of life; C. Smith, 'Introduction: Rethinking the Secularization of American Public Life', 76-7.

conflict. All four investigations have engaged us theological discourse. However, the first three suggest a foundational role for the spirit world and for creational theology in scientific endeavour, while the fourth requires us to regard such possibilities as 'unscientific' and bar them from our professional discourse.

At the surface level, this conflict might be taken as another instance of the supposed ongoing conflict between religious faith and modern science.[66] Since the first three foundations of scientific endeavour constitute the deep structures of scientific endeavour and are the furthest removed from everyday experience in the modern world, their continuing role in scientific endeavour is not so readily apparent as that of the fourth foundation, which everyone can see in industrial technologies and universities around us. However, the thick description of scientific endeavour we have developed indicates that the situation is rather more complex. The conflict is not between science and theology as such, but among the various deposits, laid down at different stages of cosmic history, that together make modern scientific endeavour possible. There is a conflict, or at least a paradox, within the very foundations of scientific endeavour, and, as we shall see, there is a comparable conflict within theological endeavour.

Our analysis of the foundations of scientific endeavour has led to another paradox, which I shall call the 'SFSS paradox', that results when Science-Fostering Social Systems are viewed in the context of the deeper cosmic, anthropological and cultural foundations on which they rest. Normally we do not give such paradoxes much thought, but they can tell us a lot about some of the difficulties we live with. In fact, many of the mental stresses that plague our lives could be the result of skirting over the paradoxes embedded in structures on which we depend. So it is worthwhile investigating them as part of our thickening description of scientific endeavour.

The SFSS paradox can be formulated in various ways. One way would be to begin with the most recently developed and immediate of the four foundations and work our way down to the earlier, deeper ones. We begin with the fact that SFSS involve restrictions on professional language and behaviour. Spirits may have been a fact of life for ancient cultures, and they may still be taken seriously by some people, but not in professional meetings or on company time.[67] Theological beliefs and divine inspiration may have inspired the founders of modern science, who mostly worked as lone individuals, but as university-trained professionals we now have to bracket them out in our research. These restrictions are necessary for eliminating contingencies and getting reproducible results as well as for inter-cultural cooperation.

---

66   The conflict of faith and science was largely an artifact of 19th-century secularizing agendas. Prior to the nineteenth century, most of the supposed conflicts were the result of tensions between different methodologies for doing science, matched by different methods for doing theology. Some were more naturalist, while others stressed the contingency of natural causation; cf. Kaiser, *Creational*, 49, 51, 53-4, 59, 101, 111, passim.

67   Berger et al., *The Homeless Mind*, 17; British edn, 22-3. The present-day clash between spirit possession and factory discipline is well documented for rapidly industrializing nations like Malaysia; Aihwa Ong, *Spirits of Resistance and Capitalist Discipline: Factory Women in Malaysia* (Albany: SUNY Press, 1987), 203-210. Countermeasures included education, the use of traditional spirit-healers for psychological effect and soothing popular music.

In this top-down approach, the paradox arises when we realize that these restrictions on professional language make it extremely difficult to converse openly about the deeper foundations that make science and industry possible – a difficulty we struggled with in our discussion of those foundations in earlier chapters. In short, the continued progress of scientific endeavour requires clear lines of demarcation that make it difficult to explain its deeper foundations in the contingent lawfulness of the universe, the Science-Fostering Intelligence of humanity, and the beliefs on which all working scientists rely on a daily basis. Or, to put it the other way around, sustained scientific endeavour occludes the very possibilities that its cosmic, anthropological, and cultural foundations require.

Another way of describing this paradox would be to begin with the cosmic, anthropological and cultural foundations and work our way forward (or upward) to the societal foundation. We find that modern scientific endeavour depends on (1) the contingency of cosmic law – a contingency that at least suggests a foundational role for a Lawgiver, (2) human ability to indwell abstract symbolic worlds – an ability that can be explained as an adaptation to the spirit world as an ecological niche; and (3) culturally sustained belief in the comprehensibility of the natural world – a belief with roots in ancient religions and creational theology. These three foundations all have deep theological connections, and they are all necessary for the origin and continuance of modern science.

The paradox, from this bottom up perspective, is that open discussion about these three foundations is virtually impossible in industrial and professional circles – their theological connections are judged to be a private matter without any shared value or even any apparent connection to the endeavour they actually foster. What makes the paradox particularly striking is the fact that this animus against discussing the deep foundations of scientific endeavour in professional, technoscientific circles is actually necessary for the progress of scientific endeavour. Without such lines of demarcation we would not have the basic structures of industrial enterprise on which scientists rely.

## A dilemma for the unity of science

So far we considered the present state of scientific endeavour from the perspective of its origins in cosmogenesis, Paleolithic prehistory, and the history of science, and we have become entangled in the SFSS paradox. If we now shift our focus toward future challenges, the paradox can be stated even more sharply, and it leads to a dilemma for the unity of scientific knowledge. The more that advanced technologies enable scientists to reach beyond the common-sense world of everyday experience and to remove the mysteries of nature by explaining what they find in terms of natural laws, the more the contingent lawfulness of the universe, the success of human intelligence, and the fact that scientists are true believers all seem like impenetrable mysteries. Yet the ongoing progress of scientific endeavour will eventually require some explanation of its feasibility, and meeting this demand will require open consideration of the very possibilities that its industrial foundation consistently shoves to the periphery.

It is not my intention to challenge the secularizing strictures of professional discourse. The special sciences should continue to progress as long as robust commercial enterprise enables the development of the needed technologies. The deeper problem has to do with the long-term quest for the unity of all science. The day-by-day work of scientists is as much a part of the space-time world that scientists want to understand as atoms or galaxies are. Since, as defined here, the goal of scientific endeavour is to explore and understand all accessible features of the space-time world, it should at some point attempt to develop a unified theory that will explain the possibility of scientists doing what they do.

The problem is that the secularizing strictures on discourse make it very difficult to discuss the preconditions for scientific endeavour with the openness needed to arrive at a consensus. Reasonable hypotheses that are needed to advance our understanding of those foundations will inevitably be regarded as metaphysical or even obscurantist. The possibility that scientific endeavour can examine its own foundations will be hindered by the very strictures on professional discourse that make technoscience possible. As a consequence, it is nearly impossible for science ever to become self-explanatory and thereby reach its goal. The SFSS paradox becomes a dilemma for the goal of a unified science.[68]

Based on what we have already said, it is clear that this unity of science dilemma can not be solved just by repudiating the industrial technology on which modern science relies. Any deliberate effort to desecularize (or resacralize) industrial systems or reintegrate scientific discourse in a framework of theology and prayer would seriously hamper the development of reliable new technologies and be ruinous for future scientific endeavour.

Those who care about the future of scientific endeavour need an eschatology – an exercise of the imagination in which possible futures are projected in an attempt to visualize resolutions to present-day dilemmas. Perhaps the very discussion of such futures will help resolve some of the paradoxes.[69] The least we can say is that it would be both fascinating and helpful for us to learn how matters will turn out long after we ourselves have ceased to live in the space-time world as subjects of its industrial strictures. As in our earlier chapters, we find that pressing our inquiry into the foundations of scientific endeavour leads us into theological discourse. Science and theology are not connected by building bridges, but by digging a deep network of tunnels.

---

68  A similar dilemma confronted physicists when the laws of quantum mechanics turned out to be incompatible with those of general relativity. The two were designed to work at different scales – cosmic and subatomic – but they must be reconciled in any unified theory that will explain cosmic origins. Some of the most creative work in physics has been stimulated by the dilemma.

69  Some options currently being discussed for the future of technological innovation are reviewed by Robert Adler, 'Are we on our way back to the Dark Ages?', *New Scientist* 187 (2 July 2005), 26-7.

**Theological challenges and resources**

I have argued that scientific endeavour depends on the industrialization of its societal foundation and thereby places severe constraints on theological discourse in professional contexts related to science and technology – constraints that result from long-term secularizing developments that neither can nor should be undone. As in previous chapters, our thick description of scientific endeavour engages us in theological discourse although it does not legitimate any particular brand of theology.

I have also shown how this analysis leads to paradoxes for our understanding of scientific endeavour. In this section we will find that it also leads to paradoxes for theological endeavour, and we shall look at some resources for addressing this challenge. As in previous chapters, such resources will be drawn from the Judeo-Christian tradition. What is at stake here is not the validity of that tradition, which must be addressed on its own grounds, but its compatibility with a thick description of scientific endeavour.

*Two common approaches and a dilemma for theology*

In order to frame our discussion, let us consider two common theological approaches to the problems raised by industrialization. One is tempted either to be countercultural or to be science-affirming. I have tried following both of these approaches myself.

The first option is to take a countercultural stance toward the science and society nexus that has so dominated modern life. Such an outlook could be based on a historic Anabaptist tradition, or the experiences of an excluded minority, or even a social-ethics crusade in a mainline denomination. The target here could be the commodification of labor, the harmful effects of exploiting natural resources, or the power of professional specialists (the 'knowledge class') over media and education. From this perspective, many of the dominant forces in our society are demonic, and the theologian's task must be to call for radical social change.

There are certainly points to affirm in this countercultural stance, but it is nearly impossible to maintain consistently either as one who willingly lives in the modern world or as an advocate of traditional theology. However dehumanizing some aspects of industrial society may appear to be, we inevitably use and even celebrate some of its benefits: whether basic technologies like automobiles and computers, or technology-dependent institutions like libraries and the media. It would be difficult to come up with a simple criterion that will differentiate the good from the bad within the complex web of society and technology.

Based on our findings about the foundations of scientific endeavour, we see that the countercultural option leads also to a theological contradiction. Those who criticize the programme of technoscientific research find themselves at variance with traditional Judeo-Christian teachings about the God-given comprehensibility of creation, described in Chapter 3. Creational teachings are just as foundational to the Judeo-Christian tradition as they are to scientific endeavour, even if scientists put their understanding of those beliefs into practice on a daily basis more than most Christians do. The idea that humans have the God-given ability to investigate creation does more than just legitimate the enterprise of natural science. Traditionally, at least, it has also meant that God intends us to use our abilities and pursue the investigation as best we can.[70] Nor is it possible to affirm traditional creational faith and try to confine our criticisms to the effects of industrialization. All modern science is technoscience and therefore linked to large-scale corporate industry. On either side of the issue, a critical, countercultural stance toward SFSS inevitably leads to contradictions and is not a viable theological option.

A common science-affirming approach to the problems of industrialization has an initial advantage over the countercultural option: it can appeal directly to the theology of creation, citing chapter and verse, and follow through on its implications for the present-day pursuit of scientific knowledge. Creational theologians can also cite many benefits that derive from modern science and industry, including the advancement of agriculture and medicine. In Scripture, feeding and healing are among the most basic signs of God's kingdom on earth. In historical theology, the profession of medicine is viewed as a direct expression of biblical teachings about creation.[71] From this creational perspective, the theologian's task must be to support scientific and industrial progress as part of the divine plan for humanity.

In spite of the fact that this science-affirming position has such great biblical and theological support, the paradoxes we have raised in this chapter lead to serious contradictions here also. Naturally, creational theologians with a strong social conscience will deplore the negative side effects of industrialization: urban sprawl, pollution, global warming, economic inequality and the rest. But other effects of SFSS are equally serious. In the first part of this chapter, we showed in some detail that the sustained progress of scientific work depends on a consumer-oriented, market-driven industrial base the development of which required the leadership of land-enclosers and corporate-business tycoons. Creational theologians can certainly advocate corrective measures for the excesses of industrialization, but they can not change the consequences like the marginalization of native peoples and the secularization of professional discourse that we have documented here. So the science-affirming theological stance toward SFSS also leads to serious contradictions.

In short, neither of these two theological strategies works consistently. As a result, we are left with a serious dilemma for theology, similar to the dilemma we just encountered in trying to understand the societal foundation of scientific endeavour. Like the previous one, this dilemma can be stated in different ways. Given that Science-Fostering Social Systems marginalize spirit peoples and bracket traditional creational theology, must we not conclude that God is no longer the trustworthy guide of history? Could God possibly bless the work of land-enclosers, spirit-marginalizers, and secularizing elites? Did God not realize what effects industrial society would have for indigenous nations or even for participants in the dominant culture? How should a theologian answer?

We can also approach the dilemma from the other direction. Given that God has been preparing the way for modern science from the very beginning – ordaining a comprehensible universe, presiding over a spirit world to which humans are adapted, and inspiring a Scripture-based tradition of creationist ideas (Chapters 1-3) – must we

---

70   See Chapter 3 on Kepler's theological argument for scientific research.

71   Kaiser, *Creational Theology*, 60-83, passim.

not conclude that the development of the massive infrastructure needed for scientific research is the inevitable fulfillment of God's purposes for the world? If so, we must also conclude that God sanctions the dehumanizing aspects of industrial society as 'collateral damage'. Or else we have been too simplistic in the way in which we think about God's ways of acting in history.

The discovery of an intellectual dilemma is an opportunity for finding and developing new ways of thinking. This is always true in the natural sciences, where paradoxes and dilemmas are often celebrated as avenues to new learning. Scientists thrive on paradoxes – always, of course, with a view toward resolving them. Paradoxes also come up in discussing the foundations of scientific endeavour as we have seen. So it should not be surprising that they crop up in theology as well, particularly in the theology of history with which we are concerned here. The question is whether traditional theology has any other resources for dealing with such paradoxes.

*Refocusing our theology of history*

In the approach taken here, theology is a human endeavour just as much as science. If natural science is the endeavour to explore and understand all accessible features of the space-time world, theology is the endeavour to understand as much as possible about aspects of the world where God, humanity and nature interrelate. Theological endeavour is not a disinterested exploration of the space-time world, but an effort to interpret the world in relation to human life and divine purposes. The 'good news' is that human life and divine purposes have been filled with paradoxes from the start: theologians did not need to wait for the emergence of industrial society to encounter such problems. They had plenty of material to work with long before the emergence of SFSS. So the tradition may well have resources that can be adapted to the present dilemma.

Here it will be helpful to refer back to our discussion of God as ecstatic Creator of all things in Chapter 1. In the act of creation, God projects God's self into the realm of finite form and enters into direct relationship with what God creates. In so doing, God takes on the forms of creation: space-time forms and various attributes like justice and mercy. It is as if white light had passed through a prism and diffracted itself into a rainbow of colours. Any one colour might be in focus at any one time. The God described in the Hebrew Bible is invested in each moment of time with colour and passion. God can be all things and do all things, but not all at once. This diffraction of the divine attributes does not fit in easily with the Aristotelian dialectic on which most Western thought is based, but it has helped generations of believers make sense of the paradoxes of their lives and their history. It also allows for an eschatological refocusing of the divine attributes, which we will discuss later.

With this background in mind, let us return to the theological dilemma described above. If, as the first three chapters of this study have argued, God has gone to the trouble of providing creation with comprehensible laws and inducing Science-Fostering Intelligence in the human species, it is hard not to agree with traditional creation-based teaching that God passionately wants humans to use their gifts to investigate the laws of creation. To this extent we must agree with the 'science-affirming' option described above. The question is whether that divine passion could conceivably override other considerations like justice (for indigenous peoples) and wisdom (concerning professional discourse).

For many people it may seem inconceivable that God would actually set aside considerations of either justice or wisdom. However, Rabbis and theologians who have attempted to understand the ways of the Deity have frequently been forced to explore such possibilities. When God acts with purpose and passion, a single attribute may be expressed in ways that appear to contradict sober deliberation. God's self-investment in the people of Israel was filled with purpose and passion, and it was quite a stormy relationship. Sometimes it was one of passionate attraction, and the God of Israel (ha-Shem) was romantic and lavish in giving (Ezek. 16:6-14). But there were also times when the Creator was furious with Israel and operated out of the attribute of judgment. More than once, Moses had to argue with ha-Shem in order to prevent the destruction of the entire nation. When Moses spoke, ha-Shem listened and eventually returned to the attribute of mercy (Exod. 32:9-14; Num. 14:11-25; Ps. 106:23).[72]

In many of these biblical accounts, God was willing to abandon acts of judgment. When the passion in question was one of love or mercy, however, God was less likely to listen to reason and more persistent in following through on the original purpose. I shall discuss two examples of such divine persistence and draw some conclusions that will help us assess the place of industrial technology, which as the societal foundation of scientific endeavour may be another of God's passions, in a theology of history. The first example comes from a classic Midrash concerning an event much earlier than the calling of Israel – the creation of humanity. The second comes from a New Testament parable about a later event – Jesus of Nazareth's attempt to broaden the kingdom of God beyond the boundaries of ethnic Israel.

*Genesis Rabbah on the creation of humanity*

In Chapter 1, we discussed several *midrāshîm* (exegetical investigations mostly compiled in the first millennium CE) that discuss the possible existence of other universes. The value of these *midrāshîm* for our discussion is that all parts of the Hebrew Bible are viewed in relation to each other and explore possibilities of divine action that a more linear reading of Scripture might miss.

Several classical *midrāshîm* raise questions that are very similar to the ones we have been considering, but in relation to the creation and history of humanity. Did God foresee the problems that would arise from creating humans on earth? If so, how could God have risked the goodness and beauty of the primeval world? On the other hand, how could God not create the one being that would have the ability to do truly good things and so embellish creation in a way that other creatures could not? The early Rabbis did not skirt around these questions: they actually dramatized and accentuated them. So the wisdom they offer may be helpful to us in thinking about the SFSS paradox and the dilemma it raises for a theology of history.

---

72  Kaiser, *Doctrine of God*, 11-13; cf. Yochanan Muffs, *Love and Joy: Law, Language and Religion in Ancient Israel* (New York: Jewish Theological Seminary of America, 1992), 33-7.

One classic midrash is found in Genesis Rabbah (*Běre'shît Rabbah*), the 'Great Genesis Collection', which dates in its present form from the fifth century CE. The discussion begins with the Genesis text, *Let us make Adam [Heb.'ādām] in our image and likeness* (Gen. 1:26). The midrash goes like this:

> When God came to create the first man [*'ādām*], he saw that both righteous and wicked descendants would come forth from him. He said, 'If I create him, wicked descendants will come forth from him. If I do not create him, how will the righteous descendants come forth from him?' What did the Holy One, blessed be he, do? He disregarded the way of the wicked and joined to himself his quality of mercy and so created him. (Gen. Rab. 8:4.1)[73]

The first of our questions is answered at the outset: God foreknew that evil would result even before humans were created. God is totally immersed in the moment and yet foreknows the future. Paradox is embedded in this very combination of attributes, and it is expressed in the form of a dilemma: to create humans, or not to create?[74] In the first case, evil would arise and God's creation would be harmed. This knowledge makes God hesitate just long enough to consider the alternative. Perhaps humanity should not be created. Then the goodness of creation would be preserved, but there would be no righteous descendents in it. The poignancy of the drama is indicated by a special phrase, 'What did the Holy One, blessed be he, do?' According to the Rabbis, there was a paradox at the very beginning of history – a dilemma even for God! Its strategic placement suggests that they viewed it as a template for subsequent dramas in history.

God's choice in the midrash was not simply a matter of taste – a little more of this, a little less of that. It was rather a clear-cut, all-or-nothing situation. The Holy and Blessed One is not portrayed as an artist thinking about a great composition, so much as a lover desiring to be a father and to have children after his own image. The 'righteous' is a standard designation for those who adhere to God's will and so prove to be God's children, created in God's image. They are God's anticipated offspring – the object of God's deep desire. Like an expectant mother or father, God longs to see them. There is no further hesitation. God's decision to create humanity is completely uninhibited: 'He joined to himself his quality of mercy and so created him'. The creation of humanity was an act of divine ecstasy, here expressed in terms of the classic attribute of mercy.

According to our midrash, the creation of humanity was motivated by passion more than reason.[75] Like God's passion for Israel, it can be compared to the desire of

---

73    Jacob Neusner, trans., *Genesis Rabbah*, 1:77. On this midrash, see David Stern, '*Imitatio Hominis*: Anthropomorphism and the Character(s) of God in Rabbinic Literature', *Prooftexts* 12 (May 1992), 166-8 (where the passage is labeled 8:3); cf. Muffs, *Love and Joy: Law*, 44-5.

74    Underlying this paradox is the dialectic of transcendence and interiority discussed in Chapter 1 ('God as ecstatic Creator of all things').

75    Among Christian theologians who have captured this idea of divine passion is Catherine of Siena: "I confess and do not deny that thou didst love me before I existed, and that thy love for me is ineffable, as if thou wast mad with love for thy creature"; *The Dialogue*

a man for his betrothed (Ezek.16:8).[76] Here God 'joins with' the attribute of mercy and bypasses the demands of strict justice and goes ahead with the plan. All of the bewildering paradoxes of history are evoked in this dramatic portrayal. They all point back to the diversity and conflict among the attributes of God.[77] Once self-projected into the realm of finite form, God could be all things and do all things, but not all at once.

From this first midrash, we learn that God may be willing to tolerate human injustice, at least temporarily, if there is no other way to ensure that there will be children capable of fulfilling divine purposes. Such passionate choice results in a non-equilibrium state. There is a temporary imbalance among God's assets: one account has been overdrawn at the expense of the other (we take up the matter of balance later). What makes this midrash about the foundations of human history particularly helpful for our purposes is the possible insight it may afford us in our effort to understand the imbalances in the foundations of scientific endeavour.

Some of us may wonder whether God made the right choice in either case: creating humans or supporting the work of scientists. If so, we are not alone. The Genesis text, *Let us make Adam in our image*, suggests that there was some sort of conversation prior to the creation of humanity, although nothing is said about the reason for the discussion. As we saw in Chapter 1, God was traditionally held to preside over a council of divine beings (angels who represent various divine 'powers' and sometimes righteous humans), where issues of government and justice were debated.[78] That possibility is further developed in the *midrāshîm* that immediately follow the one we just discussed.

In the sequel, there are two distinct versions of the discussion that preceded the creation of humanity. In the first, God seeks to know the mind of his associates. 'Shall we make man [*'ādām*]?' God asks (Gen. Rab. 8:4.2). Apparently a bit suspicious, the angels ask for more information on the new creature: 'What will be his character?' The angel's attitude suggests that they already had everything they needed and were happy with creation in its natural state. Like all 'haves' for whom life is good as it is, they are leery about innovations.

As in the previous midrash, God foreknows the future of humanity, but God also anticipates the possible responses of the angels: if they were to know the full truth,

---

*of the Seraphic Virgin, Catherine of Siena*, trans. Algar Thorold (London: Burns, Oates & Washbourne, 1925), 343.

76   The Babylonian Talmud compares God's impatience to indwell Israel with a man's impatience to possess his bride; *b. Ketuvôt* 62b; Jeffrey Rubenstein, trans, *Rabbinic Stories* (New York: Paulist Press, 2002), 143, 282n.10. The 18th-century Hasidic writer, Jacob Joseph of Polonnoye, stated that human sexual desire actually had its origin in the divine attribute of mercy; Raphael Patai, *The Jewish Mind* (New York: Charles Scribner's Sons, 1977), 203. The 'maleness' of God may be figurative, but, given the culture. it perfectly expressed the sense of risk and drive that the Rabbis attributed to ha-Shem.

77   In *Avôt de-Rabbi Natan* 4, God is said to create with the attribute of mercy alone; Psalm 89:2 (Hebrew 89:3) is cited for support. In Gen. Rab. 12:15, however, the attributes of mercy and justice are perfectly balanced in creation, based on the names 'Lord' and 'God' in Gen. 2:4. Fruitful explorations need not all follow the same line of thought.

78   See Chapter 1 under 'God as interpersonal Lord'.

they would take the side of justice and try to veto God's plan. So God only tells them about the 'righteous descendents' of Adam and withholds the part about the wicked. Of course, the Rabbis would never suggest that God was untruthful or unjust, but, in this case at least, the desire to create and behold righteous children outweighed considerations of truth and justice.

The second version of the divine council in Genesis Rabbah makes the point even more forcefully than the first. Here the angels do not need to ask God about the character of humanity. None of them has the whole picture, but each one is associated with a single divine attribute (or power) and is thereby able to foresee a single aspect of the future (Gen. Rab. 8:5). As a result, the angels take sides and debate the issue. The angels representing the attributes truth and peace vehemently oppose the idea of creating humanity. 'He will perform acts of mercy', says Mercy. No, 'he is a complete fake', says Truth. But 'he will perform acts of righteousness', says Righteousness. 'He is one mass of contention', says Peace. The sides are evenly matched, and the deliberation is inconclusive. God must break the stalemate. The democratic process was a great idea – at least, it absolved God of the charge of untruthfulness – but the result makes the previous version look good by comparison. God's plan for creatures that reflect the divine image is on the verge of collapse.[79]

'What then did the Holy One, blessed be he, do?' God took hold of Truth and threw it to the ground. Impossible? We are given biblical support and, at the same time, promised that Truth will be restored in due time: *Truth will spring up from the ground [and Righteousness will look down from the sky]* (Ps. 85:11). We need to reconsider the promise of Truth in a later section.

The very fact that Genesis Rabbah preserves several different versions of the dilemma involved in creating humanity indicates how significant this issue was to the Rabbis in the early centuries CE.[80] No doubt their investigations were motivated by the paradox of hopes and fears that followed the destruction of the Second Temple and the Christianization of the Roman Empire.[81] But the problem had been a familiar one throughout Jewish history, and the pattern found in Genesis Rabbah would find echoes in many other contexts. One can well imagine similar celestial deliberations about the building of the Jerusalem Temple under Solomon – using foreign craftsmen and Jewish forced labour (1 Kgs. 5; 2 Chron. 2) – or the later

---

79  The Rabbis were viewing the whole matter retrospectively in a polemical environment. It was a fact that humans had been created. But by whom? Many Gnostics viewed creation as a disaster and attributed it to the egotistic Demiurge who blundered at every step of the way. So the Rabbis had to preserve the sovereignty of their God in order to maintain hope for a fulfillment of the divine promises.

80  Another version is found in *b. Sanhedrin* 38b. Here God creates and destroys angels until he gets a company that agrees with his plan (parallel to the *midrāshîm* on multiple universes discussed in Chapter 1). In other versions, God overrules angelic opposition to his revealing the Torah to Israel and his sending the Shekhinah-Glory to dwell in the Tabernacle. The parallel between the creation of humanity and the revelation of the Torah is discussed by Gary A. Anderson, *The Genesis of Perfection: Adam and Eve in Jewish and Christian Imagination* (Louisville: Westminster John Knox Press, 2001), 30-35, 165.

81  See Jacob Neusner, *Transformation in Ancient Judaism: Textual Evidence for Creative Responses to Crisis* (Peabody, Mass: Hendrickson, 2004), esp. chaps 4 and 5.

rebuilding of the Temple under the patronage of foreign kings like Darius and Herod. God desperately wanted to live in and among the people of Israel. The desire to have a place in which to dwell was evidently great enough to overcome immediate concerns for strict justice or cultic purity in many stages of the history of Israel.

Before looking at another source for some help with paradoxes of history, let us summarize the basic pattern in the texts we have reviewed so far, which we may take as a paradigm for subsequent cases. At times, God is not satisfied with prior accomplishments and desires to introduce some innovation even though the expected results are mixed at best. Reflection on the matter is based on an inner dialectic of divine attributes or else on deliberation among God's associates who represent those attributes. The forum for discussion is the divine council, where objections can be raised and God's desires can be opposed or even thwarted (cf. Exod. 32:30-34; Job 1:6-12). In the present age, God is more likely to listen to ideas (like those of Abraham and Moses) that favour the objects of God's desire, than to those that favour strict justice.[82] If opposed, God may overrule the demands of justice in favor of high-risk projects. As in all of life's paradoxes, finding an ideal way to accomplish the desired result is a luxury. The real question is whether the result can be even accomplished.

After a brief look at a New Testament parallel (and a second look at the demands of Truth), we shall return to the SFSS paradoxes and draw some conclusions for a possible eschatological resolution of the dilemma.

## New Testament parables about the kingdom of heaven

The New Testament is concerned with several historical innovations that parallel the creation of humanity and the calling of Israel. Although the New Testament writings antedate the collections of *midrāshîm* by a few centuries, the hermeneutical strategies and dramatic analogies are similar in many ways. The main difference is that the Rabbis were motivated by disappointing circumstances to explore past events as paradigms for the present, whereas New Testament writers saw the paradigms as pointing toward a new dispensation of God's grace.

The basic pattern is particularly clear in the expanded version of the sayings of Jesus that is found in the Gospel of Matthew. The motif of debate within the divine council underlies Jesus' confrontation with Peter over the way of the Cross (Matt. 16:21-23) and several of the 'parables of the kingdom' (Matt. 13; 18; 20; 21; 22; 25). Like the *midrāshîm* we have studied, the Matthean parables feature God as the chief protagonist in the drama.[83] Parables that deal with God's actions in the present age are particularly helpful for our purposes because they often portray God as an ordinary woman or man who has to make a choice between conflicting values. As in

---

82   The appeal to justice and truth is sometimes associated with the Accusing Angel, *ha-shātān* ('Satan' in English); cf. Gary Anderson, *The Genesis of Perfection*, 167-8, 183. Precedent for this attribution can be found in the Hebrew Bible itself; 1 Chron. 21:1 (cf. 2 Sam. 24:1); Job 1:6-12. Like the Angel of Truth, Satan is cast down to the earth in Life of Adam and Eve 13-16 (Charlesworth, ed., *Old Testament Pseudepigrapha*, 2:262); Rev. 12:9.

83   Cf. David Stern, *Parables in Midrash: Narrative and Exegesis in Rabbinic* Literature (Cambridge, Mass: Harvard University Press, 1991), 19-21.

the *midrāshîm*, the Holy One, blessed be he, follows the goal of his desire rather than playing it safe. We shall look at a few examples.

First we look at two very short parables to establish the basic idea. They occur side by side in Matthew 13:

> The kingdom of heaven is like a treasure hidden in a field, which someone found and hid; then in his joy he goes and sells all that he has and buys that field. (Matt. 13:44)

> Again, the kingdom of heaven is like a merchant in search of fine pearls; on finding one pearl of great value, he went and sold all that he had and bought it. (Matt. 13:45-6)

These kingdom parables were selected by the Evangelist and are placed together, much as various creation *midrāshîm* were placed together by the Rabbis, in order to reinforce a common theme.[84] If we may admit Genesis Rabbah as a witness to the hermeneutical strategy, the pearl collector or merchant in these parables must be God. The Deity is portrayed as a person of wealth who searches for objects of unique beauty and value – buried treasure, pearls, etc. – the more rare ('hidden') the better.[85]

One treasure turns up that excels all others, but it costs an exorbitant amount. The drama of the story arises from the fact that God must sell everything – everything already possessed – in order to buy this one treasure. What was the Holy One, blessed be he, to do? As in the classic midrash, God's decision is uninhibited. Without any bargaining or deliberation, God sells everything just to have this one beautiful thing. The high-risk impulsiveness of this Collector clearly resonates with the Creator in Genesis Rabbah.

Jesus' parables are intended to shock readers into rethinking their ideas about God. In this case, the shock value is based on an implicit conflict of values. How many of us would risk everything we own so spontaneously? How many of us would even counsel a friend to do so? Surely not in everyday business affairs. The only context in which we are normally impelled to take such risks is in affairs of the heart. That is how God is portrayed here – as a passionate lover of beauty rather than a thrifty householder or a successful investor.[86]

Here is the principal point of contact with the *midrāshîm* about the creation of humanity. God desires to create a new situation even knowing that venture is risky and the results will be mixed at best. As the first of these parables explicitly states: 'in his joy [*apò tês charâs*] he goes and sells all that he has' (Matt. 13:44). The Greek

---

84  The two closest parallels in the Gospel of Thomas (Logia 76 and 109) are unrelated to each other. There are no direct parallels in the Gospel of Luke.

85  Intertextual reference to Prov. 2:1-9 and the 'parable of the rich young man' in Matt. 19:16-22 might suggest that the collector-investor here is a wise young person who desires to be perfect and thereby gain eternal life. However, the exact same combination of terms – seeking, finding, joy – occurs in the 'parable of the lost sheep' in Matt. 18:12-14, where the shepherd clearly is God. The parables of the kingdom are all about desire and the delight in possession, not the discipline and achievement of a sage but the passion of a bridegroom. Another reading to consider would be that the protagonist is Jesus himself (Matt. 13:44; cf. Matt. 16:21-23; Heb. 12:2).

86  Contrast the parallel versions in the Gospel of Thomas, Logia 76, 109, where the buyer is described as making a prudent and even a shrewd investment.

term used here to express the joy of God (*chará*) often has a rather ordinary sense of emotion, but the term was also used in the Septuagint (Greek) translation of the prophets to describe the joy of a woman who has successfully delivered her first child, or the mutual joy of a bride and bridegroom (Isa. 66:10-11; Jer. 16:9; 25:10).

If the parables are viewed alongside the *midrāshîm*, several questions arise. One thing missing in Matthew 13 is any explicit reference to the 'righteous descendents' whose presence God so deeply desires. Perhaps they are represented by the treasure and the pearl, but what would God be selling to purchase them? And what would be the risk involved? And where were God's advisors in this crucial moment? What would they have said about God's letting go all the gains of previous accomplishments? In the Matthean context, the more sensible (angelic) parties that Jesus is clearly speaking against are the elites of his nation (cf. Matt. 12:2, 14, 24, 38). Unlike the *midrāshîm*, however, there is no actual dialogue in these two parables: their very brevity precludes such detail.

With these questions in mind, we turn to a much longer, more developed example – the 'parable of the wedding banquet' in Matthew 22. Here is the kernel with which it begins:

> The kingdom of heaven may be compared to a king who gave a wedding banquet for his son. He sent his slaves to call those who had been invited to the wedding banquet, but they would not come. Again he sent other slaves, saying, 'Tell those who have been invited: Look, I have prepared my dinner, my oxen, and my fat calves have been slaughtered, and everything is ready; come to the wedding banquet.' But they made light of it and went away, one to his farm, another to his business…. Then he said to his slaves, 'The wedding is ready, but those invited were not worthy. Go therefore into the main streets, and invite everyone you find to the wedding banquet.' Those slaves went out into the streets and gathered all whom they found, both good and bad; so the wedding hall was filled with guests. (Matt. 22:1-5, 8-10)

This time the king clearly represents God. As in previous *midrāshîm* and parables, the theme is God's desire for a particular object – in this case an expensive wedding feast for his son. Similarly to the creation *midrāshîm*, there is a council of servants (angels or prophets) with whom the king discusses his plan and who are expected to carry it out.[87] As in previous *midrāshîm*, God's desires can be thwarted – not this time by the reluctance of servants, but by the invited guests. These guests are evidently longstanding friends of the family, and, in the New Testament context, they represent the Torah-observant, Temple-supporting elite of Israel (the chief priests and Pharisees; cf. Matt. 21:23, 45). They are also well-to-do farmers and businessmen with many projects of their own. Being responsible, sensible stewards of their own gifts, they refuse to abandon their businesses and family obligations.[88]

---

87  Compare Jesus' parable with Gen. Rab. 8:6, where a creation without humanity is likened to a tower that a king has stocked with enough food for a banquet but that still lacks guests; Neusner, trans., *Genesis Rabbah*, 1:79.

88  A similar idea is developed in Gospel of Thomas, Logion 64, though the issue there is one of material accumulation.

The king's safest course of action would be to keep faith with the people whom he knows and trusts. But that would mean either canceling his son's wedding (out of the question) or going ahead with an empty banquet hall. The shocking truth is that 'haves' who are responsible about the use of their time and resources are often, unlike God, too conservative to take risks and too cautious to join the celebration.[89] So what is the Holy and Blessed One to do?

Based on what we have seen before, the extreme action of the king is no surprise. But still it comes as a shock. The would-be father of the groom throws out the entire original guest list and starts over.[90] This time the servants are commanded to go out and invite anyone they can find. There is no time to check into their backgrounds or test out their piety, because 'everything is ready'. So all are invited, both good and bad.

It is not clear just who these new guests are supposed to be, but they would spook the angels. Given God's high standards of purity and righteousness, the risk would be great enough if they were simply nonobservant Jews ('people of the land') or even Christian Jews. It would be even greater if they were Gentiles brought up in a lifestyle of idolatrous practices. Regardless of the risk, there was a full banquet hall and the wedding of the king's son was duly celebrated. As in the creation of humanity, the Holy and Blessed One opted to relax the demands of strict justice rather than forgo the desired goal, at least, for the time being.[91] The issue for God was not how best to accomplish the desired goals within the ideal of ritual purity, but how to accomplish it at all.

We shall return to this parable and consider its sequel momentarily. But first we should review our results thus far and consider its application to the SFSS paradoxes described earlier.

*The perspective of mercy: a theology of Science-Fostering Social Systems*

Our point of contact between biblical studies and the societal foundation for scientific endeavour lies in the paradoxes embedded at the heart of each of these fascinating subjects. The rabbinic *midrāshîm* and New Testament (Matthean) parables offer

---

89   The same idea is found in other Gospel passages like Luke 7:37-47; 10:38-41; 14:12-14; 16:1-8.

90   Matt. 22:7 (omitted above) states that the king sent his troops to destroy those who had rejected his invitation and to burn their city – part of an interpolation not found in the parallel version in Luke 14:21. Aside from a secondary reference to the destruction of Jerusalem (70 CE), the theme of the fiery destruction of those who oppose God's plan fits the pattern of the midrash about the creation of humanity in b. Sanh. 38b: 'Thereupon he stretched out his little finger among them and consumed them with fire'; *Hebrew-English Edition of the Babylonian Talmud: Tractate Sanhedrin*, ed. Epstein, 38b. In our parable, the invited guests fill the role of the opposing angels.

91   Another parable, the 'parable of the wheat and the tares', also places the attribute of mercy ahead of justice (Matt. 13:29-30). Note that mercy for one group or interest ('people of the land' and/or Gentiles) coincides with judgment for the other (the Torah-observant Jews); cf. the 'midrash of the guardian angels' described by James Kugel, 'The Ladder of Jacob', *Harvard Theological Review* 88 (April 1995), 212-16.

important insights both for a theology of history and for our understanding of the imbalances in the foundations of scientific endeavour.

Let us return to the questions we were left with after discussing the theological dilemma that results from the SFSS paradox. Did God realize what would result from the industrialization and secularization required to foster technoscience? Did God foresee the effects for people living in industrial societies and for indigenous nations on the fringes? Could God possibly bless the work of land-enclosers, spirit-marginalizers and secularizing elites? Is the continued development of science consistent with belief that God is the author and ruler of history?

Insofar as the *midrāshîm* and the parables may still be taken as templates for understanding how God acts in history, the answer to all of these questions would be 'yes' on one special condition – that there be a sufficient object of God's desire in view. If God desires something deeply enough, the normal standards of caution and the demands of justice may be set aside. In fact, if God desires something as much as God desired righteous descendents to exhibit the divine image, or as much as God desired a filled banquet hall to celebrate his son's wedding, the values of caution and justice must be positively overruled.

We now draw some conclusions regarding the societal foundation of scientific endeavour. The *midrāshîm* and the parables can help us address the SFSS paradox on one special condition – we must assume God's intention to be that scientific endeavour develop to the point that the laws and history of the universe (or metaverse) of which God is the Lawgiver and Animating Governor be investigated and understood by someone other than members of the divine council. [92]

According to the first midrash we studied, God wanted 'righteous descendents'. Why? Because by adhering to the Torah of Moses, they would learn to appreciate God's own righteousness and resemble it, as most children learn to appreciate and resemble their natural parents. So God created humanity with full awareness of the evil side-effects of his plan. Righteous descendents are the image of a righteous God.

The same thinking can be applied to the case of scientific endeavour. Evidently God wanted 'descendents' with the intelligence, beliefs and technology needed to explore and understand all accessible features of the space-time world. Why? Because by developing their gifts of intelligence and creativity, these descendents would learn to appreciate and emulate God's own intelligence and creativity. God blessed the development of industrial society in order to make this possible, even with full awareness of the evil side-effects. [93]

There are several reasons for believing this scenario to be reasonable. For one thing, the assumption that scientific endeavour is part of a divine plan is consistent

---

92    In order to apply the *midrāshîm* and parables to modern contexts, it is necessary to relax the assumption that the righteous and unrighteous are two separate classes of people. In many texts, the tendencies toward good and evil coexist in each individual (for example, m. Ber. 9:5; Gen. Rab. 9:7; Rom. 7:22-4).

93    Like the Rabbis, we are viewing the whole matter retrospectively. Industrial society is a fact of history. Theologically it is necessary to preserve the sovereignty of God in order to avoid contemporary Gnosticism (the world is ruled by an evil force) and maintain hope for a fulfillment of the divine promises.

with the traditional idea that God created humans in the divine image in order that they might investigate the created order and appreciate the divine wisdom it exhibits. In Chapter 3, we saw this belief forcefully stated in the words of the early seventeenth-century astronomer, Johannes Kepler.[94] Another influential example was the later seventeenth-century naturalist, John Ray.[95] So the idea was instrumental for the early modern founders of Western science.

The idea that God always intended humans to appreciate the created order actually goes back to the founders of the Christian theology. In the late fourth century, Gregory of Nyssa explained it this way:

> This then is the implication of our argument: that he who is God the Word and Wisdom and Power created human nature.... For it was not right that light should remain unseen, or glory unwitnessed, or goodness unenjoyed, or that any other aspect that we observe of the divine nature [in the natural world] should lie idle with no one to share or enjoy it. (*Catechetical Oration* 5)[96]

For early theologians as for early modern scientists, the very idea that God would create a cosmos without inviting others (besides angel colleagues) to explore it was as unthinkable as an artist painting a masterpiece without inviting anyone to view it ('that light should remain unseen, or glory unwitnessed'). Gregory's analysis of the creation of humanity is similar to the classic midrash: God created humans in order to have descendents. Only in the former case, the focus is more on knowledge than on righteousness.

The idea that God desired to have children with the intelligence and the technology needed to appreciate the creation can also be approached from our discussions of theological resources in earlier chapters. God created at least one lawful universe out of the desire to express divine creativity ('God as ecstatic Creator'). God created at least one species that is capable of comprehending and appreciating the universe. God inspired at least one theological tradition that would enable that species to believe in the possibility of understanding the heights and depths of the universe. To arrive at such conclusions and then thwart God's desire for the SFSS needed for humans to act on those beliefs, use that intelligence, and explore that creation might be to side with the angels at the risk of denying God's actions and intentions from the beginning of time.[97] God's exercise of intelligence in creating must be imaged in the exercise of human, science-fostering intelligence in scientific endeavour.

---

94 Letter to Johannes Georg Herwart von Hohenburg, 9/10 April 1599; cited in Chapter 3.

95 John Ray, *The Wisdom of God Manifested in the Works of Creation* (1691).

96 Gregory of Nyssa, *Or. Cat.* 5; ET in Hardy and Richardson, eds, *Christology of the Later Fathers*, 276. The idea is also found in apocalyptic texts like 1 Enoch 36:4; 2 Enoch 24:1-4; 36:3^A, where God promised that human knowledge of creation would excel that of the angels (see the discussion in Chapter 3).

97 The argument has a Hebrew Bible parallel in the idea that the construction of a Tabernacle was the Lord's intention from the foundation of creation; Moshe Weinfeld, 'Sabbath, Temple and the Enthronement of the Lord: The Problem of the *Sitz im Leben* of Genesis 1:12-2:3', in A. Caquot and M. Delcor (ed.), *Mélanges bibliques et orientaux en l'honneur de M. Henri Cazelles*, Keveleaer: Butzon & Bercker, 1981, pp. 501-512. Similarly, the *tāmîd* service could be viewed as the completion of the plan of creation, at least, for

Of course, God may have other reasons for blessing the development of industrial society besides sustaining scientific endeavour. There have been unprecedented advances in travel and international contact. Modern technologies also provide immense improvements for medical care and reduced mortality rates. But our aim here is not to legitimate industrial society as such. What commends the assumption of God's desiring infrastructure for scientific endeavour for our purposes is that it helps us address the unity of science dilemma created by the rift we discovered among the foundations of scientific endeavour.[98] A theology of Science-Fostering Social Systems can make a positive contribution to the quest for the unity of scientific knowledge.

What about all those land-enclosers and corporate-business tycoons? Those of us whose social consciences are still intact will wince when we read about the measures they took to provide us with the industrial technologies upon which modern science relies and to which it contributes. According to the exegetical traditions reviewed here, however, the God who directs history is motivated by passion more than perfection. Modern robber-barons and warlords stand in a long line going back to Adam and Eve ('in God's image'), David ('after God's own heart'), Solomon ('a son to me'), Cyrus ('his anointed'), Darius, and Herod.[99] Sinners all, but agents of change that would never have been made without their 'evil' inclinations.[100]

Theology of history is not for the sentimental or tender-hearted. Given the complex tangle of human motivations, God's challenge is not how to find people who are above reproach, but how to find people, 'both good and bad' (Matt. 22:10), who are capable of imagining new possibilities and seeing them through in practice. God's vision was too risky for the angels at the time of creation. It was too revolutionary for the Jerusalem elites at the time of Jesus. And it was too secularizing for most church leaders in early modern Europe and America. God's challenge was not how to sustain existing scientific knowledge within the limits of moral and theological norms, but how to further human endeavour toward the goal for which humans were created.

*The perspective of justice: an eschatology of scientific endeavour*

Within the realm of finite form, God can be and do all things, but not all things at once.[101] Like the sage who reflects the divine image, our wise God works with an

---

Israel; Sir. 50:19c; cf. Carter T.R. Hayward, *The Jewish Temple: A Non-Biblical Sourcebook* (London: Routledge, 1996), 79.

98   The rift is addressed but not eliminated. Since it is matched with a dialectic of the divine attributes, the rift is resolved only by referring back to the primordial diffraction of divine attributes and ahead to their eschatological refocusing (see below).

99   The texts cited are Gen. 1:26 (Adam and Eve); 1 Sam. 13:14 (David); 2 Sam. 7:14 (Solomon); Isa. 45:1 (Cyrus). Darius and Herod were God's servants in the rebuilding of the Temple.

100   The 'evil inclination', *yētser hâ-râ'* in Hebrew, is the God-given ambition or desire without which no one would build a house, get married, or have children (Gen. Rab. 9:7). Adherence to the Torah keeps it in check but does not completely repress it (Babylonian Talmud, Qiddushin 30b). The greater the person, the greater his/her 'evil inclination' (Sukkah 52a).

101   Chapter 1 under 'God as ecstatic Creator of all things'.

array of options. One option may be the desire for human creativity and recognition. Another is the exercise of judgment and the administration of justice.

How long will the Holy and Blessed One postpone the demands of justice? Industrial societies have overpopulated God's world; polluted the land, sea and sky; developed weapons of mass destruction; suppressed, and in some cases even exterminated, indigenous cultures; and marginalized the spiritual and creational beliefs on which modern technoscience is historically and culturally founded. As the Angel of Peace foresaw in Genesis Rabbah, humanity is 'one mass of contention' (8:4). If this was the truth for humanity in the time of the Rabbis, it is exponentially truer today. The angels were overruled opposing God's desire, but they certainly had a case to argue.

There should be no question about God's complying with the demands of justice in the long run: the pattern set by biblical history is quite consistent on this point. Early in the Genesis narratives, the creation of humans was already resulting in all sorts of evil, and the Holy and Blessed One responded with the Great Flood. The change of heart on God's part is breathtaking:

> The LORD was sorry that he had made humankind on the earth, and it grieved him to his heart. So the LORD said, 'I will blot out from the earth the human beings I have created … for I am sorry that I have made them.' (Gen. 6:6-7)

The voice we hear at this point in the narrative is that of Truth, the very voice that was silenced and banished to earth in the last of the creation *midrāshîm* we looked at (Gen. Rab. 8:5). The ideal balance of divine attributes is a dynamic, long-term process; its manifestation may take many generations.[102]

Recall that the midrash had a brief sequel in which we were promised that one day Truth would be restored to its rightful place: *Truth [or, Faithfulness] will spring up from the ground* (Ps. 85:11a). No timeframe was specified, but the implication was that the demands of justice and peace would eventually be met. The restoration of justice would take place within human history; it did not have to wait until the world to come.

The exact same pattern occurs in the sequel to the 'parable of the wedding banquet' in Matthew 22. Recall that the king went ahead with the wedding banquet, gave up on the people originally invited, and opened the gates to all comers, 'both good and bad'. What happens when the king gets a closer look at the folks he let in? In the Matthean sequel, we find a self-correction similar to the one we have seen in the Genesis 6 and the midrash:

> But when the king came in to see the guests, he noticed a man there who was not wearing a wedding robe, and he said to him, 'Friend, how did you get in here without a

---

102 The same pattern of blessing followed by judgment can be seen in the events surrounding the building and rebuilding of the Jerusalem Temple; cf. 1 Kgs. 9:3-9; Sir. 47:12-21; 4 Ezra 10:44-54; 13:36; Mark 13:2; 14:58; b. Yoma 9b; Pesiqta Rabbati 35:1. Moshe Idel argues that God's shifting weight from one attribute to the other (*du-parzufin*) establishes a more stable system of theology (*Absorbing Perfections*, 223-4, 226-8) – something like Einstein's quest for invariance in the laws of physics.

wedding robe?' And he was speechless. Then the king said to the attendants, 'Bind him hand and foot, and throw him into the outer darkness...' For many are called, but few are chosen. (Matt. 22:11-14)[103]

The process of sifting the results of God's inclusive invitation ('many are called') is dramatic in the case of a single individual. The gracious acceptance of unworthy guests is now balanced by rigorous judgment ('few are chosen').[104] The 'attendants' or 'servants' (Greek, *diákonoi*) here are clearly angels who, as in the *midráshîm*, represent the attribute of justice (cf. Matt. 13:39-42, 49-50). The important result for the parable as a whole, however, is that God's main purpose has been fulfilled. The banquet hall was full, and the wedding of the king's son was duly celebrated. Mercy and justice have both been satisfied.

How do these developments affect the result of our discussion of the SFSS paradox? If the classic *midráshîm* and Matthean parables of the kingdom may once again be used as a template, the result is a fairly clear eschatology of scientific endeavour. Insofar as industrial social structures minimize the public role of spiritual practices and marginalize indigenous spirit peoples, they must be deconstructed once the purposes for which God blessed them are fulfilled.[105] Laws that define people's identity in abstraction from their ethnic and religious groupings will eventually be relaxed. Market systems will be balanced or even replaced by local, bioregional marketplaces. The infrastructure of the spirit world will be restored. Indigenous peoples will regain the political and economic independence needed for their chosen lifestyles and spiritualities. The spirit-niche to which our species is adapted and in which the vast majority of the world's people have found meaning for their lives will one day provide us with 'sacred canopies' to sustain all our endeavours – scientific as well as theological.[106]

From a sociology of knowledge perspective, the process of reversing the effects of industrialization and professionalization need not alter the overall inventory of cultures, subcultures and finite provinces of meaning. The changes envisioned have more to do with the relationships among these constituents of the social order. The industrial matrix will become optional, and the sacred periphery will regain interpersonal 'objectivity'. In theological terms, the LORD God will continue to display multiple attributes in the realm of finite form, but a shift will take place

---

103 Matt. 22:11-14 is thought to be an independent parable that the Gospel of Matthew added as a corrective to the 'parable of the wedding banquet'.

104 In Matt. 22:7, the friends who declined the earlier invitations were destroyed like the opposing angels in b. Sanh. 38b (see above). Is it possible that the king later repented of this impulsive action as in the case of the angel of Truth and raised them up again (Gen. Rab. 8:5)? That eventuality is consistent with *midráshîm* like *Êikhāh* (Lamentations) *Rabbah*, Proem 24; excerpted in David Stern and Mark J. Mirsky, eds, *Rabbinic Fantasies: Imaginative Tales from Classical Hebrew Literature* (New Haven: Yale University Press, 1990), 49-51.

105 As in the *midráshîm* and parables, the idea of God's purposes being fulfilled is heuristic and can not be used to make predictions. A personal goal is accomplished when the person who sets it says so.

106 Berger, *The Sacred Canopy: Elements of a Sociological Theory of Religion* (Garden City, N.Y.: Doubleday, 1967).

from the attribute of mercy to that of justice, at least, as far as industrial society and indigenous cultures are concerned.[107]

The eschatology of scientific endeavour developed here is based on sources from the Judeo-Christian tradition and is similar to traditional eschatologies in many ways. However, it also is also different in its range of application, its ethical implications, and its underlying rationale. As to its applicability, the eschatology developed here can not promise restoration to Jews or Christians alone: it must extend to all spiritual traditions that have been displaced or marginalized in industrial societies, particularly those of indigenous peoples who probably recapitulate the spiritual experiences of our common ancestors most nearly. The history of industrialization, professionalization and other secularizing developments have affected people all around the world. The promise of restitution must be equally extensive.

Another difference from the traditional models is that our eschatology does not have very straightforward implications for ethics. In most Bible-based eschatologies, the projected characteristics of the world to come have clear implications for the present conduct of believers. Those who long for the coming of the Messiah and the rebuilding of the Temple must pray for a speedy realization of their ideal and devote their lives to hastening its coming (m. Ta'an. 4:8). Those who anticipate a kingdom of peace and justice must try to live in accordance with those values in this present age (Rom. 14.13-23). Believers live in the present as a way of preparing for the age to come.

Some similar ethical guidance can be drawn from our eschatology of scientific endeavour. Those who support scientific endeavour certainly ought to be sensitive to the social costs of what amounts to an irrelevant luxury for many minority cultures. We should advocate on behalf of indigenous peoples. We ought to reconceptualize our world as a 'metaverse' and restructure our lives in such a way that the fundamental reality of the spirit world can be more evident. My writing this book is an effort along those very lines.

However, the bottom line in this chapter is that God wills and blesses the industrial society we live in for all of its (and our) faults. The secular, spirit-peripheralizing order of things pleases the God who created a universe capable of being comprehended, a species capable of comprehending it, and a culture believing in both capabilities. We should realize that the industrial social order will not go on forever, but we should also share God's delight in it and contribute as much as we are able to its fulfillment. In so doing we can participate in an eschatological refocusing of the divine attributes, but it is beyond our abilities to bring about that refocusing ourselves. What is needed is a divine act of atonement.[108]

Most of all, our eschatology of scientific endeavour differs from traditional eschatologies in its very rationale. The reversals anticipated here are implications from our discussion of the societal foundation of scientific endeavour supplemented

---

107 As in the case of the 'parable of the wedding banquet', mercy for one group or interest may coincide with judgment for another.

108 Refocusing or rebalancing the divine attributes is essential to the Kabbalistic interpretation of Jewish rituals; for example, Idel, *Absorbing Perfections*, 13. It is also one aspect of the Pauline understanding of the atoning work of Jesus Christ (1 Cor. 15:25-8; Eph. 1:9-10; Col. 2:9-10).

by insights from classical Jewish *midrāshîm* and New Testament parables. Those reversals may or may not agree with projections based on current societal trends. They may or may not agree with the eschatologies of traditional religions. What brings them to our attention and commends them is not a preconceived demand for justice or a predilection for old-time religion, but a quest for the unity of scientific knowledge. This eschatology addresses the paradoxes raised in our discussion of the foundations of scientific endeavour.

Undoubtedly there are many other ways to address these paradoxes and to advance the unity of scientific knowledge. It suffices for us to demonstrate the importance of addressing the paradoxes and to show that theological resources are available that can help in the quest for the unity of science. A thick description of scientific endeavour leads to a thick description of the history and the attributes of God – past, present and future. The advancement of science – even in its secularizing industrial stages – is not an obstacle, but a stimulus to theological endeavour.

# CHAPTER FIVE

# Foundations of Scientific Endeavour and the Unity of Knowledge

Scientific endeavour consists of two quests that must be pursued simultaneously: the quest for new knowledge about the space-time world and a further quest to unify all such knowledge using the most powerful formalisms and the most widely applicable concepts available.[1] Biologists, for example, discover new species and seek to relate them systematically using the tools of morphology, genetics and ecology. Systems theory attempts to unify various levels of organization in organisms. Chemists demonstrate the unity of the material elements in terms of periodicity and valence. Physicists search the unity of the fundamental forces and elementary particles in terms of underlying symmetries. Biochemistry and chemical physics seek unification across disciplinary lines.

Both of these quests are patronized by modern industrial societies. Our support is funded by corporate industry and governmental agencies, and it is institutionalized in universities and research institutes. As far as the general public is concerned, however, the technical content and significance of scientific developments are poorly understood. The more newsworthy innovations are broadcast in the media. Practical applications are available in the form of new technologies; some are even available to consumers as goods and services. Those who work in technical fields get to know quite a bit about their special disciplines. But the possibility of analysing scientific endeavour as a whole is generally relegated to philosophers. The possibility of integrating it with religious beliefs is left to theologians. Given this context of specialization, the goals of this study may seem overly ambitious. For a university trained person of faith like myself, they are necessitated by the need to live reflectively and with integrity in a highly fragmented world.[2]

In this brief conclusion, I shall first review the steps toward unification we have taken in previous chapters. Following that, I will suggest some further steps that can be taken when the four chapters are viewed together in relation to each other.

## Toward the unity of knowledge

Our deliberations have been part of a larger quest for the unity of knowledge. We have sought a wider frame of rationality to demonstrate the unity between scientific endeavour and the preconditions or foundations that support it. We have also mined the Judeo-Christian tradition for insights that can help address some of the challenges

---

1    Bohr, 'Unity of Knowledge' (1954), discussed in Chapter 2.
2    Kaiser, 'Wearing Different Hats: Christian Living in a Fragmented World'.

and paradoxes that arose in that quest. In so doing, we have tried to further the unity of science and theology as human endeavours in an even wider frame of rationality.[3]

In the Introduction, we sought to move beyond the usual understanding of science as a growing body of knowledge (cosmology, biology, etc.) toward a realistic, 'thick' description of the endeavour that produces such knowledge and the preconditions or foundations that support it. Scientific endeavour requires a special kind of universe (or multiverse), special form of intelligence (SFI), a historically conditioned culture of belief (SFB), and an industrial infrastructure (SFSS).[4] These four conditions are cumulative and forward-contingent: each condition depends on all prior ones, though none of them is necessitated or predetermined by prior conditions.

For each of these conditions, our analysis has challenged the idea that scientific endeavour can be tidily demarcated from theological discourse (or vice versa). Our analysis did not legitimate any particular confessional tradition, but it did raise theological questions that need to be addressed by confessional traditions, even if that requires restructuring the tradition to make its resources more evident.

- In Chapter 1 we discussed the seemingly intractable problem of the origin of cosmic laws and showed the necessity for theological discourse in addressing possible resolutions. We argued that the Cosmic Lawgiver that can be posited to resolve the issue need not be an impersonal being removed from nature and history – the God of the physicists is not incompatible with the God of the prophets.
- In Chapter 2 we tackled the paradox of Science-Fostering Intelligence – a foundation of scientific endeavour that should be included among the subjects of scientific investigation. The paradox can be resolved provided one allows for a multilayered spirit world as one of the environmental niches to which early humans adapted in accordance with Darwinian evolution.
- In Chapter 3 we confronted the disciplinary separation of historical theology from the history of science. Science-Fostering Beliefs are rooted in a continuous theological tradition that extends from ancient Babylon and Egypt to the efforts of modern scientists from Johannes Kepler to Albert Einstein.
- In Chapter 4 we argued that the specialization needed for Science-Fostering Social Systems requires the de facto separation of science and spirituality and thereby contradicts the results of all three previous analyses – a paradox that calls for a theology of history and an eschatology of scientific endeavour.

---

3    Newbigin, *Foolishness to the Greeks*, 90; Polkinghorne, 'The Reason Within and the Reason Without', 181.

4    Other preconditions we discussed include the Anthropic Principle; a habitable planetary environment; a left-brain interpreter (Gazzaniga); ancient city-state governments; and whatever drove Western Europe toward the industrial revolution. Our short list of four preconditions suffices to illustrate the methodology.

As bodies of knowledge science and theology are quite distinct, but as human endeavours they are entangled at all levels.[5] We have suggested the metaphor of tunnels to replace the more common idea of bridges. Insofar as science and theology are separate bodies of knowledge, it may be helpful to build bridges between them. In order to view them as human endeavours, however, it is better to think of ourselves digging down to the supportive foundations, where the questions that scientists themselves raise are profoundly theological and the most plausible concepts overlap with traditional doctrines. Our overall agenda is the unity of knowledge – a unity that manifests itself in the foundations that make knowledge possible rather than in bodies of information.

So much for the steps toward unification for each of the four foundations. It is also possible to discern connections among the foundations we have examined. Some overlap is a straightforward result of the fact that the four foundations we have studied are cumulative and forward-contingent. For example, the natural evolution of a species capable of doing science would not be possible without the operation of basic laws governing molecules and the forces between them. Similarly, the development of technoscience in the 19th and 20th centuries would not have been possible without the beliefs that sustained the development of modern science. So there are clear links between the first and second foundations, and between the third and fourth (shown along the diagonal in Figure 5.1).

What about the intermediate pair: the anthropological and cultural foundations of scientific endeavour? A culture might transmit belief in the possibility of comprehending the natural world even if humans had no such ability. But the paleoshamanic engagement with the spirit world that provided the environmental niche needed for the emergence of built-in SFI also left a legacy of confidence in the possibility of cosmic exploration. Soul journey continued to be practiced in prehistoric city states and well into historical times. Its beliefs were restated in terms of the cosmologies of city states and embedded in many of the myths and rituals that underlie the prophetic and wisdom traditions. So the legacy of paleoshamanism may have provided the prehistoric backdrop for stories about the cosmos-exploring intelligence of ancient kings, prophets, and apocalyptic heroes.[6] In other words, the early human cultivation of spirit niches may have fostered the birth of the historic creationist tradition as well as that of modern science.

We see that the interrelations of the foundations of scientific endeavour are more complex than the simple, linear progression of topics we have used to order the chapters of this study. Various lines of influence (necessary, if not sufficient) diverge and converge, as shown in Figure 5.1.

---

5    The quantum-mechanical metaphor of entanglement is suggested by the facts that aptitude for science and aptitude for religious ecstasy emerge from the same innate psychic capabilities (Chapter 2), and that the working beliefs of scientists and creational beliefs of Jews and Christians derive from the same historic creationist tradition (Chapter 3).

6    See the studies by Lindblom, Muffs, Alexander, Davila, Hawkes and West cited in chapters 2 and 3.

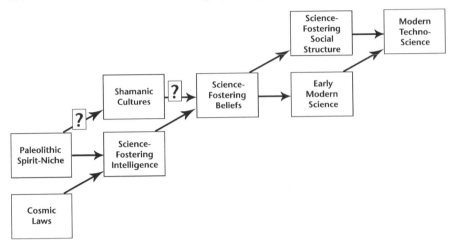

**Figure 5.1 Flow chart of the descent of modern technoscience**

The main topics in Chapters 1 to 4 are shown in the boxes along the diagonal line beginning at the lower left. They correspond to the four foundations shown in Figure 1 in the Introduction. Auxiliary themes appear as off-diagonal elements. The two question marks surrounding the 'Shamanic Cultures' box indicate significant gaps in our knowledge about cultural transmission in prehistoric times. The important point here is a representation of the ideal unity of scientific knowledge in areas as diverse as cosmology, the history of religions and sociology.

## Toward a theology of scientific endeavour

The outline sketched above is based on a thick description of scientific endeavour, not on the tenets of theology. Even though theological endeavour has entered our discussion of the foundations at every level, neither the outline nor the method was dictated by theology itself. Our purpose was rather to identify resources in the Judeo-Christian tradition that might be pertinent in addressing the challenges and dilemmas raised by examining the foundations of scientific endeavour. The theological result is a refocusing of traditional tenets from a secular perspective – a 'theology of scientific endeavour'.

When viewed from the perspective of the traditional 'loci' of theology, the theological topics we have identified may seem rather disjointed: attributes of God were discussed in Chapter 1 and again in Chapter 4; eschatology came up in Chapters 2 and 4, and so forth. So a traditionalist might question whether systematic theology is well served by such an approach.

Yet recurring themes have revealed other connections among our main topics that might not be evident in standard treatments of theology. Consider the idea of humanity created in the image of God, for example. In Chapter 1 we focused on the ancient idea of God's ecstatic self-projection in the act of creation. In Chapter 2 we found that the ritual experience of soul journey was a likely environmental niche for the evolution of distinctive features of the human psyche (SFI). Hence we may view the evolution of the psyche as the mirror image of the self-projection of God (the Logos) in creation.[7] Approaching theology from the perspective of the sciences can contribute to our understanding of ideas like the divine image and relate them directly to present-day endeavours.

In Chapter 3 the traditional idea of the divine image provided one of the primary vectors for belief that humans could comprehend the heights and depths of the cosmos. This belief provided ideological support for early modern science and has continued to sustain scientific endeavour to this day. In Chapter 4 we returned to the idea of the ecstatic nature of God's involvement in history and applied it to God's current desire that the story of creation be revealed through the development of technoscience. So the correlated ideas of divine ecstasy in creation and its image in human exploration run through the foundations of scientific endeavour in a classic ABBA sequence. When viewed in terms of these two ideas, rather than traditional 'loci', the theology of scientific endeavour becomes much more coherent.

Another recurring theme has been the divine council and its corollary, the social nature of God. In Chapter 1 we arrived at this idea from the Hebrew Bible as a way of understanding the inherently relational nature of the Creator and thereby mitigating the sense of distance suggested by God's governing the world through cosmic laws. In Chapter 2 we arrived at the same idea from a different direction. Having postulated the existence of a spirit world (accessed through ritual) as an evolutionary niche for the evolution of Science-Fostering Intelligence, we found that the unity and regularity required of that world pointed to the existence of a 'Lord of spirits' who presides over it. In Chapter 3 the divine council provided the conceptual backdrop for the idea of divinely decreed laws that gave rise to the Science-Fostering Belief in a lawful universe. The idea came to our aid once again in Chapter 4 as a midrashic device for exploring the dialectic of divine attributes. It is remarkable that such an ancient concept should prove so useful in addressing four of the foundations of modern scientific endeavour.

Theological ideas like the image of God and the divine council derive from ancient cultures for which the spirit world was as real as that of ordinary space and time. Their notions were just as practical for them as ideas about weather forecasts and stock indexes are for us today. We can use such ideas to recover a sense of the divine presence in our lives and work today without becoming antiquarian, provided we refocus them in light of a secular discipline like scientific endeavour.

**Seven theses and four conclusions**

Our primary concern has been to develop a methodology for exploring the foundations of a secular endeavour like natural science and finding the deep connections (tunnels) to theological discourse. The main results can be summarized in seven theses:

---

7     A similar mirror image occurs in Christology: the possibility of human participation in the divine realm (the new Adam/Eve) is the reciprocal of divine participation in the human (the Word made flesh); cf. Kaiser, 'Christology and Complementarity', *Religious Studies* 12 (1976), 37-48.

1. Modern science should be viewed as a continuing endeavour as well as a set of ideas.
2. Scientific endeavour has 'thickness' – a good description must include preconditions or foundations that support scientific work.
3. Applying the tools of cosmology, anthropology, history and sociology to these foundations leads to fundamental questions and paradoxes that extend beyond the safe demarcations of separate disciplines.
4. Pursuit of these questions engages theological discourse and raises significant challenges for any theological tradition.
5. Mining the Judeo-Christian tradition in order to address these challenges refocuses traditional teachings – some long neglected – and rearranges them in light of a prominent secular endeavour.
6. A thick description of natural science leads to a thick description of nature, humanity, history and God.
7. The work of scientists can be seen as a stimulus rather than a threat to theological endeavour.

This study was undertaken as an effort to pry theological discourse free of the constraints and demarcations embedded in professionalized (particularly academic) discourse and to recover something of the wholeness that characterized theology in pre-industrial times. In each of the earlier chapters, we have focused on a thesis that helps recover that wholeness:

1. The laws and symmetries of the space-time world directly manifest the word of God (Chapter 1).
2. The ability of scientists to discern those laws is an inheritance from our species' long-term participation in a spirit world (Chapter 2).
3. The ability of scientists to meet increasingly difficult intellectual challenges relies on beliefs that go back to biblical teachings about creation (Chapter 3).
4. Modern technoscience relies on industrial and educational systems that further one of God's most cherished purposes in history (Chapter 4).

There is more to human endeavour than science. Here we have offered a method that can be applied to any secular discipline. The role of theology may not be obvious on the surface, but theology is embedded in the very depths of our life and work. Seeing it only requires the discipline of thick description and persistent questions.

# Bibliography

Adler, Robert (2005), 'Are we on our way back to the Dark Ages?', *New Scientist* **187**, 2 July, 26-7

Alcock, John (1998), *Animal Behavior: An Evolutionary Approach*, 6th edn, Sunderland, Mass.: Sinauer Associates.

Aldhouse-Green, Miranda and Stephen Aldhouse-Green (2005), *The Quest for the Shaman: Shape-Shifters, Sorcerers and Spirit-Healers in Ancient Europe*, London: Thames and Hudson.

Alexander, Philip S. (2002), 'Enoch and the Beginnings of Jewish Interest in Natural Science', in C. Hempel, A. Lange, and H. Lichtenberger (eds), *The Wisdom Texts from Qumran and the Development of Sapiential Thought*, Leuven: Leuven University Press, 223-43.

Alexander, Philip S. (1998), 'From Son of Adam to Second God: Transformations of the Biblical Enoch', in Michael E. Stone and Theodore A. Bergren (eds), *Biblical Figures Outside the Bible*, Harrisburg, Penn.: Trinity Press.

Alexander, Philip S. (1977), 'The Historical Setting of the Hebrew Book of Enoch', *Journal of Jewish Studies* **28**, Autumn, 156-80.

Ancient Christian Writers (1949 to date), ed. Johannes Quasten et al., New York: Paulist Press.

Anderson, Gary A. (2001), *The Genesis of Perfection: Adam and Eve in Jewish and Christian Imagination*, Louisville: Westminster John Knox Press.

Ante-Nicene Fathers (1885-96), ed. Alexander Roberts and James Donaldson, 10 vols, Buffalo and New York, N.Y.

Arieti, Silvano (1976), *Creativity: The Magic Synthesis*, New York: Basic Books.

Arsuaga, Juan Luis (2002), *The Neanderthal's Necklace: In Search of the First Thinkers*, New York: Four Walls Eight Windows.

Arsuaga, Juan Luis (2003), 'Requiem for a Heavyweight', *Natural History* **111**, Jan., 43-8.

Athanasius of Alexandria (1971), *Contra Gentes and De Incarnatione*, ed. Robert W. Thompson, Oxford Early Christian Texts, Oxford: Clarendon Press.

Atkinson, Jane Monnig (1992), 'Shamanisms Today', *Annual Review of Anthropology* **21**, 307-330.

Atwell, James E. (2000), 'An Egyptian Source for Genesis 1', *Journal of Theological Studies* **51**, October, 441-77.

Augustine of Hippo (1967), *Concerning the City of God against the Pagans*, trans. Henry Bettenson (ed. David Knowles), Harmondsworth: Penguin Books.

Augustine of Hippo (1991), *Confessions*, trans. Henry Chadwick, Oxford: Oxford University Press.

Babbage, Charles (1838), *The Ninth Bridgewater Treatise: A Fragment*, 2nd edn, London: John Murray.

Bacon, Francis (1857-74), *The Works of Francis Bacon*, ed. James Spedding, Robert Leslie Ellis, and Douglas Denon Heath. 14 vols, London: Green, Longman and Roberts.

Balfour, Arthur James (1895), *The Foundations of Belief being Notes Introductory to the Study of Theology*, London: Longmans, Green and Co.

Barbour, Ian G. (1974), *Myths, Models and Paradigms: The Nature of Scientific and Religious Language*, London: SCM Press.

Barbour, Ian G. (1990), *Religion in an Age of Science*, San Francisco: Harper & Row.

Barbour, Ian G. (2000), *When Science Meets Religion*, San Francisco: HarperSanFrancisco.

Barker, Peter and Bernard R. Goldstein (2001), 'Theological Foundations of Kepler's Astronomy', in John Hedley Brooke, Margaret J. Osler and Jitse Van der Meer (eds), *Science in Theistic Contexts: Cognitive Dimensions* (*Osiris* 16), Chicago: University of Chicago Press, pp. 88-113.

Barrett, L., et al. (2004), 'Habitual Cave Use and Thermoregulation in Chacma Baboons (*Papio hamadryas ursinus*)', *Journal of Human Evolution* **46**, February, 215-22.

Barrow, John D. (1998), *Impossibility: The Limits of Science and the Science of Limits*, Oxford: Clarendon Press.

Barrow, John D. (1989), 'The Mathematical Universe', *The World and I* **4**, May, 306-311.

Barrow, John D. (1991), *Theories of Everything: The Quest for Ultimate Explanation*, Oxford: Clarendon Press.

Barrow, John D., and Frank J. Tipler (1986, 1988), *The Anthropic Cosmological Principle*, Oxford: Oxford University Press.

Baumgardt, Carola (1951), *Johannes Kepler: Life and Letters*, New York: Philosophical Library.

Behringer, Wolfgang (1998), *Shaman of Oberstdorf: Chonrad Soelckhlin and the Phantoms of the Night*, trans. H.C. Erik Midelfort, Charlottesville: University of Virginia Press.

Berger, Peter L. (1967), *The Sacred Canopy: Elements of a Sociological Theory of Religion*, Garden City, N.Y.: Doubleday.

Berger, Peter L. (1973), *The Social Reality of Religion*, Harmondsworth: Penguin.

Berger, Peter L., Brigitte Berger, and Hansfried Kellner (1973), *The Homeless Mind: Modernization and Consciousness*, New York: Random House.

Berger, Peter L., and Thomas Luckmann (1967, 1971), *The Social Construction of Reality: A Treatise in the Sociology of Knowledge*, Harmondsworth: Penguin Books.

Bernardus Silvestris (1973), *The 'Cosmographia' of Bernardus Silvestris*, trans. Winthrop Wetherbee, New York: Columbia University Press.

Berry, Hugues, Daniel Gracia Pérez, and Olivier Temam (2005), 'Chaos in Computer Performance', available at http://arxiv.org/abs/nlin.AO/0506030.

Beyerlin, Walter (ed.) (1975), *Near Eastern Religious Texts Relating to the Old Testament*, London: SCM Press; German original, Göttingen.

Bodde, Derk (1991), *Chinese Thought, Society, and Science: The Intellectual and Social Background of Science and Technology in Pre-Modern China*, Honolulu: University of Hawaii Press.

Bohr, Niels (1958), *Essays 1932-1957 on Atomic Physics and Human Knowledge*, New York: Wiley.

Bojowald, Martin (2005), 'Original Questions', *Nature* **436**, 18 August, 920-21.

Borgen, Peder (1996), 'Moses, Jesus, and the Roman Emperor: Observations in Philo's Writings and the Revelation of John', *Novum Testamentum* **38**, April, 145-59.

Bower, Bruce (1997), 'Humanity's Imprecision Vision', *Science News* **152**, 21 July, 26-7.

Boyarin, Daniel (2004), *Border Lines: The Partition of Judaeo-Christianity*, Philadelphia: University of Pennsylvania Press.

Boyer, Carl B. (1987), *The Rainbow: From Myth to Mathematics*, Princeton: Princeton University Press.

Boyle, Alison (2001), 'The Edge of Infinity', *New Scientist* **171**, 29 September, 26-9.

Breasted, James H. (1959), *Development of Religion and Thought in Ancient Egypt*, New York: Harper (first edn, New York: Scribner's, 1912).

Broadie, A. and J. MacDonald (1978), 'The Concept of Cosmic Order in Ancient Egypt in Dynastic and Roman Times', *L'Antiquité classique* **47**, 106-128.

Brooks, Michael (2003), 'The Impossible Puzzle', *New Scientist* **178**, 5 April, 34-35.

Brush, Stephen G. (1992), 'How Cosmology Became a Science', *Scientific American* **267**, August, 62-70.

Bultmann, Rudolf (1953), 'The New Testament and Mythology', in Hans Werner Bartsch (ed.), *Kerygma and Myth: A Theological Debate*, trans. Reginald H. Fuller, London: SPCK, pp. 1-44.

Burkert, Walter (2004), *Babylon, Memphis, Persepolis: Eastern Contexts of Greek Culture*, Cambridge, Mass.: Harvard University Press.

Burkert, Walter, and Margaret E. Pinder (1992), *The Orientalizing Revolution: Near Eastern Influence on Greek Culture in the Early Archaic Age*, Cambridge, Mass.: Harvard University Press.

Burtt, Edwin Arthur (1932), *The Metaphysical Foundations of Modern Physical Science: A Historical and Critical Essay*, 2nd edn, London: Kegan Paul; New York: Humanities Press.

Butler, Declan (2001), 'Are You Ready for the Revolution?' *Nature* **409**, 15 February, 758-60.

Butterworth, Brian (1999), *What Counts? How Every Brain Is Hardwired for Math*, New York: Free Press; published in the UK as *The Mathematical Brain*, London: Macmillan.

Calvin, William H. (2002), *A Brain for All Seasons: Human Evolution and Abrupt Climate Change*, Chicago: University of Chicago Press.

Carruthers, Peter (2002), 'Human Creativity: Its Cognitive Basis, its Evolution, and its Connections with Childhood Pretense', *British Journal for the Philosophy of Science* **53**, 225-49.

Casti, John L. (1996), 'Confronting Science's Logical Limits', *Scientific American* **275**, October, 102-5.

Cathcart, Brian (2004), *The Fly in the Cathedral*, New York: Farrar, Straus and Giroux.

Catherine of Siena (1925), *The Dialogue of the Seraphic Virgin, Catherine of Siena*, trans. Algar Thorold, London: Burns, Oates & Washbourne.

Charlesworth, James H. (ed.) (1983), *The Old Testament Pseudepigrapha*, 2 vols, Garden City, N.Y.: Doubleday.

Chilson, Clark, and Peter Knecht (2003), *Shamans in Asia*, London: RoutledgeCurzon.

Chown, Marcus (2002), 'Cycles of Creation', *New Scientist* **173**, 16 March, 26-30.

Chown, Marcus (2004), 'Einstein's Rio Requiem', *New Scientist* **181**, 6 March, 50-51.

Clottes, Jean and David Lewis-Williams (1998), *The Shamans of Prehistory: Trance and Magic in the Painted Caves*, New York: Abrams.

Corley, Jeremy (2003), 'Wisdom versus Apocalyptic and Science in Sirach 1,1-10', in F. García Martínez (ed.), *Wisdom and Apocalypticism in the Dead Sea Scrolls and in the Biblical Tradition*, Leuven: Leuven University Press/Uitgeverij Peeters, 269-85.

Coukell, Allan (2001), 'Spellbound (Could mysterious figures lurking in Australian rock art be the world's oldest shamans?)', *New Scientist* **169**, 19 May, 34-37.

Cragg, Gerald R. (1962), *The Church and the Age of Reason, 1648-1789*, Harmondsworth: Penguin Books.

Crombie, A. C. (1959), *Augustine to Galileo: The History of Science AD 400-1650*, 2nd edn, 2 vols, Oxford: Heinemann.


d'Aquili, Eugene, and Andrew Newberg (1999), *The Mystical Mind: Probing the Biology of Religious Experience*, Minneapolis: Fortress Press.

Dales, Richard C. (1973), *The Scientific Achievement of the Middle Ages*, Philadelphia: University of Pennsylvania Press, 1973.

Dales, Richard C. (1978), 'A Twelfth-Century Concept of the Natural Order', *Viator* **9** 179-92.

Davies, Paul (1995), *Are We Alone? Philosophical Implications of the Discovery of Extraterrestrial Life*, Harmondsworth: Penguin.

Davies, Paul (1988), *The Cosmic Blueprint: New Discoveries in Nature's Creative Ability to Order the Universe*, New York: Simon and Schuster.

Davies, Paul (1983), *God and the New Physics*, New York: Simon and Schuster.

Davies, Paul (1993), 'The Intelligibility of Nature', in Robert John Russell, Nancey Murphy and C. J. Isham (eds), *Quantum Cosmology and the Laws of Nature: Scientific Perspectives on Divine Action*, Vatican City State: Vatican Observatory, pp. 145-61.

Davies, Paul (1992), *The Mind of God: The Scientific Basis for a Rational World*, New York: Simon & Schuster.

Davies, Paul (1994), 'The Mind of God', in Jan Hilgevoord (ed.), *Physics and Our View of the World*, Cambridge: Cambridge University Press, pp. 226-38.

Davies, Paul (1994), 'The Unreasonable Effectiveness of Science', in John Marks Templeton (ed.), *Evidence of Purpose: Scientists discover the Creator*, New York: Continuum, pp. 44-56.

Davies, Paul (1990), 'Why Is the Universe Knowable?' in Ronald E. Mickens (ed.), *Mathematics and Science*, Singapore: World Scientific, pp. 14-33.

Davila, James (1994), 'The Hekhalot Literature and Shamanism', in Eugene H. Lovering, Jr (ed.), *SBL Seminar Papers 1994*, Atlanta: Scholars Press, pp. 767-89.

Deacon, Terrence W. (1997), *The Symbolic Species: The Co-Evolution of Language and the Brain*, New York: Norton.

Debus, Allen G. (1978), *Man and Nature in the Renaissance*, Cambridge: Cambridge University Press.

Debus, Allen G. (1968), 'Mathematics and Nature in the Chemical Texts of the Renaissance', *Ambix* **15**, Feb., 1-28.

Devlin, Keith (2001), *The Math Gene: How Mathematical Thinking Evolved and Why Numbers are Like Gossip*, New York: Basic Books.

Devlin, Keith (2005), *The Math Instinct: Why You're a Mathematical Genius (Along with Lobsters, Birds, Cats, and Dogs)*, New York: Thunder's Mouth Press.

Diamond, Jered (1996), 'Why Women Change', *Discover* **16**, July, 131-7.

Dobbelaere, Karel (1999), 'Towards an Integrated Perspective of the Processes Related to the Descriptive Concept of Secularization', *Sociology of Religion* **60**, Fall, 229-47.

Douglas, Kate (2006), 'Evolution and Us', *New Scientist* **189**, 11 March, 30-33.

Drees, Willem B. (1990), *Beyond the Big Bang: Quantum Cosmologies and God*, LaSalle, Ill.: Open Court.

Drees, Willem B. (1994), 'Problems in Debates about Physics and Religion', in Jan Hilgevoord (ed.), *Physics and Our View of the World*, Cambridge: Cambridge University Press, 188-225.

Drees, Willem B. (1996), *Religion, Science and Naturalism*, Cambridge: Cambridge University Press.

Duhem, Pierre (1969), *To Save the Phenomena: An Essay on the Idea of Physical Theory from Plato to Galileo*, trans. Edmund Doland and Chaninah Maschler, Chicago: University of Chicago Press.

Easterbrook, Gregg (1997), 'Science and God: A Warming Trend?', *Science* **277**, 15 August, 890-93.

Edwards, Jonathan (1957-2004), *The Works of Jonathan Edwards*, ed. Perry Miller and John E. Smith, New Haven: Yale University Press, 27 vols.

Einstein, Albert (1954), *Ideas and Opinions*, London: Alvin Redman.

Einstein, Albert (1950), *Out of My Later Years*. New York: Philosophical Library.

Einstein, Albert (1935) *The World As I See It*, London: John Lane.

Ellis, George (2005), 'Physics and the Real World', *Physics Today* 58, July, 49-54.

Ellul, Jacques (1970), *The Meaning of the City*, trans. Dennis Pardee, Grand Rapids, Eerdmans.

Epstein, Isidore (ed.) (1969), *Hebrew-English Edition of the Babylonian Talmud: Tractate Sanhedrin*, London: Soncino Press.

Eswaran, Vinayak, Henry Harpending, and Alan R. Rogers (2005), 'Genomics Refutes an Exclusively African Origin of Humans', *Journal of Human Evolution* **49**, 1-18.

Eusebius of Caesarea (1903), *Preparation for the Gospel*, trans. Edwin Hamilton Gifford, 2 vols, Oxford: Clarendon Press, repr. Grand Rapids: Baker, 1981.

Falk, Dan (2004), 'The Anthropic Principle's Surprising Resurgence', *Sky and Telescope* **107**, March, 43-47.

Feist, Gregory J. (2006), *The Psychology of Science and the Origins of the Scientific Mind*, New Haven, Conn.: Yale University Press.

Feuerbach, Ludwig (1957), *The Essence of Christianity*, trans. George Eliot, New York: Harper and Row.

Fichman, Martin (2001), 'Science in Theistic Contexts: A Case Study of Alfred Russel Wallace on Human Evolution', in John Hedley Brooke, Margaret J. Osler, and Jitse Van der Meer (ed.), *Science in Theistic Contexts: Cognitive Dimensions*, *Osiris* **16**, Chicago: University of Chicago Press, pp. 227-50.

Fishbane, Michael (1998), *The Exegetical Imagination: On Jewish Thought and Theology*, Cambridge, Mass.: Harvard University Press.

Forster, Peter and Shuichi Matsumura (2005), 'Did Early Humans Go North or South?' *Science* **308**, 13 May, 965-6.

Fox, Robert (1984), 'Science, the University, and the State in Nineteenth-Century France', in Gerald L. Geison (ed.), *Professions and the French State, 1700-1900*, Philadelphia: University of Pennsylvania Press, pp. 66-145.

Frankfort, Henri (1948a), *Ancient Egyptian Religion*, New York: Columbia University Press.

Frankfort, Henri (1948b), *Kingship and the Gods: A Study of Ancient Near Eastern Religion as the Integration of Society and Nature*, Chicago: University of Chicago Press.

Frankfort, Henri, et al. (1946), *The Intellectual Adventure of Ancient Man: An Essay on Speculative Thought in the Ancient Near East*, Chicago: University of Chicago Press.

Frege, Gottlob (1950, 1959), *The Foundations of Arithmetic: A Logico-Mathematical Enquiry Into the Concept of Number*, Oxford: Blackwell.

Funkenstein, Amos (1986), *Theology and the Scientific Imagination from the Middle Ages to the Seventeenth Century*, Princeton: Princeton University Press.


Gaál, Botond (2003), *The Faith of a Scientist: James Clerk Maxwell*, Debrecen: István Hatvani Theological Research Centre.

Gardner, Howard (1983), *Frames of Mind: The Theory of Multiple Intelligences*, New York: Basic Books.

Gardner, Howard (1999), *Intelligence Reframed: Multiple Intelligences for the 21st Century*, New York: Basic Books.

Garin, Eugenio (1983), *Astrology in the Renaissance: The Zodiac of Life*, trans. Carolyn Jackson and June Allen, London: Routledge & Kegan Paul.

Gazzaniga, Michael S. (1998), *The Mind's Past*, Berkeley: University of California Press.

Gazzaniga, Michael S. (1989), 'Organization of the Human Brain', *Science* **245**, 1 Sept., 947-52.

Ghiselin, Brewster (1985), *The Creative Process: A Symposium*, Berkeley: University of California Press (first edn, 1952).

Giberson, Karl (1997), 'The Anthropic Principle: A Postmodern Creation Myth?', *Journal of Interdisciplinary Studies* **9**, 63-90.

Giddens, Anthony (1990), *The Consequences of Modernity*, Stanford: Stanford University Press.

Gilkey, Langdon (1959), *Maker of Heaven and Earth: A Study of the Christian Doctrine of Creation*, Garden City, N.Y.: Doubleday.

Gillispie, Charles Coulston (ed.) (1970-80), *Dictionary of Scientific Biography*, 16 vols, New York: Scribner's.

Goodacre, John (1994), *The Transformation of a Peasant Economy: Townspeople and Villagers in the Lutterworth Area, 1500-1700*, Aldershot, UK: Scolar Press.

Goubert, Jean-Pierre (1989), *The Conquest of Water: The Advent of Health in the Industrial Age*, Princeton: Princeton University Press.

Gould, Stephen Jay (2002), *The Structure of Evolutionary Theory*, Cambridge, Mass.: Belknap Press.

Gould, Stephen Jay and R. Lewontin (1979), 'The Spandrels of San Marco and the Panglossian Paradigm: A Critique of the Adaptationist Programme', *Proceedings of the Royal Society of London*, Series B **205**, 581-98.

Gould, Stephen Jay and Elisabeth Vrba (1982), 'Exaptation: A Missing Term in the Science of Form', *Paleobiology* **8**, 4-15.

Grant, Edward (1979), 'The Condemnation of 1277, God's Absolute Power, and Physical Thought in the Late Middle Ages', *Viator* **10**, 211-44.

Grant, Edward (1981), *Much Ado About Nothing: Theories of Space and Vacuum from the Middle Ages to the Scientific Revolution*, Cambridge: Cambridge University Press.

Grant, Robert M. (1952), *Miracle and Natural Law in Graeco-Roman and Early Christian Thought*, Amsterdam: North Holland.

Greeley, Andrew M. (1995), 'The Persistence of Religion', *Cross Currents* 45, Spring, 24-41.

Greene-McCreight, Kathryn E. (1999), *Ad Litteram: How Augustine, Calvin, and Barth Read the 'Plain Sense' of Genesis 1-3*, New York: Peter Lang.

Gregory Palamas (1983), *The Triads*, ed. John Meyendorff, Classics of Western Spirituality, New York: Paulist Press.

Gribbin, John (1986), *In Search of the Big Bang: Quantum Physics and Cosmology*, Toronto: Bantam Books.

Griffin, David (1973), *A Process Christology*, Philadelphia: Westminster Press.

Grosseteste, Robert (1996), *On the Six Days of Creation*, trans. C. F. H. Martin, Oxford: Oxford University Press.

Gruenwald, Ithamar (1980), *Apocalyptic and Merkavah Mysticism*, Leiden: Brill.

Gunton, Colin (1998), *The Triune Creator: A Historical and Systematic Study*, Grand Rapids: Eerdmans.

Guth, Alan H. (1997), *The Inflationary Universe: The Quest for a New Theory of Cosmic Origins*, Reading, Mass.: Addison-Wesley.

Guthrie, Dale (2006), *The Nature of Paleolithic Art*, Chicago: University of Chicago Press.

Hahn, Roger (1981), 'Laplace and the Vanishing Role of God in the Physical Universe', in Harry Woolf (ed.), *The Analytic Spirit: Essays in the History of Science in Honor of Henry Guerlac*, Ithaca: Cornell University Press, pp. 85-95.

Halifax, Joan (1982), *Shaman: The Wounded Healer*, New York: Crossroad.

Hamming, R. W. (1980), 'The Unreasonable Effectiveness of Mathematics', *American Mathematical Monthly* **87**, February.

Hardy, Edward Rochie and Cyril C. Richardson (eds) (1954), *Christology of the Later Fathers*, Library of Christian Classics 3, London, SCM Press; Philadelphia: Westminster Press.

Harman (Heimann), Peter M. (1972), 'The Unseen Universe: Physics and the Philosophy of Nature in Victorian Britain', *British Journal for the History of Science* **6**, June, 73-9.

Harpending, Henry C., et al. (1998), 'Genetic Traces of Ancient Demography', *Proceedings of the National Academy of Sciences of the United States* **95**, 17 February, 1961-7.

Hartshorne, Charles (1948), *The Divine Relativity: A Social Conception of God*, New Haven: Yale University Press.

Harwit, Martin (1984), *Cosmic Discovery: The Search, Scope, and Heritage of Astronomy*, Cambridge, Mass.: MIT Press.

Harwit, Martin (2003), 'The Growth of Astrophysical Understanding', *Physics Today* **56**, November, 38-43.

Hauser, Marc D. (2000), 'What do Animals Think About Numbers?', *American Scientist* **88**, March-April, 144-51.

Hawkes, David (1974), 'The Quest of the Goddess', in Cyril Birch (ed.), *Studies in Chinese Literary Genres*, Berkeley: University of California Press, pp. 42-68.

Hawkes, David, trans. (1985), *The Songs of the South: An Ancient Chinese Anthology of poems by Qu Yuan and Other Poets*, London: Penguin Books.

Hawking, Stephen (1988), *A Brief History of Time: From the Big Bang to Black Holes*, Toronto: Bantam Books.

Hayward, Carter T. R. (1996), *The Jewish Temple: A Non-Biblical Sourcebook*, London: Routledge.

Heaton, E. W. (1974), *Solomon's New Men: The Emergence of Ancient Israel as a National State*, London: Thames and Hudson.

Heelen, Patrick A. (1970), 'Quantum Logic and Classical Logic', *Synthese* **21**, 2-33.

Heidel, Alexander (1951), *The Babylonian Genesis: The Story of Creation*, 2nd edn, Chicago: University of Chicago Press.

Heller, Michael (1995), 'Chaos, Probability, and the Comprehensibility of the World', in Robert John Russell, Nancey Murphy, and Arthur R. Peacocke (eds), *Chaos and Complexity: Scientific Perspectives on Divine Action*, Vatican City State: Vatican Observatory, pp. 107-121.

Helvenston, Patricia A., and Paul G. Bahn (2003), 'Testing the "Three Stages of Trance" Model', *Cambridge Archaeological Journal* **13**, October, 213-24.

Hengel, Martin (1974), *Judaism and Hellenism: Studies in their Encounter in Palestine during the Early Hellenistic Period*, trans. John Bowden, 2 vols, London: SCM Press.

Heninger, S. K., Jr (1977), *The Cosmographical Glass: Renaissance Diagrams of the Universe*, San Marino, Cal.: Huntington Library.

Henshilwood, Christopher and Curtis W. Marean (2003), 'The Origin of Human Behavior', *Current Anthropology* **44**, December, 629-31.

Hershbell, Jackson P. (1981), *Pseudo-Plato, Axiochus*, Chico, Calif.: Scholars Press.

Heschel, Abraham J. (1970), 'God, Torah, and Israel', in Edward LeRoy Long, Jr, and Robert T. Handy (eds), *Theology and Church in Times of Change*, Philadelphia: Westminster Press, pp. 71-90.

Himmelfarb, Martha (1993), *Ascent to Heaven in Jewish and Christian Apocalypses*, New York: Oxford University Press.

Hoffman, Lawrence A. (ed.) (1997), *My People's Prayer Book: Traditional Prayers, Modern Commentaries, Vol. 1 – The* Sh'ma *and Its Blessings*, Woodstock Ver.: Jewish Lights.

Holden, Constance (2004), 'Life Without Numbers in the Amazon', *Science* **305**, 20 August, 109.

Holland, Thomas Erskine (1896), *The Elements of Jurisprudence*, St Paul, Minnesota: West.

Holmes, Robert (2001), 'In Search of God', *New Scientist* **170**, 21 April, 25-8.

Holton, Gerald (1973, revised 1988), *Thematic Origins of Scientific Thought: Kepler to Einstein*, Cambridge, Mass.: Harvard University Press.

Hubisz, John (2003), 'Middle-School Texts Don't Make the Grade', *Physics Today* **56**, May, 50-54.

Hull, David L. and Michael Ruse (eds) (1998), *The Philosophy of Biology*, New York: Oxford University Press.

Hultkrantz, Åke (1973), 'A Definition of Shamanism', *Temenos* **9**, 25-37.

Hutton, Ronald (2001), *Shamans: Siberian Spirituality and the Western Imagination*, London: Hambledon and London.

Hyde, Krista L., and Isabelle Peretz (2004), 'Brains that are Out of Tune but in Time', *Psychological Science* **15**, May, 256-60.

Idel, Moshe (2002), *Absorbing Perfections: Kabbalah and Interpretation*, New Haven: Yale University Press.

Idel, Moshe (1988), *Kabbalah: New Perspectives*, New Haven: Yale University Press.

Idel, Moshe (1989), *Language, Torah and Hermeneutics in Abraham Abulafia*, Albany: State University of New York Press.

Ihde, Don (1983), 'The Historical-Ontological Priority of Technology Over Science', in Paul T. Durbin and Friedrich Rapp (eds), *Philosophy and Technology*, Dordrecht: Reidel, pp. 243-65.

Jackson, Myles W. (2001), 'From Theodolite to Spectral Apparatus: Joseph von Fraunhofer and the Invention of a German Optical Research-Technology', in Bernward Joerges and Terry Shinn (eds), *Instrumentation Between Science, State and Industry*, Dordrecht: Kluwer Academic, pp. 17-28.

Jackson, Myles W. (2000), *Spectrum of Belief: Joseph von Fraunhofer and the Craft of Precision Optics*, Cambridge, Mass.: MIT Press.

Jacobs, Louis (1977, 1996), *Jewish Mystical Testimonies*, New York: Schocken Books.

Jacobsen, Thorkild (1976), *The Treasures of Darkness: A History of Mesopotamian Religion*, New Haven: Yale University Press.

Jammer, Max (1966), *The Conceptual Development of Quantum Mechanics*, New York: McGraw-Hill.

Jammer, Max (1999), *Einstein and Religion: Physics and Theology*, Princeton: Princeton University Press.

Jardine, Nick (2004), 'Etics and Emics (Not to Mention Anemics and Emetics) in the History of the Sciences', *History of Science* **42**, 261-78.

Jastrow, Robert (1978), *God and the Astronomers*, New York: Norton.

Jenkins, Philip (2002), *The Next Christendom: The Coming of Global Christianity*, Oxford: Oxford University Press.

Jones, Lindsay (ed.) (2005), *Encyclopedia of Religion*, 2nd edn, 15 vols, Detroit: Thomson Gale.


Kaiser, Christopher B. (1988), 'Calvin's Understanding of Aristotelian Natural Philosophy: Its Extent and Possible Origins', in Robert V. Schnucker (ed.), *Calviniana: Ideas and Influence of Jean Calvin*, Kirksville: Sixteenth Century Journal Publishers, pp. 77-92.

Kaiser, Christopher B. (1976), 'Christology and Complementarity', *Religious Studies* **12**, 37-48.

Kaiser, Christopher B. (2003), 'Climbing Jacob's Ladder: John Calvin and the Early Church on Our Eucharistic Ascent to Heaven', *Scottish Journal of Theology* **56**, 247-67.

Kaiser, Christopher B. (1991), *Creation and the History of Science*, London: Marshall Pickering; Grand Rapids: Eerdmans.

Kaiser, Christopher B. (1997), *Creational Theology and the History of Physical Science: The Creationist Tradition from Basil to Bohr*, Leiden: E. J. Brill.

Kaiser, Christopher B. (1993), 'The Creationist Tradition in the History of Science', *Perspectives on Science and Christian Faith* **45**, June, 80-89.

Kaiser, Christopher B. (2001), *The Doctrine of God: A Historical Survey*, revised edn, Eugene, Oregon: Wipf and Stock.

Kaiser, Christopher B. (1997/98), 'Extraterrestrial Life and Extraterrestrial Intelligence', *Reformed Review* **51**, Winter, 77-91.

Kaiser, Christopher B. (1994), 'From Biblical Secularity to Modern Secularism: Historical Aspects and Stages', in S. Marianne Postiglione and Robert Brungs (eds), *Secularism versus Biblical Secularity*, St Louis: ITEST Faith/Science Press, pp. 1-43.

Kaiser, Christopher B. (1988), 'Holistic Ministry in a Technological Society', *Reformed Review* **41**, Spring, 175-88.

Kaiser, Christopher B. (1989), 'How Can a Theological Understanding of Humanity Enrich Artificial Intelligence Work', *Asbury Theological Journal* **44**, Fall, 61-75.

Kaiser, Christopher B. (2001), 'Humanity in an Intelligible Cosmos: Non-Duality in Albert Einstein and Thomas Torrance', in Elmer M. Colyer (ed.), *The Promise of Trinitarian Theology: Theologians in Dialogue with T. F. Torrance*, Lanham, Md.: Rowman & Littlefield, pp. 239-67.

Kaiser, Christopher B. (1996), 'The Integrity of Creation and the Social Nature of God', *Scottish Journal of Theology* **49**, 261-90.

Kaiser, Christopher B. (1996), 'The Laws of Nature and the Nature of God', in Jitse Van der Meer (ed.), *Facets of Faith and Science*, Lanham, Md.: University Press of America, Vol. 4, pp. 185-97.

Kaiser, Christopher B. (1996), 'Scientific Work and Its Theological Dimensions: Toward a Theology of Natural Science', in Jitse Van der Meer (ed.), *Facets of Faith and Science*, Lanham, Md.: University Press of America, Vol. 1, pp. 223-46.

Kaiser, Christopher B. (1999), 'Wearing Different Hats: Christian Living in a Fragmented World', in Craig E. Van Gelder (ed.), *Confident Witness, Changing World: Rediscovering the Gospel in North America*, Grand Rapids: Eerdmans, pp. 16-25.

Kane, Gordon (2003), 'The Dawn of Physics Beyond the Standard Model', *Scientific American* **288**, June, 68-75.

Kepler, Johannes (1937-88), *Gesammelte Werke*, 20 vols, ed. Walther von Dyck, Max Caspar, et al., Munich: Becksche Verlagsbuchhandlung.

Kepler, Johannes (1997), *The Harmony of the World*, trans. E. J. Aiton, A. M. Duncan, and J. V. Field, Philadelphia: American Philosophical Society.

Kepler, Johannes (1981), *Mysterium cosmographicum: The Secret of the Universe*, trans. A. M. Duncan, Introduction and Commentary by E. J. Aiton, New York: Abaris Books.

Kimelman, Reuven (1980), 'Rabbi Yohanan and Origen on the Song of Songs: A Third-Century Jewish-Christian Disputation', *Harvard Theological Review* **73**, 567-95.

Klein, Aaron E. (1970), *Threads of Life: Genetics from Aristotle to DNA*, Garden City, N.Y.: Natural History Press.

Klein, Cecelia F., Eulogio Guzman, Elisa C. Mandell, and Maya Stanfield-Mazzi (2002), 'The Role of Shamanism in Mesoamerican Art: A Reassessment', *Current Anthropology* **43**, June, 383-401.

Klein, Cecelia F., and Maya Stanfield-Mazzi, 'On Sharpness and Scholarship in the Debate on "Shamanism" – Reply', *Current Anthropology* 45 (June 2004), 404-406.

Klein, Jan, Naoyuki Takahata, and Francisco J. Ayala (1993), 'MHC Polymorphism and Human Origins', *Scientific American* **269**, December, 82-3.

Klein, Ursula (2005), 'Introduction: Technoscientific Productivity', *Perspectives on Science* **13**, Summer, 139-41.

Knoeff, Rina (2002), *Herman Boerhaave (1668-1738): Calvinist Chemist and Physician*, Amsterdam: Edita KNAW.

Koester, Helmut (1968), 'NOMOS PHYSEŌS: The Concept of Natural Law in Greek Thought', in Jacob Neusner (ed.), *Religions in Antiquity: Essays in Memory of Erwin Ramsdell Goodenough*, Leiden: Brill, 521-41.

Koestler, Arthur (1959), *The Sleepwalkers: A History of Man's Changing Vision of the Universe*, New York: Macmillan.

Koryé, Alexandre (1957), *From the Closed World to the Infinite Universe*, Baltimore: Johns Hopkins University Press.

Kragh, Helge (1999), *Quantum Generations: A History of Physics in the Twentieth Century*, Princeton: Princeton University Press.

Krings, Matthias, et al. (1999), 'DNA Sequence of the Mitochondrial Hypervariable Region II from the Nedandertal Type Specimen', *Proceedings of the National Academy of Sciences of the United States* **96**, 11 May, 5581-5.

Kugel, James (1995), 'The Ladder of Jacob', *Harvard Theological Review* **88**, April, 209-227.

Kuhn, Thomas S. (1970), *The Structure of Scientific Revolutions*, 2nd edn, Chicago: University of Chicago Press.

Kung, Joan R. (1982), 'Review Essay on *Magic, Reason and Experience*, by G. E. R. Lloyd', *Nature and System* 4, 101-105.

Laenen, J. H. (2001), *Jewish Mysticism: An Introduction*, trans. David E. Orton, Louisville: Westminster John Knox Press.

Leith, John H. (1963), *Creeds of the Churches: A Reader in Christian Doctrine from the Bible to the Present*, 3rd edn, Atlanta: John Knox Press.

Lewis, Bernard (2002), *What Went Wrong? The Clash Between Islam and Modernity in the Middle East*, New York: Oxford University Press.

Lewis-Williams, David (1997), 'Harnessing the Brain: Vision and Shamanism in Upper Paleolithic Western Europe', in Margaret W. Conkey et al. (eds), *Beyond Art: Pleistocene Image and Symbol*, San Francisco: California Academy of Sciences, pp. 321-42.

Lewis-Williams, David (2002), *The Mind in the Cave: Consciousness and the Origins of Art*, London: Thames & Hudson.

Lewis-Williams, David (2004), 'Neuropsychology and Upper Paleolithic Art: Observations on the Progress of Altered States of Consciousness', *Cambridge Archaeological Journal* 14, April, 107-111.

Lindberg, David C. (1992), *The Beginnings of Western Science: The European Scientific Tradition in Philosophical, Religious and Institutional Context*. Chicago: University of Chicago Press.

Lindberg, David C., and Ronald L. Numbers (1987), 'Beyond War and Peace: A Reappraisal of the Encounter between Christianity and Science', *Perspectives on Science and Christian Faith* 39, 140-49.

Lindberg, David C., and Ronald L. Numbers (eds) (2003), *When Science and Christianity Meet*, Chicago: University of Chicago Press.

Lindblom, Johannes (1973), *Prophecy in Ancient Israel*, Oxford: Blackwell.

Linde, Andrei (1994), 'The Self-Reproducing Inflationary Universe', *Scientific American* 271, November, 48-55.

Linklater, Andro (2002), *Measuring America: How the United States Was Shaped by the Greatest Land Sale in History*, London: Penguin Books.

Lloyd-Hart, Michael (2003), 'Taking the Twinkle out of Starlight', *IEEE Spectrum* 40, December, 22-9.

Loew, Cornelius (1967), *Myth, Sacred History, and Philosophy: The Pre-Christian Heritage of the West*, New York: Harcourt, Brace & World.

Lossky, Vladimir (1957), *The Mystical Theology of the Eastern Church*, Cambridge: James Clarke; French original, Paris, 1944.

Loveman, Mara (2005), 'The Modern State and the Primitive Accumulation of Symbolic Power', *American Journal of Sociology* 110, May, 1651-83.

Lü Buwei (2000), *The Annals of Lü Buwei*, trans. John Knoblock and Jeffrey Riegel, Stanford: Stanford University Press.

Luther, Martin (1955-76), *Luther's Works: American Edition*, 55 vols, ed. Jaroslav Pelikan and Helmut T. Lehmann, St Louis and Philadelphia: Concordia and Fortress Press.

MacCormac, Earl R. (1971), 'Meaning Variance and Metaphor', *British Journal for the Philosophy of Science* **22**, 145-59.

MacCulloch, Diarmain (2004), *The Reformation*, New York: Viking.

McBrearty, Sally, and Alison Brooks (2000), 'The Revolution That Wasn't: A New Interpretation of the Origin of Modern Human Behavior', *Journal of Human Evolution* 39, 453-563.

McClenon, James (2002), *Wondrous Healing: Shamanism, Human Healing, and the Origin of Religion*, Dekalb, Ill.: Northern Illinois University Press.

McDonald, H. D. (1981), *The Christian View of Man*, London: Marshall, Morgan & Scott.

McDonald, Kim A. (1993), 'Science Confronts the Ultimate Question: Does the Universe Hold Clues to God?', *The Chronicle of Higher Education* **39**, 12 May, A6-A9.

McGinn, Bernard (1991), *The Foundations of Mysticism*, New York: Crossroad.

McGrath, Alister E. (2001-2003), *A Scientific Theology*, 3 vols, Edinburgh: T&T Clark; Grand Rapids: Eerdmans.

McMullin, Ernan (1988), 'Natural Science and Belief in a Creator: Historical Notes', in Robert John Russell, William R. Stoeger, and George V. Coyne (eds), *Physics, Philosophy, and Theology: A Common Quest for Understanding*, Vatican City State: Vatican Observatory, pp. 49-79.

McNutt, Paula M. (1990), *The Forging of Israel: Iron Technology, Symbolism, and Tradition in Ancient Society*, Sheffield: Almond Press.

Mackintosh, N. J. (2000), 'Evolutionary psychology meets *G*', *Nature* **403**, 27 January, 378-9.

Marcus, Gary F. (2004), *The Birth of the Mind: How a Tiny Number of Genes Creates the Complexities of Human Thought*, New York: Basic Books.

Margenau, Henry (1961), *Open Vistas: Philosophical Perspectives of Modern Science*. New Haven: Yale University Press.

Margenau, Henry and Roy Abraham Varghese (eds), (1992), *Cosmos, Bios, Theos: Scientists Reflect on Science, God, and the Origins of the Universe, Life, and Homo Sapiens*, LaSalle, Ill.: Open Court.

Margolis, Howard (2002), *It Started with Copernicus: How Turning the World Inside Out Led to the Scientific Revolution*, New York: McGraw-Hill.

Marsden, George M. (1992), 'The Soul of the American University: An Historical Overview', in George M. Marsden and Bradley J. Longfield (eds), *The Secularization of the Academy*, New York: Oxford University Press, pp. 9-45.

Marsden, George M. (1994), *The Soul of the American University from Protestant Establishment to Established Nonbelief*, New York: Oxford University Press.

Matsuzawa Tetsuro (2006), 'What Only a Chimp Knows', *New Scientist* **190**, 10 June, 48-9.

Mayr, Ernst (1983), 'How to Carry Out the Adaptationist Program', *American Naturalist* **121**, 324-34.

Mayr, Ernst (2001), *What Evolution Is*, New York: Basic Books.

Mazur, Barry and Peter Pesic (2005), 'On Mathematics, Imagination and the Beauty of Numbers', *Daedalus* **134**, Spring, 124-30.

Merkur, Daniel (1989), 'The Visionary Practices of Jewish Apocalypticists', *The Psychoanalytic Study of Society* **14**, 119-48.

Meyendorff, John (1964), *A Study of Gregory Palamas*, London: Faith Press; French original, Paris, 1959.

Meynell, Hugo A. (1982), *The Intelligible Universe: A Cosmological Argument*, Totowa, N.J.: Barnes & Noble.

Meynell, Hugo A. (1987), 'More Gaps for God?', in John M. Robson (ed.), *Origin and Evolution of the Universe: Evidence for Design?*, Kingston, Ontario: McGill-Queen's University Press, pp. 253-4.

Migne, Jacques Paul (ed.) (1857-66), *Patrologiae Cursus Completus... Series Graeca*, 162 vols (Paris: Garnier Fratres.

Migne, Jacques Paul (ed.) (1844-79), *Patrologiae Cursus Completus... Series Latina*, 221 vols, Paris: Garnier Fratres.

Miller, Arthur I. (1996), *Insights of Genius: Imagery and Creativity in Science and Art*. Cambridge, Mass.: MIT Press.

Mithen, Steven (1996), *The Prehistory of the Mind: A Search for the Origins of Art, Religion and Science*, London: Thames & Hudson.

Mithen, Steven (2001), 'Symbolism and the Supernatural', in Frans B. M. de Waal (ed.), *Tree of Origin: What Primate Behavior Can Tell Us about Human Social Evolution*, Cambridge, Mass.: Harvard University Press, pp. 147-69.

Moltmann, Jürgen (1985), *God in Creation: A New Theology of Creation and the Spirit of God*, London: SCM Press.

Moltmann, Jürgen (2003), *Science and Wisdom*, trans. Margaret Kohl, Minneapolis: Fortress Press.

Muffs, Yochanan (1992), *Love and Joy: Law, Language and Religion in Ancient Israel*, New York: Jewish Theological Seminary of America.

Muir, Hazel (2005), 'Particle Smasher Gets a Super-Brain', *New Scientist* **186**, 21 May, 10-11.

Mullen, E. Theodore, Jr (1980), *The Divine Council in Canaanite and Early Hebrew Literature*, Chico, Cal.: Scholars Press.

Murphy, Nancey and George F. R. Ellis (1996), *On the Moral Nature of the Universe: Theology, Cosmology, and Ethics*, Minneapolis: Fortress Press.

Murray, Robert (1992), *The Cosmic Covenant: Biblical Themes of Justice, Peace, and the Integrity of Creation*, London: Sheed & Ward.

Nagel, Thomas (1986), *The View from Nowhere*, New York: Oxford University Press.

Navon, Robert (ed.) (1986), *The Pythagorean Writings: Hellenistic Texts from the 1st Cent. B.C. – 3d Cent. A.D. On Life, Morality, Knowledge, and the World*, Key Gardens, N.Y.: Selene Books.

Nebelsick, Harold (1985) *The Circles of God: Theology and Science from the Greeks to Copernicus*, Edinburgh: Scottish Academic Press.

Needham, Joseph and Wang Ling (1956), *Science and Civilisation in China, Volume 2: History of Scientific Thought*, Cambridge: Cambridge University Press.

Neugebauer, Otto (1981), *The 'Astronomical' Chapters of the Ethiopic Book of Enoch (72 to 82)*, København: Munksgaard.

Neusner, Jacob (2004), *Transformation in Ancient Judaism: Textual Evidence for Creative Responses to Crisis*, Peabody, Mass.: Hendrickson.

Neusner, Jacob, trans. (1985), *Genesis Rabbah: The Judaic Commentary to the Book of Genesis*, 3 vols, Atlanta: Scholars Press.

Newberg, Andrew, and Eugene d'Aquili (2001), *Why God Won't Go Away: Brain Science and the Biology of Belief*, New York: Ballantine Books.

Newbigin, Lesslie (1986), *Foolishness to the Greeks: The Gospel and Western Culture*, Grand Rapids: Eerdmans.

Newman, Judith H. (2004), 'The Democratization of Kingship in Wisdom of Solomon', in Hindy Najman and Judith H. Newman (eds), *The Idea of Biblical Interpretation: Essays in Honor of James Kugel*, Leiden: Brill, 309-328.

Nicene and Post-Nicene Fathers, Second Series (1890-1900), ed. Philip Schaff and Henry Wace, 14 vols, Buffalo and New York.

Nicolas of Cusa (1954), *Of Learned Ignorance*, trans. Germain Heron, London: Kegan Paul: New Haven: Yale University Press.

Noble, David F. (1997), *The Religion of Technology: The Divinity of Man and the Spirit of Invention*, Harmondsworth: Penguin Books.

Noll, Richard (1985), 'Mental Imagery Cultivation as a Cultural Phenomenon: The Role of Visions in Shamanism', *Current Anthropology* **26**, 443-61,

Nye, David E. (1990), *Electrifying America: Social Meanings of a New Technology, 1880-1940*, Cambridge, Mass., MIT Press.

Odling-Smee, F. John, Kevin N. Laland, and Marcus W. Feldman (2003), *Niche Construction: The Neglected Process in Evolution*, Princeton: Princeton University Press.

Odom, Herbert H., (1966) 'The Estrangement of Celestial Mechanics and Religion', *Journal for the History of Ideas* **27**, October, 533-48.

Ofek, Haim (2001), *Second Nature: Economic Origins of Human Evolution*, Cambridge University Press.

Olson, Daniel C. (2004), *Enoch, A New Translation: The Ethiopic Book of Enoch, or 1 Enoch, Translated with Annotations and Cross-References*, North Richland Hills, Texas: Bibal Press.

Ong, Aihwa (1987), *Spirits of Resistance and Capitalist Discipline: Factory Women in Malaysia*, Albany: SUNY Press.

Origen of Alexandria (1936), *On First Principles*, ed. G. W. Butterworth, London: SPCK; New York: Harper & Row, 1966.

*Oxford Dictionary of the Jewish Religion* (1997), ed. R. J. Zei Werblowsky and Geoffrey Wigoder, New York: Oxford University Press.

Paper, Jordan (1995), *The Spirits Are Drunk: Comparative Approaches to Chinese Religion*, Albany: SUNY Press, 1995.

Parker, T. H. L. (1952, 1969), *Calvin's Doctrine of the Knowledge of God*, Edinburgh: Oliver and Boyd.

Patai, Raphael (1977), *The Jewish Mind*, New York: Charles Scribner's Sons.

Pedersen, Olaf (1992), *The Book of Nature*, Vatican City: Vatican Observatory Publications.

Peirce, Charles S. (1931-58), *Collected Papers*, ed. Arthur W. Burks et al., 8 vols, Cambridge, Mass.: Harvard University Press.

Pennings, Tim (2003), 'Do Dogs Know Calculus?', *The College Mathematics Journal* **34**, May, 178-82.

Pfeiffer, John E. (1982), *The Creative Explosion: An Enquiry into the Origin of Art and Religion*, New York: Harper & Row.

Philo of Alexandria (1929-62), *Philo*, Loeb Classical Library, 10 vols and 2 supplementary vols, Cambridge, Mass.: Harvard University Press.

Pickthall, Mohammed Marmaduke, trans. (1953), *The Meaning of the Glorious Koran*, New York: New American Library.

Pingree, David (ed.) (1986), *Picatrix: The Latin Version of the Ghâyat Al-Hakîm*, Studies of the Warburg Institute, 39, London: Warburg Institute.

Plato of Athens (1961), *The Collected Dialogues of Plato*, ed. Edith Hamilton and Huntington Cairns, Princeton: Princeton University Press.

Polanyi, Michael (1966), *The Tacit Dimension*, New York: Doubleday-Anchor.

Polkinghorne, John (1990), 'The Reason Within and the Reason Without', in Ronald E. Mickens (ed.), *Mathematics and Science*, Singapore: World Scientific, pp. 173-82.

Polkinghorne, John (1989), *Rochester Roundabout: The Story of High Energy Physics*, New York: Freeman.

Pollard, William G. (1961), *Physicist and Christian: A Dialogue between Two Communities*, New York: Seabury Press.

Potts, Richard (1996), 'Evolution and Climate Variability', *Science* **273**, 16 August, 922-3.

Potts, Richard (1996), *Humanity's Descent: The Consequences of Ecological Instability*, New York: Morrow Books.

Premack, David (2004), 'Is Language the Key to Human Intelligence?', *Science* **303**, 16 January, 318-20.

Proclus (1970), *A Commentary on the First Book of Euclid's Elements*, trans. Glenn R. Morrow, Princeton: Princeton University Press.

Puett, Michael J. (2004), *To Become a God: Cosmology, Sacrifice, and Self-Divinization in Early China*, Cambridge, Mass.: Harvard University Press.

Randles, W. G. L. (1999), *The Unmaking of the Medieval Christian Cosmos, 1500-1760: From Solid Heavens to Boundless Ether*, Aldershot, Hants: Ashgate.

Raymo, Chet (1998), *Skeptics and True Believers: The Exhilarating Connection Between Science and Religion*, New York, MJF Books.

Reid, T. R. (1984), *The Chip: How Two Americans Invented the Microchip and Launched a Revolution*, New York: Simon and Schuster.

Richardson, Cyril C. (ed.) (1953), *Early Christian Fathers*, Library of Christian Classics 1, London, SCM Press; Philadelphia: Westminster Press.

Robinson, H. Wheeler (1944), 'The Council of Yahweh', *Journal of Theological Studies* **45**, 151-7.

Rubenstein, Jeffrey, trans. (2002), *Rabbinic Stories*, New York: Paulist Press.

Runia, David (1988), 'God and Man in Philo of Alexandria', *Journal of Theological Studies* **39**, April, 48-75.

Sagan, Carl (1980), *Cosmos*, New York: Random House.

Saunders, Nicholas (2002), *Divine Action and Modern Science*, Cambridge: Cambridge University Press.

Sawyer, Deborah F. (ed.) (1993), *Midrash Aleph Beth*, Atlanta: Scholars Press.

Schäfer, Peter (2002), *Mirror of His Beauty: Feminine Images of God from the Bible to the Early Kabbalah*, Princeton: Princeton University Press.

Schäfer, Peter (2004), 'In Heaven as in Hell: The Cosmology of Seder Rabbah di-Bereshit', in Ra'anan S. Boustan and Annette Yoshiko Reed (eds), *Heavenly Realms and Earthly Realities in Late Antique Religions*, Cambridge; Cambridge University Press, 233-74.

Schilpp Paul Arthur (ed.) (1949), *Albert Einstein: Philosopher-Scientist*, LaSalle, Ill.: Open Court.

Schivelbusch, Wolfgang (1988), *Disenchanted Night: The Industrialization of Light in the Nineteenth Century*, Berkeley: University of California Press.

Schrödinger, Erwin (1944), *What Is Life?* Cambridge: Cambridge University Press.

Schutz, Alfred and Thomas Luckmann (1973), *The Structures of the Life-World*, trans. Richard M. Zaner and H. Tristram Engelhardt, Jr, Evanston, Illinois: Northwestern University Press.

Scribner, Robert W. (1997), 'Reformation and Desacralisation: From Sacramental World to Moralised Universe', in R. Po-Chia Hsia and Robert W. Scribner (eds), *Problems in the Historical Anthropology of Early Modern Europe*, Wiesbaden: Harrassowitz, pp. 75-92.

Seife, Charles (2003), 'Physics Tries to Leave the Tunnel', *Science* **302**, 3 October, 36-8.

Seneca (1917-71), *Seneca in Ten Volumes*, Loeb Classical Library, Cambridge, Mass.: Harvard University Press.

Sextus Empiricus (1933-49), *Sextus Empiricus*, Loeb Classical Library, 4 vols, Cambridge, Mass.: Harvard University Press.

Shermer, Michael (2003), 'Demon-Haunted Brain', *Scientific American* **288**, March, 47.

Sills, David L. (ed.) (1968), *International Encyclopedia of the Social Sciences*, 17 vols, New York: Macmillan.

Singh, Simon (1997), *Fermat's Enigma: The Epic Quest to Solve the World's Greatest Mathematical Problem*, New York: Anchor Books.

Smith, Christian (ed.) (2004), *The Secular Revolution: Power, Interests and Conflict in the Secularization of American Public Life*, Berkeley: University of California Press.

Smith, Jonathan Z. (1968), 'The Prayer of Joseph', in Jacob Neusner (ed.), *Religions in Antiquity: Essays in Memory of Erwin Ramsdell Goodenough*, Leiden: Brill, pp. 253-94.

Stark, Rodney (1999), 'Secularization, R.I.P.', *Sociology of Religion* **60**, Fall, 249-73.

Stark, Rodney and Roger Fink (2000), *Acts of Faith: Explaining the Human Side of Religion*, Berkeley: University of California Press.

Steiner, Mark (1998), *The Applicability of Mathematics as a Philosophical Problem*, Cambridge, Mass.: Harvard University Press.

Stern, David (1992), '*Imitatio Hominis*: Anthropomorphism and the Character(s) of God in Rabbinic Literature', *Prooftexts* **12**, May, 151-74.

Stern, David (1991), *Parables in Midrash: Narrative and Exegesis in Rabbinic Literature*, Cambridge, Mass.: Harvard University Press.

Stern, David and Mark Jay Mirsky (eds) (1990), *Rabbinic Fantasies: Imaginative Tales from Classical Hebrew Literature*, New Haven: Yale University Press.

Stone, Michael E. (1976), 'Lists of Revealed Things in the Apocalyptic Literature', in Frank Moore Cross, Werner E. Lemke, and Patrick D. Miller, Jr (eds), *Magnalia Dei, The Mighty Acts of God: Essays on the Bible and Archaeology in Memory of G. Ernest Wright*, Garden City, New York: Doubleday, 414-52.

Susskind, Leonard (2005), *The Cosmic Landscape: String Theory and the Illusion of Intelligent Design*, New York: Little, Brown, and Co.

Tait, Peter Guthrie, and Stewart, Balfour (anon. 1875), *The Unseen Universe or Physical Speculations on a Future* State, New York: Macmillan.

Tattersall, Ian (1998), *Becoming Human: Evolution and Human Uniqueness*, New York: Harcourt Brace.

Tegmark, Max (1998), 'Is "The Theory of Everything" Merely the Ultimate Ensemble Theory?', *Annals of Physics* **270**, 1-51.

Tegmark, Max (2003), 'Parallel Universes', *Scientific American* **288**, May, 41-51.

Templeton, Alan R. (2002), 'Out of Africa Again and Again', *Nature* **416**, 7 March, 45-51.

Theophilus Presbyter (1963, 1979), *Theophilus, On Divers Arts: The Foremost Medieval Treatise on Painting, Glassmaking and Metalwork*, trans. John G. Hawthorne and Cyril Stanley Smith, London: Constable; repr. New York: Dover.

Thomas, George M., Peck, Lisa R. and De Haan, Channin G. (2004), 'Reforming Education, Transforming Religion, 1876-1931', in Christian Smith (ed.), *The Secular Revolution: Power, Interests and Conflict in the Secularization of American Public Life*, Berkeley: University of California Press, pp. 355-94.

Thrupp, Sylvia L. (1948, 1989), *The Merchant Class of Medieval London*, Ann Arbor: University of Michigan Press.

Tillich, Paul *Systematic Theology*, Vol. 1 (1951), Chicago: University of Chicago Press.

Torrance, Thomas F. (1981), *Christian Theology and Scientific Culture*, New York: Oxford University Press.

Traweek, Sharon (1988), *Beamtimes and Lifetimes: The World of High Energy Physicists*, Cambridge, Mass.: Harvard University Press.

Trefil, James S. (1983), *The Moment of Creation: Big Bang Physics from before the First Millisecond to the Present Universe*, New York: Charles Scribner's Sons.

Trinh Xuan Thuan (1995), *The Secret Melody: And Man Created the Universe*, trans. Storm Dunlop, New York: Oxford University Press.

Turner, Frank M. (1978), 'The Victorian Conflict Between Science and Religion: A Professional Dimension', *Isis*, **69**, September, 356-76.

Turner, R. Steven (1971), 'The Growth of Professional Research in Prussia, 1818 to 1848', *Historical Studies in the Physical Sciences* **3**, 137-83.

Turner, Victor (1975), *Revelation and Divination in Ndembu*, Ithaca: Cornell University Press.

Urbach, Ephraim E. (1987), *The Sages: Their Concepts and Beliefs*, Cambridge, Mass.: Harvard University Press.

VanderKam, James C. (1984), *Enoch and the Growth of an Apocalyptic Tradition*, Washington, D.C.: Catholic Biblical Association of America.

Van der Leeuw, Gerardus (1938, 1964), *Religion in Essence and Manifestation*, London: Allen & Unwin, 393-402.

Van Huyssteen, J. Wentzel (2006), *Alone in the World? Human Uniqueness in Science and Theology*, Grand Rapids, Eerdmans.

Vaux, Roland de (1961, 1965), *Ancient Israel, Its Life and Institutions*, London: Darton, Longman & Todd.

Wallace, Alfred Russel (1890), *Darwinism: An Exposition of the Theory of Natural Selection with Some of Its Applications*, London: Macmillan.

Wallis, Roy and Steve Bruce (1992), 'Secularization: The Orthodox Model', in Steve Bruce (ed.), *Religion and Modernization: Sociologists and Historians Debate the Secularization Thesis*, Oxford: Clarendon Press, 8-30.

Walsh, Roger N. (1990), 'Shamanic Cosmology: A Psychological Examination of the Shaman's Worldview', *ReVision* 13, Fall, 86-100.

Walsh, Roger N. (1990), *The Spirit of Shamanism*. Los Angles: Tarcher.

Ward, Peter, and Don Brownlee (2002), *The Life and Death of Planet Earth: How the New Science of Astrobiology Charts the Ultimate Fate of Our World*, New York: Times Books.

Ward, Peter, and Don Brownlee (2000), *Rare Earth: Why Complex Life is Uncommon in the Universe*, New York: Copernicus Books.

Watts, Ian (2001), 'The Origin of Symbolic Culture', in Frans B. M. de Waal (ed.), *Tree of Origin: What Primate Behavior Can Tell Us about Human Social Evolution*, Cambridge, Mass.: Harvard University Press, pp. 113-46.

Weinberg, Steven (1992), *Dreams of a Final Theory*, New York: Pantheon Books.

Weinberger, Norman M. (2004), 'Music and the Brain', *Scientific American* 291, November, 89-95.

Weinfeld, Moshe (1981), 'Sabbath, Temple and the Enthronement of the Lord: The Problem of the *Sitz im Leben* of Genesis 1:12-2:3', in A. Caquot and M. Delcor (ed.), *Mélanges bibliques et orientaux en l'honneur de M. Henri Cazelles*, Keveleaer: Butzon & Bercker, pp. 501-512.

West, Martin Litchfield (1983), *The Orphic Poems*, Oxford: Clarendon Press.

West-Eberhard, Mary Jane (1992), 'Adaptation: Current Usages', in Evelyn Fox Keller and Elisabeth A. Lloyd (eds), *Keywords in Evolutionary Biology*, Cambridge, Mass.: Harvard University Press, 13-18, reprinted in David L. Hull and Michael Ruse (eds) (1998), *The Philosophy of Biology*, Oxford: Oxford University Press, pp. 8-14.

Westman, Robert S. (1975), 'The Melanchthon Circle, Rheticus, and the Wittenberg Interpretation of the Copernican Theory', *Isis* 66, June, 165-93.

Wetherbee, Winthrop (1988), 'Philosophy, Cosmology, and the Twelfth-Century Renaissance', in Peter Dronke (ed.), *A History of Twelfth-Century Western Philosophy*, Cambridge: Cambridge University Press, chap. 1.

Whitehead, Alfred North (1925), *Science and the Modern World*, New York, Macmillan.

Whitehead, Alfred North (1929), *Process and Reality: An Essay in Cosmology*, New York: Macmillan.

Wiebe, Philip H. (2004), 'Finite Spirits as Theoretical Entities', *Religious Studies* **40**, September, 241-50

Wigner, Eugene P. (1960), 'The Unreasonable Effectiveness of Mathematics in the Natural Sciences', *Communications on Pure and Applied Mathematics* **13**, February, 1-14; reprinted in idem (1967), *Symmetries and Reflections: Scientific Essays*, Bloomington: Indiana University Press, pp. 222-37.

Wigner, Eugene P. (1967), *Symmetries and Reflections: Scientific Essays*, Bloomington: Indiana University Press.

Wildiers, N. Max (1982), *The Theologian and His Universe: Theology and Cosmology from the Middle Ages to the Present*, trans. Paul Dunphy, New York: Seabury Press.

Wilson, David Sloan (2002), *Darwin's Cathedral: Evolution, Religion, and the Nature of Society*, Chicago: University of Chicago Press.

Wilson, Edward O. (1998), *Consilience: The Unity of Knowledge*, New York: Random House.

Winkelman, Michael James (2002), 'Shamanism and Cognitive Evolution', *Cambridge Archaeological Journal* **12**, 71-101.

Winkelman, Michael James (2004), 'Shamanism as the Original Neurotheology', *Zygon* **39**, March, 193-217.

Winkelman, Michael James (1990), 'Shamans and Other "Magico-Religious" Healers: A Cross Cultural Study of Their Origins, Nature, and Social Transformations', *Ethos* **18**, September, 308-52.

Winiarski, Douglas L. (2004), 'Souls Filled with Ravishing Transport: Heavenly Visions and the Radical Awakening in New England', *William & Mary Quarterly* **61**, January, 3-45.

Winston, David (1979), *The Wisdom of Solomon, A New Translation*, Anchor Bible 43, New York: Doubleday, 1979.

Wolfson, Henry Austryn (1970), *The Philosophy of the Church Fathers: Faith, Incarnation, Trinity*, third edn, Cambridge, Mass.: Harvard University Press.

Worthing, Mark William (1996), *God, Creation, and Contemporary Physics*, Minneapolis: Fortress Press.

Yukawa, Hideki (1973), *Creativity and Intuition: A Physicist Looks at East and West*, Tokyo: Kodansha.

Yulsman, Tom (1999), 'Give Peas a Chance: Could an exotic object known as a pea instanton have given birth to our universe?', *Astronomy* **27**, September, 38-46.

Zaleski, Carol (1987), *Otherworld Journeys: Accounts of Near-Death Experience in Medieval and Modern Times*, New York: Oxford University Press.

Zizioulas, John D. (1985), *Being as Communion: Studies in Personhood and the Church*, Crestwood, N.Y.: St Vladimir's Seminary Press.

# Index of Names

# Index of Subjects

# Index of Biblical Texts

# Index of Biblical Texts